To Roger—

Had I seen your question earlier, I might have been moved to add a subtitle to the book: on the <u>productivity</u> of cappucino & fashion strolls!

With best wishes,

Ron

April 1998

The political economy of dictatorship

Much of the world still lives today, as always, under dictatorship. Yet the behavior of these regimes and of their leaders often appears irrational and mysterious. In *The Political Economy of Dictatorship*, Ronald Wintrobe uses rational choice theory to model dictatorships: their strategies for accumulating power, the constraints on their behavior, and the reasons why they are often more popular than is commonly accepted. The book explores both the politics and the economics of dictatorships, and the interaction between them. The questions addressed include: What determines the repressiveness of a regime? Can political authoritarianism be "good" for the economy? After the fall of a dictatorship, who should be held responsible for crimes against human rights?

The book contains many examples and case studies, including chapters on Nazi Germany, Soviet communism, South Africa under *apartheid*, the ancient Roman Empire, and modern capitalist–authoritarian regimes such as Pinochet's Chile. It also provides a guide to the policies toward dictatorships that should be followed by the democracies.

The political economy of dictatorship

Ronald Wintrobe

University of Western Ontario

PUBLISHED BY THE PRESS SYNDICATE OF THE UNIVERSITY OF CAMBRIDGE
The Pitt Building, Trumpington Street, Cambridge CB2 1RP, United Kingdom

CAMBRIDGE UNIVERSITY PRESS
The Edinburgh Building, Cambridge CB2 2RU, United Kingdom
40 West 20th Street, New York, NY 10011-4211, USA
10 Stamford Road, Oakleigh, Melbourne 3166, Australia

First published 1998

Printed in the United States of America

Typeset in Times Roman

Library of Congress Cataloging-in-Publication Data
Wintrobe, Ronald.
The political economy of dictatorship / Ronald Wintrobe.
p.   cm.
Includes bibliographical references (p.   ).
ISBN 0-521-58329-2 (hb)
1. Dictatorship.   2. Rational choice theory.   3. Economic
development.   I. Title.
JC495.W55   1998
338.9–dc21   97-24262
                                                           CIP

A *catalog record for this book is available from*
the British Library.

ISBN 0 521 58329 2 hardback

Contents

to Diana

Acknowledgments

Over the years in which this book has been in progress, many people have commented on and made suggestions about the arguments in it. These people are too numerous to thank by name, but I must at least mention the universities at which seminars have been presented and the names of the seminar organizers. In this way, I hope to thank them and the participants for comments and helpful discussions: in Canada, Carleton (Stan Winer), McMaster (Stuart Mestelman), Toronto (Albert Breton), and Western Ontario (Bob Young); in Europe, Alessandria and Torino (Giorgio Brosio, Alberto Cassone, and Mario Ferrero), Catania (Isadora Mazza and Ilde Rizzo), Institut d'Etudes Politiques de Paris (Jean-Jacques Rosa, Pierre Salmon, and Alain Wolfesperger), Modena (Michele Grillo), Naples (Massimo Marelli), University of Paris I (Jean Bénard and Pierre Salmon), Perugia (Gianluigi Galeotti), Rome (Galeotti again!), and Siena (Ugo Pagano); and in the United States, George Mason (Roger Congleton), Stanford (Hilton Root and Barry Weingast), and Yale (Henry Hansmann and Alan Schwartz). Parts of the book were also presented as the lecture "Dictatorships and Democracies," which was given on the Canadian Broadcasting System's radio show "Ideas"; I wish to thank Hans and Grace Scheel for their help in facilitating that presentation, and the producer of that program, Sara Wolch, for many helpful comments on the material. A number of chapters were presented for the first time at seminars of the Villa Colombella Group for the Economics of Institutions. I wish to extend a special thanks to my colleagues in that group for many discussions and debates over the years: Albert Breton, Gianluigi Galeotti, and Pierre Salmon. I also wish to thank my colleagues in the Department of Economics and the Political Economy Research Group at the University of Western Ontario for their comments: Robin Cowan, Joel Fried, Peter Howitt, David Laidler, Christophe Rühl, Terry Sicular, and especially Robert Young. I wish to thank Christine Bies for her able research assistance at a crucial point in the preparation of the final manuscript. For financial support, I am very grateful to the Lynde and Harry Bradley Foundation for its generous assistance, which, among other things, allowed time off from teaching over the past three years. Without that support the book would never have been written. I wish to extend a most special thank you to my secretary, Yvonne Adams, who has typed and retyped the chapters of this book with unfailing efficiency and dedication, and who has always been a great pleasure to work with.

Part I

Introduction

1 The problem

1 The questions

Why was Caesar assassinated? Why have some dictatorships been stable and long-lasting (those in the USSR, China, Cuba, Iran), whereas others have proved to be unstable and very short-lived (such as many of the regimes in Africa and Latin America in the 1960s and 1970s)? Why did the regimes in South Africa and the former USSR collapse? Just as important, why didn't they collapse sooner than they did? Why have countries such as South Korea, China, and Chile grown so fast in recent years? Is political dictatorship good for economic growth? Why are some regimes (Stalin's Russia, Hitler's Germany, Pinochet's Chile) extremely repressive, whereas others are less so? Why do even relatively repressive regimes have periods of thaw in which the level of repression is temporarily reduced? Have dictators such as Cuba's Fidel Castro or Iraq's Saddam Hussein stayed in office so long because of their capacities to repress their peoples, or because they are popular? Can the answer be: both? Was Adolf Eichmann, the transportation coordinator of the Final Solution to the Jewish question, himself guilty of the crimes committed by the Nazi regime, or was he just a cog in the machinery of mass murder? Should functionaries in other regimes – such as those in Argentina, South Africa, or China, which committed massive violations of human rights – be tried for the activities practiced by those regimes?

All of these questions, and others like them, concern different aspects of the *behavior* of dictatorships. That is, they describe the conduct of the ruler, his or her administration, or those who are ruled in a political system in which the rights of the people to decide by whom and how they will be governed have been abrogated by the ruler. In this book I assume that this behavior is explainable and (statistically) predictable. In other words, although not all dictatorships are alike, they follow patterns which can be understood in rational-choice terms and which can be predicted given certain broad characteristics of the regime.

Several dimensions of the behavior of dictatorships are important, including the level of political repression, economic policy (toward economic growth, property rights, or redistribution of wealth), the level of economic efficiency, and attitudes toward other states (open or autarkic, peaceful or threatening). Perhaps the central point of departure in what follows is that although the dictator may have a formal monopoly with regard to political power, the policies pursued on all these matters is conditioned by constraints which arise both from the behavior of other actors – including the administration or bureaucracy, as well as the military – and from the extent of support or opposition from the dictator's subjects.

Formally, the dictator has power over all these groups. But no matter how great the dictator's powers, he or she cannot simply issue commands and expect them to be obeyed. For one thing, there are just too many people to be controlled this way. For another, how can the dictator be sure that his or her orders will be carried out? It is easy to threaten punishment, but can the punishers be trusted to remain loyal? Finally, it is important to notice that a ruler's rights are themselves circumscribed. Although the dictator may believe otherwise, he or she doesn't *own* the regime and usually cannot transfer the rights of office to a designated successor. This limitation makes the dictator's position peculiarly vulnerable. Of course, the people have good reason to fear the ruler. But this very fear (as well as jealousy) will make many among them look for ways to get rid of the dictator. So the ruler has every reason to suspect that there are plots against the regime, and one common method of removing a dictator from office has indeed been assassination. If the regime is to have any permanence, institutions must be created or maintained which deal with this problem by regularizing payments to its supporters and by providing for the systematic marginalization or elimination of its enemies. These institutions of repression and redistribution define the dictatorship.

Examples of political and economic institutions which (among other things) play these roles – and which are analyzed in this book – include the totalitarian party; the pass system in *apartheid* South Africa; the ethnic or religious reservation of jobs and other privileges in such countries as South Africa, Nazi Germany, and contemporary Iran; and the system of gifts or *clientela* in ancient Rome and in many less developed countries today. All these institutions provide for the distribution of payments to the regime's supporters on a systematic basis, and they simultaneously repress or tax the opposition.

Given this perspective, the book addresses the following abstract versions of the questions, which were posed at the beginning of this chapter, *viz*:

1. What are the primary tools that dictators use to stay in power?
2. What determines the repressiveness of a regime? How does the level of political repression respond to economic forces such as changes in the regime's economic performance (e.g., the rate of growth in GNP), and to political forces (e.g., changes in popularity)?
3. What circumstances (economic and political) contribute to the stability or instability of authoritarian regimes?
4. Are dictatorships more capable of superior economic growth than democracies? Are they less subject to rent-seeking or redistributional pressures?
5. Does the introduction of free markets inevitably lead to the decline of political dictatorship?
6. What circumstances contribute to the fall of democracy and the rise of dictatorship?
7. How does nationalism arise and how and why do dictators promote it?
8. What is the responsibility of bureaucratic functionaries for crimes committed by the regime? (This is the Eichmann question.)
9. What policies should Western democracies follow toward autocratic regimes?
10. How does a study of dictatorships shed light on the workings of democracy?

Although there is no shortage of thoughtful discussion on these issues in the literature, analysis is seldom based on an explicit model capable of explaining the behavior of different regimes, or even of the same regime at different times. I develop a general model of dictatorship in this book which provides a consistent set of answers to these questions (some of which the reader will no doubt find more satisfying than others). The model uses the tools of economic theory. However, the economic methods used are not the traditional ones; they are instead the tools of the "new economics of institutions," and they are explained in some detail in Chapter 2.

The use of economic methods implies that I assume dictators (and their subjects) to be rational, in the standard sense that given their goals, they choose the best means of achieving them. On the whole (with one exception), I do make this assumption, and I do so because in that way I can comprehend their behavior. However, assuming that dictators are rational does not mean that they are perfectly informed or that they are incapable of error. If they were, their control of the machinery of the state would guarantee that they would never lose power; they would be able to uncover any plot against their regimes and prevent its fulfillment. On the contrary certain classic errors of dictators are very much the subject matter of this book. In this way, and in others, I associate particular regimes with "fables" – lessons that help us to understand the nature of that regime (and dictatorship in general). Thus, although the models used are themselves abstract, I use certain regimes or historical figures to illustrate them. Some regimes are discussed in detail: Nazi Germany, the Communist government in the former Soviet Union, the *apartheid* system in South Africa, the Pinochet regime in Chile, and the ancient Roman Empire. Other regimes are mentioned, but they are examined less thoroughly: Mobutu's Zaire, Haiti under "Papa Doc" Duvalier, and contemporary China and other Asian dictatorships. Sometimes the conduct of a particular dictator is used simply to illustrate a particular theoretical point. As for the regimes studied in detail, they are selected partly on the basis of their importance, partly on the basis of the availability of materials, but mostly on their interest. I have relied on standard historical and other sources for the facts alluded to in these "case studies." I hope the theory developed here contributes to an understanding of these regimes – how their institutions worked and why particular dictators did what they did. At any rate this is the main purpose of the book.

The book thus attempts to fill and to bridge gaps in and between two literatures. On the one hand the literature known as the economics of politics (or "public choice") has, with important exceptions (e.g., North and Thomas 1973; North and Weingast 1989; Olson 1993; Root 1989; and Tullock 1987), focused on modeling democracy. Because most of the world for most of human history has lived under dictatorship, there is obviously a deep need for more work in this area. Moreover, every democracy contains aspects of autocracy, and indeed, all too often autocratic solutions have been suggested as ways to compensate for one or another failure of democracy. The most obvious examples are all those situations in which it is proposed that policy on certain matters be taken out of the democratic process and put into the hands of an independent authority. Thus, it is said "independent" central bankers are the only ones who can be counted on to control a nation's money supply, constitutional prohibitions are required to prevent overspending by democratically elected governments, and so on. The literature on public choice is particularly rife with these policy prescriptions. Yet all of them involve the substitution of authority for democracy in the sense that the right to decide these matters is withdrawn from the citizenry. Why should an independent authority, a person who is not responsible to the people, do what is best for them? If an argument along these lines can be successfully made in central banking or on the deficit, why can't it be extended to other areas of public decision making? What's wrong with an independent Pentagon? I contend that one cannot answer these questions without an understanding of autocracy. And, finally, I suggest that one cannot really understand how democracy works if one does not understand its converse.

The other literature to which this book is addressed is the vast and often fascinating literature on particular regimes developed by historians and political scientists. Although the theory developed here is very different from the kind of account usually found in these works, I have in fact used them extensively, not only in the cases studied but also as a way of thinking about the problem of autocracy. In particular, I have extracted four archetypes, or "images," of dictatorship. These correspond to the four possible equilibria of the basic model developed in this book. Of course, there are many other typologies and points of view, but the ones cited here are those that I have found most useful, and they do encompass a good deal of the literature. And I hope the reader will find it interesting that all four can be generated from the same simple, rational-choice–based model. So my goal is not to develop yet another typology, but to show that although very different kinds of regimes can emerge under different conditions, all dictatorships can be analyzed the same way. These images of dictatorship are presented in the next section.

2   Images of dictatorship

Important contributions to our understanding of dictatorship have been made in a large number of different fields of specialization, including, most obviously, in history and political science, but also in psychology, economics, and fiction. I will not make any attempt to survey this literature here, but I do believe that as viewed from the perspective of this book, we can discover a small number of what I think it is useful to conceive of as *images* of dictatorship that tend to recur over and over in it. The four types of dictatorship we will be examining are totalitarianism, tinpots, tyranny, and timocracy.

A. Totalitarianism

There are a number of classic sources for this concept of dictatorship. In fiction they include, most notably, George Orwell's *1984* (1949), Arthur Koestler's *Darkness at Noon* (1941), and Aldous Huxley's

Brave New World (1946). The fundamental problem of all novels is an individual's – a character's – identity (Kundera 1995, p. 22), and so these books were concerned with the effects of brainwashing, thought control, and indoctrination on the individual spirit. The word *totalitario* itself comes from Mussolini's Italy, which is sometimes classified as a totalitarian regime; but often his regime is not so classified, because, it is believed, the level of repression or state control under Mussolini never reached the levels that it did in Germany or Russia. The analytics of the concept were fleshed out by Hannah Arendt in *The Origins of Totalitarianism* (1951/1973) and by Carl Friedrich and Zbigniew Brzezinski in their *Totalitarian Dictatorship and Autocracy* (1965). Both drew a sharp distinction between totalitarianism and previous forms of autocracy. Friedrich and Brzezinski defined totalitarianism as a syndrome (note the analogy to medical disease) consisting of six interrelated characteristics, including an official ideology, a single party typically led by one individual, a terrorist police force, monopoly of mass communications, monopoly of armaments, and state control of the economy. The underlying logic of this type of regime – how it functioned and what its goals were – was never made clear. That task was performed by Arendt in monumental fashion. More than forty years after her book's publication, the conceptual and analytic power of her reasoning is undiluted, and although the regimes described in it are thankfully both gone, the book is as fresh as ever. One reason, apart from the skill of the author and the frightening nature of the regimes discussed in it, is that the book on one level is simply an attempt to portray, in stupefying, mind-altering clarity, the most perfect nightmare of everyone who values freedom: the possibility of being completely subjected, in every sphere of life, to domination by the state. So totalitarianism as a political system is defined as one which aspires to total domination – "the permanent domination of each single individual in each and every sphere of life" (Arendt 1951/1973, p. 326). In part, this goal is achieved through the "atomization" of human relationships – the destruction of classes, interest groups, and other relationships between people. Another one of her books, *Eichmann in Jerusalem* (1976), became famous for its introduction of the concept "the banality of evil" and for its personification in the functionary Eichmannn, who, in sending millions to their deaths, argued that he was just "carrying out orders" and who appeared as dehumanized himself as the victims of the terror in which he played a substantial part.

With so much emphasis within the concept of totalitarianism on the state's control over the minds of its subjects, it was natural that psychologists would become interested in the problem. Two of the most famous works in this vein, each of which spawned an enormous literature, were that of Theodor Adorno, Else Fenkel-Brunswik, Daniel Levinson, and R. Nevitt Sanford [*The Authoritarian Personality* (1950)] and that of Stanley Milgram, an account of whose experiments was published as *Obedience to Authority* (1974). In the former work a scale (the "F" – for Fascism – scale) was devised on the basis of interviews to isolate a constellation of personality traits which correlated, sometimes in a nonobvious way, with a disposition toward authoritarianism. Although some of the original ideas have been discarded, work on scales of this nature has continued, and new scales were developed, notably the one measuring "Right-Wing Authoritarianism" by Bob Altemeyer (1981, 1988, 1996), which he has developed and refined over a period of twenty years or so.

In Milgram's experiments the question was to measure how much people would be willing to obey a recognized authority figure. For this purpose Milgram had an actor pose as a "scientist," purportedly one conducting a learning experiment, who would instruct the hapless sub-jects to administer shocks of ever-increasing magnitude to a fake "learner" (also an actor); the fake learner, in turn, was instructed to keep giving wrong answers to the questions asked. Milgram found that the subjects obeyed the authority figure to an astonishing degree, even when they had nothing to gain by doing so and even when cooperation with the scientist appeared to mean inflicting considerable pain on the "victim." To my knowledge the results have never been discredited, although no university will allow experiments like this one to be performed any longer (the subjects found their own behavior, after the fact, to be as distressing as the reader presumably does).

The experiences of the 1930s also had an impact on economics. Al-though the subject matter of economics is less concerned than that of novels or psychology with the emotions, restrictions on the freedom of individuals to invest or on the capacity of managers of firms to operate them the way they like can be every bit as horrifying to the modern free-market–oriented economist as thought control, political repression, or psychological domination are to other scholars. Because government control over the economy was much greater in the Soviet system than in Nazi Germany (even at its height), it was the Soviet experience which stimulated the most research and debate within the economics profes-sion. One important issue was that of the efficiency and functioning, in strictly economic terms (i.e., apart from the question of liberty), of such a system. Initially, there was a considerable debate – stimulated by Friedrich Hayek in his *Collectivist Economic Planning* (1935) and by Oskar Lange's response, *On The Economic Theory of Socialism* (1938/ 1964) – about how central planning could "mimic" the price system and thus obtain the efficiency of capitalism without its concomitant vices of "external effects" (which could be solved by simply choosing the right shadow prices) and income inequality.

In the end what emerged as the standard picture of the economy of a Soviet-type system was a vision very much like that of the picture of totalitarianism in political theory in this one respect: It led to a so-called command economy, a giant bureaucracy in which all decisions are made at the center. In such economies, orders filter down to those at lower levels, who are responsible for doing the actual work. The difference is that, to an economist, this picture appears pathetic rather than threatening. The standard theory of markets implies that a society of over 250 million people – in which everything is decided at the center and in which everyone else follows orders – would be shot through with inefficiency, and this belief also became part of the typical picture. Thus, as Alec Nove wrote in 1980, "[I]n most instances *the centre does not know* just what it is that needs doing, in disaggregated detail, while the management in its situation *cannot* know what it is that society needs unless the centre informs it" (p. 89).

Moreover, even if the center had the correct information, it would have difficulty communicating it. As Nove asserted, "The trouble lies in the near impossibility of drafting micro economic instructions in such a way that even the most well-meaning manager will not be misled" (p. 89). Finally, there is the veritable host of inefficiencies that result from the use of substitutes for the set of perfect instructions – this is the so-called success indicator problem – all of which are nicely illustrated by the well-known cartoon depicting a group of Soviet managers from a nail factory who are gazing with satisfaction at a single enormous nail and congratulating themselves on overfulfillment of the plan for nails, which was expressed in tons.

However, it is noteworthy that until at least the late 1970s, assessments of actual Soviet economic performance by top Western experts, those based either on official Soviet data or on those of the CIA, were typically extremely positive (e.g., see the estimates of Soviet productivity growth in Abram Bergson 1978 – the estimates were revised in 1987 and 1992; for a general survey, see Ofer 1987). So if the Soviet Union was inevitably doomed to self-destruct, it was not always clear before the fact. The question which remains, and which is discussed later, is, how could Soviet-type economies appear so successful for such a long period of time if they were not? And if they were indeed successful, why did this success erode so badly over time?

In any case many of the arguments that were used to buttress the case for the economic strength of communism during the Cold War are still around, only now they have been transferred to a different style of dictatorship: the newly industrialized and industrializing countries of Asia. The threat is posed by the same forces as before: a mysterious group loyalty of the citizenry to the state or to the firm, an alleged superior capacity to make collective decisions, and an apparent ability to control the economy in socially beneficial ways of which no democracy is deemed capable, all buttressed by impressive statistics on economic growth. The difference is that these regimes (even contemporary China) are not totalitarian; I will be referring to them as "tyrannies." Before turning to that category, however, let me first discuss another type of regime, one which in many respects is the polar opposite of totalitarian dictatorship. I refer to the unstable, chimeric, short-lived, or weak dictatorships common in Africa and Latin America, especially from the 1960s to the 1980s, a category with many different labels but one which I will label "tinpots."

B. Tinpots

Tinpots are regimes in which the ruling government does not disturb the traditional way of life of the people; instead, it represses them only to the modest extent necessary to stay in office and collect the fruits of monopolizing political power (Mercedes Benzes, palaces, Swiss bank accounts, and so on). Examples of this latter type include the ex-rulers Somosa of Nicaragua, the Shah of Iran, Ferdinand Marcos of the Philippines, and General Noriega of Panama. There is no standard label for this type of regime, which in my view encompasses some traditional autocracies (Kirkpatrick 1982, following Friedrich and Brzezinski 1965, distinguished two types of regimes: totalitarian regimes and traditional autocracies). Other labels include "sultanism," "patrimonial" and "neo-patrimonial" rule, and "personal" rule. Military dictatorships are often of this type. The revolving Latin American or African dictator is the classic popular image.

Kirkpatrick argued that U.S. foreign policy should be relatively tolerant toward traditional autocracies, not because these regimes display very much that is appealing to lovers of freedom, but because (1) although their leaders are dictators, they tend to be pro-Western and (2) because such regimes are less repressive and less stable than totalitarian regimes, the United States often abets their downfall by taking a hostile attitude toward their repression of civil liberties, only to see them succeeded by regimes of the totalitarian type. Hence, she argued that a "double standard" could be recommended to lovers of freedom in their attitude toward dictatorship, and she fought for such a standard while serving as American ambassador to the United Nations.

Now all policy conclusions depend on a model, and so it is reasonable to ask what the underlying model of dictatorship is in this case. I think it is fair to say that in Kirkpatrick's view, the essential tool or instrument of governments under either traditional or totalitarian dictatorships is *repression*, or coercion of the citizenry. Consequently, the only – or at least the main – difference between traditional and totalitarian dictatorships is their *level* of repression. This way of looking at dictatorship is, I believe, common to much of political science.

One difficulty with Kirkpatrick's theory is that some of the regimes which appear as relatively harmless traditional autocracies in her categorization were very repressive indeed. The most obvious cases are the military regimes of Brazil and that of Pinochet in Chile. A general empirical test of the theory was performed by Neil Mitchell and James McCormick (1988). They constructed two measures of human rights violations for a large number of countries – one measuring the frequency of use of torture and the other the number of political prisoners taken – and they found that military regimes and traditional monarchies actually used torture more frequently than totalitarian (Marxist) governments (although they used imprisonment less often). And when repression was operationalized as an aggregate index incorporating both imprisonment and torture, they found no significant difference between the two types of regimes.

This analysis suggests, first, that the argument for double standards may be misplaced and, second, that there is a need for another category of dictatorship, one which is not totalitarian but in which the level of repression is high. Since totalitarianism is a new (twentieth century) phenomenon, whereas repression, even at extensive levels, is a very old one, this second point seems obvious enough. I follow a venerable tradition in political philosophy and describe such regimes as "tyrannies."

C. Tyranny

The label "tyranny" was commonly used in the ancient world. In his magisterial *Bread and Circuses* (1990), Paul Veyne gives three definitions of the word as used in ancient Greece and Rome:

1. a regime in which the tyrant keeps himself[1] in power through violence

---

[1] I have been unable to discover any female dictators in history (with the possible exception of Indira Gandhi for a short period), an interesting point emphasized here and throughout the book by the use of the male pronoun when referring to dictators of the past.

2. a regime run by a man whose policy runs contrary to the material interests of a section, large or small, of his subjects
3. a regime controlled by a man whose delight in the exercise of power derives entirely from the servitude that he imposes on some of his subjects (p. 405).

All these definitions appear consistent with the concept as used here – that is, a regime in which repression is high but which lacks or abjures the instruments of mass communication and control that make totalitarianism possible. Another term which describes the same phenomenon is "despotism," a term which describes the reigns of the unenlightened monarchies of the seventeenth and eighteenth centuries. Of course, a moment's reflection confirms that such regimes are not uncommon in the modern world; the most obvious examples are the Duvalier regime in Haiti and those in Chile and Argentina in the 1970s. Africa has had its share of tyrants as well, a number of whom are catalogued and described in an article which was appropriately titled "His Eternity, His Eccentricity, or His Exemplarity? A Further Contribution to the Study of H.E. the African Head of State" (Kirk-Greene 1991). Of course, tyrants do not usually identify themselves as such, but often, as Kirk-Greene points out, they emphasize a claim to legitimacy through the use of appropriate titles, including "The Guide" (Mobutu), "Conquerer of the British Empire" (Idi Amin), or simply "The Emperor of Ethiopia," followed by "The Elect of God, Son of David, Son of Solomon, King of Kings, and Lion of Judah" (Haile Selassie).

The most important theorizing about contemporary tyrannies has concerned itself with Latin American regimes, possibly because of their proximity and importance to the United States, where most contemporary theorizing on most subjects in the social sciences seems to take place. One celebrated contribution was the "Bureaucratic–Authoritarian" model invented by Guillermo O'Donnell (1973), which explained the rise of authoritarianism in Latin America in the 1960s as the result of economic pressures. Specifically, he suggested both that these economies had reached the limits of import substitution as a means of economic growth and that further development required capital "deepening," thus requiring, in turn, military rule backed by an alliance with the domestic bourgeoisie and foreign capital. However, in the 1970s the same pressures for economic growth produced another form of military rule called "Market–Authoritarian" by John Sheahan (1987). Karen Remmer (1989) has recently provided evidence that contradicts the conjectures implicit in these models about the superior capacity of military regimes to solve crises or to promote development. Still, the idea that some form of authoritarianism is superior to democracy in promoting economic growth has, as I have already mentioned, lost none of its appeal (the leading examples cited today include the "soft authoritarian" regimes of Southeast Asia, the lasting economic successes of Pinochet's reforms, and the new "Free-Market Communism" of China).

Can tyrants really be the heroes they claim to be, if not in genuine popularity while in office, at least in posterity or the bond market? Perhaps Kwame Nkrumah of Ghana did not, in the end, deserve the accolades "Man of Destiny," "Hero of the Nation," "His High Dedication," "The Messiah," and others by which he was only too willingly known (Kirk-Greene 1991, p. 178), but can similar accolades really belong to Pinochet for his legacy of low long-run interest rates and privatized pensions? This question brings us to our final, perhaps mythical category: timocracy.

D. Timocracy

I borrow this term (perhaps inappropriately) from Plato (in *The Republic* [1974]). I use it to refer to a benevolent dictatorship, one in which the dictator genuinely cares for his or her people. It was not Plato's ideal form of rule – it ranked second to rule by the Philosopher–King in his scheme. Still, the Greek root of timocracy is *Thymos* – to love. In any case the allure of the concept of benevolent dictatorship is well known – whether it is indeed the rule of a philosopher–king, an enlightened despot, Fidel Castro or the Nicaraguan Sandinistas in their salad days, the dictatorship of the proletariat, the stern but growth-oriented regimes of Lee Kwan Yew of South Korea or Pinochet of Chile, or the social welfare function of modern economic theory. I do not know whether a genuinely benevolent regime has ever existed, but the idea has a never-ending appeal. So for this reason I include it here, defining it as a regime in which repression is low but which produces a dictator who is capable of staying in office because his or her love for the people is reciprocated by them. The historian Edward Gibbon (1981) suggested that the Antonine Age of the ancient Roman Empire was the happiest time the world had ever known. This provides me with an appropriately mythical historical context in which to theorize about how such a regime might operate.

To summarize this subsection, I have suggested four images of dictatorship which are common in the literature. Although it does a grave injustice to the works mentioned, from the point of view of this study, the four types can be usefully conceived of simply as different combinations of the variables "loyalty" and "repression." Thus, totalitarian regimes combine high repression with a high capacity to generate loyalty to the totalitarian party. In tyranny the regime stays in power through high repression alone; in such a regime, loyalty is low. A tinpot regime is low on both counts. And timocracy implies that loyalty is high even at low levels of repression. Consequently, in one sense the different regimes simply represent different solution levels of these variables, which suggests that all four regimes could in principle be obtained from a single general model. In this model the dictator maximizes a utility function in which utility depends on his or her own consumption, power, security, and so on. The constraints on the dictator's maximization are both political and economic. For example, the dictator cannot allow power to fall below the level required to remain in office, and maintaining this level of power requires scarce resources. The regime's institutions of repression and redistribution help to define these constraints. This model is developed in some detail in this book. The methodology behind it is introduced in Chapter 2. The next and final section of this chapter outlines the rest of the book.

3   Plan of the book

The first, previously cited questions to be pursued in this study are:

1. What are the primary tools that dictators use to stay in power?
2. What determines the repressiveness of a regime? How does the level of political repression respond to economic forces such as changes in the regime's economic performance (e.g., the rate of growth in GNP), and to political forces (e.g., changes in popularity)?
3. What circumstances (economic and political) contribute to the stability or instability of authoritarian regimes?

Part II of the book (Chapters 3, 4, and 5) suggests a simple abstract model which confronts these questions. In the model all dictators remain in power through the use of two broadly defined instruments: political repression and the accumulation of loyalty. One way to create loyalty, which is very common in the modern world, is to stimulate economic growth. Chapter 3 considers two types of regimes: totalitarian and tinpot. A totalitarian regime uses these instruments of repression and loyalty to maximize power over the population, whereas a tinpot regime seeks no more power over its citizenry than is required to remain in power and collect the fruits (Mercedes-Benzes, palaces, Swiss bank accounts) of that office. The basic institution of control in the totalitarian regime is the totalitarian party (Communist, Nazi, Ba'thist), which in some cases dominates the economic as well as the political sectors. Many tinpot regimes, on the other hand, are short-lived, are often military-backed or run, and do not deeply alter the economy.

Given these assumptions, we will develop a model in Chapter 3 that both displays the equilibrium levels of power, repression, and loyalty for each of these two types of regime and shows how levels of these political variables respond to changes in a regime's economic performance or to exogenous shocks such as the imposition of external sanctions or the offer of aid or trade. Some novel predictions are derived: For example, an improvement in economic performance tends to reduce repression under a tinpot regime but to *increase* it in a totalitarian one. This provides the basis for addressing question (9): What policies should Western democracies follow toward autocratic regimes? Chapter 3 develops the basic policy implications of the book; these implications are generalized further in Chapters 5 and 8 and summarized again in Chapter 14.

Chapter 4 develops a similar model for the other kinds of regimes considered here: tyrants and timocrats. The chapter begins by looking at life from the dictator's point of view. The leader's dilemma is that, given that he or she has such power over the regime's subjects, how can he or she know whether they really support the regime or are merely pretending to do so while secretly plotting his or her downfall? Put differently, is it better to be a tyrant or a timocrat? Although the model of tyranny is a straightforward extension of the totalitarian version, that of timocracy requires us to develop some new ideas. I ask whether a dictator who really loved his or her subjects would tend to prosper in office. The proposition that love tends to be reciprocated in this way was suggested long ago by the Greek philosopher Xenophon. I analyze how such a regime could be expected to function if it did exist, and I illustrate it with a possible historical example about which so little is known that the conjecture (by Gibbon 1981) that it was indeed benevolent rule could be true. In any case the label bears the stamp of Gibbon's authority. The regime referred to is that of the Antonine rulers of ancient Rome – especially Marcus Aurelius, the author of the famous *Meditations* (1964).

Chapter 5 generalizes the model developed in Chapters 3 and 4. I show there how the four types of dictatorship may be thought of simply as special cases of a very simple general model. This model also shows, in a precise way, the limits of the dictator's power.

Part III looks at the functioning of the economy under dictatorship. It is mostly devoted to questions (4) and (5), which were posed in the first section of the chapter:

4. Are dictatorships more capable of superior economic growth than democracies? Are they less subject to rent-seeking or redistributional pressures?
5. Does the introduction of free markets inevitably lead to the decline of dictatorship?

The first chapter in this part, Chapter 6, discusses alternative approaches to autocratic economies and presents the basic elements of the approach taken here. Part III then examines two examples of the economy of tyranny. Chapter 7 examines the case for the superior economic performance of contemporary free-market dictatorships and in particular asks whether there is any foundation to the idea that this superior performance results from the fact that dictatorships are less subject to rent-seeking or redistributional pressures than other forms of government (e.g., democracies). The cases of Pinochet's Chile and South Korea under the generals are examined in this light. This discussion is clearly relevant to question (10): How does a study of dictatorships shed light on the workings of democracy? Indeed, all of Part III compares, if sometimes only implicitly, the economic institutions of dictatorship and democracy. Chapter 8 turns to the economics of redistribution under the *apartheid* regime in South Africa. Two models are developed, one in which the regime exploited black labor for the benefit of white labor and one in which this exploitation benefited white capital. These models are also of general interest insofar as they show how economic exploitation can be carried out in markets. I also show why the regime collapsed – that is, I develop a simple autopsy for *apartheid*. Chapters 9 and 10 are devoted to the political and economic institutions of communism. Chapter 9 develops a model of Communist economics. This married totalitarianism to an economic system in which production was organized within a single bureaucratic system controlled by the Communist party. Chapter 10 applies this model to an understanding of the history of this system, first explaining how it worked under Stalin, and then turning to an examination of the economic decline of the system after the 1960s. It suggests an explanation of why in China the system was successfully transformed into a market economy whereas similar attempts by Gorbachev in the former Soviet Union simply led to the collapse of the regime.

Part IV looks at various questions concerned with the dynamics (rise and fall) of dictatorship, and thus it compares the political institutions of dictatorship and democracy. Chapter 11 models the breakdown of democracy in terms of a failure of democratic competition. I show that under certain circumstances political party competition ends up in the "inaction zone," a region in which both parties prefer to do nothing other than to propose a controversial course of action. This is more likely both when voters' preferences are relatively polarized and rigid and when there is little trust between voters and politicians. This formalizes and expands arguments developed in the political science literature by Samuel Huntington (1976), Giovanni Sartori (1976), and others that political polarization tends to breed an incapacity on the part of the political system to solve important problems, and that this failure, in turn, often leads to the breakdown of the democratic system and a turn toward authoritarianism. So Chapter 11 provides one point of view on question (6):

6. What circumstances contribute to the fall of democracy and the rise of dictatorship?

Chapter 12 continues the investigation of this subject, and it also turns to question (7):

7. How does nationalism arise and why do dictators promote it?

I develop a model of ethnic group relations and show why there is always a potential for conflict among ethnic groups, as well as why this conflict is not reduced by market forces.

Moreover, when political competition is based on conflict or competition among ethnic or racial groups, it is particularly likely to lead to polarization instead of compromise solutions. I introduce the concept of "ethnic capital"[2] and discuss the attractiveness of ethnicity or nationalism as a way of reducing transaction costs. Ethnicity is modeled as a capital good that reduces obstacles to both political and market exchange among those who have invested in it. Investments in ethnic capital naturally increase the importance of the group relative to the individual and therefore give rise to a demand for political leadership to manage that capital stock. Hence, their attractiveness to dictators. This same analysis also explains conflicts *between* groups and why the market mechanism cannot eliminate them as well as why democratic political mechanisms also do not solve these conflicts. Dictators resolve these conflicts through repression: Dictators give one group the capacity to impose its will on another. I use these concepts to examine the roots of the Nazi dictatorship. Throughout this chapter, I try to show the usefulness of the concept of ethnic capital in explaining the economic, political, and even psychological origins of Fascism.

---

[2] The term is George Borjas' (1992), although he does not model it the way I do here.

Chapter 13 discusses one aspect of the fall of dictatorship. It is devoted to an ethical and legal issue, namely question (8):

8. What is the responsibility of bureaucratic functionaries for crimes committed by the regime?

This question was, of course, most famously addressed by Hannah Arendt in her book, *Eichmann in Jerusalem* (1976), on the Nazi Final Solution to the Jewish question. The general question is this one: How is it possible to hold bureaucrats responsible for crimes committed by the regime if, in perpetrating those crimes, they are only following orders from their superiors? This issue reappears again and again. It was raised with respect to the behavior of the Argentinean military after the reassertion of civilian control there; it reappeared in Germany after the release of the files of the Stasi; and it became an issue in Poland and in Russia, where Yeltsin once suggested putting the Communist party itself on trial! The defense is always the same: "I acted under orders, so I can't be held responsible." I argue, with specific reference to the Eichmann case, that this line of defense was false in that it rested on an invalid picture of the way the Nazi regime functioned. Evidence from standard historical sources is used to show that Eichmann and others like him were in fact extremely competitive and entrepreneurial. They were not simply acting on orders; a host of agencies were "competing" to solve the Jewish question. Once this fact is understood, there is no difficulty in convicting them of guilt.

Part V (Chapter 14) summarizes the argument on a number of themes in simple English and concludes the book.

2   The Dictator's Dilemma

1   Sympathy for the dictator

The most obvious feature of dictatorship is that dictators typically have enormous power over their people. Yet there is one thing that even dictatorial powers cannot give them: the *minds* of their subjects. Dictators cannot – either by using force or the threat of force, or by promises even of vast sums of money or chunks of their empires (if any are available) – know whether the population genuinely worships them or worships them because they command such worship. The case of the Roman emperor Nero provides a good illustration.[1] Of all of his accomplishments, Nero was most proud of his lyre playing and, while emperor, he often entered musical contests. The art scene in Rome did not satisfy him and he headed for Greece. According to the profile of him by Gaius Suetonius, in his celebrated *The Twelve Caesars* (1957):

> His main reason [for leaving Rome] was that the [Greek] cities which regularly sponsored musical contests had adopted the practice of sending him every available prize for lyre playing; he always accepted these with great pleasure, giving the delegates the earliest audience of the day and invitations to private dinners. Some of them would beg Nero to sing when the meal was over, and applaud his performance to the echo, which made him announce: "The Greeks alone are worthy of my efforts, they really listen to music." (p. 224)

It is of course possible that the Greek audience may have been influenced by Nero's position. If that were not enough, Suetonius continued, there were other constraints on their behavior. He wrote,

> No one was allowed to leave the theatre during his recitals, however pressing the reason. We read of women in the audience

[1] Although they did not use the title "dictator" (only Julius Caesar had been granted that title permanently, and he did not, as it turned out, hold it for long), the emperors most surely had that power, as discussed in detail in Chapter 4.

giving birth, and of men being so bored with listening and applauding that they furtively dropped down from the wall at the rear, since the gates were kept barred, or shammed dead and were carried away for burial. (p. 225)

Jon Elster analyzes this general problem, which he refers to as the basic paradox of the Hegelian master–slave dialectic. He stated,

> The master cannot simultaneously enjoy his absolute power – which exists only insofar as he can abuse it . . . – *and* draw satisfaction from the recognition that the slave offers him. It would be like a nation seeking diplomatic recognition from one of its own colonies, like the person checking the news in the paper by buying a second copy . . . (1993, p. 67)

However, this way of thinking about dictatorship does not originate with Hegel, but was known in ancient times. Consider the dialogue by Xenophon, "Hiero, or Tyrannicus," apparently the only ancient dialogue devoted entirely to the subject of tyranny, and which Leo Strauss has resurrected and written an extensive commentary on (Strauss, 1963/1991). In the first part of the dialogue, the tyrant (Hiero) complains at length about the miseries that tyranny causes the *tyrant* himself. Flattery is no solace to him. He laments,

> "What pleasure . . . do you think a tyrant gets from those who say nothing bad, when he knows clearly every thought these silent men have is bad for him? Or what pleasure do you think he gets from those who praise him, when he suspects them of bestowing their praise for the sake of flattery?" (Xenophon, reprinted in Strauss 1963/1991, p. 5)

The basic problem is that the tyrant could trust no one, not even those closest to him. Because of this, love was denied to him as well. According to Hiero,

> ". . . [i]t is never possible for the tyrant to trust that he is loved. For we know as a matter of course that those who serve through fear try by every means in their power to make themselves appear to be like friends by the services of friends. And what is more, plots against tyrants spring from none more than from those who pretend to love them most. . . . How should they believe they are loved by anyone else, inasmuch as they are so hated by such as are inclined by nature and compelled by law to love them?" (pp. 7–8, 10)

Instead of trust or love, the tyrant's life is governed by fear. He continued,

> "To fear the crowd, yet to fear solitude; to fear being without a guard, and to fear the very men who are guarding; to be unwilling to have unarmed men about me, yet not gladly to see them armed – how could this fail to be a painful condition? . . . to trust strangers more than citizens, barbarians more than Greeks; to desire to keep the free slaves, and be compelled to make the slaves free – do not all these things seem to you signs of a soul distracted by fears?" (p. 13)

The poor tyrant! And yet his or her dilemma cannot be dismissed, and it must be investigated. To do so, let us begin by noting that this dilemma is inherent in any dictatorship – that is, in any system in which the rulers are self-appointed and in which there is no legal procedure for removing them. The problem is obviously magnified when procedures for succession are unclear. On the other hand the dilemma is partly solved if the identity of the successor is known for certain, as in dynastic rule. There is no point in assassinating a dictator if by doing so, you will only get his or her idiot son instead. This knowledge soothes the dictator.

The dilemma is also a paradox: As the dictator's *power* over his or her subjects increases, his or her problem appears to become larger. The more threatened they are by the ruler, the more the subjects will be afraid to speak ill of or to do anything which might conceivably displease him or her. Therefore, it would seem, the less the dictator knows what they are really thinking, and the more reason for him or her to be insecure! Hence the paradox: The greater the dictator's power, the more reason he or she has to be afraid. Finally, and most important, the problem is *two-sided*. The dictator's dilemma could equally be called the subject's dilemma: As much as dictators want to be loved, the subjects want them to believe that they *are* loved, for only then are the people safe from them. If they can make their dictator believe that they truly worship (or even that they support) him or her, then he or she need not fear them; and if in turn the ruler does not fear them, they need not fear him or her. This was the solution to the Dictator's Dilemma suggested by the character Simonides (an economist!) in Xenophon's dialogue. He told the emperor that if only he cared for his people, they would care for him in return, and then not only would he have nothing to fear from them, he would be the happiest of men. We will later examine (in Chapter 4) this strategy in more detail.

Stalin is a good modern illustration of a dictator in the grip of the dilemma – and of a different type of solution to this problem. According to the historian Alan Bullock, he thirsted for recognition from his former allies, the Old Bolsheviks, and it was this thirst which explains his fantastic efforts to extract confessions from them in the great show trials of the 1930s. Stalin wanted these allies to recognize, Bullock (1991) noted,

> not just that he had won, but that his victory was deserved and that they accepted him, as they had accepted Lenin, of their own volition, as the *Vozhd* (leader). This explains his insistence over and over again during the period of the trials that the accused, the generation of the Old Bolsheviks, should confess in humiliating terms that they had been wrong, and Stalin always right. (p. 358)

But it was not just this demand for recognition but fear itself that motivated Stalin. "His suspicion never slept," Bullock wrote. "[I]t was precisely the Bolshevik Old Guard whom he distrusted most. Even men who had been closely associated with him in carrying out the Second Revolution, as members of the Politburo or the Central Committee, were executed, committed suicide, or died in the camps" (p. 377).

Stalin was like Julius Caesar insofar as he attempted and was seen to be attempting to substantially augment his own personal power. But Caesar was popular. He won popularity not just through glory, but through generosity. He built a new forum with the spoils taken in Gaul. He doubled the pay of the army and made gifts of prisoners, thousands at a time, or loans of troops whenever asked, without first obtaining official permission from the Senate or the Roman people. He also presented the principal cities of Asia and Greece with magnificent public works, and he did the same for those of Italy, Gaul, and Spain (Suetonius 1957, p. 25). He always accepted honors, even when they might appear excessive: It was whispered at one point that at the next meeting of the Senate the title "King" (hated by many Romans) would be conferred on Caesar (p. 48). Stalin was "haunted by the fear of an attempt on his life" (Bullock 1991, pp. 364–5). No fewer than sixty men took part in Caesar's assassination.

The modern African dictator also suffers from insecurity. For many regimes, this insecurity is unsurprising, given the frequency of coups in and the notoriously short life of many African regimes.[2] However, even a long-lasting regime like that of Zaire's Mobutu, which survived for 31 years, was dominated by insecurity. According to Michael Schatzberg's

---

[2] John Londregan and Keith Poole (1990) provide evidence that the frequency of coups in Africa is caused by the poverty of that region, thus suggesting that no separate "Africa effect" is needed to explain this frequency.

(1988) portrait of the regime, "[t]he insecurity of its leaders is never far from the surface" (p. 49). One reason for this insecurity, apparently, was the difficulties Zairian officials experienced in obtaining information from the hinterland. The leader's problem (Schatzberg 1988; see also Callaghy 1984) is that his relationships with the people were filtered through the bureaucracy. The bureaucracy had its own interests, apart from giving Mobutu accurate information as to what was going on under his rule. In particular the regime's extensive use of coercion made bureaucrats afraid to turn in negative information – information that things were not going well in the hinterland – which might raise the possibility that there were people in some parts of Zaire who were not ecstatic about life under Mobutu. The bureaucrat who reported this information ran the risk associated with being the bearer of bad news. Thus, one of the important "information networks" used by the Zairian state was the CND (Centre National de Documentation), the direct successor of the Belgian Colonial Sûreté. Some CND reports read like this:

> During this ten day period all remains calm across all the area of Mongola. All the people work in joy, doubling their energy thanks to the continuity of the new regime. The recent ministerial reshuffle accomplished by the Father of the Nation brought forth a great joy among the population which promises him a sincere attachment. (Schatzberg 1988, p. 47)

Would reports like this one have made Mobutu feel more secure – or less? Perhaps sensing this problem, the CND employ the mantra "situation is calm" to soothe the dictator. The soothing action of the phrase was limited, however, as a result of its use in the following bizarre manner:

> You are informed that on 26 May 1974 the Zone Commissioner presented to the public 36 robbers who were sowing terror in the City of Bumba. These thieves are being kept in the central prison of Bumba which is not well maintained and their escape is to be feared. The operation continues. The situation is calm. (p. 47)

And then, one month later came this report: "Daily situation: of the 36 robbers arrested in Bumba, only 12 were brought to the prosecutor's office at Lizalla. Twenty-four escaped from the prison at Bumba. Situation is calm" (p. 48).

Thus, one problem with the coercive solution to the Dictator's Dilemma is that there is a cost to the dictator in imposing so much risk on the bureaucracy. It makes its members unwilling to report harmful – but truthful – information. Carl Friedrich and Zbigniew Brzezinski (1965) refer to this as the "vacuum effect" surrounding the dictator. In contemporary principal–agent theory, similar problems arise whenever the principal imposes too much risk on the agent. So it is not necessarily easy for dictators to displace their own risks onto those under them.

Of course, dictators typically enjoy income, privileges, and perquisites of office unknown to any democratic leader. But they also experience the other end of the spectrum of consumption possibilities: One common method of removing a dictator is assassination. In other words the dictator's rewards are great; his or her risks equally so. The dictator's fundamental difficulty in getting real information on just how popular he or she is compounds this risk–reward structure.[3]

Expressing it in terms of rational-choice theory, we would say that dictators and their subjects have a mutual communication or "signaling" problem; alternatively, they do not *trust* each other (Breton and Wintrobe 1982; Coleman 1990); or they have a problem of making "credible" commitments (North and Weingast 1989); or there is a problem of "enforcing" commitments (Przeworski 1991). Dictators may promise not to harm their subjects, but such promises are unenforceable. So are the citizens' promises of support. The insecurity of dictators follows from this line of reasoning: Mutual signaling is more costly between dictators and their subjects than between the government and the people in a democracy.

2   The method of analysis: economics and the enforcement problem

The Dictator's Dilemma, considered in abstract terms, is a set of circumstances in which there are gains from "exchange" (between the dictator and his subjects) but in which promises and obligations are not enforceable. For example, in exchange for their support, the dictator could promise to implement the kinds of policies that his or her subjects wish. However, what guarantee does each party have that the other party will live up to its commitment? Dictators could promise to change their policies in order to quell a riot, to appease an important interest group, or to break up a plot against them within the military or civilian bureaucracy. What commits dictators to keep their word after the crises are over? In the same way, any of these groups may profess their undying

---

[3] The general problem of knowing what the population really thinks is nicely described by Timur Kuran: It is caused by the disjunction between the *private beliefs* and *publicly expressed opinions* of the citizens of an autocracy (Kuran 1991, 1995). Kuran suggests that revolutions are, for this reason, fundamentally unpredictable.

support to calm a dictator. What prevents them from taking part in an assassination plot as soon as the ruler lets down his or her guard?

Viewed this way, we see that the Dictator's Dilemma is merely an extreme version of a very common problem. It exists in democratic politics, within firms and government bureaucracies, in families, and even in many markets. For example, consider the arena of democratic politics (interpreted here as political exchange). Particularly during elections, politicians promise policies in exchange for votes or for support from interest groups. What motivates the citizens or interest groups to believe the politicians will keep their promises? They cannot sue a politician in court for breaking a campaign promise. So what guarantee do they have that he or she will keep it after obtaining their votes? The world of bureaucratic politics is also often modeled in exchange terms. Bureaucrats trade favors with each other and with politicians. But a bureaucrat who reneges on a promise to do a favor for a politician or for another bureaucrat can't be taken to court. So how can the exchange take place? The same problem arises in primitive societies (in which often there are no courts) – and of course in many markets (some promises, e.g., that a good is "high quality" are obviously unenforceable, and many more are difficult to enforce). Even within families, the same problem arises if relations there are interpreted as exchange (e.g., a child may promise to "repay" his or her parents for the care he or she receives by promising to support them in their old age, but at present, at least in the United States, the parents can't sue the child if he or she reneges).[4]

In recent years a great deal of work has been done to apply the methods of economic theory to these problems, much as economic theory has been applied to areas traditionally in the domain of other disciplines such as law, politics, organizational relations, and the family. Partly as a result of this work, which has necessitated considerable adaptations to the tools of economic theory, and partly as a result of new developments in the theory of markets itself, it has been discovered that when economic rights and obligations are unclear, difficult to establish, or difficult to enforce, many of the standard propositions in economic theory do not hold and indeed are sometimes turned on their head. At the same time, this line of thought makes it possible to understand a great deal about social, political, legal, and even market relationships that is otherwise mysterious.

To see how the analysis works, consider the standard economic model

---

[4] Of course, one cannot rule out the development of such possibilities (citizens suing politicians, parents suing their children) in the future.

of the labor market. Note first that the same enforceability problem arises in this context. Firms hire employees and pay them a wage in exchange for the performance of tasks as specified by the employer. But what if the employer reneges and doesn't pay, or what if the employee "shirks" or otherwise performs badly? Implicitly, it is assumed the other party can sue in court and obtain satisfaction at little (theoretically zero) cost. Given this assumption – and some other standard ones – we know that the market for labor clears, producing an equilibrium wage W^* and employment level L^* in which everyone willing to work at that wage has a job.

Now suppose the assumption of costless enforceability is dropped. Instead, assume, say, that workers can shirk or in other ways perform their tasks poorly but that employers may have difficulty discovering this fact. One reason for this situation is that it may simply be hard to tell how well they are performing their tasks. For example, if employees are bond traders, it may be hard for the employer to ascertain if they are taking undue risk and exposing the firm to possible bankruptcy. If they are doing some form of creative work, it may be that an employee gets his or her best ideas while lying horizontally on a couch. In short, for various reasons, the performance of the employee may be difficult to monitor. What difference does this make? Suppose an employee shirks and the employer happens to discover this fact. The employer may threaten to fire him or her. However, by definition of the market-clearing wage W^*, any employee can get another job at that wage. Under these assumptions, the employee's rational response is to say, "Go ahead. The market clears, so if you fire me, I can always get another job at exactly the same wage as the one you're paying me!" In other words, as long as the market clears, no employee has any incentive to fulfill his or her contract as long as shirking is preferable to working. The reason this is so is that the employer has no means of punishing workers as long as a dismissed worker can always get another job on exactly the same terms as the one he or she already holds.

How can the employer solve this problem? One way is to offer a wage higher than that obtainable elsewhere. Then an employee can be credibly disciplined, because in that case the employee has something to lose (the wage premium) if he or she is caught shirking. However, all employers have exactly the same incentive to do this. So each firm will attempt to raise wages above those paid at rival firms, and the net result will simply be that the equilibrium wage at all firms rises to above market-clearing levels. In the end the problem does get solved, not because some firms pay higher wages than others (in equilibrium, they all pay the same wage), but because at the nonmarket-clearing wage, not only will some workers be involuntarily unemployed, but also every worker will face some *prospect* of unemployment. This situation gives employers *power* or authority over their workers. Employers can tell a worker to do something and threaten dismissal and the prospect of unemployment if he or she does not comply. As Carl Shapiro and Joseph Stiglitz (1984) put it, the prospect of unemployment serves as a "worker discipline" device.

The prospect of unemployment is not the only possible disciplinary mechanism. For example, Jeremy Bulow and Lawrence Summers (1986) suggested that if the economy can be divided into two sectors, one with "good" jobs (which pay high wages, offer some prospect of promotion and some job security, and so on) and one with "bad" jobs (with none of these attributes – McJobs, as they are popularly known), then the prospect of unemployment is not needed to discipline workers in good jobs. Dismissal poses a threat as long as the worker can fall into the bad jobs sector. Such a prospect is sufficient to discipline the labor force. Moreover, in this model many of the standard propositions of economic theory do not hold. For example, free trade is no longer optimal, because it is desirable to protect the good jobs sector.

Prior to the development of this type of model, economic theory identified power in economic relations solely with market power – that is, with some form of monopoly. These models showed that in the absence of costlessly enforceable property rights, power is not only consistent with but also essential to the workings of competition. Another implication of these models is that the institutions of exchange – and who controls them – make a difference. One reason this is so derives from the fact that the firm can deter employee shirking in either of two ways: by supervising workers more closely or by paying them a higher wage. To the firm, money spent on supervision and money spent on higher employee wages are both costs, and the firm will simply choose the cost-minimizing means to deter a given amount of employee shirking. But from the point of view of the economy, money spent on supervision uses up real resources, whereas paying higher wages does not, because it is merely a transfer from the firm to its employees. Consequently, from society's point of view, resources will be wasted in excess supervision (Bowles 1985; Shapiro and Stiglitz 1984). Moreover, alternative employment systems will give different results. Gordon (1990), for example, presents data on the ratio of administrative and managerial employees as a percentage of nonagricultural employment for various countries. In 1985 this ratio was 11.7 percent for the United States, but it was approximately 4 percent for Japan and West Germany, and 2.7 percent for Sweden. An interesting recent development is the "just-in-time system."

(In this system, as workers receive the next piece which they are supposed to work on, they are expected to see that it has come to them with no defects.) The system essentially *eliminates* supervisory personnel as such, because under such a system, workers are motivated to monitor each other.

In the labor market, then, *power* solves the enforcement problem. In other markets (and even in the labor market), there are alternative mechanisms that can perform this task. For example, consider the market for high-quality goods. Suppose that prior to purchase, consumers cannot distinguish high quality from low. What prevents the firm from producing low-quality goods and selling them as if they were of high quality? Carl Shapiro (1983, following Klein and Leffler 1981) showed that three conditions are required if a firm is to be discouraged from trying to cheat its customers:

1. There must be a prospect of future sales.
2. The firm must have a reputation, built in the past, as a seller of high-quality goods.
3. The firm must receive a price *premium* on high-quality goods, both to compensate it for its past investments in reputation and to serve as a deterrent to cheating.

According to the *no-cheating condition*, the present value of the premiums received from future sales must be large enough to overcome the one-time gains from cheating ("milking" the firm's reputation). In essence the existence of the price premium provides the consumer with a reason to trust the firm. Or, as Klein and Leffler put it, the consumer pays the firm "protection money" in the form of a price premium to ensure contractual fulfillment. In this context *trust* rather than power substitutes for legally enforceable property rights in solving the enforcement problem. But in another sense, the two solutions are the same: In both, *overpayment* (the wage or price premium) solves the cheating problem.

Now let us apply this way of thinking to political life. Begin by noting that all governments, democratic or dictatorial, provide services to citizens: They build roads, hospitals, and schools; and they provide policing and defense services which protect the population and (in dictatorships) repress it. The government provides these goods and services to the citizenry in exchange for political support. Or politicians may "supply" interest groups with policies that amount to some form of favorable regulation – a subsidy, a tariff, control over entry into an industry, favorable tax treatment, and so on – in exchange for campaign contributions. However, in any of these forms of political exchange, the problem, once again, is that there is no third party enforcement of the "contract" between politicians and citizens. Indeed, no formal contract is ever drawn up.

Because there is no contract, what prevents politicians from reneging on the exchange? Of course, they often do renege. The accusation that a government has "broken its promises" is one of the most commonly heard charges in any election campaign. However, if politicians *always* broke their promises, there would be little point in accusing them of doing so in any individual instance. So the question remains: Why do politicians keep their promises as often as they do? A similar question exists on the "demand" side of the political marketplace: What motivates citizens and interest groups to deliver support?

One solution is analogous to the one which was just given for labor and product markets: Cheating can be prevented when

1. There is a prospect of future interaction between the parties.
2. The parties have built up a reputation for not cheating.
3. The parties receive a premium on the exchange, both to compensate them for their past investments in reputation and to serve as a deterrent to cheating.

Now political parties are long-lived institutions both with reputations based on their past performance in office and with a substantial stake in their reputation in the future (Galeotti and Breton 1986; Weingast and Marshall 1988; Wintrobe 1987); and rational politicians have the same incentive as rational sellers in economic markets: to provide citizens with some reason to believe their promises (Wittman 1983). Similarly, rational politicians need to guard against "cheating" by citizens – that is, they will search for mechanisms which guarantee that citizens or interest groups can be counted on to deliver support. In general I suggest that the reciprocal problem of cheating is solved in political markets by "investments" which bind the parties to one another – that is, by engendering *political loyalty* or support. I define loyalty as a long-term attachment on the part of an individual to an organization or institution (for similar definitions see, e.g., Schaar 1968; also see Hirschman 1970). For the most part I will be talking about "rational" loyalty: For example, if Shapiro's conditions (1) to (3) are satisfied, the attachment is rationally motivated.

Substituting political parties for individuals as the central institutional actor in the political life of a democracy makes it possible to see how political exchange can take place. Conditions (1) and (2) are satisfied by democratic political competition when there is some trust in or loyalty to political parties. Of course, political parties may fall into disrepute, and many have. The fates of the Progressive Conservative Party in Canada or the Christian Democrats in Italy are recent cases which come readily to mind as examples of the severe punishment that voters can mete out to parties in which a pattern of cheating has been discovered.

This interpretation of political life also yields a simple explanation for the role of political *ideologies*, one which differs from the classic analysis of Downs (1957): A party's ideology is simply a set of promises, against which the actual performance of the party's representatives can be measured to ascertain whether cheating (deviating too far from its ideology) has occurred. This ideology gives the party a considerably larger role than simply assembling and nominating candidates (the roles assigned to it by Downs). It is the guardian of the voters' trust.

What is the political analogue of condition (3) – the premium? As far as politicians are concerned, the rewards – the income, prestige, and power – to holding political office are so large in most democracies that, by themselves, they constitute a substantial deterrent to political cheating. In a sense the premium here arises naturally from the dichotomous nature of political office – politicians are either "in" or "out." The more interesting question is what motivates loyalty on the part of citizens or interest groups. I suggest that the distribution of political *rents* (earnings that exceed productivity) often plays this role. Two examples which generate rational loyalty are pork-barrel projects and political patronage. Both are frequently discussed in the literature on congressional politics (Ferejohn 1974; Shepsle and Weingast 1981).

Suppose, for example, that a politician obtains a dam or bridge or other pork-barrel project for the citizens in his or her district. A proper cost–benefit analysis will reveal that the project is wasteful. Indeed, if the project is not wasteful, citizens have no reason to give their support to that politician in exchange for the dam or bridge, because the politician is making no sacrifice on their behalf but is simply doing what any technocrat would do. On the other hand, to the extent that the project *is* wasteful (i.e., a genuine pork-barrel project), citizens have some reason to believe that that politician or that political party is responsible for getting them the project and will thus look after their interests in the future, provided they reciprocate with their support. More precisely, the element of waste in the project is precisely the sign that the politician can claim credit for the project, as suggested by Ferejohn (1974) and others. A patronage job acts in exactly the same way. So pork-barrel projects and patronage jobs are the exact analog (in political markets) to price and wage premiums (in economic markets). The size of the premium is measured by the amount of waste in the project or by the excess of wages over marginal productivity in the case of a patronage job.

In general, the stock of loyalty capital may be measured by the total value of rents distributed by the political party in office. The total costs of rent-seeking (Posner 1975; Tullock 1967) – frequently measured in recent years – may be waste in the economic marketplace, but in the political marketplace these costs are useful investments which reduce the transactions costs of political exchange.

To recapitulate, we can say that the group which receives a monopoly privilege or other rent from a political party immediately has some reason to believe that that political party will look after its interests in the future. Because the rents can be withdrawn, politicians are justified in their belief that the favored group will provide the politicians with loyal support in return. The rents thus supply the necessary premium to compensate the group for its support or loyalty to the party, and they also serve as a deterrent to cheating. Consequently, pork-barrel projects and political patronage are investments which solve the problem of political cheating by citizens and interest groups (in political markets) in exactly the same manner as wage and price premiums (in labor and goods markets). We will call the total stock of such investments a politicians' "loyalty capital." These stocks are measurable and have been measured directly by Gianluigi Galeotti and Antonio Forcina (1989), who provide estimates of "loyalty ratios" for U.S. political parties.

Of course, these solutions are "second-best"; they involve waste and corruption, and in a sense they constitute a perversion of the democratic ideal. In the ideal scenario the citizenry trusts its politicians to implement their promises, and politicians can count on the citizenry in turn to fight for their political beliefs. But the ideal implicitly assumes that enforcement costs are zero. *So there is a precise parallel between the economist's ideal of markets and the political scientist's ideal of politics: Both function in the way they are supposed to only if the costs of enforcement are ignored.*

Still, we should not remain blind to the enormous gap between the pork-barrel and patronage-style solutions to the enforcement problem, on the one hand, and the democratic ideal, on the other. And this recognition should alert us to the fact that there are many other, better ways in which democracy might work and sometimes does. The basic problem for democratic politicians is to get the citizenry to believe in them and to motivate its voters to act on this belief by supporting them. There are many ways parties can do this. J.R. Lott (1987), for example, suggests that one important device by which politicians can precommit themselves is *ideology*. His many papers provide considerable evidence for this view (see, e.g., Lott 1987, 1990; for a general survey, see also Lott and Bender 1996). William Landes and Richard Posner (1975) suggested another mechanism to solve the enforcement problem: The independent judiciary, by making legislation harder to reverse in the future, helps to serve as a precommitment device. No doubt there are many other institutions that serve this function, and an illuminating book could probably be written about democracy from this point of view. In the present context, perhaps the most interesting point is that by limiting the power of the ruler over his or her subjects, by ensuring a free press which not only frees the subjects to criticize the ruler but also enables the ruler to discover what his or her subjects are really thinking, and by providing formal constitutional means for the ruler's removal, democratic institutions allow relations of trust to develop, credible commitments to be made, or signals to be sent much more simply and directly than is possible under dictatorships. Consequently, however badly democracy may sometimes perform in these respects, on theoretical grounds, we should expect it to do better than the alternative! With this point in mind, let us return to the subject of dictatorship and see what strategies are available to the dictator for solving the Dictator's Dilemma.

3   The instruments of political power

The message of our brief tour of the economics of self-enforcing exchange in the preceding section is that there are a number of devices which can substitute for the missing external enforcement mechanism, devices which allow exchange to take place.[5]

As far as the strategies available to the dictator are concerned, I suggest that all of them may be grouped into two classes: *repression* and *loyalty*.

By repression I refer to restrictions on the rights of citizens to criticize the government, restrictions on the freedom of the press, restrictions on the rights of opposition parties to campaign against the government, or,

---

[5] A second implication of this analysis is that markets do not solve the enforcement problem by themselves, and there is therefore a role for some other external force – which could be legal enforceability or the rule of law, but which could also be the dictator's political power – that helps markets to function. In other words, even within the realm of pure neo-classical economic theory, in the absence of a perfectly and costlessly functioning legal system, one cannot rule out the unpleasant idea that political and even autocratic interventions might be beneficial to economic efficiency or growth. The notion that markets spontaneously solve these problems by themselves, so widely believed and propagated, is simply logically incorrect. The lesson is perhaps by now well understood after the disastrous results of the attempt to simply "liberalize" the economy in Russia. There is thus no alternative, in assessing the operation of an economic system, to inquiring into how it works in some detail, and one cannot dismiss every autocratic intervention into the economy as one which necessarily reduces economic efficiency; as we will see (in Part III, where this issue is extensively discussed), many of them do, but not all, and not always in the ways expected.

as is common under totalitarian dictatorship, the outright prohibition of groups, associations, or political parties opposed to the government. To be effective, these restrictions must be accompanied by the monitoring of the population and by sanctions for disobedience. The existence of a political police force and of extremely severe sanctions for expressing and especially for organizing opposition to the government (such as imprisonment, internment in mental hospitals, torture, and execution) is the hallmark of dictatorships of all stripes.

How does the use of repression get around the Dictator's Dilemma? In part, of course, it does not (indeed, it *engenders* it), for as we have seen, the more the citizens are ruled by repression, the more the dictator has to fear from them. However, there is a way to solve this problem: Increase the level of repression further. Eventually, the dictator's own fear will begin to subside, for the simple reason that he or she need only be afraid of the people *if* (and it is a big *if*) they can organize or get their hands on the means to depose him or her. Increasing repression reduces this likelihood. However, it does cause another problem: In order to accomplish this goal, the dictator's security forces must themselves be given sufficient power, and their own uncertain reliability may, in the end, constitute the main threat to the ruler's regime. One obvious way to solve this problem is to overpay the security forces. But this is not the only way; there is another one that was typified by Stalin. Alan Bullock (1991) described his strategy when he wrote,

> ... [a]s a man of the people himself, not an intellectual or a former emigé, he alone understood that the Russian people had always been ruled, and could only be ruled, by fear, by suffering. And the key to that, as Peter the Great and Ivan the Terrible had understood before him, was to keep the *apparat* itself in a state of fear which it would in turn pass on to the people. Convictions might change, but fear lasted. ... After Yagoda had completed two years as head of the secret police, Stalin decided that the time had come to liquidate him. He was succeeded by Yezhov, after whom the worst period of the terrors is known in Russia as the *Yezhovschina*; Yezhov also lived in fear, and when Stalin decided that the time had come, he, too, was liquidated. (p. 357)

This description of Stalin's strategy is not yet complete. One other important element in the successful inducement of fear (and the accurate revelation of information about culpability) is to ensure *competition* among agencies. Seweryn Bialer (1980) describes how this was part of Stalin's strategy as well:

The secret police itself, the main tool but also the main danger to Stalin, was not permitted to grow too powerful *against* Stalin. It was checked by a number of administrative arrangements and policies. Besides Stalin's private secretariat, the most important of those were:

The existence in the secretarial apparatus of the party's Central Committee of a Special Department [later named Department of Administrative Organs] which was empowered to supervise the internal affairs of the secret police;

Stalin's retention of the power to appoint high police officials who were often selected from competing factions in order to minimize the possibility of a monolithic command and collusion;

The retention of a military intelligence apparatus [GRU], semi-autonomous from the secret police, which provided an independent channel of information and an investigative body in strong competition with the police;

The infrequent but significant reorganizations of the police apparatus, the most important of which consisted of dividing the enormous machine into two command structures – the MVD (NKVD) and MGB (NKGB) – and the separation of the internal intelligence and counterintelligence service from control over the militarized internal security units [VVB]. (p. 35)

So repression itself is, after all, one way to "solve" – or at least to ameliorate – the Dictator's Dilemma. The complications arising from its use (from the dictator's point of view) can be handled in several ways: There can be sufficient further repression; the security forces can be overpaid; such forces can be kept in a state of fear by means of competition among the different agencies; and so on.

Substantial evidence exists on the extent of repression in different regimes. Although the level of political repression may be difficult to measure conceptually, a number of indices are available, among which perhaps the best known is the "Civil Liberties Index," which has been issued by Freedom House annually since 1973 for a very large number of countries. Countries are ranked subjectively from 1 (most free) to 7 (least free) on the basis of such factors as the number of political prisoners, freedom of expression, freedom of the press, and so on. The rankings are reviewed by a distinguished panel of academics.

Economists have not, until recently, made much use of these data. The basic reason is undoubtedly the absence of a good theory of the determinants of political repression. On the other hand it is an article of faith among many economists that at least some of the important determinants of political freedom are economic. Using the Gastil data, John Bilson (1982) attempted to test for the influence of these factors and other economic variables on political freedom. However, the results were not very definitive. For example, the level of government intervention turned out not to be a significant determinant of political repression in his analysis. Neither did the growth rate of GNP, the average level of government expenditure, the ratio of exports to GNP (an index of "openness" to foreign influences), or population size. The only important explanatory variable was the level of income per capita, which is negatively correlated with political repression. However, the hypothesis that all the coefficients are equal to zero was also rejected. This possibility and the likelihood that all the independent variables themselves are highly correlated suggest that the main obstacle to progress in this area is that we do not understand how the variables are related to one another. R.H. Barrow (1949/1987) used the Civil Liberties Index in a multiple regression analysis to investigate the determinants of economic growth. Adam Przeworski and Fernando Limongi (1993) summarized the findings of a number of studies in an attempt to see if there is any correlation between dictatorship and economic growth, and they found very mixed results. Perhaps the most robust finding in this literature is the correlation between political stability and economic growth reported by Silvio Borner, Aymo Brunetti, and Beatrice Weder (1995). There is also the interesting finding of Stephen Knack and Philip Keefer (1995) that the protection of property rights, independent of regime type, is positively related to growth. But the main obstacle to discovering the determinants of repression – and the effects of repression on economic variables – appears to be not a lack of data but the lack of theory.

The other way to accumulate power is to accumulate political loyalty. One way to do this, as we have already suggested, is by means of the distribution of rents. But if this unsavory practice is common in democratic regimes, we will see that they pale in this respect in comparison with dictatorships. This subject is considered in detail in Part III of the book. In the meantime, readers might satisfy themselves on the plausibility of this point by recalling the well-known practice of this art under, say, Marcos in the Philippines, Hwan and Woo in South Korea, or communism as practiced everywhere. Note that on theoretical grounds we already have some reason to expect dictatorships to engage in greater rent distribution than democracies. Many of the institutions which can be used to create trust directly in democracy are exactly those forsworn by dictators. Nevertheless, there are other, more subtle strategies available to a dictator to gain the trust of his or her subjects. Some of them can be illustrated by examining the practices of the Roman emperor

Augustus. Augustus was one of the most skilled individuals at accumulating power the world has ever known, a ruler who (with Antony) defeated Brutus and then Antony (and Cleopatra), and founded the Roman Empire.

Suetonius describes some of the techniques Augustus used to solve the Dictator's Dilemma. For example, he often committed adultery, but according to Suetonius, he did so only for reasons of state: "[H]e wanted to discover what his enemies were at by getting intimate with their wives or daughters" (1957, p. 92). He nearly always restored the kingdoms which he had conquered to their defeated dynasties, and he followed a policy of linking together his royal allies by mutual ties of friendship or intermarriage (p. 82). One reason he fought wars, Suetonius says, is "because he wished to offer his secret enemies, and those whom fear rather than affection kept with his party, a chance to declare themselves by joining [his enemy] Lucius Antonius; he would then crush them, confiscate their estates, and thus manage to pay off his veterans" (p. 61). After what happened to Julius Caesar, he was wise enough to refuse offers of excessive honors. Thus, "when the people would have forced a dictatorship on him he fell on his knee and, throwing back his gown to expose his naked breast, implored their silence . . ." (p. 84). And "[he] did his best to avoid leaving or entering any city in broad daylight, because that would have obliged the authorities to give him a formal welcome or sendoff" (p. 84).

According to Suetonius, he was known for his generosity to all classes of people (p. 77). "None of Augustus' predecessors had ever provided so many, so different or such splendid public shows" (p. 78). But he always tried to demonstrate that he did this *not* to win popularity, but simply to improve the public welfare – that is, because he cared for the people, and wanted to be generous to them. But this did not mean that he could be taken advantage of. If the people demanded largesse which he had in fact promised, he responded, "I always keep my word." But he refused to grant demands for largesse for which no promise had been given (p. 78).

All of these strategies are ways to accumulate loyalty,[6] an ability which, I will argue, is characteristic of stable or long-lived dictatorships. As even Napoleon is said to have realized, "[T]errorist methods are a sign of weakness rather than of strength" (Cobban 1971, p. 90). The fact that both Hitler and Mussolini amassed considerable popular support is

---

[6] Although he was not averse to creating fear. "Once for instance, while addressing a soldiers' assembly at which a crowd of civilians were [*sic*] also present, he saw a Roman knight named Pinarius transcribing his speech; and had him stabbed there and then as taking too close an interest in the proceedings" (Suetonius 1957, p. 68).

well known (see, e.g., the studies in Larsen, Hagtvet, and Mykelbust 1980) and the basis for the famous claim by Seymour Lipset (1960) and others that the masses are a threat to democracy when politically active. In the next chapter we will show how the structure of totalitarian parties facilitates investments in loyalty. Chapter 4 returns to the Roman Empire and examines still other techniques used by the emperors to accumulate support.

In summary, the Dictator's Dilemma sounds like a paradox. In particular, what appears paradoxical is the proposition that the more power dictators have, the more insecure they are. Was Julius Caesar not powerful? And was it not for that reason that he was killed? But the paradox is really an artifact of the command model often used implicitly in discussions of power, a model in which the only instrument of power available to the dictator is commands backed by sanctions. A more general analysis, which we have begun in this chapter, shows that there are many ways for the dictators to accumulate power without increasing their insecurity.

Indeed, all of the techniques mentioned – the accumulation of loyalty (Augustus), the exercise of surveillance (Mobutu), and the use of bureaucratic competition to create fear (Stalin) would appear to increase the dictator's security as well as his or her power, thus invalidating the simple paradox of an apparent correlation between insecurity and power. Other strategies enable dictators to increase their level of security – and the security of their assets – at the expense of their power. Examples of such expenditures abound: The most obvious are the Swiss bank account; the plane on the landing strip, both ready and fueled; or the Praetorian Guard. Another technique is the practice of rotating – and requiring turnover among – staff and senior officers. Indeed, the simplest technique is to accept formal checks or limits on his or her power. Douglas North and Barry Weingast (1989) explain the Glorious Revolution in England – from which Parliament obtained from the king the capacity to insist that he repay his debts – in this manner. They point out that accepting this constraint on his power subsequently allowed the king to raise more revenue, because his promises to repay would, for the first time, be credible. By contrast, the French king, whose authority was not similarly limited, was at a disadvantage, a disadvantage which ultimately led to the bankruptcy of the state and to the French Revolution. In the same way, on the basis of our analysis, the population would have less to fear from the dictator if there were limits on his or her power. Such a dictator would also have less to fear from the people – and thus be more secure. So, in all these ways, a dictator can exchange power for security if he or she so desires.

In short, there are a number of techniques a dictator can use to circumvent the paradox of power. Behind the paradox, however, lies a fundamental truth about dictatorship: The absence of a legitimate, regularized procedure for the dictator's removal from office makes him or her relatively insecure in it. So, on perfectly rational grounds, the characteristic personality trait of dictators is paranoia.

4   Conclusion

The Dictator's Dilemma results from the fact that using his or her power to threaten people can increase his or her own insecurity in office. As the threat to the people increases, the people become more afraid to speak out or to do anything which might displease the ruler; as a result, the less the dictator knows about what they are really thinking or planning, and the more reason he or she has to fear them. On the other hand, if the subjects can convince the dictator of their support, then he or she need not fear them, and they therefore need not fear him or her. In terms of rational-choice theory, the dictator and the subjects have a problem of credibly "signaling" support or trust in one another. I discussed a number of reasons why this problem is important for the dictator's subjects; one of them is the fact that the insecurity of the dictator results in excessive repression (Stalin is the classic modern example).

From one point of view, the dilemma is simply an extreme case of the general problem of building or accumulating trust between two parties when their assets are very unequal – for example, in wealth, beauty, or fame, as well as in power. (For example, a woman who won a lottery declared on television afterward that from now on, she would be "stuck with the friends she has" – that is, now that she was wealthy, friendly overtures from people who were not themselves wealthy could only be greeted with suspicion.) From another point of view, the dilemma arises when there are gains from exchange but when promises and obligations are not enforceable. This problem occurs in many situations: in democratic politics, within firms and government bureaucracies, in families, and even in many markets. One general solution to this problem involves *overpayment* or the use of a price premium to motivate loyalty or trustworthiness. I explained how this solution works in the context of the labor market and the "market" for votes (democratic politics). I then looked at some of the ways autocrats have solved this problem, including Stalin, the Roman emperor Augustus, and Mobutu of Zaire, and I suggested that all these solutions can be grouped into two types: repression and loyalty.

Part II

Equilibrium political repression

3 The tinpot and the totalitarian

1 Introduction

One of the most provocative and controversial contemporary studies of dictatorship was that of Jeane Kirkpatrick, in her book *Dictatorship and Double Standards* (1982).[1] The essence of her argument, as already mentioned in Chapter 1, is that there are two kinds of dictatorships. The first type, commonly referred to as "totalitarian" dictatorship, is characterized by massive government intervention into the economic and social lives of the citizenry, an intervention motivated by utopian goals of one kind or another and exemplified by Communist dictatorships, Nazi Germany, and possibly contemporary Iran. The second type is what Kirkpatrick, following Carl Friedrich and Zbigniew Brzezinski (1965), calls "traditional autocracies" and which I call "tinpot" dictatorships, ones in which the ruling government does not intervene very much into the life of the people, represses them only to the modest extent necessary to stay in office, and uses its rewards of monopoly of political power to maximize personal wealth or consumption. Examples include Anastasio Somoza of Nicaragua, the Shah of Iran, Ferdinand Marcos of the Philippines, and General Noriega of Panama. In short, in Kirkpatrick's model, the basic tool dictators use to remain in power is the instrument of repression, and tinpot and totalitarian dictatorships differ mainly in their level of repression.

Perhaps surprisingly, in view of the controversy generated by these ideas, very little effort has been made to answer the simple question: How much of the actual behavior of dictatorships can be explained with this type of model? For example, although all dictatorships are repressive, the level of repression does not appear to be constant under any particular regime, whether totalitarian or tinpot. In the former Soviet Union and in Eastern Europe, for example, from time to time there appeared periods of permissiveness or "thaws," such as those that occurred in the Soviet Union under Khruschev and later under Gorbachev.

[1] Some of the material in this chapter originally appeared in Ronald Wintrobe (1990).

43

In Latin America there was a resurgence of authoritarianism in the 1970s (see, e.g., Collier 1979). In the 1980s this trend was reversed and a period of democratization ensued, which persists as of this writing (1997). How can these changes be explained?

A second question concerns the behavior of *military* dictatorships (a very common form in the modern world). If coercion or repression is the basic tool of dictatorial rule in general, one would expect military governments to have a comparative advantage here; military dictatorships should be among the most successful dictatorships, in the sense that they would be stable and long-lived. Instead, we find precisely the opposite. Military regimes tend to be relatively short-lived and unstable, and (what could be more ignominious) often they hand power over to a civilian government after fewer than five years in power (Nordlinger 1977, p. 139; Paldam 1987). What explains the instability of military regimes, and why do military governments sometimes voluntarily cede power to civilians?

Third, consider totalitarian regimes. Although we have very little direct evidence about the popularity of these regimes in the form of opinion polls or electoral results, we do have some information about them. For example, we know that after the end of World War II, a large proportion of the German population still supported Hitler (see the results of various polls in Larsen, Hagtvet, and Mykelbust 1980). It is also well known among scholars of comparative economic systems that the economic record of Communist regimes, at least as measured by economic growth rates over long periods of time, was remarkably good (Ofer 1987). Economic performance declined in the 1970s and rather dramatically in the 1980s, but measured performance compared very favorably with that of capitalist countries from the 1920s to the 1970s. Performance in Communist China in the 1980s and 1990s, as measured by growth rates, has been astonishing (Perkins 1994). One traditional explanation of the periods of apparent popularity or dynamism of totalitarian regimes is that the people in those societies are brainwashed by the government. Repression is carried out not only against actions but also against thought. Kirkpatrick's (1982) definition of totalitarian government is "one prepared to use governments' coercive power to transform economic and social relations, beliefs, values and psychological predispositions" (p. 101). A "totalitarian ideology" is the first of Friedrich and Brzezinski's (1965) six characteristics of totalitarian government. Gordon Tullock (1987) develops an evolutionary argument to suggest that human beings are "readily indoctrinable" (p. 94) and will accept any regime that has been in office for some time, although he does not accord this factor much importance in explaining the survival of dictatorship.

One obvious problem with these explanations, when viewed from a contemporary standpoint, is that if totalitarian propaganda was success-ful in the past, what explains its obvious failure in the 1989–91 period in Eastern Europe and then in the Soviet Union? But the more general problem with ideology as an explanatory variable is simply that we do not understand it very well. Thus, Friedrich and Brzezinski, after giving ideology pride of place in their explanation of the workings of totalitari-anism, also suggest that the populations in these societies have a pro-found distrust of what they are told. But if the ideology is not believed, what function does it serve? Kirkpatrick (1982), having laid even greater emphasis on the importance of ideological indoctrination to explain the survival of totalitarian government, brings herself at last to the cen-tral question. She writes, "But have they [the Politburo leaders] man-aged to reform human consciousness? Have they managed to educate Soviet citizens so that they would freely choose to behave according to the norms of Soviet culture *if the constraints of coercion were removed*? The answer of course is that we do not know" (emphasis in original, p. 123).

After the fall of communism in the Soviet Union and Eastern Europe, it appears that we do know the answer to this question, and it is "no."

In this book I will not assume that dictatorships – even totalitarian ones – can capture the souls of men and women. They may, however, obtain their loyal support, which is quite a different matter and one entirely within the domain of rational choice. So a dictator can use two instruments – repression and loyalty – to accumulate power over the population. Section 2 of this chapter shows the equilibrium levels of repression and loyalty for a tinpot dictator, one who simply maintains the minimum amount of power necessary to stay in and enjoy the fruits of office. This model is then used to address two issues: first, the relation-ship between economic performance and political repression, and, sec-ond, the instability of military dictatorships. Section 3 extends the model to totalitarian regimes – that is, regimes which maximize power – and develops the connection between economic performance and political repression for that type of regime. These two sections imply, surprisingly, that an improvement in economic performance tends to lower the level of political repression in a tinpot regime but to raise it in a totalitarian regime. Finally, Section 4 of the chapter looks at policy implications. It derives the policies which democratic governments should pursue to-ward dictatorships, assuming that the objective is simply to promote more freedom in those countries (i.e., neglecting possible strategic considerations).

2   The model of a tinpot regime

A. Equilibrium levels of loyalty and repression

To this point I have argued that dictators typically use two instruments to build and maintain political power over the population under their governments. The first instrument involves political repression – that is, removing the threat of opposition to their policies by outlawing it. The use of this instrument requires resources devoted to producing repressive legislation, to publicizing these laws, to policing their obedience, and to punishing offenders. Alternatively, dictators can bind parts of the population to them as loyal supporters through the creation and distribution of political rents. Rents cost resources and in addition generate a deadweight loss to the economy (of course, expenditures on repression are also deadweight losses). The dictator who wishes to remain in office therefore faces a trade-off between these two alternatives. The interrelationships between them, however, are complex. The main complication is that whereas loyalty and repression both use up resources (and in that sense are alternative "inputs" into the creation and maintenance of political power), their levels are not independent of one another: The level of repression affects the supply of loyalty. In order to sort out the various relationships involved, I now construct a simple model of the equilibrium levels of repression and political loyalty.

First, I assume that the relationship between the inputs of loyalty (L) and repression (R) and their output (power) can be represented by the production function:

(1) $\pi = \pi(L, R)$.

The production function for power (π) is assumed to be "well-behaved" – that is, $\pi_L, \pi_R > 0, \pi_{LR} > 0, \pi_{LL}, \pi_{RR} < 0$. These relationships imply that the continued use of either instrument alone leads to diminishing returns in the production of power and that there is some complementarity between repression and loyalty in the production of political power. Figure 3.1 depicts this production function in the form of a set of isopower lines in which, as is usually the case, higher isopower lines denote higher power.

Second, I assume that the amount of loyalty available to the dictator is, like any capital good, fixed in the short run but variable in the long run.

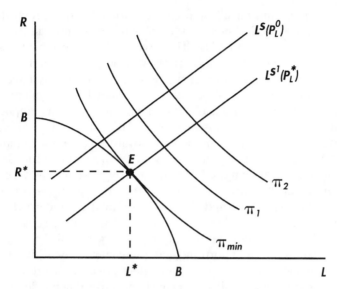

Figure 3.1. Equilibrium levels of repression and loyalty under a tinpot.

On the other hand the level of repression is variable in the short as well as in the long run.

Third, I distinguish two kinds of dictators: totalitarians and tinpots. Totalitarian dictatorships use the instruments of mass control to maximize power over the population under their jurisdiction. I believe this objective function is consistent with the characterization of totalitarianism in Hannah Arendt (1951/1973), Friedrich and Brzezinski (1965), or Friedrich Hayek (1944).[2] The objective function of a tinpot dictator, on the other hand, is to minimize the resource cost of staying in office. In Figure 3.1 the tinpot dictator seeks no more power over the population than that represented by the lowest isopower line in the figure, π_{min}. At any lower level of power, the tinpot will be deposed. Should tinpots obtain more resources than required to attain $\pi = \pi_{min}$ (resource constraints will be discussed shortly), they do not spend them on repression or loyalty, but on their own personal consumption or that of their families. Since tinpots always remain at π_{min} (as long as they stay in office), it immediately follows that there is an inverse relationship between the amounts of L and R demanded by the tinpot: An increase in R results in a fall in the level of L demanded.

Now consider the supply of loyalty to tinpot dictators. I assume that

---

[2] See, especially, Arendt, pp. 320ff., and the discussion in R. Burrowes (1968).

although tinpots may have a monopoly of formal political office, they do not monopolize political power in their countries but instead face opposition in the form of potential alternatives to the government. Citizens and interest groups may establish (possibly covert) ties with these potential opposition leaders. In other words such dictators may have a monopoly of formal (legal) political power, but they have no monopoly on political loyalty. What happens to the supply of loyalty to a tinpot if the level of political repression is increased? To analyze a typical citizen's response, recall that, in our framework, loyalty to the government or to opposition leaders is a capital asset which is accumulated in order to facilitate political exchanges. Each citizen may be viewed as accumulating an optimum "portfolio" of these assets, taking into account their expected rates of return and their risk. As in the standard theory of portfolio choice (see, e.g., Arrow 1971 for an exposition), a change in the riskiness or in the rate of return of any asset will lead the investor to change his or her desired portfolio, and this change may be decomposed into the usual income and substitution effects. In other words citizens or interest groups who speak out against the government, demonstrate against it, and so on are essentially offering their loyalty to someone willing to offer an alternative policy. An increase in repression affects the risks that are associated with accumulating these assets as well as the return on such assets.

The increase in repression may take the form of an increase in the range of activities prohibited, in the level of policing of forbidden activities, or in the size of the sanctions imposed on those caught engaging in them. Whichever form it takes, the risks of disloyalty among the citizens are increased, and the expected rate of return is diminished. Consequently, from the point of view of citizens and interest groups, the attractiveness of dealing with the opposition decreases, and the relative attractiveness of exchanges with the dictator, or with his or her representatives, increases. This substitution effect implies that a typical citizen's loyalty – and hence the aggregate supply of loyalty to the dictator – will be positively related to the level of repression. However, there is an income effect that works in the opposite direction. An increase in repression either increases the likelihood that the individual will be the victim of a sanction, or it increases the size of the sanction imposed, and this is so even if he or she is for the most part loyal. This fact reduces the individual's wealth, and, as long as investments in political loyalty are a normal good, it reduces investments in political loyalty to the regime (as well as to the opposition). At low levels of repression, this effect will be small for most individuals. For example, if, as in the early years of Nazi Germany, repression is directed mainly at obvious opponents of the regime (e.g., at Jews), the loyalty of these groups would obviously be reduced, but individuals who do not fall into such a category could reasonably assume that they would not be the victims of the regime's repressive policies. Consequently, as long as the level of repression is relatively low, it seems reasonable to assume that the substitution effect dominates the income effect for most citizens. If this is the case, the aggregate supply of political loyalty is positively related to the level of repression, as depicted by the two L^S curves in Figure 3.1.

The supply of loyalty to the dictator will also depend on other variables apart from the level of repression. In our framework, citizens and interest groups supply loyalty because they expect to receive in return some portion of the gains from political exchange. This return or rent to suppliers can be represented as a "price" received per unit of loyalty supplied (P_L). The distinction between the price received and the price paid will be discussed shortly. I assume the supply of loyalty is positively related to this price. In Figure 3.1 an increase in P_L from P_L^0 to P_L^* therefore results in a rightward shift of the supply curve, as depicted.

Finally, the supply of loyalty also depends on the economic performance of the regime (PE). For example, suppose that performance were better than expected. Then the value of a given fraction of the rents from political exchange will tend to rise, and the supply of loyalty will increase.

For these reasons, the supply of loyalty function can be written as

(2) $L^S = L^S(R, P_L, PE)$

where

$$\frac{\partial L^S}{\partial R} > 0, \ \frac{\partial L^S}{\partial P_L} > 0, \ \frac{\partial L^S}{\partial PE} > 0.$$

The model can be completed by formally introducing the resource costs to the dictator of repression and loyalty. The costs per unit of repression, P_R, are the costs of obtaining manpower and capital equipment for the police, prisons, and the court system. It seems reasonable to assume that these per unit costs are not under the tinpot's control, although some dictators may be able to "produce" repression more efficiently than others, as will be discussed shortly. So we will assume they are fixed (i.e., $P_R = \bar{P}_R$).

The cost to the dictator of creating and maintaining loyalty (P_L) includes the costs of creating and distributing monopoly rents, of building dams or bridges, of doing favors for the citizenry, and so on. The production of loyalty is a rather subtle process, because it essentially involves the creation of a belief on the part of the citizens that the dictator can be counted on to look after their interests. The costs involved therefore include the costs of communicating, in addition to the literal costs of such pork-barrel projects as dams and bridges. It follows that the demand price, the price *paid* for a unit of loyalty capital by the dictator (P_L^D), differs from the supply price, the price *received* by suppliers of loyalty (P_L^S), because the former includes all the costs incurred by the dictator to create and maintain loyalty, whereas the latter includes only the portion actually received by the suppliers of loyalty. Normally, the two prices will move together, but, for example, an increase in the efficiency of producing loyalty implies a lower P_L^D, but not necessarily a lower P_L^S. Apart from such exogenous changes, we shall assume that the ratio P_L^D/P_L^S is fixed. In what follows, the superscripts S or D will be dropped to simplify the notation whenever they are not required.

In order to represent the dictator's expenditure function, it is convenient to rewrite equation (2) with P_L instead of L as the dependent variable. In other words,

(2)′ $P_L = P_L(L, R, PE)$,

in which case $\dfrac{\partial P_L}{\partial L} > 0$, $\dfrac{\partial P_L}{\partial R} < 0$, $\dfrac{\partial P_L}{\partial PE} < 0$.

The dictator's expenditure function is then simply:

(3) $B = P_R R + P_L(L, R, PE)L$.

Equation (3), which incorporates the supply of loyalty relationship of equation (2)′, is depicted by the concave budget line *BB* in Figure 3.1. The variable B does not represent the total budget of the government, because it does not include resources spent for the dictator's personal consumption. Rather, B represents the resource costs to the dictator of staying in office. Dictators are not constrained by any particular level of B, because at least to some extent their powers enable them to increase the resources under their control through increased taxation, borrowing, or simple confiscation (although these methods may of course have deleterious effects on the economy and therefore on the dictator's future consumption prospects). A simple way of representing the dictator's total budget is discussed shortly. For the moment we simply note that resources spent on R or L to maintain the hold on power are thereby diverted from the tinpot's personal consumption. For this reason the dictator will strive to minimize the resource costs of staying in office.

Consequently, he or she will be sensitive to P_L/P_R, the relative per unit costs of R and L.

The tinpot's problem is to minimize the resource costs of staying in office – that is, to minimize (3) subject to (1), as in

(4) $Min \ V = \overline{P}_R R + P_L(L, R, \overline{PE})L + \lambda[\pi_{min} - \pi(L, R)]$

with respect to the choice of R and L. (PE is assumed exogenous for the time being – i.e., $PE = \overline{PE}$.)

This yields

(5) $\dfrac{\partial V}{\partial L} = \dfrac{\partial P_L}{\partial L}L + P_L - \lambda\dfrac{\partial \pi}{\partial L} = 0$

(6) $\dfrac{\partial V}{\partial R} = \dfrac{\partial P_L}{\partial R}L + \overline{P}_R - \lambda\dfrac{\partial \pi}{\partial R} = 0,$

which may be combined to obtain the familiar-looking expression

(7) $\dfrac{\pi_L}{\pi_R} = \dfrac{P_L + LP_{LL}}{P_R + LP_{LR}}$

where $\pi_L = \dfrac{\partial \pi}{\partial L}$, $\pi_R = \dfrac{\partial \pi}{\partial R}$, $P_{LL} = \dfrac{\partial P_L}{\partial L}$, $P_{LR} = \dfrac{\partial P_L}{\partial R}$.

Equation (6) resembles the usual condition for cost-minimization, except that the marginal cost of repression $P_R + LP_{LR}$ is less than its price, because an increase in R allows the dictator to obtain loyalty at a reduced price $\left(\dfrac{\partial P_L}{\partial R} < 0\right)$.

The long-run equilibrium described by (6) is represented by point E in Figure 3.1, and it is unique if the production function is well-behaved and if the budget line is concave. The upward-sloping supply of loyalty function does not pose an additional constraint (i.e., it must pass through point E), because this relationship is incorporated into the budget constraint. Its main usefulness will be apparent shortly when we turn to comparative statics (in Section 3B).

An interesting special case of this general model may be described if we further assume that the tinpot's total budget (i.e., one including government resources diverted to his or her personal use, either for personal consumption or perhaps to be deposited in Swiss bank accounts) arises solely from a proportional revenue-maximizing income tax. As in G. Brennan and James Buchanan (1980), let t = tax rate, and Y_0 = initial (pretax) income. The tax reduces work effort – and therefore income – by η (the elasticity of income with respect to the tax rate). Tax revenue is then $tY_0(1 - \eta t)$. Assume also that the rate of growth of disposable income of the population $(\dot{Y}_D)$ is a good proxy for PE, the dictator's economic performance.[3] Then the tinpot may be described as maximizing "profits" – that is, the difference between total revenue and total costs of staying in office, as in

$$(8) \qquad MAX\ Z = tY_0(1-\eta t) - \bar{P}_R R - P_L(R,L,\dot{Y}_D)L + \lambda\left[\pi_0 - \pi(L,R)\right]$$

where

$$\dot{Y}_D \equiv \text{the rate of growth of } (1-t)Y_0(1-\eta t).$$

Maximizing (8) with respect to t, R, and L yields the same first order conditions for R and L which were described in equations (5) and (6) [or (7)], and it yields this further condition for t:

$$(9) \qquad \frac{\partial Z}{\partial t} = Y_0(1-2\eta t) - \frac{\partial P_L}{\partial t} L = 0, \text{ or}$$

$$(9)' \qquad Y_0(1-2\eta t) - \frac{\partial P_L}{\partial t} L$$

where

$$\frac{\partial P_L}{\partial t} \equiv \frac{\partial P_L}{\partial \dot{Y}_D}\frac{\partial \dot{Y}_D}{\partial t} > 0.$$

The left-hand side of (9)', $Y_0(1-2\eta t)$, is the marginal revenue from an increase in the tax rate, and the right-hand side, $\frac{\partial P_L}{\partial t}L$, is the marginal cost, which arises because higher taxes reduce political support or loyalty and must be compensated for by the payment of a higher price for loyalty to keep L from falling and reducing π below π_0.

From (9), we find that the optimum tax rate is

$$(10) \qquad t^* = \frac{1}{2\eta}\left(1 - \frac{\frac{\partial P_L}{\partial t}L}{Y_0}\right).$$

---

[3] See the literature on the political business cycle, which relates political popularity to various macroeconomic indexes, such as the growth in per capita real disposable income. Alesina (1995), in Jeffrey Banks and Eric Hanushek (1995), reviews this literature.

This differs from Brennan and Buchanan's revenue-maximizing tax rate, which is simply $t^* = \frac{1}{2}\eta$. The "profit maximizing" tax rate described in (9) is lower than this, since $\frac{\partial P_L}{\partial t} > 0$.

The present analysis is more general than theirs, because it incorporates the concern facing any dictator that raising tax rates increases opposition to his or her regime. No such problem arises for Brennan and Buchanan's Leviathan, who is assumed to have no difficulty in staying in office even at confiscatory tax rates.

B. Effects of economic performance on the behavior of a tinpot

To illustrate the workings of the model, let us suppose first that the economic performance of the regime improves and that the regime is able to claim credit for this development. The analysis is straightforward, as a simple graphic proof shows. In Figure 3.2, E_0 depicts the initial equilibrium of the system, at which R, L, and P_L are given by R_0, L_0, and P_L^0. The improvement in economic performance shifts the supply of loyalty to the right: to L^S. In the short run there is now an excess supply of loyalty ($L_1 - L_0$). At L_1, R_0 of repression is unnecessary to remain in power, and the dictator will relax R to R_1, implying a new short-run equilibrium at E_1. In the long run, however, the excess supply of loyalty implies that the dictator can allow the price paid for it, P_L, to fall. This shifts L^S back partially to $L^{S''}$, and it also changes the slope of the budget line (to BB_1). Since (P_L/P_R) falls, the final long-run equilibrium must be at a point to the right of E_0 – for example, at E_2 in the figure (on B_2B_2, which is parallel to BB_1) – thus implying an increase in L (to L_2) and a fall in R (to R_2). Under a tinpot dictatorship, in other words, an improvement in economic performance unambiguously results in an increase in loyalty and a fall in the level of political repression.

Note that if strong economic performance were to continue over a period of time, the level of repression would continue to fall, and ultimately, it is possible that the tinpot would need to use very little repression to stay in office and could even hold and win a reasonably free election.

Suppose, on the other hand, that there is a deterioration in economic performance. The supply of loyalty shifts to the left (from L^S to $L^{S'}$), as shown in Figure 3.3. At R_0, the supply of loyalty has fallen to L_1, and R_0 of repression and L_1 of loyalty are insufficient to keep the dictator in

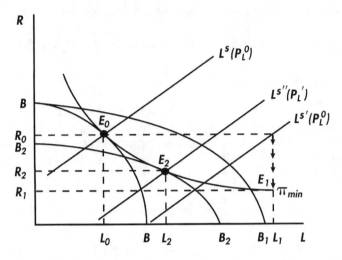

Figure 3.2. Improvement in economic performance lowers repression under a tinpot regime.

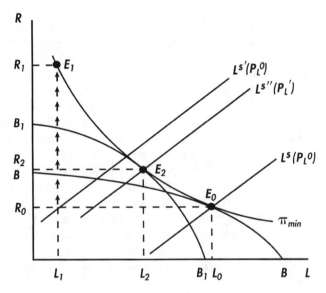

Figure 3.3. Decline in economic performance raises repression under a tinpot regime. [*Note*: The short-run increase in repression in Figure 3.3 $(R_1 - R_0)$ is larger than the decrease $(R_0 - R_1)$ in Figure 3.2.]

office (i.e., $\pi < \pi_{min}$). The proper short-run response by the dictator is to increase R at least to R_1, implying a new short-run equilibrium at E_1. Thus, the short-run response to changes in economic performance is asymmetric – a deterioration in performance calls for a sharp rise in repression, whereas an improvement results only in a slow relaxation of much smaller magnitude (compare $R_1 - R_0$ in Figure 3.3 to $R_0 - R_1$ in Figure 3.2). The asymmetry arises for two reasons: First, the increase in repression when performance declines is necessary for survival (in office), whereas only greed motivates a fall in R when performance improves; and, second, the diminishing marginal rate of substitution between R and L implies that the absolute size of the increase in R required to stay in office when performance declines is larger than the decrease possible when performance improves. Because of this asymmetry, a cross-sectional regression between some index of economic performance (such as the growth rate of national income used in Bilson's 1982 study as well as in many other studies) and a repression index (such as the Freedom House index of civil liberties) will not necessarily reveal the true relationship between these two variables.

Of course, dictators, especially tinpots, are not perfect, and they sometimes make mistakes. If they did not, then, provided they had command over sufficient resources to obtain π_{min}, they would never be deposed. The classic error for a tinpot dictator is to respond to worsening economic conditions by relaxing repression rather than increasing it. (For reasons that will become apparent later, I call this the error of tinpots who confuse themselves with totalitarians.) For example, there is evidence that the Shah of Iran responded in this fashion to the unrest resulting in part from the considerable deterioration in economic conditions after 1976, and the result was his ouster (Arjomand 1986).

In the long run, maintaining repression at R_1 is both expensive (because R_1, L_1 is not the cost-minimizing solution) and unnecessary (because at R_1, the supply of loyalty will expand beyond L_0). Consequently, in the long run, the dictator can allow R to drift down, provided that P_L is increased to eliminate the shortage of L which would arise again if R were to fall back to R_0. The rise in P_L from P_L^0 to P_L^1 shifts L^S partially back to $L^{S'}$ and twists the budget constraint in the direction shown in Figure 3.3, so that the new long-run equilibrium is at E_2, thus implying (compared with the initial equilibrium) a fall in L and an increase in R. In other words a deterioration in the economic performance of a tinpot regime results in a fall in loyalty and an increase in political repression.

C. Military regimes

A number of different types of military regimes can be distinguished, depending on the degree of civilian power-sharing. Here, we follow Eric Nordlinger (1977, p. 3) and consider a military regime to be one in which power was obtained through a coup, in which the highest governmental officials have served (or continue to serve) in the armed forces, and in which the governors are primarily dependent upon the support of the officer corps for the retention of power.

As mentioned in the introduction to this chapter, there are two issues of particular interest concerning military regimes, namely:

1. Why are they so unstable?
2. Why do they often voluntarily hand power over to civilian governments?

To begin the analysis, we will assume that, compared with a civilian regime, a military regime has a comparative advantage at repression and a comparative disadvantage at accumulating political loyalty. The assumption that the military would have an advantage at repression is easy to understand. After all, the central skill of the military is, in Lasswell's well-known phrase, "the management of violence." In addition, it has often been argued that, compared with civilian regimes, military regimes are disadvantaged when it comes to building a civilian political base. Thus, A. Stepan (1971) suggests that "a military government does not easily tolerate a normal level of dissension and debate needed to build or maintain coalitions with civilians" (p. 263). Amos Perlmutter and Valerie Bennett (1980) note that historically, military regimes have shown "an inability to tolerate political participation" (p. 20), and they suggest that this is true because such regimes tend to equate mass participation with political turbulence and the possibility of violence. Thus, although no quantitative evidence has, to my knowledge, been assembled on this issue, the general consensus among observers of these regimes seems to be, as summed up by Eric Nordlinger (1977), that "few [military regimes] have attempted to build mass parties and where they have been created they turned out to be ineffectual structures because genuine participation was not permitted" (p. 58).

Assume, then, that the resource constraint for the military is steeper than that for a civilian regime (e.g., BB compared with B_2B_2 in Figure 3.2). The initial equilibrium for the military regime is at a point like E_0 in Figure 3.2 (compared with E_2 for the civilian regime), thus implying the use of more repression, R, and less political loyalty, L (compared with the civilian regime). What makes this military regime unstable? To answer this question, one has to probe into the motives behind the intervention of the military into political life. Although these reasons are undoubtedly many and complex, ranging from disgust at the behavior of civilian politicians and fear of Communist takeover to the desire to restore order to political life, there is one motive that stands out for its simplicity and generality: the desire to increase the budget of the military. There is considerable evidence to support the importance of this motive. Robert Putnam (1967) classified twenty Latin American countries according to the extent of military intervention and found a positive correlation between this variable and defense spending as a percentage of GNP. Phillipe Schmitter (1971) classified Latin American countries into three groups according to the level of military intervention, and he found that central government expenditures devoted to the military ranged from 9 to 14 and then to 19 percent as the level of military intervention increased. Nordlinger (1977) found that the average proportion of GNP allocated to defense expenditures was almost twice as high in countries with a praetorian officer corps than in those in which the military accepted civilian control.

In other words, one straightforward way to explain military intervention in politics is to model the military as a budget-maximizing bureau and to note that intervention is a strategy available to the military for increasing its budgets in countries with weak political systems. As argued elsewhere (Breton and Wintrobe 1975, 1982; Wintrobe 1997), budget maximization is too specific a maximand to satisfactorily represent the objectives of most bureaus, mainly because of the existence of substantial opportunities for mobility among the different bureaus in most bureaucracies. However, this objection does not apply to the military, which tends to be a closed hierarchy. Since career opportunities for military personnel tend to be limited in bureaus outside the military hierarchy, budget maximization is often the most attractive strategy available to raise the salaries, prestige, and power of military personnel. Consequently, the objectives of military dictators are not necessarily the same as those of tinpot regimes generally.

Suppose, then, that the military takes power from a civilian regime. As a result, the equilibrium shifts from E_2 to E_0 in Figure 3.2. The military then proceeds to do what military governments do best – namely, raise the salaries of military personnel. This has a peculiar consequence, which is that it raises the price of repression, P_R (i.e., it destroys the comparative advantage of the military in governing). In Figure 3.2 the budget constraint BB would pivot downward toward the origin from point B on the horizontal axis (not shown) – that is, its slope would flatten out. Consequently, having achieved its primary aim (increasing the military budget), a military government which was acting rationally would hand power over to a civilian regime – but, of course, only after having received suitable guarantees of immunity from prosecution and from budget cuts by the new regime. Of course, a military government which seeks to remain in office not merely to raise the military budget will sense the danger that would be posed by excessive salary increases – such action could undermine its capacity to govern – and it may therefore attempt to limit them or to restrict them to certain subgroups in the military. This action, however, tends to breed internal dissension, to destroy the internal cohesiveness of the military hierarchy, and possibly to breed a countercoup. Countercoups are quite common in military governments – according to Gavin Kennedy's (1974) study they were twice as likely in a military as in a civilian regime, and the vast majority involve the overthrow of one military government and its replacement by another.

Consequently, it is not difficult to explain either the instability of military regimes or why the vast majority of such regimes tend to end in a voluntary withdrawal of the military from power. There is nothing peculiar about the fact that the military, once in power, tends to reward its supporters; all political regimes presumably do this. Political parties that are backed by unions presumably reward unions when in power; political parties backed by business groups presumably reward *them* when in power; and so on. What is peculiar about military governments is that in the process of rewarding their supporters, they tend to weaken, rather than strengthen, their own capacity to govern. Although this point is obviously not a complete explanation of these regimes, it does explain both the instability of military regimes and why they typically end in a voluntary transfer of power to civilian regimes.

3   Totalitarian regimes

The differences between the totalitarian and tinpot regimes are reflected in their respective maximands. In a totalitarian regime I assume that the dictator, or the Leader (Hitler, Stalin), or "Great Helmsman" (Mao) uses the instruments of repression and loyalty to maximize power over the population under his or her control. I believe this objective is consistent with the descriptions of such regimes in Arendt (1951/1973), Friedrich and Brzezinski (1965), and Hayek (1944). The classic historical examples are Nazi Germany and Stalin's Russia in the 1930s. For example, at the height of Hitler's power, the population of Germany was held to be subject not to any laws but exclusively to the will of the Führer as divined from his speeches and other remarks; subjection to laws would amount to circumscribing the power of the Leader (Arendt 1951). How useful the various concepts of totalitarian rule are – and how much they are applicable to other societies (such as Russia between Stalin and Gorbachev or contemporary China) – is a much-debated question.[4] We will be presenting some evidence on this matter later in this section. In any case, extreme cases are often useful analytically, and this conception of totalitarian regimes is useful insofar as it places tinpot and totalitarian regimes at opposite extremes. Most real world dictatorships undoubtedly lie somewhere in between these two extremes.

From an economic point of view, the central question is not so much the maximand but the nature of the constraint on the totalitarian Leader's maximization of power. Budget considerations may pose a constraint,[5] particularly at the point at which revenue-maximizing taxes have been imposed on every available tax base. However, the Leader can always nationalize or confiscate resources directly. Deleterious economic effects such as deadweight losses (which, according to Becker's 1983 formulation, constrain the behavior of ruling interest groups) may cause problems, but they do not, at first blush, necessarily reduce the power of the Leader. Suppose, then, for the sake of argument, that we ignore budgetary and price constraints (they are discussed in full in Chapter 5). Is there any other constraint on the totalitarian Leader's maximization of power?

From the Leader's point of view, the key consideration is the loyalty of the population. The Leader's problem is depicted in Figure 3.4. So long as the aggregate supply of loyalty curve is upward sloping, the dictator can increase his or her power over the population by increasing the level of repression. Consequently, if the L^s curve were upward sloping throughout its range, the only possible equilibrium would be a corner solution involving the perfect repression of the population, a goal which, Arendt often suggested, the Nazi regime had set itself – namely, "the permanent domination of each single individual in each and every sphere of life" (1951/1973, p. 325) – and one which, she sometimes implied, it had attained. However, considerable evidence has been amassed subsequently that this goal was not achieved by the Nazi regime (see, e.g., Broszat 1981). In addition, theoretical considerations suggest that there is a conflict between perfect repression and the maximization of power over the population.

---

[4] See, for example, Burrowes (1968), and references therein.

[5] Where budgetary considerations do pose a binding constraint, the reader can easily verify that a totalitarian regime that maximizes power subject to a budget constraint will respond in exactly the same way to exogenous changes in economic performance as one subject to a loyalty constraint (developed in the text shortly).

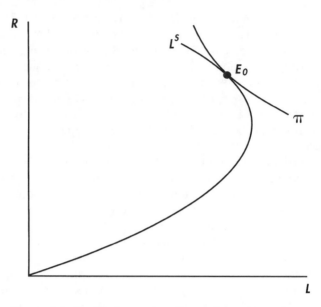

Figure 3.4. Equilibrium repression and loyalty under a totalitarian regime.

To see this, recall from Section 3A earlier that an increase in repression induces opposing effects on the supply of loyalty to the regime. The substitution effect (the change in the amount of loyalty supplied as a result of a fall in the return or of an increase in the risk of disloyalty) always favors the regime. On the other hand, an increase in the probability of being discovered for having links to actual or potential opposition movements, or an increase in the sanction imposed for this offense, reduces expected wealth; and this reduction in wealth has an income effect which leads an individual to reduce all investments in political loyalty, including those with the regime. At low levels of repression, it is reasonable to assume that the income effect is small for most people, so that their response is dominated by the substitution effect (as argued earlier in the context of our analysis of tinpot dictatorships). However, as the level of repression increases, the income effect gets larger. In addition, as the level of repression increases, the number and the size of groups that are opposed to the regime become smaller, and at very high levels of repression, opposition to the regime tends to get wiped out. Consequently, the substitution effect becomes vanishingly small as the level of repression becomes very large. Ultimately, then, a point must be reached at which the income effect overwhelms the substitution effect for most citizens, causing the aggregate supply of loyalty to the regime to bend backward (as depicted in Figure 3.4).

This point is reinforced if we note that the process of repression will usually be subject to error. The real opponents of the regime do not typically identify themselves as such, and actual or potential opposition to the regime will have to be inferred from certain behavior and characteristics. At low levels of repression the identification of opposition leaders is a relatively simple task. At higher levels of repression it becomes more and more difficult. Consequently, even perfectly loyal individuals will have to be more and more careful in establishing or maintaining network links. It may turn out that their investments will, ex post, turn out to have been made with the "wrong" people. Such a possibility explains the great effort during the Stalinist purges of the Communist party in the late 1930s to wring fabricated confessions from the accused in the infamous Moscow show trials. The more that doubts persisted within the party as to the real guilt of the accused, the more that party members could reasonably be expected to withhold making any investments, even from perfectly loyal motives, for fear that they themselves would become the victims of the terror. Indeed, there is some evidence that by the late 1930s even Stalin felt that the purges had gone too far (Schapiro 1971, pp. 435ff.). This fact explains both the subsequent "liquidation of the liquidators" and the ultimate relaxation of the terror at the end of 1938.

If the supply of loyalty becomes backward-bending, "optimality" for the totalitarian dictator is at a point like E_0 in Figure 3.4, where the backward-bending supply curve is tangent to the highest attainable isopower line.

Formally, the Leader chooses R and L to maximize power – but subject to the constraint posed by the supply of loyalty. That is, his or her problem is

(11) $Max\ \pi(L,R)+\lambda\left[L^S - L^S(R,\overline{PE})\right].$

The solution is simply

(12) $\dfrac{\pi_R}{\pi_L} = \dfrac{\partial R}{\partial L},$

which shows that if the supply of loyalty is the only constraint, the slope of the supply curve must be the same as that of the isopower line at the optimum point (E_0 in Figure 3.4). Note that the dictator might still be able to increase his or her power by better than expected performance

(*PE*) or by raising the price of loyalty (P_L), as will be discussed shortly. But at E_0 the limits of repression as a means of increasing power over the population have been reached.

One implication of this model is that in a totalitarian regime, repression is carried to the point at which at the margin, an increase in repression reduces the supply of loyalty. The opposite prediction holds for a tinpot. Consequently, one test of whether a dictatorship is totalitarian or tinpot concerns the marginal behavior of the supply of loyalty in response to a change in the level of repression at the equilibrium point. Interestingly, some evidence on this question has been collected for the former Soviet regime. Using data from the Soviet Interview Project, D. Bahry and D. Silver (1987) computed a "KGB differential" – the relationship between the estimated competence of the KGB and the degree of support for various goals of the regime. That is, the subjects (2,793 Soviet emigrés) were asked to rank the leaders of various Soviet institutions on different scales, including a scale for competence. They were also asked how much they supported various regime goals. Bahry and Silver found that although support for regime goals was positively related to the estimated competence and honesty of various institutional leaders, excluding the KGB, it was (significantly) negatively related to the estimated competence of the KGB. Thus, whatever the limitations of the procedure and the data,[6] the results do indicate that at least as far as these respondents were concerned, the Soviet Union under Brezhnev was still a totalitarian regime.

A totalitarian regime also differs from a tinpot in its response to exogenous shocks. Suppose, for example, that the performance of the regime were to improve, and that the Leader could claim credit for this improvement. The improvement can be, as with tinpots, in any kind of performance, including success in war or in solving some major political problem, but we focus here on economic performance, such as an improvement in the rate of economic growth, a reduction in inflation or unemployment, and so on. An improvement in any of these dimensions of performance shifts the supply of loyalty curve to the right, as depicted in Figure 3.5. The new equilibrium is at E_1. The power of the regime over the population increases unambiguously (because the supply of loyalty shifts to the right, the new L^S curve, $L^{S'}$, must be tangent to a higher isopower line than L^S, the old supply curve). And for the most obvious cases (e.g., a parallel shift of the backward-bending supply curve, and homogeneous isopower lines), the level of repression tends to

---

[6] The main problem is that the emigrés were often atypical – for example, 85 percent of them were Jewish, and 30 percent read *Samizdat* (banned underground literature).

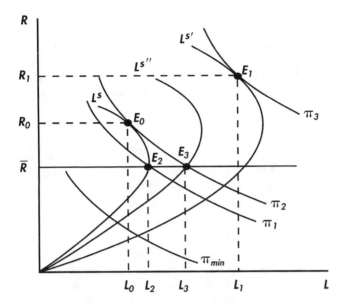

Figure 3.5. How equilibrium levels of repression and loyalty under a totalitarian regime are affected by changes in economic performance and Western policy.

increase as well. The reason is simple: The increase in the supply of loyalty as a consequence of the improvement in performance provides the Leader with an opportunity to amass more power. Since the Leader maximizes power (unlike a tinpot, who would simply squander the extra resources on personal consumption), he or she takes this opportunity to do so.

In the former Soviet Union and in the satellite Communist countries of Eastern Europe, this performance for many years was surprisingly good. From the 1960s onward, however, economic performance, as measured by the rate of growth of national income or productivity, steadily declined (Ofer 1987). Our model predicts that in response to this decline, the levels of power, loyalty, and repression will all diminish. Even before the collapse of communism in the former Soviet Union and Eastern Europe, there was evidence supporting this proposition. Stephen White (1986), for example, argued that as economic performance in Eastern Europe declined during the 1980s, the parties looked for other ways to secure "legitimacy," and he noted the following: (1) *Increasing use of the electoral mechanism.* Whereas multiple candidacies in Communist "elections" were an isolated phenomenon in the 1960s, they were characteristic of over half of the countries of Eastern Europe in the 1980s. (2) *Political incorporation*. The proportion of the population that belonged to the party increased steadily from 3–4 percent in the 1950s to 6–10 percent in the 1970s and 1980s. (3) *Associational incorporation*, and (4) *The instigation in successive countries of the practice of allowing letters to be written to the party, the state, and the press*. Of course, the events following the 1989–91 period in the Soviet Union and Eastern Europe, however difficult to imagine before the fact, are consistent with this model. So is the fact that in Communist China, where the economy has been liberalized and growth is substantial, political repression shows no sign of easing. That is, events in both the former Soviet Union and its satellites, as well as in Communist China, are consistent with the positive correlation between the level of economic performance and the level of repression as predicted here for totalitarian regimes.

Finally, and perhaps most important, the model implies that the average level of repression and the average level of loyalty are positively correlated in totalitarian regimes. In Figure 3.5, both repression and loyalty increase for movements along a given supply curve (except at the margin); This fact suggests that as long as such methods are successful, the level of loyalty to the regime in totalitarian regimes is high compared with tinpot regimes. Informal evidence that this is true is summarized and interpreted in Chapter 13 for the Nazi regime, and in Chapter 10 for the Soviet regime. It is also worth noting that when communism failed economically – and when its support declined – the various regimes collapsed. So the collapse of communism is consistent with the fact that it was based in part on the support of the population. When that support vanished as the result of the failure of the regime to deliver on its promises, so did the regime.

The interpretation of totalitarian regimes suggested by this model, then, is quite different from those that are common in the literature, including those put forth by both proponents of the concept of totalitarianism and their critics. It is also very different from the "command economy" construct widely used in the economic literature on socialist countries. The basic idea here is that the repression characteristic of totalitarian societies helps to build a core of loyal supporters whose relationship with the regime is primarily one of exchange rather than of coercion. The regime accommodates these offers of support through an institutional mechanism that facilitates the accumulation of loyalty and enforces exchanges. This institution is the totalitarian party.

In order to fulfill this role, the Communist party of the Soviet Union, for example, was organized in a particular way. First, the Party controlled the productive system. This was true in a formal sense (Article VI of the Soviet constitution specified that the Party was the "leading and directing force of Soviet society") and, in the industrial sector at least, in an informal sense (insofar as the Party permeated the productive system). Every factory of even modest size contained a Party cell.

Consequently, the Party had much stronger control over the bureaucracy than the governing party in a democracy has over the civil service. The Party controlled promotions and access to a vast range of perquisites, including housing, the closed system of hospitals, special shops, and so on (see Matthews 1978, who describes these privileges in detail). The Party used these resources as prizes to encourage subordinates to compete with each other to loyally advance the goals of the Party – possibly as in a Lazear–Rosen–style "tournament" (see Lazear and Rosen 1981). When the system functioned efficiently, subordinates competed to loyally advance the goals of their superiors by showing initiative, dedication, enterprise, and flexibility (rather than to simply obey orders, as discussed at much greater length in Chapter 10). In return the Party ensured that the "implicit contract" that loyal performance would be rewarded was kept – that is, superiors within the government, ministry, or Party hierarchies did not renege on promises to subordinates. In this way the Communist party substituted for enforceable property rights to solve the problem of mutual cheating which is characteristic of exchange when law-based property rights are absent.

One reason the Party could fulfill this role was that it was expected to be a long-lived institution. So exchanges over time – for example, across generations – were possible. This fact explains one commonly noted feature of totalitarian regimes: their orientation toward economic growth. Otherwise, it is not obvious why such policies would be in the interest of the regime; the leaders could simply exercise their monopoly power by lavish living. Why should they sacrifice present consumption for a future when they will no longer be in office? Why should they make such a sacrifice when it was unlikely that their sons and daughters would succeed them? If membership at the top – for example, in the Politburo – were transferable through sale, the leaders of the Politburo could collect the capitalized value of their offices and would have an incentive to preserve it.[7] It is obvious why this route was not taken. An alternative, however, is provided if the Communist party facilitated exchanges between the young and the old. In that case, differences in time preference would be eliminated through trade – the old (the leadership) would pursue growth-orientated policies, and the young would offer loyal per-

---

[7] This point is also made in David Schap (1988).

formance in exchange. This explains the peculiar "futuristic" look of all totalitarian parties – the Thousand Year Reich, the early associations of Fascism with the artistic movement known as Futurism, and the enormous program of forced industrialization carried out by Stalin.

In addition to enforcing exchange, a totalitarian party possesses a number of features which facilitate investments in loyalty to the party. These features are described in detail in Chapter 10 (on the former Soviet system) and in Chapter 13 (on the Nazi regime). The way this worked may be gleaned from the following points about the former Soviet system, most of which apply to the contemporary (and very much alive) Chinese system (see, e.g., Walder 1986), as well as to the defunct Soviet one. First, in contrast to a democracy, there was no "free-rider" problem with respect to political participation in the former Soviet Union: Political participation (one way of investing in loyalty) was demanded, monitored, and rewarded (for details on these and other practices, see Hough and Fainsod 1979; also see Schapiro 1971 for a historical treatment). Second, membership in the party was an exclusive privilege. Exclusive membership made expulsion possible, and the threat of expulsion for disloyalty – whether on an individual or a mass basis (the party purge) – was obviously a powerful incentive device. Third, the party was centrally organized. All factions and groups *within* the party were officially prohibited in the party's statutes; communication and decision making were organized along strictly hierarchical lines (the principle of "democratic centralism"). To the extent that these three incentives were effective, loyalty was diverted toward the party and its hierarchy and not to other (proscribed) political groupings within it – or to dissident groups outside it. (From the party's point of view, dissidence threatens exchanges in the same way that crime threatens both property rights and efficiency in a capitalist economy.)

A fourth, and more subtle, point concerns the role of the totalitarian party's ideology. At a basic level the party's ideology was just a set of promises which established its goals. The ideology of Marxism–Leninism is often seen as a critique of capitalist societies which did not fundamentally guide (or hinder) the actual functioning of the former Soviet system. But this critique also reinforced the party's promises and helped to promote loyalty to the party. One obvious way that it did this was by identifying heroes and villains as well as by glorifying successes and minimizing the failures of the party.

An even more subtle point is that the party's totalitarian ideology and propaganda may have succeeded in building its reputation, irrespective of whether the party line was believed or not, in the same way that, according to Klein and Leffler (1981), advertising promotes the reputation of and brand loyalty to a capitalist firm. In their model it is not the content of advertising but its volume (the accumulated stock) that provides information. Because better products are advertised more – or, more precisely, because producers have a greater incentive to accumulate a larger stock of advertising capital for higher quality products – advertising can signal quality: The buyer who knows nothing about two different products except that one has been advertised more than the other can still correctly infer that it is indeed of higher quality. However, that repetitive quality is surely even more characteristic of totalitarian ideology and propaganda. That is, it is not the content of a message but the number of times it is repeated (the magnitude of the party's investments in its promises) that contributes to reputation and promotes loyalty.

Of course, words are cheap – hence the typical resort to exaggeration, hyperbole, and repetition, in part, as a way of compensating for this truth. Why would Pravda devote two-thirds of its space for nine months to the publication of greetings to Stalin on the occasion of his seventieth birthday? As in the case of advertising, one cannot discover the meaning of ideology by looking solely at its content ("Happy Birthday, Stalin!"). One important aspect of the communication is not its content, but the frequency with which the message is repeated.

Finally, less subtly, but perhaps most important, the Party controlled the distribution of rents. One simple interpretation of the legendary shortages characteristic of Soviet-type systems, shortages which are otherwise rather difficult to explain (the difficulties have been discussed extensively by Kornai 1980), is simply that the shortages create rents, and the rents are controlled by the party. Consequently, they are an excellent device for building party loyalty. In this interpretation the shortages are a permanent feature of Soviet-type systems, and no economic reform can be expected to remove them.[8]

This brief description of the workings of the system (for more detail and for an explanation of why loyalty within the system tends to corrode over time, see Chapters 9 and 10 on the Soviet system, and Chapter 13 on the Nazi regime) suggests that in totalitarian societies, the organizational technology for operating an economic system on what might be called

---

[8] Recently, Adi Schnytzer and Janez Susteric (1996) investigated the impact of the distribution of economic rents on the popularity of the Communist party in the six Yugoslav Republics over the 1953–88 period, and they compared this factor with other variables, such as the level of repression or economic conditions. The dependent variable (the index of popularity) is membership in the Communist party. Their results indicated that rents distributed were the most important determinant of membership, thus suggesting that the political exchange approach is superior to other approaches in explaining the behavior of these regimes.

loyalty-based property rights is far more advanced than it is in other political systems.

4   Policy implications

Perhaps surprisingly, in view of its simplicity, the model developed here does yield rather strong implications with respect to the policies which should be followed by democratic countries vis-à-vis both tinpot and totalitarian dictatorships. I assume throughout that the only aim of Western governments is to promote freedom – that is, that the countries of the West have no strategic or economic interests other than the promotion of freedom for their people. This is obviously an idealistic point of view, but it does represent the oft-stated aim of much of Western policy.

A. Aid policy toward tinpots

One major policy issue with respect to tinpot dictatorships is whether to extend economic aid to them or not and, if aid is given, whether this aid should be tied to improvements in the human rights record of such regimes. Figure 3.6 displays the policy dilemma faced by democracies with respect to tinpot regimes. The initial equilibrium is at E_0. Consider first the policy of giving aid with no strings attached. Aid in this form does not change the relative costs of repression by and loyalty to the dictator. It implies only that more resources ($B'B'$ rather than BB in Figure 3.6) could be spent on repression and loyalty while maintaining the dictator's personal consumption at its initial level. However, if, as depicted, the original budget constraint provides enough resources for the dictator to remain in office (it is at least tangent to π_{min}), the dictator will simply spend the aid on personal consumption. If the tinpot could not remain in office without foreign assistance (i.e., if BB were to be everywhere below π_{min}), the aid would have an effect which is to maintain the dictator in office as long as the aid is continued. Otherwise, the equilibrium levels of R and L at R_0 and L_0, respectively, would be unchanged.

An alternative policy that is often advocated is to tie the aid to a constraint on violations of human rights by the tinpot. Assuming that this constraint can be made effective – that is, assuming that violations can be properly monitored and that the constraint is binding – we find that the tinpot will be constrained to impose a level of repression lower than R_0 (e.g., one no greater than $\bar{R}$ in Figure 3.6). As Figure 3.6 clearly shows, the effect of the binding constraint is to destabilize the regime. In the

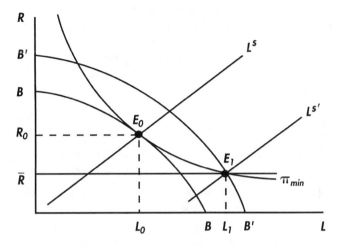

Figure 3.6. Optimum Western policy toward a tinpot regime.

short run, loyalty is fixed at L_0, and with $\bar{R}$ of repression and L_0 of loyalty, the dictator has insufficient power to stay in office, no matter how high the level of external assistance.

Neither of these two policies, then, is effective in reducing repression. The first policy (aid with no strings attached) is ineffective because although it may maintain the tinpot in office, it creates no incentives for the tinpot to substitute loyalty for repression as a means of staying in power. The second policy (aid with a binding human rights constraint) is ineffective because it gives the tinpot no chance to make such a substitution but rather puts the tinpot in immediate danger of being deposed. (If the aim of the policy is to cause the tinpot's downfall, why extend aid at all?) Moreover, both policies may have other effects which are counterproductive. For example, if the aid is continued for a long time, the tinpot is freed from dependence on the loyalty of his or her supporters and may substitute for such loyalty a dependence on foreign aid, especially if he or she finds it easier to get the aid than to maintain loyalty. Alternatively, if the tinpot is deposed, the regime which replaces him or her may be even less palatable (Kirkpatrick's point).

There is, however, a third policy which has some chance of success. This is a policy of aid, combined with a long-term human rights constraint – that is, one that becomes successively more stringent over time. The aim is to force the tinpot to a new long-run equilibrium at E_1. The long-run constraint ensures that in the future the tinpot will only be able to stay in office at a level of repression no greater than R_0. The aid provides the tinpot with sufficient resources to "purchase" the extra loyalty required at no sacrifice to his or her personal consumption, and the long-term nature of the constraint implies that sufficient time is allowed for the dictator's investments to yield the required support. Consequently, this policy alone among those considered provides the correct incentives to the tinpot to reduce repression.

B. Aid policy toward totalitarians

The central issues for the democracies in dealing with a totalitarian government are:

1. Should democracies engage in economic relations (trade and investment) with it in the hope that these relationships are likely to improve the economic performance of such a government, or should they pursue policies such as an arms race or economic sanctions which can, among other possible effects, worsen the totalitarian regime's economic performance?
2. Should the democracies push for human rights?

Again, the point of view in addressing these questions is a scientific one: Given the assumptions of our model, we want to know which policies will reduce the optimal level of repression chosen by the totalitarian Leader.

We can begin with aid policy. Figure 3.5 displays the policy dilemma of the democracies in dealing with totalitarian governments. E_0 is the initial equilibrium. If as a result of the aid (or of trade or other favorable economic relationships with the democracies), the economic performance of the regime improves, and if the regime can take at least part of the credit for this improvement, the supply of loyalty to the regime L^S shifts to the right: to $L^{S'}$. The most plausible result (see the earlier discussion in Section 3) is a new equilibrium like E_1 in Figure 3.5, with the dictator obtaining more power and more loyalty and being more repressive. In this case the direct result of the aid is to worsen the political rights of the people (even if it raises their standard of living), so that these policies, by themselves, tend to be ineffective in increasing freedom. On the other hand a human rights constraint (e.g., one binding at $\bar{R}$), if imposed alone, would simply reduce the power of the regime and therefore be unacceptable to the Leader. This can be seen in Figure 3.5: The new optimum for the dictator with a long-term binding human rights constraint of $\bar{R}$ is at E_2, a lower level of power than E_0. Again, however, although neither policy is effective when used alone, the two can be effective in combination. The principle is simple: A long-term binding human rights constraint can be suggested to the regime, provided it is accompanied by the offer of sufficient aid to allow the dictator to increase loyalty to L_3. At these levels of repression and loyalty (E_3 in Figure 3.5), the dictator has as much power as before. Repression, however, is successfully reduced (from R_0 to $\bar{R}$). Consequently, slightly more aid will increase the dictator's power – and therefore be acceptable to him or her – while still reducing the level of repression under the regime.

A more acute dilemma confronts the democracies in dealing with totalitarian dictatorships in decline and seeking to reform. The analysis in Figure 3.5 suggests, as indicated earlier, that the proper response to economic decline for a totalitarian government is some relaxation of repression (e.g., from R_1 to R_0 in Figure 3.5). The next step in the sequence, however, is economic reform and not full political liberalization. Substantial liberalization (any $R < R_0$) will simply reduce loyalty (and power) further. Moreover, if the Leader expects economic reforms initially to cause widespread hardship (e.g., producing unemployment or price increases) and hence to produce the potential for political unrest, the Leader's problems would only be exacerbated by political liberalization (which allows the opposition to organize and a bandwagon effect to develop). Consequently, the optimal sequence of reforms for the leader of a totalitarian regime is some relaxation of repression followed by economic reforms to increase the supply of loyalty before major political reforms are attempted. Given this important result, we conclude that the dilemma for democracies is that if the economic reforms are successful and if the Leader can claim the credit for this improvement so that loyalty increases in the long run, any power-maximizing Leader will then be tempted to renege on his or her promises of political liberalization and respond by increasing rather than decreasing political repression. That is, the new power-maximizing equilibrium at higher L (L_1 compared with L_0) implies higher R. Again, therefore, from the point of view of democracies, which are considering whether to expand economic relations with such a regime, there is no substitute for the principle of insistence on a long-term binding human rights constraint if their objective is to minimize the repressiveness of the dictator's regime.

So we have a very simple guide – a *single standard* – to the policies that should be pursued by foreign governments interested in reducing repression: Human rights observance should be the cornerstone of Western policy. Aid to any type of regime can be expected to produce beneficial effects provided it is accompanied by a long-term human rights constraint, one which becomes progressively more stringent over time.

Without the human rights standard, the effects of aid will be ineffective or perverse.

C. Trade policy

Another policy dilemma is whether to trade with dictatorships. Trade policy is a bit more complicated than aid policy. We can distinguish the following effects:

1. Trade may be expected to increase the national income of the target regime directly, because its income will rise as a result of both the availability of imported inputs at a lower price and the increase in demand for the target's exports. To the extent that the regime can successfully claim credit for this improvement in welfare, loyalty to the regime may be expected to increase.

2. Since the richer people are, the more they tend to demand liberty, the increase in income tends to reduce loyalty to the dictatorship as people increasingly demand their rights (Bilson [1982], Londregan and Poole [1996]). However, note that the estimated size of this effect is very small. Thus, as Londregan and Poole conclude their analysis of this effect in non-European countries, "Those expecting income growth to promote the development of democratic institutions must be very patient indeed" (pp. 22–3).

3. The increase in trade creates further links between foreign businesses and domestic producers, possibly resulting in the development of independent power bases within the target regime. This is particularly likely when the trade is not organized through the central government (as it is in Cuba, for example). Thus, in China, regional governments in particular have built up substantial connections with outsiders and with the private sector, and they rely much less on the central government for revenue than they did before Deng launched the revolution he blandly called "socialism with Chinese characteristics" (cited in MacFarquahar, [1997], p. 15). To the extent that this happens, loyalty to the regime may fall. On the other hand, it has been argued, perhaps most forcefully by Huntington (1996), that trade between different types of civilizations actually increases mistrust, because the increased intensity of contacts simply breeds hostility. He points out, for example, that World War I occurred at precisely the last peak of the "openness" of the international system. If Huntington is right, trade might gener-

ate a short-run fall in loyalty to the regime due to the initial increase in foreign contacts, but in the longer run, further contacts simply breed nationalism and possibly *increased* support for the dictatorship in the target regime.

4. The rise in income may increase tax revenues, and as a result, dictators may have *more* resources at their disposal. These resources may be used either for their own consumption or to further their hold on power by increasing expenditures on either repression or loyalty.

To disentangle the implications for policy, note that the question with respect to points 1–3 is simply whether the net effect of the trade agreement is to increase or decrease loyalty to the regime. Point 4 concerns the dictator's budget, and detailed analysis of this issue will have to be left to Section 4 in Chapter 5. Considering points 1–3, then let us suppose first that, as seems likely, support for the regime increases as the result of the trade agreement. Suppose also that the ruler is a tinpot. Then it can be argued that with increased support, the tinpot will be motivated to relax repression, and there is thus no need for a human rights constraint. But note that even in this case, the human rights constraint does no harm; it simply asks the dictator to do what he or she would do in any case, and therefore it should be acceptable to him or her. On the other hand, if, on balance, loyalty to the regime were to decrease as a result of trade, the tinpot would want to raise repression in order to stay in office, and the human rights constraint is absolutely necessary for the trade agreement to lower, not raise, repression.

Suppose now that we are dealing with a totalitarian dictator. Here, if loyalty were to increase, on balance, as the result of the trade agreement, the dictator would tend to raise repression, and the binding human rights constraint would be necessary to prevent a loss of freedom. The only case for a trade agreement with a totalitarian regime is where the opposite happens – that is, where loyalty to the regime decreases from the trade agreement. In that case, repression falls as well. *This is the only case where trade with a totalitarian regime makes sense.* But note that the totalitarian leader, in pursuing this trade agreement, cannot fail to be aware of the likely consequences of the trade agreement for the regime's hold on power – namely, that its capacity for repression, the loyalty of the citizenry, and its power are all going to diminish as a result of his or her signing up. So, if this analysis were correct, it requires us to believe that the totalitarian Leader, in pursuing trade, is either unaware of, or deliberately acting contrary to, his or her own long-run interest. It is noteworthy also that all the totalitarian regimes which have collapsed historically did so as a result of falling, not rising, real incomes, and that the increase in income in China has resulted in not the slightest relaxation of repression there after almost two decades of reform and spectacular economic growth. The case for trade with totalitarian regimes, therefore, is particularly weak.

Finally, suppose that the human rights constraint cannot be implemented, either because the target regime is too powerful or because no binding agreement can be reached among the countries involved in implementing the policy. Then there is a difficult choice between a policy of sanctions, on the one hand, and trade agreements with no human rights constraint, on the other. Of course, the actual choices are never this stark, and the actual policies that are followed will be a mixture of trade and sanctions, but the basic principle involved in the choice remains one of engagement or isolation. In that case, the analysis here implies that the least harm is likely to come from a trade agreement with a tinpot regime, and that the most harm will come from trade with a totalitarian.

These policies are strictly "second best" in the economist's terminology. Note that an analogous set of second-best policies exist for aid as well – aid in the absence of a progressively tightening human rights constraint will probably do less harm to a tinpot's subjects (in the sense that rather than actually increase the level of repression, the aid will just be wasted) than to those living under a totalitarian regime. However, the single standard, based on the progressive human rights constraint, remains the first best policy. The analysis also suggests that the key to unraveling the dictator's hold on power is to attack the instruments that are used to maintain that hold on the population – namely repression and loyal support. There are other policies that can be used for this purpose, even where agreement and coordination among the democracies is weak. One example is to provide external support for dissidents and for resistance movements inside the regime; such a tactic was used in South Africa, but it is often neglected in the case of China. Perhaps even more important, the message here is that dictators survive on the basis of the support of segments of the population, and attacking these bases of support is an important tool in trying to undermine the regime.

Of course, a number of other policies could be considered, including applying economic sanctions, giving aid to international agencies rather than to the dictator, earmarking the aid for specific investment projects, and so on. Their effects can easily be analyzed within the present framework. Although I shall not do so here in detail, there is one point about sanctions which is worth emphasizing: Sanctions are not just the reverse of aid, and policies like those pursued by the United States and the UN vis-à-vis regimes like Castro's Cuba, Hussein's Iraq, or Milosevic's Serbia may superficially resemble those described here, but in fact they work very differently. In all these cases, the United States or UN imposed sanctions and then offered to lift them as a reward for better behavior. For example, the Americans have, as of mid-1997, continued to block Belgrade's admission to such world institutions as the International Monetary Fund and the World Bank, demanding that Milosevic first open a dialogue with his political opponents and allow more political freedom.[9] Such policies are not necessarily wrongheaded, but they do not work in the manner of those advocated here. The sequence is reversed: The regime has to liberalize *first* – that is, before the sanctions are lifted and before trade is allowed to resume and aid to flow. This means that the regime cannot use the benefit of aid or trade to build loyalty prior to liberalization, which is the effect of the policies advocated here. Dictators who agree to liberalize put themselves in immediate danger of being deposed, and it is no surprise that Castro, Hussein, and Milosevic have all been reluctant to do so. The policies work only if they succeed in coercing or bullying the dictator into submission. There is nothing necessarily ethically wrong with this policy, since all these leaders oppress their peoples. It's just that such policies have failed: The United States has bullied Castro for thirty years, but after all that time he is, as of this writing, still in power, and his regime is, according to Freedom House reports (Freedom House, 1997), as oppressive as ever. Coercive strategies have also failed, as of this writing, to dislodge or liberalize Saddam Hussein's regime.

Finally, it is worth mentioning some other problems with sanctions. Their use may perversely stimulate nationalistic support for the dictator (the "rally round the flag" effect), and they may actually strengthen his or her hold on power by isolating the regime from Western influence. And their use requires coordination of policy among and enforcement by the sanctioning countries in order to prevent businesses in non-sanctioning countries or in countries where the sanctions are loosely monitored from moving in to exploit the opportunities available from evading the sanctions. Aid and trade agreements have none of these problems. Of course, sometimes sanctions and even stronger measures, including a declaration of war, may have to be used. But toppling an entrenched dictator is seldom easy.

The policies advocated here give the dictator the opportunity to substitute a policy of building loyalty for repression as a means for staying in power, and they therefore have a greater chance of being acceptable to

---

[9] *The Toronto Globe and Mail* (December 11, 1996), p. A18.

the dictator. They do carry a real danger insofar as the dictator could agree to the aid or trade and promise liberalization down the road only to renege when the time comes to make good on the promise, as just discussed. But that just means the agreements have to be monitored and enforced. If the United States or UN has the will to do so, the policies advocated here have a much greater chance of success than others, simply because they appeal to the dictator's self-interest and try to accommodate it; and they also have the virtue of maintaining the UN's commitment to human rights.

5   Conclusion

In this chapter, I used basic tools of economic theory to construct a simple model of the political behavior of dictatorship. Two extreme cases were considered: a tinpot dictatorship, defined as one in which the dictator wishes only to minimize the costs of remaining in power so that he or she can continue to collect the rewards of office; and a totalitarian dictatorship, defined as one in which the totalitarian Leader maximizes power over the population. I derived some novel predictions: For example, an improvement in economic or other type of performance implies that a tinpot dictator will reduce the extent of his or her repression of the population; a totalitarian, on the other hand, tends to respond by increasing it. I presented some evidence that supports this prediction for totalitarian dictatorships. The model also explains why military dictatorships (a subspecies of tinpots) tend to be short-lived and why they often voluntarily hand over power to a civilian regime. Finally, the model also explains a number of features of totalitarian regimes, for example, the persistence of shortages in Soviet-type regimes, the preferences of their leadership for economic growth, and the structure of totalitarian party organization.

Perhaps surprisingly, the simple model developed here yields rather strong policy implications with respect to how democratic regimes should deal with dictatorships, on the assumption that democracies wish to maximize freedom in the world. In particular, an insistence on the observance of human rights under either type of regime, provided such a policy is imposed in the right way and accompanied by sufficient aid, trade, or investment, is shown to be not only a sensible but also a necessary condition if economic relations with either type of regime are to increase, and not decrease, human freedom.

4　Tyranny and timocracy

It was dangerous to trust the sincerity of Augustus; to seem to distrust it was still more dangerous.

Gibbon, *The Decline and Fall*
of the Roman Empire (1981)

1　Love and hate in the Roman Empire

The ancient Roman Empire still remains the example of greatness to which many dictators aspire. It was the model for Mussolini and Hitler, who tried to emulate it in both architectural style and longevity – and who failed on both counts. As an illustration of absolute power, what was perhaps most remarkable about the empire was its extent: Whoever commanded the empire monopolized political power in the civilized world. As Gibbon (1981) expressed it,

> The object of [a modern tyrant's] displeasure, escaping from the narrow limits of his dominions, would easily obtain, in a happier climate, a secure refuge, a new fortune adequate to his merit, the freedom of complaint, and perhaps the means of revenge. But the empire of the Romans filled the world, and when that empire fell into the hands of a single person, the world became a safe and dreary prison for his enemies. . . . "Wherever you are," said Cicero to the exiled Marcellus, "remember that you are equally within the power of the conqueror." (pp. 111–12)

The emperors themselves did not use the title "dictator," but they most surely had those powers. The main other contenders for power were the Senate and the people of Rome. The people were largely tamed as a result of the struggles at the end of the Roman Republic, and the Senate by the emperor Augustus. Thus, according to the historian Paul Veyne (1990),

> There was nothing they [the Senate] could do. The army, the Fiscus [Treasury], foreign policy, all were in the Emperor's

> domain . . . They confined themselves to rubber stamping the
> Emperor's decisions, while hoping that he would be tactful
> enough not to do them the dubious and dangerous honor of
> asking their advice, and that he would be kind enough to await
> their acclamations without demanding them: They would never
> be delivered late. (p. 412)

Thus, the emperors had tremendous formal powers. How did they
make them effective? How could they secure their hold on power, especially in the absence of a formally specified method of succession and in
the presence of numerous rivals?

Modern autocrats typically attempt to earn the loyalty of their subjects
through the pursuit of economic growth. In the ancient world technology
was largely static (Finley 1973), and the issue of the pursuit of economic
growth, so dear to the modern heart, did not really present itself. As
Picard has nicely put it, "[t]he fundamental problem in the history of the
Roman Empire was the meagre opportunity for creative investment,
which obliged it to live from day-to-day, spending its profits without
care for the future" (quoted in Veyne 1990, p. 55). Veyne adds that as a
result of big differences in income, a large part of the surplus was concentrated in the hands of the possessing class, and this class used it for
"splendors that were out of proportion to the level of prosperity attained
by society as a whole" (pp. 55–6). As far as the overt repression of the
population was concerned, the police were virtually nonexistent
(MacMullen 1988, p. 58). Of course, at higher levels, murdering actual
and potential rivals (especially relatives) was common. Still, what has to
be explained is how, at its height, a vast empire of 60 to 70 million people
was controlled by a tiny imperial apparatus. (Its precise size is very
difficult to estimate – MacMullen suggests a figure of 500,000 – but no
one thinks it was very large. See, e.g., Barrow 1949/1987; Dudley 1975; or
Grant 1978.)

Four mechanisms of control are usually discussed:

1. gifts
2. conquest
3. clientage
4. ideology – the imperial cult.

The third and fourth mechanisms raise no new theoretical issues, and,
institutionally, they are too complicated to discuss in the space available
here. (On clientage, the interested reader may consult Veyne 1990, pp.
216ff.; Grant 1978, pp. 60ff.; or Dudley 1975, Chapter 8; on ideology, see
Veyne 1990, especially Ch. 4.) We focus here, therefore, on gifts and

conquest – or war. These topics are discussed, respectively, in Sections 4 and 3 of this chapter.

Apart from the issue of control, how can the behavior of the Roman emperors be modeled? The typical Roman emperor is obviously no tinpot. On the other hand the political and bureaucratic institutions of the ancient Roman Empire are entirely unlike those of a modern totalitarian regime, with its instruments of mass communication and control, and especially its capacity to stimulate, monitor, and reward political participation by a vast proportion of the population through the institution of the mass party. Accordingly, some new categories are needed.

Section 2, which follows, classifies these regimes as either tyrannies or timocracies, and it extends the economic analysis of dictatorship developed in the last chapter for tinpot and totalitarian regimes to tyranny. Section 5 develops the model of timocratic (benevolent) rule. I suggest the Roman emperor Marcus Aurelius as a possible historical example of a timocrat and use the economic theory of the family (the benevolent dictator is the "father" of his people) to explain the workings of this seductive but flawed form of government. Section 6 shows how a regime can degenerate from timocracy into tyranny, and it illustrates this transition with the story of the emperor Commodus (Aurelius' son and successor). Section 7 concludes the chapter.

2   Timocracy and tyranny

In the preceding chapter, I categorized modern dictatorships as either tinpot or totalitarian. Both types of regimes use the instruments of repression and loyalty to accumulate power. The tinpot leader is essentially a rent-seeker, who seeks no more power over the population than the minimum needed to stay in office, using the rest of the resources of the state for his or her own purposes (palaces, Mercedes Benzes, Swiss bank accounts, and so on). The totalitarian Leader (Hitler, Stalin, the Ayatollah), on the other hand, maximizes power over the population. The constraint on the totalitarian's power maximization is the supply-of-loyalty curve. As long as increased repression increases the loyalty of the population, it increases the power of the totalitarian Leader as well. However, once the supply of loyalty curve bends backward, further repression reduces loyalty, ultimately by enough to reduce power. The totalitarian leader's power is therefore maximized at the point at which the backward-bending supply of loyalty curve is tangent to an isopower line curve, as shown in the preceding chapter (e.g., Figure 3.5).

As already suggested, neither the tinpot nor totalitarian images are appropriate for the Roman Empire. The people of Rome constituted less than 1 percent of the Roman Empire. At their peak the armed forces of Rome numbered 500,000–600,000 or so. The Senate was a small and ineffectual body. And the bureaucracy and the institutions for operating the state were of course very primitive – for example, fixed, regular, annual taxes were not instituted until very late in the empire. So the emperor relied on both very large penalties as a technique of repression (to compensate for the technological lack of monitoring capacity) and bread and circuses and other gifts to accumulate loyalty.

However, there is one respect in which Roman leaders resemble the modern totalitarian dictator – in the use of propaganda. One way they did this was through building. For example, Augustus states in his *Res Gestae* – his testimonial (carved on his tomb) to his accomplishments as ruler of the people of Rome, which included a careful accounting of the funds that he spent personally for their welfare on buildings and entertainments – that the Rome he inherited was made of rubble, but that by the end of his reign he had turned it into marble. Modern totalitarian leaders such as Mussolini, Hitler, and Stalin copied this mania for building directly from the Roman Empire.

Nevertheless, the political institutions of the Roman Empire lacked the crucial nexus between repression and loyalty (that over a wide range, increased repression generates more loyalty) which, I have argued, is characteristic of totalitarian societies. Instead these regimes appear – and did in fact appear to contemporaries – as either tyrants (characterized by high repression and low loyalty), or timocrats (characterized by high loyalty with low levels of repression). The range of possible equilibria is illustrated in Figure 4.1. I borrow the term "timocracy" from Plato (in *The Republic*), who designated by it what is obviously a benevolent dictatorship, although this type of regime ranked second to rule by the Philospher–King in Plato's scheme. Still, the Greek root of the word "timocracy" is *Thymos* – to love. That these two (timocracy and tyranny) are the possible equilibria is also another way of illustrating the Dictator's Dilemma – the dictator does not know (although he will have his suspicions) whether he is loved or hated by the population (i.e., whether he is regarded as a timocrat or tyrant).

The equilibrium for a tyrant is depicted in Figure 4.2. Like a totalitarian, the tyrant also maximizes power. But the tyrant lacks the mass party and other political institutions that permit the totalitarian leader to monitor and reward political participation or loyalty on a grand scale. In the Roman Empire, the tyrant's capacity to build loyalty was with the groups we have discussed in the previous section – the people of Rome,

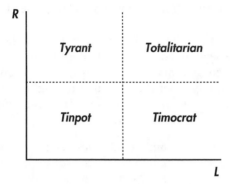

Figure 4.1. Types of equilibria under dictatorship.

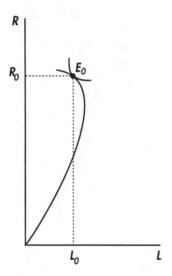

Figure 4.2. Tyranny.

the army, and the Senate. As a result, the supply curve of loyalty is much more steeply sloped than that of a totalitarian leader (see, e.g., Figure 3.4 or 3.5). Equilibrium is at E_0 in the figure, with loyalty L_0 and repression R_0.

The analysis is obviously very simple, but the equilibrium so depicted does illustrate all three of the definitions of tyranny in antiquity:

1. a regime in which the tyrant keeps himself in power through violence
2. a regime run by a man whose policy runs contrary to the material interests of a section, large or small, of his subjects
3. a regime controlled by a man whose delight in the exercise of power derives entirely from the servitude that he imposes on some of his subjects. (The three definitions are given by Veyne 1990, p. 405.)

By virtue of the first definition, tyranny is the only regime of the four possibilities in Figure 4.1 in which repression is overwhelmingly the primary tool used to maintain power. By virtue of the second, the fact that the tyrant's policies are unpopular partly explains why the supply of loyalty to the regime is so low. And by virtue of the third, the tyrant's delight in exercising power is illustrated in Figure 4.2 by the fact that he maximizes it. Thus, the three properties of the tyrant's equilibrium correspond well with the three definitions of tyranny in antiquity.

Of course, tyrannies are not limited to the ancient world. Chapters 7 and 8 discuss some contemporary examples – Pinochet's Chile in Chapter 7 and the *apartheid* government of South Africa in Chapter 8. What is perhaps unique to the ancient world is that it furnishes a possible example of timocracy. This subject is discussed in Section 5, after which we show how a regime can lapse from timocracy into tyranny.

One way to understand the forces which may result in tyrannical rule is to recall a point made in the preceding chapter about the effect of improved economic performance on the fortunes of a tinpot. I suggested there that improved economic performance does not *necessarily* lead to greater loyalty to the tinpot because it has two effects on the typical subject:

1. a substitution effect – economic growth will typically raise the subjects' return on their investments in the regime
2. an income or wealth effect – to the extent that economic growth raises an individual's wealth, he or she is led to increase all of his or her investments, including those with opposition forces.

For the latter reason, it is possible that economic growth may, if it leads the subject to invest more with the opposition than with the regime, actually *diminish* the dictator's security in office.

This outcome suggests another possible strategy for the astute dictator: Under some circumstances *immiserizing* the population may be more attractive than enriching it. This strategy may be attractive to dictators for two reasons:

1. Looting, taxing, confiscating, or otherwise taking the money of their subjects for themselves gives dictators funds they can use to spend for their own purposes – or to buy off those whose active support they need the most (the army, close political associates, and so on). The pursuit of economic growth, on the other hand, forces dictators to refrain from overtaxation, overregulation, or confiscation, because of their possibly deleterious effects on growth.
2. Impoverishing the population implies it will have fewer resources which could be used to oppose the regime. And, as is well known, poor people tend to participate less in politics.[1]

This fact provides one rationale for tyranny. Dictators who pursue a strategy of immiserization will not be loved, but most of the population will be too poor to actively oppose them, and what little opposition does arise can be controlled directly through the use of repression. The army and other groups, whose loyalty *is* essential, can be bought off with the resources taken from everyone else. This strategy of immiserization is clearly more attractive in societies in which the prospects of successful economic growth are slim – that is, in those in which the population is undereducated (models of endogenous growth, e.g., that of Azariadis and Drazen 1990, emphasize the importance of this factor in generating growth), in which it is primarily rural (and therefore least likely to benefit from growth, because growth usually means holding down the prices of primary products in order to benefit urban centers [see Bates 1981]), and in which there is considerable income inequality (see Alesina and Rodrik 1990; Persson and Tabellini 1990; both studies show that income inequality and growth are negatively correlated).

A good example of a modern country with a regime that appeared to have followed this strategy is Haiti under the Duvaliers. All of the conditions just listed were certainly present; in addition, one of the regime's most important allies was the *houngans* or voodoo priests, who were natural community leaders because of the religious functions they fulfilled, and who were inherently antigrowth because growth or modernization could easily threaten their own position if it weakened the capacity of the masses to believe in the supernatural (Lundahl 1984).

---

[1] As an illustration, Kathy Cohen and Michael Dawson (1993) provide evidence that among Afro-Americans, neighborhood poverty has an identifiable and substantial impact on perceptions of the effectiveness of political acts, perceptions of community efficacy, and perceptions of group influence; in their study, they found that the residents of the poorest neighborhoods demonstrated the most consistent effects (p. 298).

3   War

The economic theory of conquest would appear to be perfectly straight-forward: Conquest is profitable if the present value of taxes, booty, and other forms of revenue from conquered territories exceeds both the costs of conquest and the expected annual maintenance costs of expenditures involved in maintaining power over the subjugated peoples – that is, expenditures either to repress revolts or to buy or otherwise obtain the loyalty of the local inhabitants. Initially, there is probably a range of increasing returns, as conquered territories supply the conqueror with more manpower and other resources. However, it seems reasonable to assume ultimately diminishing returns to additional conquests, as territories which are farther away or more difficult to conquer – or whose peoples are more difficult to subjugate – are progressively encroached upon. Assuming for simplicity that all members of society share equally in the costs and benefits of foreign adventures, we find that the marginal adventure is that in which the marginal expected payoff is just equal to the marginal extra costs of conquest, administration, or subjugation.

The marginal payoff to the *dictator* or other political leader may be very different from this one. For example, under the Roman Republic, a Roman general could raise an army, go and conquer a foreign territory, use the proceeds to pay off his veterans, and, at least formally, keep the proceeds for himself! Because under the Republic, Roman armies were very effective, there was no shortage of ambitious men willing to under-take this task, especially because, apart from the money, foreign con-quest was the surest route to glory and a future in politics. Indeed, most of what later became the Roman Empire was in fact obtained under the Republic. Analytically, the result of a status-seeking competition like this is, naturally, *overexpansion*, because as with other status-seeking games (see Frank 1985), everyone cannot simultaneously move up the hierarchy. Indeed, it is often argued that it was the oligopolistic competition for power among the generals that ultimately resulted in the civil war which ended the Roman Republic (Barrow 1949/1987, pp. 58ff.).

This last difficulty was resolved by Augustus, who solved the problem of destructive oligopolistic competition by substituting for it the principle of monopoly rule or dictatorship (although he always refused the title "dictator"). He assumed control of all of the armed forces of the state, whose members were then required to take an oath of loyalty to him. He took control of the appointment of the provincial governors (previously, the Roman generals or warlords) and established checks and balances on their powers (Dudley 1975, p. 154). He also completely reorganized the system of administrating newly conquered territories with his policies of "Romanization" (pp. 160–1 and 228–9) and local government. And he soothed nationalistic feelings in the conquered territories by granting local self-government in exchange for loyalty to Rome (Barrow 1949/ 1987, p. 57; Dudley 1975, pp. 160–1).

However, Augustus and later emperors were still prone to overexpansion – as are all dictators. To see why, recall our general proposition that dictators are more insecure than democratic leaders. That proposition provides a simple explanation for the oft-noted fact that dictators fight wars more often than democratic leaders. First, dictators have more to fear from other regimes than democratic leaders. Dissidents within their own regime can ally with external forces; communications media in other countries can counteract a dictator's propaganda; perhaps most important, the dictator's promise *not to attack other countries* is less credible than a similar promise from a democratically elected leader. The democratic leader's promise will have been formally ratified between the executive and legislative bodies of the democracy, which in turn makes it binding on the executive. Dictators have no similar way of making their promises to a foreign leader credible. Second, there is perhaps no surer way to inspire loyalty from one's people than with the glory and the booty which result from foreign conquest. In this way, possibly unlike any other, dictators can displace their own fear onto those who would attempt to remove them from office. Finally, war is a controversial and difficult decision, and in any democracy, there will undoubtedly be groups and forces opposed to it. As a result, democratic societies can be plagued by inaction, as discussed further in Chapter 11. Dictators, on the other hand, do not need to forge a consensus in favor of war to be able to engage in it.

These ideas can be compared with the classic Kantian explanation of why dictatorial regimes fight wars more frequently than do democracies, an idea revived recently by Schweller (1992); this explanation rests on the proposition that democracies fight fewer wars than do dictatorships because in a democracy, the consent of the citizenry is required in order to initiate war, and "nothing is more natural than that those who would have to decide to undergo all the deprivations of war will very much hesitate to start such an evil game" (Kant, quoted in Schweller, p. 241). Dictators, on the other hand, may "resolve for war from insignificant reasons, as if it were but a hunting expedition" (Kant, quoted in Schweller, loc. cit.; see also Lake 1992), because they do not bear the costs of war.

With respect to the Kantian argument, the important issue is the likely fate of a leader who loses a war. Bruce Bueno de Mesquita, Randolph Siverson, and Gary Woller provided empirical evidence on this issue.

Using a large sample of countries during the 1823–1974 period, they showed that there is a strong relationship between losing a war and drastic changes in political leadership, with 29.5 percent of the losers, and only 9.1 percent of the winners experiencing a violent regime change. Finally, in considering the costs of defeat to a dictator, it is perhaps worth pondering the case of the Roman emperor Valeran, who was defeated and captured by the Persians. For the emperor it was a permanent humiliation. "For the rest of his life," Trevor-Roper (1965) wrote, "he was carried about in chains to be a living footstool for the Persian King when he mounted his horse" (p. 54). In short, the Kantian argument is wrong: Costs of defeat to a dictator are not necessarily smaller, and they can be substantially larger than they would be for any democratic leader.

4   Gifts

Linked to conquest, but apart from it, was the other important mechanism for accumulating loyalty under both the Roman Republic and the empire: the practice of *euergetism* (as Veyne [1990] calls it), beneficence, or gift-giving. Apart from the executive (the magistrates), the three other contenders for power in ancient Rome were the army, the Senate, and the people of Rome. One way to describe the history of ancient Rome is to say that there was a steady loss of power, first by the people, and then by the Senate to the army and the executive (the magistrates). Of course, this is an oversimplification. There were many shifts of power among these four groups over the 1,000 years of history from about 500 BC to about AD 500. Throughout that history, however, only these groups were those with the power to unseat a ruling oligarch under the Republic – and later an emperor. They were also the main recipients of gifts. The army received *donativum* (bonuses), the Senate various privileges, and the people of Rome bread and circuses.

How can the extensive practice of gift-giving, common in many modern as well as in ancient dictatorships, be explained? The economic theory of gifts has been discussed by George Akerlof (1984), Gary Becker (1974), and Colin Camerer (1988). Becker discussed gifts in the context of altruism, an important subject to which we turn in the next section. Akerlof notes that the root for the word "gift" in the two major ancient languages – ancient German and ancient Greek – is the same as the root for the word "poison." He suggests that this is because of the reciprocal character of gifts: gifts "given" usually demand gifts in return. A more specific interpretation of the poisonous quality of gifts is that accepting a gift puts the recipient in a position of debt – and therefore in a circumspect and responsive (poisonous) relation to the donor as long as the gift goes unrequited. Perhaps there is no better example of the poisonous quality of gifts than that of the gift by Constantine of Roman citizenship to all the citizens of the provinces ruled by Rome: With this "gift," the Roman government acquired the right to levy taxes on those people!

None of these authors discuss political gifts, which may have different functions. Many of these are traced out with great skill by the historian Paul Veyne (1990) in his justly celebrated *Bread and Circuses*. But before returning to the case of ancient Rome, let us consider the case of Zaire's Mobutu. Mobutu was known for distributing largesse to the Zairian people, and the press there constantly catalogued his magnanimous gestures. According to Michael Schatzberg's (1988) account,

> Whenever a new development project is completed – be it a renovated building, a new construction, road or hospital – the press presents the new or rebuilt facility as a gift from the President founder to his children, the Zairian population ...even a hearse for the City of Nbuji-mai...[they] are all "gifts" from "the Father" that demonstrate his eternal love and solicitude. (p. 77)

In turn, the people were required to repay the Guide (as Mobutu was known) with their taxes. As Schatzberg put it, "[t]he billions of dollars he extracts from the Zairian people is therefore only his due. The Father bestows gifts on his children and what he receives in return is merely repayment of an outstanding and never-ending obligation. . . . No theft, no corruption, no exploitation; only grateful 'children' repaying their generous 'Father'" (p. 81).

Thus, one important meaning of gift-giving under dictatorship is to confirm the dictator's "ownership" of the assets of the state. Theoretically, gifts solve a Coaseian bargaining problem. Two parties can only exchange, even if transactions costs are low, when property rights are established – that is, if it is known what belongs to whom. When dictators make a gift to the public or some part of it, from the public treasury, they are asserting that it is their right to give that money, and by accepting the gift, the recipient is agreeing to this fact. The gift confirms that the dictator "owns" the resources of the state. Whereas the people are *compelled* to pay their taxes and to accept the confiscations of the dictator, the dictator may, as a matter of his or her own choosing, *give* (out of his or her own pocket) public expenditures to them. By accepting these as gifts, the people confirm the dictator's power.

Yet there is one important sense in which the establishment of property rights in this way differs from the legal establishment of property rights that facilitates market exchange. Whereas dictators may "legitimize" their right to hold office through gifts, they do not thereby acquire the power to transfer those rights. This problem – the lack of an established succession mechanism – recurs throughout the history of the Roman Empire. It also distinguishes this type of dictatorship (Caesarism, as we shall refer to it, following Veyne [1990], p. 410) from some other types in which this problem is (more or less) solved – for example, by dynastic succession or divine right. Of course, the idea that a ruler can acquire the right to hold office in any of these ways rather than by the granting of this right by the people is what fundamentally distinguishes dictatorship from democracy.

The emperor Augustus knew the meaning of gift-giving. According to Gaius Suetonius (1957), he was extraordinarily generous with his gifts, but

> ... [W]hen his house on the Palatine Hill burned down, a fund for its rebuilding was started by the veterans, the guilds, and the tribes; to which people of every sort made further individual contributions according to their means. Augustus, to show his gratitude for the gift, took a token coin from each heap, but no more than a single silver piece. (p. 86)

Truly, for an emperor, it may be said that it is better to give than to receive! And there are many other nuances to the practice of political gift-giving in ancient Rome. For example, one function of euergetism both in Greece and Republican Rome as well as in the empire was to limit entry to politics to those who could afford to give gifts. Another was to build support, because the population loved games – "all sex and violence," as the historian MacMullen put it (1988, p. 45). Consequently, the notables tried to outdo each other in providing lavish entertainments. The population, in turn, egged them on, in John Chrysostom's beautiful description:

> The theatre fills, and the whole citizenry is seated up there, presenting the most brilliant spectacle made up of so many faces, that the very top-most gallery and its covering is blocked out by men's bodies ... Upon the entrance of that benefactor who brought them together, they leap to their feet, uttering a salute as from a single mouth, with one voice calling him guardian and leader of their common city. They stretch forth their arms; then at intervals they compare him to the greatest of all rivers; they

liken the grandeur and flow of his civic generosity, in its abun-
dance, to the waters of the Nile, and they call him a very Nile of
gifts, himself; and some who flatter still more, declaring the
comparison with the Nile too mean, set aside rivers and seas and
bring in Ocean, and they say that is what he is, as Ocean among
waters, so he in his gifts. They omit no possible term of
praise . . . He himself bows to them, and by this pays his respects,
and so he seats himself among the blessings of all, who, everyone
of them, pray to be such as he – and then to die . . . And while he
revels in his heart's desire like a person drunk with vain glory, to
the point that he would spend his very self, he can take in no
least sensation of his losses. But when he is at home . . . then at
that moment he understands they were no dream but a reality in
hard cash. (quoted in MacMullen, pp. 45–6)

So the games provided an opportunity not only for the notable to
signal how much he cared for the people, but also for the people to signal
their support for the notable or even the emperor. The people in the
crowd were (relatively) safe from political retaliation and could express
their true sentiments. Thus, on some occasions, the audience could be
considerably less than enthusiastic. For example, the emperor himself
had his favorite gladiators, so that when the audience booed them, this
could be taken to be an expression of opposition. The shows were also
sometimes scenes of political disturbances. According to Veyne (1990),
"[I]t was at a show that the crowd successfully pressed Galba to execute
Tigellinus, complained about the high price of corn, desperately en-
treated Gaius [Caligula] to cut down imports and grant some relief from
the burden of taxes and chanted their desire for peace" (p. 401). Under
the emperor, there were months of festivals, spaced out in a series of
several days at a time. The people of Rome spent these months in the
emperor's company. The Senate was also at the circus or in the
amphitheater when, at the games, the emperors had themselves ac-
claimed by the people. This was acceptable unless it went too far. Veyne
says that

> the worst stage was reached when certain Emperors demanded
> to be acclaimed by the Senate itself; these were usually the same
> ones who decimated the ruling group by driving senators to
> suicide by accusing them of high treason or, as it was put, lese-
> majesty . . . In the reigns of such men the senators looked on the
> Emperor as an idol, red with their blood, that they were forced
> to worship. (p. 407)

The other major recipient of gifts was the army. The *donativum* was born with Claudius on his accession. The Praetorians placed him on the throne, and he needed to thank them for their support and to seal his accord with them, especially because the Senate was slow to confirm the Praetorians' choice. He promised the men 150 gold pieces each and bound them by oath so that they would remain loyal to him (Suetonius 1957, p. 191; Veyne 1990, p. 341). At the death of Claudius, Nero promised a *donativum* after his father's example, and the tradition became fixed. The next emperor, Galba, promised a larger bonus than usual, but then he announced that he would not honor it, saying "it is my custom to levy troops, not to buy them" (Suetonius 1957, p. 255). Five days later, the guards launched a coup d'etat under the leadership of Otho. Just before his death, Galba is said to have promised the bounty after all (p. 257).

Thus, the gift of the *donativum* to the army was always made in exchange for the army's vow of loyalty – that is, the army's recognition of the donor's "ownership" of the state and his right to the office of emperor. This changed by the third century AD; as the barbarian threats steadily increased, the army became more and more important, and the power of the generals grew. The soldiers made and unmade emperors. On at least one occasion the throne was literally auctioned off to the highest bidder (Veyne 1990, p. 336). The emperors pampered the military more and more, raising their pay and gratuities, rewarding them with lands and suffering their petty tyranny over the civilian population (Barrow 1949/1987, p. 165). Finally, the empire turned into a vast administrative machine designed to produce taxes to maintain the army (Barrow, p. 171), who no longer accepted gifts but demanded payment.

5   All you need is love: timocracy

A. The economic theory of altruism

A number of motives for giving have just been discussed, including signaling, establishing the property rights of the emperor over the resources of the state, and creating barriers to entry to political office. But is there not still the possibility that a dictator could be genuinely altruistic and give to the people because he or she cares for them? If so, how would such a dictator rule? Turning to contemporary economic theory for advice on this matter and recalling the previously discussed analogy of the dictator as the "father" of his people – a favorite metaphor of dictators of all stripes – suggests that we consult the economics of the family. Here we indeed have economic models of the effects of altruism on behavior. Of course, even if a genuinely benevolent dictator – a timocrat – existed, he or she could not be expected to know these models, but if they point to effects which a wise politician could be expected to discover from experience, then they will be relevant to his or her conduct. So we will begin our analysis of timocracy by reviewing the main results in the economics of altruism within the family. These results are then used to analyze timocratic rule.

Becker (1974, 1976) was the first to attempt a formal demonstration of the effects of altruistic giving. In the famous "Rotten Kid Theorem," he visualized an altruistic parent (the father) interacting with a selfish ("rotten") kid. The model assumes that the kid – let's assume, for argument's sake, a son – has opportunities to provide benefits to his father at a cost to himself. Ordinarily, because the son is selfish, it could safely be assumed that he would not do such a thing. However, if the father is altruistic, he will want to make income transfers to his son in order to make the son happy. The level of these transfers, in turn, depends on the father's own income or wealth. Even though the boy is selfish, he might therefore be motivated to behave *as if* he were altruistic toward his father, because by increasing his father's wealth, he also increases the size of the transfers the father makes to him in return. Becker showed that if the father is sufficiently benevolent, the prospect of these transfers will motivate the kid to act as if he were unselfish and to jointly maximize the income of father and son. It immediately follows that altruism can "pay off," not merely in utility terms (the increase in the father's utility from an increase in his son's consumption possibilities), but also in terms of the father's *own consumption*: If the son chooses the joint maximizing solution when the father is altruistic, but not when the father is selfish, it is possible, if the parameters are right, for the father's own consumption to increase. Figure 4.3 (adapted from Hirshleifer 1977) depicts this possibility. The kid's consumption level is measured on the vertical axis, and the father's on the horizontal axis. *PP* is the kid's production possibility curve. Note that as depicted, the kid has some opportunities to increase his own consumption at the expense of that of his father – that is, by moving from *J* to *R*. If the father were selfish, the kid would obviously choose *R*. But if the father is altruistic and makes transfers to the kid, then the kid will realize that he is better off maximizing the joint income of the family and choosing *J* rather than *R*, because the altruistic father (whose indifference curves are like *AA'*) will more than compensate him for this choice by making a transfer so that the kid ends up at *A**.

Xenophon was aware of the logic behind the "Rotten Kid Theorem" and of its application to dictatorship. In his dialogue on tyranny, the poet

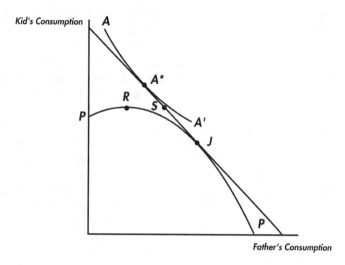

Figure 4.3. Effects of altruistic giving.

Simonides recommends love and generosity to the tyrant (Hiero) as the solution to his (the dictator's) dilemma:

> "You must not, Hiero, shrink from spending from your private possessions for the common good ... your contest is against others who rule cities; if you make the city you rule the happiest of these, know well that you will be declared by herald the victor in the most noble and magnificent contest among human beings. First, you would at once secure the love of your subjects, which is the very thing you happen to desire. Further, the herald of your victory would not be one, but all human beings would sing of your virtue. Being an object of attention you would be cherished not only by private men, but by many cities; marvelled at not only in private, but in public among all as well. ... Every man present would be your ally, and every man absent would desire to see you. Therefore, you would not only be liked, you would be loved by human beings. ...
>
> "But enrich your friends with confidence, Hiero; for you will enrich yourself. Augment the city, for you will attach power to yourself. Acquire allies for it. Consider the fatherland to be your estate, the citizens your comrades, friends your own children, your sons the same as your life, and try to surpass all these in benefactions. For you prove superior to your friends in benefi-

cence, your enemies will be utterly unable to resist you ..."
(Xenophon, in Strauss 1963/1991, p. 21)

However, there is a flaw in Becker's argument (and therefore in Xenophon's): Implicitly, the comparison being made is that between a *short-sightedly* selfish and an *altruistic* father.[2] A father who is selfish but who can anticipate the gains from obtaining his son's cooperation would also provide transfers to his son for purely selfish reasons (the gains to him from the kid's cooperation). Moreover, the selfish father's own consumption would always exceed that of the altruistic father – that is, although altruism might pay off compared with short-sighted selfishness, far-sighted selfishness pays off better than altruism. The reason is simple. A far-sighted father will "give" to his kid the same way a banker "gives" a loan: to maximize profits on the exchange. An otherwise identical but *altruistic* father must give more than this, so he must be giving too much from the point of view of maximizing profits or from the point of view of his own consumption. Thus, in Figure 4.3, the far-sighted but selfish father transfers enough so that the kid ends up at S, which is just above R. The kid will still choose J, because he is better off at S than at R. But the selfish father ends up with more of his own consumption at S than the altruistic one (at A^*). The same proposition obviously holds for dictatorship. But in either case, giving is shown to be a rational strategy.

Another implication is that a father (really the "head" of the household, male or female) who makes transfers to other members of the household, whether for selfish or unselfish reasons, has considerable *power* over them. Thus, Becker shows that if one child were to attempt to appropriate the income or wealth of another, his or her effort would have no effect: The head would simply compensate by making a transfer to the child who had lost, and he would withdraw transfers from the child who had gained until the two incomes were at the optimum level from *his* (the head's) point of view. As long as the transfers from the head are large enough, he and he alone determines how much income each child will have: They have no say in the matter. A similar result would hold between a dictator and the citizenry under his or her control, so long as the taxing and spending powers of the regime are unconstrained.

Since the donor has power over the recipient, gifts or the promise of gifts can be used to induce the recipients to do things that they might not do otherwise. B. Bernheim, A. Shleifer, and L. Summers (1985) assumed that parents want their children to visit them and are willing to pay for these visits in the form of larger bequests. In the model, children may not

---

[2] See Ronald Wintrobe (1981, 1983) for the original arguments on these points.

mind visiting their parents at first, but after awhile they get tired of doing so, so that further visits bring disutility. Parents never tire of seeing their children (at least, never before their children tire of visiting them), and so, at the margin, parents trade larger bequests for more visits. Amazingly, data do exist on the level of attention children give to their parents, in the form of indices of the number of weekly visits paid by children to their parents. Bernheim, Shleifer, and Summers' analysis of the data showed that the larger the potential bequest, the more frequent the visits. Most sadly, perhaps, visits to parents who were poor and became ill dropped off, whereas those to parents who were rich and became ill increased.

Another interesting aspect of the relationship between a donor and recipient is what James Buchanan (1975) has called the "Samaritan's Dilemma." Put simply, recipients can be "spoiled" by gifts: They can turn lazy or fail to plan appropriately for the future, relying instead on anticipated gifts from the donor. Or they can spend time and effort trying to figure out ways to get more gifts instead of engaging in more productive behavior. A similar result is described in the literature on rent seeking: The possibility of a "gift" from the government causes potential recipients to compete for this rent, and as a result, the entire value of the gift is squandered during this wasteful competition. This same point is also made in the literature on government welfare programs: It is said that welfare allegedly reduces the incentives on the part of recipients to look for a job, to work, to save, and to do other things that benefit society but that require effort and energy.[3] One important implication of this argument is that it explains why donors, whether parents or governments, typically monitor and try to control the behavior of recipients: They want to minimize deleterious effects. Thus, within the family, parents try to impose rules and regulations on their children, the children try to evade them or to outwit their parents in various ways, and the parents threaten them with sanctions when the rules and regulations are not followed. A government will typically impose stringent regulations on the recipients of transfers – such as unemployment insurance, welfare, and so on – and then it will monitor their behavior intensely. The central point is that in the absence of monitoring, giving can clearly have an effect that is precisely the reverse of that specified in the "Rotten Kid Theorem" – that is, it can turn a good child (or citizen) "rotten."

In summary, there are a number of propositions in the theory of giving

---

[3] See Wintrobe (1983) and Neil Bruce and Michael Waldman (1990) for formalizations of this argument.

that should be of interest not only to the timocratic dictator but to all dictators. They are:

1. Through the use of gifts, a donor, whether selfish or altruistic, can obtain power over recipients and induce their cooperation toward his or her own objectives.
2. An altruistic donor can do this even if he or she is unaware of the fact that his or her gifts can induce cooperative behavior on the part of recipients (the rotten kid theorem). However, an altruistic donor will give too much from the point of view of maximizing his or her own consumption.
3. All donors have to monitor the behavior of each recipient to ensure that the gifts are not corrupting that recipient, and they will calibrate the size of their gifts to the possibility of monitoring recipients, giving less (or nothing) when monitoring is difficult or impossible.

B. Benevolent dictatorship

Now let us apply these ideas to try to discover how a timocratic dictator will operate. For the purpose of exposition, we will consider a "pure" timocrat – that is, one who cares only abut the welfare of his or her people and not at all about him- or herself. It is doubtful whether such a benefactor has ever existed, although there is no shortage of political leaders who have pretended to be motivated in this way. But extreme cases are always useful analytically. The reader who wishes to imagine a concrete example of pure timocracy might consult the authoritative judgment of Edward Gibbon and ponder the Age of the Antonines, of which Gibbon (1981) declared:

> If a man were called to fix the period in the history of the world during which the condition of the human race was most happy and prosperous, he would, without hesitation, name that which elapsed from the death of Domitian to the accession of Commodus [Aurelius' successor]. The vast extent of the Roman empire was governed by absolute power, under the guidance of virtue and wisdom. The armies were restrained by the firm and gentle hand of four successive emperors whose characters and authority commanded involuntary respect. . . . The labours of these monarchs were overpaid by the immense reward that inseparably waited on their success; by the honest pride of virtue

and by the exquisite delight of beholding the general happiness
of which they were the authors. (p. 107)

Whether in fact this was such a happy time has of course been much
debated, but at least some contemporary historians (e.g., Grant 1994, pp.
148ff.) are not completely opposed to Gibbon's judgment. We do know
that this was a time of general prosperity and of the celebrated *Pax
Romana.* As to what made the Antonine emperors capable of this form
of behavior, however, Gibbon is unclear. Two rulers in particular are
singled out for praise: Antoninus Pius and Marcus Aurelius. But little is
known about the first ruler (Gibbon 1980, p. 105), although it is known
that he died tranquilly in AD 161 – a not unremarkable event in the
context of the period. Indeed, Grant (1994) says that it "was the first
really serene death that any Roman emperor had experienced" (p. 21).
The second emperor, Marcus Aurelius, has left us his famous *Meditations* (1964), in which he expressed his philosophy of rule in purely
timocratic terms – that is, in statements like "Let every action aim solely
at the common good" (quoted in Grant 1994, p. 55). Philosophy was in
fact his favorite subject, possibly confirming Hicks' (1935) oft-quoted
aphorism that "[t]he best of all monopoly profits is a quiet life" (in Stigler
& Boulding 1952, p. 369). However, the constant invasions of the period
meant that he did not have enough time to pursue this interest.

Two questions stand out for the economic theory of timocracy:

1. How would a timocrat rule? In particular, would a timocrat need
   to – or want to – use the instrument of repression, and if so, what
   are the equilibrium levels of repression and support under
   timocracy?
2. Is timocratic rule stable – that is, could it last?

A moment's reflection will convince the reader that the answer to the
first question (would a genuine timocrat repress his subjects?) is yes. To
see why, one need only note that although the timocrat may have enormous power and may have every intention of using it to benefit his or her
subjects, this does not mean that there are no constraints on his or her
behavior. Three constraints are particularly worthy of attention.

1. *The necessity to hold onto power.* What is the point of wise and
   magnanimous rule if the only result is displacement from office
   by a tyrant with a surer grasp of the levers of power? Thus, even
   a pure timocrat cannot allow power to fall below π_{min}, the minimum level of power needed to stay in office.
2. *The Samaritan's Dilemma.* The timocrat, like the loving father in
   the theory of the family, will be aware of the Samaritan's Di-

lemma – that is, of the disincentive effects of gifts on the people who receive them. Moreover, the timocrat's subjects are obviously much more numerous – and the task of monitoring them more complicated – than would be the case within the family. The expectation of gifts from the timocrat can be expected to give rise to widespread rent-seeking and sycophancy as each individual among the citizenry tries to convince the dictator that he or she is the most worthy of his or her largesse.

3. *The Rotten Kid Theorem*. This factor leads to results that are the opposite of those produced by the first two, and it simplifies rather than complicates the timocrat's task. In the context of timocratic rule, the theorem implies that the people can be expected to respond positively to compassion and to support the regime in order to preserve the leader's wealth and hence the size of the gifts to them. Again, in the context of dictatorship, this factor operates more strongly than it does within the family. Under dictatorship, it is a very real possibility that the timocrat will be replaced by someone less generous, and this possibility gives the citizens, especially those who do particularly well under his or her regime, a powerful motive to support him or her.

All of these considerations and the interaction among them can be understood better if we put them together into a simple formal model. Thus, assume the timocrat maximizes the welfare of the citizenry – that is, he or she maximizes

(1) $\Sigma_i w_i U_i \left[Y_i (1-t) + G_i \right]$

where w_i indicates the weight that the timocrat gives to person i's welfare; U is i's utility, which depends on Y_i, the person's income (saving is omitted); G_i is the size of the gift to i; and t is the tax rate, assumed to take the form of a constant tax rate on income for simplicity only (there were no income taxes in the Roman Empire).

The first of the constraints just mentioned is that power cannot be allowed to fall below π_{min}. That is,

(2) $\pi \geq \pi_{min}$, where

(3) $\pi = \pi(L, R)$, as before.

The second constraint is on the dictator's budget:

(4) $F + tY(G) = P_L(R, G)L + P_R R + G$

where

$$Y = Y(G), \ Y' < 0, \ Y'' > 0 \text{ and } P_L = P_L(R,G), \ \partial P_L / \partial G < 0$$

In the budget constraint, F is foreign income, and it is assumed to be constant. The purpose of introducing it into (4) is just to emphasize that not all gifts are simply redistributions of the taxpayer's own money. F could also represent any other source of the emperor's budget which is independent of the taxes on or incomes of the population. The variable t, the tax rate, is assumed to be a uniform tax on income (Y) for simplicity as before; G represents the aggregate costs of the gifts from the timocrat to the population. The Samaritan's Dilemma is incorporated in the negative dependence of Y on G. That is, as gifts increase, the aggregate income earned by the citizenry falls as the population increasingly resorts to rent-seeking and other forms of unproductive behavior. The rotten kid effect is represented by the negative effect of G on P_L – that is, gifts enable the dictator to obtain loyalty at a lower price. Note that apart from these two effects, the problem is formally identical to the tinpot's problem, except that timocrats maximize the welfare of the citizenry subject to the constraint that they stay in office, whereas tinpots maximize their own consumption or welfare subject to the same constraint.

This resemblance is easily seen if we illustrate the timocrat's equilibrium graphically, as is done in Figure 4.4. Note that the budget constraint BB depicted there is the power budget constraint $B = P_R R + P_L L$ only, and it is not the total budget constraint described in equation (4) – that is, it doesn't include the timocrat's gifts. But it does show the effect of giving on P_L – in Figure 4.4, the supply of loyalty is high even at low levels of repression, because people are eager to avail themselves of the largesse of the timocrat. However, even the timocrat will find, like the altruistic father, that some repression – rules, prohibitions of certain activities, penalties for antisocial behavior – improves the supply of genuine loyalty, so the L^S curve slopes up with respect to R. Timocrats maximize the welfare of the citizenry, so they are in equilibrium at the cost-minimizing combination of R and L (given their capacity to accumulate L at low cost because of the effects of gifts in reducing P_L). However, timocrats will seek no more power than this, so they stay on π_{min}. In this sense, they resemble tinpots. Indeed, the dynamics of the timocrat's responses are identical to those of the tinpot: If performance deteriorates or for some other reason the supply of loyalty to the timocrat falls, the timocrat is forced to increase the level of repression or lose office. The pattern will also be the same as that discussed earlier for the tinpot: an initial sharp increase of repression, followed by a subsequent fall to a level which is still higher than the original one. Most alarmingly, like the

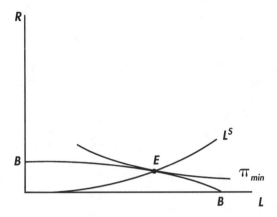

Figure 4.4. Timocracy.

tinpot, the timocrat's rule is fragile – because he or she does not maximize power, he or she is always on the verge of losing it to one who
does.

What about the Rotten Kid Theorem? And Xenophon's advice to
give, give, give to the people? Figure 4.4 shows that that advice is flawed.
The love and protection of the citizenry for timocrats do not help them
out of this dilemma, for their very magnanimity means that they squander any potential cushion of available power (any $\pi > \pi_{min}$) by increasing
their gifts until the cushion is dissipated.

To reveal the second flaw of timocratic government, examine the
equilibrium conditions for timocrats. Their choice levels of G, R, and L
to maximize (1) subject to the constraints (2)–(4) yields both the familiar
cost-minimizing conditions for R and L derived earlier for the tinpot and
a new condition for the optimal level of G:

(5) $w_i U_i' \left[1 + Y_G (1-t) \right] = \lambda \left(1 - t Y_G + L\, \partial P_L / \partial G \right),$

in which λ is the marginal utility of money (extra budgetary resources).
From equation (5), we find that an increase in G has the following
effects:

1. The citizens benefit directly (the first term on the left-hand side
   of [5]).
2. National income falls (Y_G on the left-hand side).
3. There is a direct cost to the treasury (the first term on the right-
   hand side).

4. There is also an indirect cost insofar as tax revenue falls as Y is reduced (the second term on the right-hand side).
5. The cost of obtaining loyalty is reduced (the last term in [5]).

Put another way, we could say that the timocrat may be thought of as equating the marginal benefits of gifts to their marginal costs. At the margin, the timocrat will increase gifts until (1) the direct benefits to the citizenry plus (2) the extra benefits due to the reduction in the cost of obtaining loyalty $[(\partial P_L/\partial G)L]$ are just equal to (3) the disutility from the reduction in national income and in tax revenue caused by the gifts plus (4) the direct costs of the gifts themselves.

Note that only a timocrat who is both wise and generous will consider all these benefits and costs. An ignorant or stupid timocrat will fail to consider the costs of giving and may "spoil" the population (as the citizens of Rome were often alleged to have been; see Gibbon 1981; Grant 1978; or Veyne 1990). On the other hand, a "simulated" timocrat – that is, one who pretends to care but only gives in order to increase his or her power or for other selfish reasons – will still make gifts to reduce P_L but will neglect the direct benefits of the gifts to the citizens. It follows that one cannot infer that a ruler is a timocrat from the size of the gifts alone, because a power-maximizer could easily give more than a timocrat. This outcome could occur because repression tends to be higher under the power-maximizer, possibly resulting in larger gifts to partially offset this increased repression. It follows then to conclude that a regime is timocratic, one needs to know the level of repression as well as the size of gifts: Large gifts combined with low repression does imply timocracy.[4]

Equation (5) illustrates a second flaw in timocratic rule, as well as the basic difference between the "head" of a family and a "head" of a state, even granting the unlikely possibility that a dictator would arise who was as altruistic toward his or her people as a father or mother toward his or her family. If the timocrat is successful, the people will increasingly come to rely on the regime's benevolence. The cost of doing so is the reduction in national income as citizens resort to unproductive forms of behavior. If the quality of the timocrat's leadership is the main determinant of social welfare – as may be true under some circumstances (e.g., during wars) – then these costs may be more than offset by the increased loyalty of the citizenry (which aids the leader in his or her tasks by freeing up

---

[4] It is worth noting that none of these constraints are incorporated into the usual social welfare function analysis in economic theory, in which the benevolent government is simply assumed to maximize the welfare of the citizenry. Nor is any inquiry made as to whether such a government would be capable of surviving in office if it ever attained that office.

resources for other purposes). However, if the efforts of the citizenry are the primary determinant of welfare (or if the timocrat's leadership is misguided!), then the costs of dependence on the timocrat will be too large. This is another reason why dictators of all types seek collective projects in which their guidance rather than the initiative and efforts of individuals is the main determinant of the outcome – by doing so, they augment their power.

The same considerations determine whether leadership by the head of a family raises or lowers welfare within the family. Clearly, the condition is more likely to be satisfied within the family, especially when children are young. Still, there is the obvious problem of the role of other adults (i.e., besides the head) within the family. The more important their efforts in determining family welfare, the greater the problems resulting from dependence and the less likely the family with a head is to maximize family welfare. So Becker's theory works best if apart from the head, the rest of the family consists of dependent children. In a similar vein, Gibbon's judgment on the wisdom of the rulers during the Age of the Antonines and the general happiness of the period is tempered by his judgment of the Roman people themselves, who, he asserts, willingly gave up democracy and supported the emperor as the man best fitted to rule over them and to support them, in turn, in their lifestyle (Gibbon 1981; see also Grant 1994, p. 152).

6   From timocracy to tyranny

Between the reign of Augustus and that of Trajan and the Antonines, Gibbon (1980) declares that Rome "groaned beneath an unremitting tyranny" (p. 108); and indeed, the period does include many of the most famous tyrants of Roman history, including Tiberius and Nero. Marcus Aurelius was succeeded by his son, Commodus, whose own rule degenerated into tyranny, thus ending Rome's golden age. Gibbon's account of his fall is instructive, and the shift from timocracy to tyranny provides a nice comparative static illustration of our model. First, he asserts that Commodus was not born vicious but was "weak rather than wicked" (p. 116). But, according to Gibbon, "a fatal incident decided his fluctuating character." He continued:

> One evening (AD 183), as the emperor was returning to the palace through a dark and narrow portico in the amphitheatre, an assassin who waited his passage rushed upon him with a drawn sword, loudly exclaiming, "*The senate sends you this.*" The menace prevented the deed; the assassin was seized by the

guards and immediately revealed the authors of the con-
spiracy . . . [it was originated by the emperor's sister] But the
words of the assassin sunk deep into the mind of Commodus and
left an indelible impression of fear and hatred against the whole
body of the senate. (p. 118)

Commodus reacted by employing informers to discover those who
could conceivably be treasonous or disaffected within the Senate, and he
executed those who were suspected. But his informers were themselves
corrupt. The result was that "[d]istinction of every kind soon became
criminal. . . . Suspicion was equivalent to proof, trial to condemnation"
(p. 118). A large number of distinguished senators were executed, and
each such execution included "the death of [those] who might lament or
revenge his fate" (p. 118).

Figure 4.5 depicts the passage of the regime from timocracy to tyranny.
The initial equilibrium under the timocratic reign of Marcus Aurelius is
at E_1. This is the position inherited by Commodus. The increase in
repression under Commodus' rule (from R_1 to R_2) would have increased
his power to π_e if L had remained at L_1. But as the suspicion of
Commodus turned everyone – loyal or treasonous – into an imagined
enemy, the supply of genuine loyalty dried up, as shown by the leftward
shift of the supply curve. The initial fall of loyalty is magnified further as
his suspicions, which may have been largely groundless to begin with,
make the senators afraid and therefore suspicious of him in turn, thus
amplifying his own suspicions and so on in a downward spiral ending at
E_2 (with $L = L_2$, and $R = R_2$). Because he could not trust the senators, they
could not trust him, and repression increasingly replaced loyalty as the
sole instrument of maintaining power.

The next stage of the regime was reached when, with his enemies
taken care of, Commodus thought he could relax in his fashion (he
mounted gladiatorial activities and gave himself over to the pleasures of
the flesh, according to Gibbon); he then employed Cleander to manage
the public business. Commodus chose him, Gibbon says, because

> . . . suspicious princes often promote the last of mankind, from a
> vain persuasion that those who have no dependence except on
> their favour will have no attachment except to the person of
> their benefactor. . . . [Moreover, Cleander] was devoid of any
> ability or virtue which could inspire the emperor with envy or
> distrust. Avarice was the reigning passion of his [Cleander's]
> soul and the great principle of his administration. (1981, pp.
> 120–1)

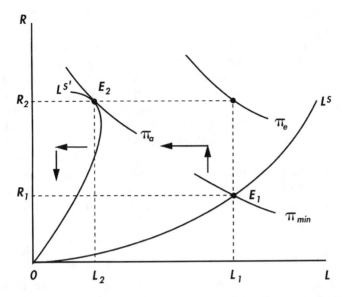

Figure 4.5. From timocracy to tyranny: the assassination of Commodus.

While Cleander plundered the public purse, Commodus degenerated further and lost all interest in affairs of state, immersing himself in the pursuit of relaxation, as just described. However, Cleander's regime was hated by the people, and its ugliness and corruption finally resulted in a revolt, which ended with a mob storming the emperor's palace, where

> Commodus lay dissolved in luxury and alone unconscious of the civil war. It was death to approach his person with the unwelcome news. He would have perished in this supine security had not two women, his elder sister Fadilla and Marcia, the most favoured of his concubines, ventured to break into his presence. Bathed in tears and with dishevelled hair they threw themselves at his feet and, with all the pressing eloquence of fear discovered to the affrighted emperor the crimes of the minister, the rage of the people and the impending ruin which in a few minutes would burst over his palace and his person. Commodus started from his dream of pleasure and commanded that the head of Cleander should be thrown out to the people. The desired spectacle instantly appeased the tumult, and the son of Marcus might even yet have regained the affection and confidence of his outraged subjects. (p. 123)

But it was not to be, for by this time Commodus "valued nothing in sovereign power except the unbounded license of indulging in his sensual appetites" (p. 123). He thought his taste for the exercise of violence, which had been amply demonstrated, was enough to control his enemies. The downward spiral of power continued, and in the end, he perished as soon as he was dreaded by his own domestics, including the same concubine Marcia, whose loyalty had previously saved him. They resolved to prevent the fate which hung over their own heads, "either from the mad caprice of the tyrant or the sudden indignation of the people" (p. 128), and they thus engaged a professional wrestler to come into Commodus' bedroom and strangle him. Commodus had finally reached the stage at which it was less risky for those closest to him to attempt to assassinate him than to leave him alive (i.e., in Figure 4.5, at the point at which $L = 0$ and therefore $\pi = 0$).

7   Conclusion

In this chapter I have explored two more solutions to the Dictator's Dilemma, tyranny and timocracy, and I have looked briefly at examples in the regimes of Mobutu of Zaire and "Papa Doc" of Haiti. I have also dwelled much more extensively on the ancient Roman Empire. In all these cases, the regime did not pursue economic growth as a means of building support. Papa Doc's Haiti and Mobutu's Zaire appeared to be "immiserizing" dictatorships – that is, the regimes impoverished their people and did not build support but survived by taxing and destroying the opposition. These regimes are examples of tyranny (characterized by high levels of repression and low public support). Economic growth was minimal in the ancient Roman Empire as well, and political support was built there through gifts to the people and through foreign conquest. I suggested that gifts served a number of political functions, including signaling; providing a barrier to entry into politics against those who couldn't afford to give such gifts; and establishing ownership (the right of the emperor to office and his right to dispose of the public purse as he wishes). Though many Roman emperors were undoubtedly tyrants who were hated by the people, not all were; and for this reason, as well as for its importance in the human imagination, past and present, I also analyzed the possibly mythical case of timocracy or benevolent dictatorship (low repression and high public support). Apart from the unlikely possibility of a genuinely benevolent dictator actually coming to power, this form of government, longed for throughout history, is flawed: The main flaws analyzed are that it is unstable and that dependence on the timocrat's largesse weakens the people as they devote themselves to lining up to receive gifts. Finally, I analyzed the transition in the Roman Empire from alleged timocracy (under Marcus Aurelius) to tyranny (under Commodus).

5   A more general model

1   Introduction

All the elements that affect the dictator's behavior are now in place. To begin with, we know some things about his or her personality. Such leaders tend to be paranoid, because they lack reliable information about what their people are really thinking about them. One of their chief concerns is staying in office, and to this end, they are engaged with more or less frequency (depending on the type of dictatorship) in buying loyalty and implementing repressive measures in order to do so. We know less about their subjects, but we do know that as long as they are at all numerous – and especially if they are unorganized – the benefits to each one of overthrowing the dictator will be small compared with the potential costs. This free-rider problem helps dictators immensely in the task of staying in office, but it doesn't solve it completely, and under the right circumstances they can be deposed, as dictators often are. This can happen in a number of ways:

1. by a cabal of associates, including those closest to the leader
2. through the loss of support of powerful bureaucracies, especially the army
3. by a revolt of the mob
4. through the intervention of foreign powers.

The behavior of a dictator's subjects was modeled in Chapter 3 as follows. Each subject faces a choice between supporting and opposing the regime. Whatever individual subjects decide, the decision is typically not revealed to the dictator, because it will usually pay to pretend that they do support him, even when they do not. The dictator's task is to face up to this state of uncertainty and devise and maintain a set of incentives that leads the subjects to make the right decision. He or she attempts to control them by either obtaining their loyalty through the distribution of rents, or by other means, and by repressing their capacity to organize any opposition to the regime.

Beyond this, our main task in the preceding two chapters has been to develop the idea that there are four different kinds of dictators and that much of their behavior that is interesting depends on their type. In this chapter we want to show that the four images may also be thought of together as different solutions to a more general way of thinking about dictatorship. This chapter develops this general model. It also shows the conditions under which each one of the four types emerges. In the model the dictator's preferences are left very general to show how different constraints shape his or her behavior. Dictators maximize utility, which depends on consumption and power, not consumption alone (like the tinpot) or power alone (like the totalitarian or tyrant). The constraint on behavior does not arise from an artificially fixed budget, nor from arbitrary limits to his or her power, but from the ultimately diminishing possibilities of transforming money into power and vice versa.

More precisely, the dictator is constrained in two ways. The first constraint – the costs of accumulating power – is governed by the political institutions of the regime; and the second – the capacity to use power to get money – by the dictator's economy. As far as the economy is concerned, what will turn out to be crucial is not whether the dictator's intervention helps or hurts the economy on the whole, but the effects of marginal (further) interventions on economic growth, efficiency, or the dictator's budget. If this marginal effect is positive, whether the total effect is positive or negative within a considerable range, the dictator will tend to be oriented more toward power than consumption, thus making him a tyrant or totalitarian. On the other hand, if the use of power tends to retard growth (and other dimensions of economic efficiency) rather than to favor it, the dictator tends to be a tinpot. So the marginal economic effects of the dictator's power help to determine whether the dictator is tinpot, totalitarian, or tyrant.[1]

This chapter models the economic organization of dictatorship in very general terms. Subsequent chapters will flesh this model out for particular systems. Thus, the relationship between the dictator's economic institutions and power is elaborated in Chapter 7 for free-market institutions, in Chapter 8 on the kinds of interventions which existed in the labor market in *apartheid* South Africa, and in Chapters 9 and 10 for the Soviet regime and the post-Mao "free-market communism" in China.

The outline of the chapter is as follows: The next section first describes the dictator's utility function and the two constraints on its maximization – the resource costs of the accumulation of power and the costs in terms

---

[1] A dictator's possibility of being a timocrat depends fundamentally on his or her preferences and not on the shape of the constraints facing him or her.

of power of raising revenue. This model is then solved for the equilibrium levels of power and budget, the dictator's consumption, and the level of repression and support. Section 3 shows how the four types of dictatorship emerge as special cases of this more general model depending on the dictator's preferences and his or her constraints, especially the capacity to convert money into power and power into money. Section 4 develops the comparative statics and policy implications of this model: how power and budgetary revenues (as well as the other variables mentioned) change in response to external shocks. Section 5 concludes the chapter.

2   The model

As just suggested, the model developed in the preceding two chapters needs to be generalized in three ways:

1. Dictators have been assumed so far to maximize either power (if totalitarian or tyrant) or consumption (if tinpot). Here we will simply assume that all dictators maximize a utility function which includes both power and consumption as arguments.
2. Dictators have been classified as tinpot, tyrant, totalitarian, or timocrat. We will show how these different types can be thought of as emerging from a more general model.
3. The constraint on the dictator's maximization has been based (in the analyses of tyrants and totalitarians) on the assumption that either the dictator's budget or the price of loyalty is fixed.

We will relax these assumptions and allow both the price of loyalty and the dictator's budget to be determined endogenously.

On the first point, the utility function for the dictator simply takes the form $U = U(\pi,C)$, where π = power, as before, and C = the personal consumption level. Thus, a dictator can spend resources in two ways:

1. to increase his or her power (π) – that is, by expenditures on repression (R) or loyalty (L)
2. on consumption goods – palaces, parties, Mercedes-Benzes, and so on

This division is shown in Figure 5.1; here the dictator's utility function, $U(\pi,C)$, is maximized subject to a budget constraint (the derivation of which is discussed shortly), yielding an equilibrium at E^*, with $\pi = \pi^*$, and $C = C^*$. Note that a "pure" tyrant or totalitarian, interested *only* in power, would be in equilibrium at the corner solution π_{max}. A "pure" tinpot, maximizing consumption subject to the minimum level of power

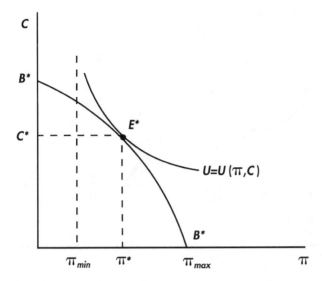

Figure 5.1. The dictator's utility maximization.

necessary to remain in office (π_{min}), is in equilibrium at the opposite corner (where $\pi \geq \pi_{min}$). Thus, most real-world dictators will be in equilibrium at an interior solution in Figure 5.1, and the closer they are to the tinpot or tyrant "ideal types," the closer they will be to either corner of the budget constraint.

The second limitation of the analysis of the last two chapters is that in analyzing tyranny and totalitarianism, we have assumed that the price of loyalty, P_L, is fixed. But this price is controlled by the dictator (the *donativum* is a good example), and if, by raising it, he or she could obtain more loyalty and more power, why would he or she not do so? To be sure, a larger budget would be required. But are there not ways for a dictator to find the extra money? To suggest, as is sometimes done, that a dictator's budget can be specified simply as that obtainable by means of the revenue-maximizing tax rate also evades the issue, for there is always the possibility of searching for new tax bases. Accordingly, we now allow the price of loyalty, P_L, to be a variable under the dictator's control. An increase in P_L would bring forth a larger supply of loyalty, L^S, for any given level of R – that is, it would shift L^S to the right, as shown in Figure 5.2, where an increase in P_L from P_L^0 to P_L^* and then to P_L^2 shifts L^S successively to the right, implying that a higher and higher budget ($B - C$) would be spent on accumulating π. Figure 5.2 therefore implies a positive relationship between the resources spent on accumu-

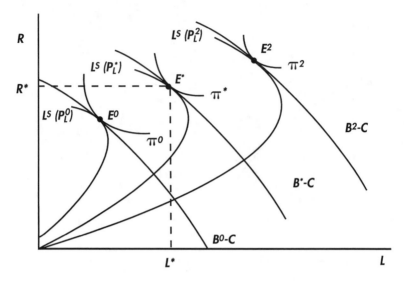

Figure 5.2. How money is transformed into power.

lating power $(B - C)$ and the level of power (π). This relationship is displayed in Figure 5.3 as the $\pi(B - C)$ curve. This curve, in effect, shows how the dictator can convert *money* into *power*.[2]

The upward-sloping $\pi(B - C)$ curve in Figure 5.3 implies a positive relationship between the amount of money spent accumulating π (the dictator's *total* budget B, minus expenditures on C) and the level of π obtained. It seems reasonable to assume diminishing returns to these expenditures – that is, to assume that the slope of the money-into-power curve is steadily increasing. In the case of loyalty, the dictator is progressively forced to forge relationships with those in the population who are less and less sympathetic or with whom it is harder and harder to communicate. In the case of repression, the dictator will be forced to employ personnel who are less and less suitable and to repress those who are more and more resistant.

The slope of the $\pi(B - C)$ curve, or, more precisely, the elasticity of π with respect to money, ε^π, is a crucial variable to which we shall return. It is obviously governed by the political organization of the regime. For example, if the dictator heads a mass political party, the supply of loyalty

---

[2] Note that although the text and the figure derive the $\pi(B - C)$ curve on the assumption that the dictator is on the backward-sloping portion of the supply of loyalty curve (and therefore is either a tyrant or a totalitarian), the same derivation would apply (and the same curve would result) if he or she were a tinpot.

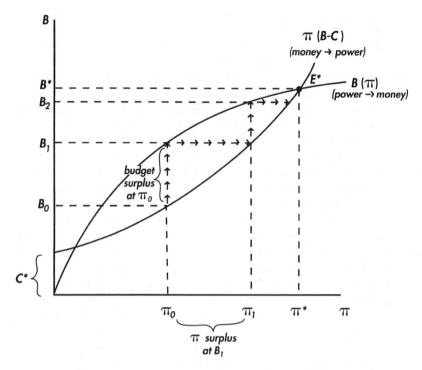

Figure 5.3. Equilibrium power and government budget under dictatorship.

will tend to be larger than otherwise, implying a relatively elastic supply at any given price; if controls on newspapers, TV, and radio are in place, and if a substantial apparatus of indoctrination and repression is available, the elasticity of repression R with respect to its price will tend to be large, producing a relatively high ε^π. The elasticity ε^π also depends on the productivity of R and L in producing power (π_R and π_L), which in turn depends on the characteristics of the population under control. If the people are disorganized or apathetic, ε^π will tend to be relatively high. Similarly, ε^π will tend to be high if the opposition is weak, the bureaucracy easily tamed, and interest groups docile or easily bought off.

What then is the limit to the dictator's power? Of course, diminishing returns to the accumulation of loyalty imply that successive increases in P_L will increase L by less and less. But as long as there is no limit to the dictator's capacity to finance the accumulation of loyalty, there is no obvious limit to the dictator's power, or to the level of loyalty or repression he or she can produce. In brief, if there is no limit to the dictator's resources, there is no limit to his or her power, because resources can always be transformed into power by the process we have just outlined. Is there any limit to the dictator's resources? As suggested earlier, it would be arbitrary to specify that the dictator's power is limited by a revenue-maximizing tax. For as long as dictators have sufficient power, they can raise more funds by imposing new tax bases and by finding other ways to raise money.[3] In short, if there is no limit to a dictator's power, there is no limit to his or her resources either.

It follows that the limits on budgetary resources and power must be simultaneously determined. We have already suggested that although budgetary considerations do not limit power, such power does become more and more costly to accumulate, as shown by the increasing slope of $\pi(B - C)$. We now turn to the dictator's economy, as summarized by the $B(\pi)$ curve in Figure 5.3. This curve describes the relationship between the exercise of political power and the consequences of that use for the dictator's budget – that is, the conversion, in effect, of *power* into *money*. Although there are diverse forms of economy under dictatorship, all of them suggest that this curve, too, displays diminishing (and sometimes negative) returns. We will explain how the intersection of these two curves (at E^*) in Figure 5.3 provides the limitation on both the dictator's budget and his or her power – that is, how it produces the equilibrium level of both power (π^*) and budget (B^*).

The derivation of the $B(\pi)$ curve is complicated for the simple reason that political dictatorship is consistent with numerous varieties of economic systems. To take only a few wildly divergent examples, all of which are discussed in more detail in the following chapters of this book, consider the forms encompassed by the Soviet system of central planning, Pinochet's free-market economy, or the regulated labor market under *apartheid* South Africa. From these cases it is immediately obvious that there can be no general model of the economy of dictatorship, except at an extremely abstract level. Moreover, in my view, the working of individual systems cannot be properly understood by analyzing each one as a set of "interferences" or "distortions" of a free-market economy. The systems are particular ways of organizing production and distribution. What can be discussed at a general level are the ways in which economic organization can generate or fail to generate resources that can then be transformed into power – that is, the extent to which the economy sustains or undermines the dictator's political regime.

---

[3] Some of these can be quite ingenious, as when Papa Doc of Haiti "sold" workers to the neighboring Dominican Republic (Lundahl 1984).

To illustrate: Perhaps the most basic process for turning power into budgetary resources is by using it to implement and collect taxes. It seems clear that there is a positive relationship between power and the capacity to raise tax revenue. At low levels of power, dictators may impose taxes, but they will face problems such as evasion and outright refusal to pay, and they will also be restricted in their choice of tax bases. The larger their apparatus of power, the more they are capable of imposing higher tax rates, closing loopholes, policing evasion, and imposing new tax bases, and the greater the level of compliance by the population, either out of fear of repression or because of loyalty. The process of the steady encroachment of the state and its taxing capacity on society has often been described for the Absolutist monarchs of Europe (see, e.g., Tilly 1975). One can also observe it in the case of the Roman Empire (see Grant 1978; also see Dudley 1975). Most recently, it has taken place in African countries (see Callaghy 1984, who describes the case of Zaire). As depicted in Figure 5.3, the power-into-money curve $B(\pi)$ also shows diminishing returns – that is, at higher levels of π, more and more power is needed to "extract" a given additional amount of revenue from the population, which again seems reasonable.

This method – *collection of taxes* – is only one process by which political power can be converted into budgetary resources. With this method, B and π are positively correlated – that is, $\partial B/\partial \pi \equiv B_\pi > 0$, although presumably, national income Y falls as taxes are increased due to the disincentive effects of taxation. Of course, at sufficiently high tax rates, the relationship could be reversed ($B_\pi < 0$). However, it is easy to imagine other processes in which the effects of the application of political power on the economy are different. Suppose, for example, that the dictator, through his or her control of the machinery of government, provides a public good or input (e.g., roads, water supplies, technological help, and so on) which raises the income of the private sector. If the tax revenues of the regime increase with national income (as would be the case with a proportional tax rate t), then $B = tY$, and $Y = Y(\pi)$, with $Y' > 0$, so that $B = tY(\pi)$, where, again, $B_\pi > 0$. In this process (*provision of a public input*), Y, π, and B all increase.

Yet another example of the application of political power to the economy is provided by *the creation of rent*. Suppose that the dictator imposes an import license for certain products and distributes this license to the private sector in exchange for a bribe. The import license reduces the efficiency of the private sector, so that (for this exercise of power) national income falls – that is, $Y = Y(\pi)$, with $Y' < 0$. However, the revenues of the government could easily increase, as long as the fall in national income is not so large as to reduce revenues by more than the amount that the bribe increases them. (If this were to happen, the dictator would be irrational to create and distribute the rent in the first place.) In this case, then, $B_\pi > 0$, but $Y_\pi < 0$.

A slight change in the example produces the result that $B_\pi < 0$. Suppose that the dictator creates a rent and, instead of receiving a bribe in exchange, gets a commitment of loyalty (which will be particularly credible if the rent can be withdrawn and given to someone else). Then the budget B falls as Y falls, although power is increased. In this process, the exercise of power reduces Y and B; that is, B_π and Y_π are both < 0.

Yet another example can be provided in which $B_\pi < 0$, but $Y_\pi > 0$. Consider the interpretation discussed earlier and advanced by Douglas North and Barry Weingast (1989) and Hilton Root (1994), who examined England's Glorious Revolution. Before the revolution, the king had difficulty raising revenue, essentially because after repeated instances of reneging, his promises to repay lacked credibility. So the king ceded some financial authority to Parliament. After that, the king's promises to repay were credible, and he could obtain loans more easily than before. In this analysis, by ceding power, the king increased his capacity to raise revenue (that is, $B_\pi < 0$), and as a result, the private sector prospered ($Y_\pi > 0$).

In general, then, the power-to-money curve $B(\pi)$ may be either positively or negatively sloped. It seems reasonable to assume that, initially, it must be positively sloped: For a ruler who starts from very low (or zero) levels of power, the provision of basic public infrastructure or the imposition of simple taxes at low rates must raise revenue. Beyond this, however, there is little to be said at a general level. As we will see in Part III, this matter depends crucially on the nature of the economic institutions of particular regimes. Specifying these institutions clarifies the slope of the power-into-money curve $B(\pi)$.

No matter what the slope of $B(\pi)$, however, equilibrium in Figure 5.3 is at the intersection of the $B(\pi)$ and $\pi(B - C)$ curves, or at E^*, implying a (total) budget of B^* and power equal to π^*. At E^*, all of the dictator's budgetary resources are spent, either on power or on consumption goods.[4] Thus, at E^*, the dictator has sufficient resources B^* to maintain power at π^* and consumption at C^*, and he or she has sufficient power to obtain the budget B^*. Given the choice of consumption at C^*, we see that the dictator cannot obtain more power (it would require more resources

---

[4] Note that E^* is an equilibrium for all dictatorships that maximize some combination of political power and consumption from government revenues, which includes all of the varieties discussed so far. Chapter 8 describes a different form of dictatorship, one in which the government may be thought of as using its political power to maximize the net private income of a private interest group (e.g., labor or capital). In this case, the equilibrium takes a different form. See Chapter 8, Section 2, and Figures 8.1 and 8.2.

than B^*) and cannot obtain a bigger budget (it would require more power than π^*). On the other hand, at any point to the left of E^*, there is a surplus, which may be measured either in money (at π_0, e.g., this is equal to $B_1 - B_0$) or in power ($\pi_1 - \pi_0$). Similarly, at any point to E^*'s right, there is a deficit (not shown) – again, there are both insufficient budgetary resources to maintain $\pi > \pi^*$ and insufficient power to maintain a budget $B > B^*$.[5]

Note that this equilibrium depends on the dictator's consumption C; if the ruler were willing to reduce this below C^*, for example, the money-into-power curve $\pi(B - C)$ would shift to the right, implying an equilibrium at the intersection of this new curve with $B(\pi)$. There is obviously a limit to the extent to which any ruler is willing to reduce consumption. But the dependency of π^* and B^* on C^* just underlines the fact that, in general, Figure 5.3 must be considered along with Figure 5.1.

In general, rulers will choose a combination of C and π, depending on their preferences for the two, as displayed in Figure 5.1. So Figure 5.1 and Figure 5.3 (or Figure 5.4) jointly determine the dictator's optimal levels C^*, B^*, and π^*.

The proof that E^* is an equilibrium is similar if $B_\pi < 0$. This case is shown in Figure 5.4.

Again, at a point to the left of E^*, there is a budget surplus (equal to $B_1 - B_0$ at π_0, e.g., or $\pi_1 - \pi_0$ at B_0). But note that here, with $B_\pi < 0$, accumulating more power "solves" the problem of the surplus by reducing the dictator's total budget B. Whereas in the former case (in which $B_\pi > 0$), either the desire for more consumption or for more power drives the dictator in the direction of E^*; in this case, only the craving for power does. Thus, with $B = B_1$ and $C = C_0$, there is a surplus, shown as $B_1 - B_0$ or $\pi_1 - \pi_0$ in the figure. The surplus can be "spent" either by accumulating more π, in which case the final equilibrium is at E^*, or by increasing C (from C_0 to C_1), in which case the final equilibrium is at E^1.

Given the dictator's choices of C, B, and π, it is then a simple matter to determine optimal R and L. Note that the optimal levels of R and L depend only on the amount of resources used to accumulate π – that is, on $B - C$, and on the production function for power (see equation [2]). These solutions have already been given in Chapter 3 and are simply the optimal conditions for cost minimization in the use of inputs to produce power, conditions which require that the marginal costs of accumulating

---

[5] Another way to see this point (that E^* is an equilibrium) is to consider a lower level of B, such as B_0. At budget B_0, $\pi = \pi_0$. But with $\pi = \pi_0$, the dictator can obtain a budget $B_1 > B_0$, which is preferable, so he or she does so. But with B_1, $\pi_1(>\pi_0)$ is available, which is preferable, so the dictator takes this, which in turn implies a still larger budget (B_2), implying more power, and so on until E^* is reached. The reverse argument shows that, from any point to the right of E^*, the dictator will return to E^*.

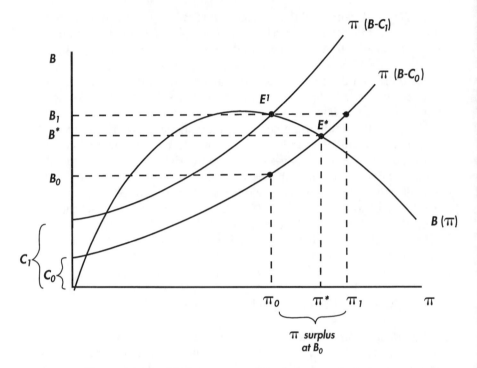

Figure 5.4. Equilibrium power and government budget when power reduces revenue.

power by means of extra loyalty be equal to that by means of the use of repression, or

(1) $$\frac{P_L + LP_{LL}}{\pi_L} = \frac{P_R + LR_{LR}}{\pi_R} = P_\pi$$

where P_π is the "price" of power, and $P_{LL} \equiv \dfrac{\partial P_L}{\partial L}$, $P_{LR} \equiv \dfrac{\partial P_L}{\partial R}$.

Consequently, the ruler can be regarded as choosing between power and consumption only – and then choosing the optimal combination of instruments to minimize the costs of π. In Figure 5.3 (or 5.4) P_π is just the slope of the money-into-power curve $\pi(B - C)$. So the ruler can safely gaze at Figures 5.1 and 5.3 (or 5.4), decide on the optimal π, B, and C, and then look at Figure 5.2 to find the division of $B - C$ between R and L. That is, in the first instance, the ruler maximizes (assuming, without loss of generality, that the price of the consumption good, P_C is equal to 1)

(2) $U = U(\pi, C)$

subject to the constraint that

(3) $B(\pi) = P_\pi \pi (B - C) + C.$

The left-hand side of the constraint (3) is just the power-into-money curve $B(\pi)$, which shows how budgetary resources are obtained. The right-hand side shows how the funds are "spent": either on consumption (C) or by accumulating power (π) by means of the money-to-power relation $[\pi(B - C)]$, with each unit of π multiplied by P_π (the money "price" of power).

The solution (first-order conditions) may be obtained by choosing π and C to maximize (2), subject to the constraint (3). Rearranging terms, it is expressed simply as

(4) $$\frac{U_C}{U_\pi} = \frac{1}{P_\pi - \pi P'_\pi - B_\pi}$$

(4)′ $$= \frac{1}{P_\pi \left(1 - \dfrac{1}{\varepsilon^\pi}\right) - B_\pi}$$

where

$$\varepsilon^\pi \equiv \frac{\partial \pi}{\partial P_\pi} \frac{P_\pi}{\pi} > 0$$

(i.e., the elasticity of π with respect to its price).

As usual, this simply implies that the marginal rate of substitution between consumption and power must be equated to their marginal rate of transformation. The left-hand side of (4) or (4)′ is just the slope of an indifference curve in Figure 5.1, and the right-hand side is the slope of the budget constraint. Since the left-hand side is positive, the right-hand side must also be positive – that is,

(5) $P_\pi \left(1 - \dfrac{1}{\varepsilon^\pi}\right) - B_\pi > 0.$

Equations (4)′ and (5) show the "full" costs of accumulating more power, which include its price (P_π), plus the increase[6] in the costs of previously accumulated units of power incurred by attempting to accu-

---

[6] I assume that the price of inframarginal units of π is the same as that for the marginal unit.

mulate more, as governed by the size of $\left(1-\dfrac{1}{\varepsilon^{\pi}}\right)$ minus (if $B_{\pi} > 0$) the increase in budgetary resources made possible by having more power. If $B_{\pi} < 0$, extra power reduces the dictator's total budget, and this is a further cost of power accumulation.

Equation (4)' displays in a particularly transparent way the three elements that enter into the dictator's calculus – the marginal costs of accumulating power $\left[P_{\pi}\left(1-\dfrac{1}{\varepsilon^{\pi}}\right)\right]$, the marginal effect of power on the dictator's budget (B_{π}), and U_c/U_{π}, the dictator's preferences for power versus consumption. The first term, as explained earlier, is governed by the dictator's political apparatus for building loyalty and for repression and the productivity of these instruments in producing power – that is, all the factors discussed in the preceding two chapters. The second term (B_{π}) shows what the accumulation of power does to the dictator's budget by virtue of its effects on the economy (e.g., its effects on economic growth, economic efficiency, and the capacity to implement taxes). As mentioned previously, these effects depend on the character of the regime; they are discussed for the Pinochet regime in Chapter 7, for the *apartheid* system in Chapter 8, and for the Soviet and Chinese systems in Chapters 9 and 10. The third factor (U_c/U_{π}) simply represents the dictator's preferences between consumption and power. Sometimes (as discussed in subsequent chapters), one can see some of the factors at work in molding these preferences – for example, how party organization or the nature of the dictator's support can drive him or her in the direction of maximizing power. But perhaps more than any other political or economic agent, political dictators have some freedom to put their stamp on society.

These three elements, in turn, determine the nature of the dictatorship – whether the regime resembles more closely that of a tinpot, totalitarian, tyrant, or timocrat, a subject to which we now turn.

3   The derivation of regimes

The derivation of the four types of regimes from this analysis is straightforward. Both the dictator's preferences and the characteristics of the political and economic constraints facing him or her are important. As far as preferences are concerned, the larger the dictator's preferences for immediate consumption relative to power, the more likely he or she is to be a tinpot. The extreme case of a pure tinpot emerges if the wealth-elasticity of consumption goods is 1; that of a pure tyrant or totalitarian emerges when the wealth-elasticity of power is 1. Only genuinely altruistic preferences on the dictator's part can lead to a timocracy.

The political constraint is the effectiveness of the political apparatus. The larger ε^π (the elasticity of power with respect to its price), the more likely the dictator is to be a totalitarian rather than a tyrant (given a relatively large taste for power). The factor ε^π in turn depends on all of the variables discussed in Chapter 3 – the prices of loyalty and repression and their marginal productivities in producing power. And finally, the more the accumulation of power favors economic growth and efficiency ($B_\pi > 0$) – or at least does not retard it very much, at the margin – the more likely the regime is to be totalitarian than tyrannical.

To illustrate these points, let us contrast very briefly two types of regime – that of Pinochet's Chile and Stalin's Russia. The Pinochet regime in Chile was undoubtedly one of tyranny[7]: Repression was high, yet no mass party was ever built, preventing the accumulation of loyalty on a substantial scale. Consequently, when repression was relaxed, Pinochet's unpopularity revealed itself. There are several reasons for this result. First, the free-market ideology adopted by Pinochet early under his regime, partly as a tool to break up the old leftist coalition (which had culminated in the socialist regime of Allende), prevented him from acquiring the system for the mass distribution of rents that could have solidified his hold on power. In short there was no political mechanism to translate either repression or the benefits of successful economic growth into loyalty. At the same time, the freeing of markets meant that the overt use of his power to interfere with the functioning of those markets or to raise taxes on a substantial scale (beyond that required to finance the increase in the military budget[8]) would have reduced the market's capacity to stimulate economic growth and efficiency; it would also have reduced his budget. This result, in turn, would have interfered with his capacity to build up the army and the police in order to enforce repression.

On the other hand, the essence of Stalinist central planning[9] is that the economic system is demonetized and that private property rights are severely attenuated so that the Communist party can control the direction of production. What determines the behavior of the regime (the levels of C, π, B, R, and L) is not whether this massive political "interference" in the economic system reduces growth or efficiency; what deter-

---

[7] Some details are presented in Chapter 7.
[8] Defense spending rose from 2 percent of Gross Domestic Product in 1969 to 7.6 percent in 1985 (Remmer 1989, p. 172).
[9] Details are given in Chapters 9 and 10.

mines this behavior are the effects of a *marginal* increase in the power of the Party on these variables. Because, as will be examined in much greater detail in Chapters 9 and 10, the enforcement apparatus of the Party in effect substituted for legal contractual enforcement, as long as the Party was controlled by its leadership and the leadership of the Party was growth-oriented, an increase in the power of the Party had a positive effect on growth and government revenues (Y_π and $B_\pi > 0$). On this analysis, the reduction in economic growth in the Soviet system in the 1970s and 1980s was therefore due to a reduction in the power of the Party. In this sense, Stalin's totalitarianism, no less than Pinochet's tyranny, was partly the result of the operation of political and economic constraints.

Of course, the overall level of efficiency of the dictator's economy plays a role in the survival of the regime. But the importance of this factor arises on the international side – that is, as a result of the competition from other regimes or regime types. This competition can be manifested in three ways:

1. to the extent that citizens of a dictatorship can get information on the standard of living (relative to their own) of those outside it
2. to the extent that the dictatorship competes by virtue of trade with other nations
3. through military competition – that is, through arms races, war, and foreign conquest.

The model identifies a set of circumstances under which dictators are particularly likely to promote nationalistic and autarchic policies – namely, when domestic conditions favor the accumulation of a large amount of power (ε^π high, $B_\pi > 0$), but when the performance of the economy compares unfavorably with that of other regimes. Of course, dictatorship by its nature tends to have a comparative advantage (relative to democracy) at building a strong military, because of the dictator's capacity to repress civilian opposition to the required sacrifice for military goods. These factors combine to reinforce the proclivity of dictatorships for international aggression, a topic which was discussed in Chapter 4.

4   Comparative statics

To illustrate the usefulness of this apparatus, let us ask the same question addressed in the preceding two chapters – namely, what is the effect of economic growth on the level of repression? Note that the analysis of

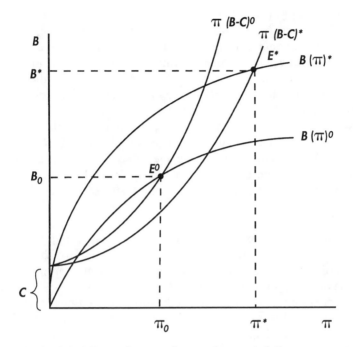

Figure 5.5. Effects of economic growth on π and B.

increased trade or foreign conquest would be similar. There are two effects. First, as a result of more growth, the population has more income, and therefore the dictator's tax base is larger. At any given level of dictatorial power, this fact in turn implies more tax revenue for the autocrat. So, in Figure 5.5, the $B(\pi)$ curve will shift upward.

Second, more growth may expand the supply of loyalty to the regime and therefore lower P_L. Because more power can now be purchased with the same budget than before, the $\pi(B - C)$ curve in Figure 5.5 shifts to the right. Note that the magnitude of this effect can be expected to differ for different regime types: In particular, it will be relatively large for totalitarian regimes, and it will be relatively small for tyrannies, for whom L^s is relatively inelastic with respect to both price and (national) income. The fall in P_L will have the usual wealth and substitution effects. The substitution effect leads to an increase in L and a *fall* in R, and the wealth effect increases both L and R.

This expansion of loyalty reinforces the effect of an enlarged tax base on B and π, both effects implying that, in equilibrium, B and π will be higher than before. The dictator's budget constraint in Figure 5.1 shows how the dictator divides the extra revenue between π and C. As long as the wealth-elasticity of π is positive (which is true for all except tinpot regimes), π will therefore increase. In general, then, the effect of improved economic performance for which the regime can claim credit is to increase B, π, C, and L, except in the case of the tinpot dictator, who spends all of the increase in B on C so that π remains unchanged. For the tinpot then, R falls whereas L increases and π remains at π_{min}, just as in the simpler analysis of Chapter 3. In all other cases, the effect on R is ambiguous: The cross-substitution effect of the fall in P_L tends to decrease R, whereas both the income effect and the increase in tax revenues tend to increase it. The larger the wealth-elasticity of π, the more likely it is that R will increase as a result of increased economic growth.

It follows that the closer the regime is to the tinpot type – that is, the greater the wealth-elasticity of consumption goods relative to power – the more likely it is that an increase in economic growth will reduce repression. On the other hand, the closer the regime approximates one that maximizes power (whether totalitarian or tyrant), the more likely it is that economic growth will raise repression. So the tinpot and totalitarian images emerge as useful special cases of the more general model developed in this chapter.

Alternatively, suppose that, contrary to this analysis, the supply of loyalty to the regime contracts as economic growth or trade results in the formation of networks with foreigners or within the private sector which are independent of the government (see the discussion of this possibility in Chapter 3, Section 4C). The contraction in loyalty to the regime implies an increase in the price of loyalty P_L, and the money-into-power curve $\pi(B - C)$ would shift to the left in Figure 5.5 (not shown) rather than to the right. By itself, this shift would tend to reduce π and B, in contrast to the upward shift in the power-into-money curve $B(\pi)$, which tends to increase these variables, as just discussed. If the first effect is sufficiently large relative to the second, π may actually fall; and if it is very large, B may fall as well.[10] But note once again that for this case to hold, dictators, in pursuing economic growth or a trade agreement, must be sowing the seeds of their own destruction (loss of power and budgetary revenue). On the other hand, if, as seems more likely, the second effect dominates, the conclusions of the analysis just conducted are unaffected, and π and B still increase. In conclusion, therefore, it is worth noting that even in the case in which loyalty to the regime falls as the result of growth or a trade agreement, the power and budgetary

---

[10] But note that R might still increase due to the substitution effect from the rise in P_L.

resources of the regime still increase, unless the drop in loyalty were of sufficient magnitude to overcome the effect of the increase in the regime's budgetary revenues on its capacity to accumulate power.

Note that policy implications similar to those derived in Chapter 3 for tinpot and totalitarian regimes also tend to emerge from this more general framework. Apart from the generalization of the utility function, the main innovation of this more general approach is that it allows us to see the effect of a trade or aid agreement on the dictator's revenues [the upward shift of the $B(\pi)$ curve in Figure 5.5]. As just discussed, the effect of this shift reinforces the effects of the trade or aid agreement in increasing B and π, assuming the trade or aid agreement increases loyalty and therefore shifts the $\pi(B - C)$ curve to the right. The first best policy therefore remains the single standard of aid or trade combined with a progressively tightening human rights constraint. This policy applies to all types of regimes (i.e., in the more general framework, regardless of the relative weights of consumption C and power π in the dictator's utility function). Although these weights and the elasticities of the power-into-money and money-into-power curves do not affect the optimal policy, they do affect the amount of harm that the "wrong" policies can do. In Chapter 3, I suggested that with a totalitarian regime, the most harm can result from trade or aid in the absence of a human rights constraint but that the least can result with a tinpot. Here, we can generalize this conclusion in two ways. The first follows from the fact that tyrannies behave the same way as totalitarian regimes but that the elasticity of π with respect to B is lower in tyrannies. This fact implies that trade or aid with tyrannies without a binding human rights constraint actually worsens repression, but not by as much as it does in the totalitarian case. So tyrants form an intermediate case between tinpots and totalitarians: The least harm will be done by trading with a tinpot regime, the most with a totalitarian, and tyrants fall in the middle.

Second, one can express the potential harm which results from the wrong policies in terms of the three elements that enter the dictator's caculus: the marginal costs of accumulating power $P_\pi\left(1 - \dfrac{1}{\varepsilon^\pi}\right)$; the marginal effect of power on the dictator's budget (B_π); and U_C/U_π, the dictator's preferences for power versus consumption. The greater the wealth-elasticity of power relative to consumption in the dictator's preferences, the greater the marginal effectiveness of power in raising the dictator's budget; and the lower the marginal cost of accumulating power, the more an aid or trade agreement without a human rights constraint will increase the dictator's power and level of repression on the population.

5   Conclusion

This chapter generalized the models developed in the last two chapters in three ways:

1. *The utility function.* In this more general model, dictators do not simply maximize either consumption or power, but they maximize a general utility function in which these variables appear as arguments.
2. *The price of loyalty and budget constraint.* In this model, neither the price of loyalty nor the budget constraint is fixed, but both are endogenously determined.
3. *The classification of dictators.* In this chapter, we showed how tinpots, totalitarians, tyrants, and timocrats materialize as special cases of the more general model. The factors which determine a dictator's type are simply the three fundamental elements that enter any autocrat's political and economic decision-making calculus – the dictator's preferences for power versus consumption, the costs of accumulating power as governed by his or her political organization, and the effect of power on the dictator's budget as determined by the organization of the economy.

Finally, I showed that more sophisticated versions of the simple predictions and policy implications derived from the basic model of tinpots versus totalitarians that was developed in Chapter 3 tend to emerge from this more general model as well.

Part III

Economics of autocracy

6 The economy of dictatorship

1 Introduction

A specter haunts democracy. Many – if not most – of the citizens of democratic countries put great value on liberty and the capacity to develop as individuals, both of which are the hallmarks of democracy. However, these freedoms have a price, one that arises from the fact that when individuals are free to develop in different ways, they will tend to take different paths. Moreover, in open societies characterized by freedom of association, individuals are free to join or form into groups, groups are free to practice and to advocate their own beliefs, and the result is what often appears to be a cacophony of different values, lifestyles, beliefs, and practices. On any given day in the United States, for example, the individual picking up a newspaper or watching television may be confronted with the views of right-to-lifers, the Christian Coalition, gun control advocates, prostitutes' associations, lesbians for Christ, advocates for the disempowered, corporate advertising of every description, advocates for the legalization of drugs, crusaders against McDonald's, people who want to fight pornography on the internet, people who think television sitcoms are a threat to family values, and so on.

Now, there are many who revel in this diversity, but for others the flourishing of alternative lifestyles and points of view that are antithetical to their own brings only discomfort. But this is not the problem which concerns us here. The problem that concerns us is an economic one: *These people have to work together.* In the workplace they have to communicate as well as coordinate their activities with one another. Politically, they all have to be able to live with the same governments. To some extent the problem is solved by competition, which in business tends to group like-minded individuals in the same firm, and different individuals in different companies. In a federal political system, competition among jurisdictions has the same effect of sorting individuals into jurisdictions. There are many other sortings as well: by family, friendships, or the natural environment. Because all these sortings cannot be done at the same time to any great degree, the result is that the typical firm in any big city in the United States, for example, has a workforce consisting of individuals with an extraordinarily diverse array of beliefs, practices, lifestyles, and habits. They can work together, but things are not as easy as they might be. And although the economic performance of the United States has been good, it does not rival that of South Korea or China over the last ten years or so. What explains the extraordinary performance, in terms of growth rates, of these countries? To many, the answer is obvious: In place of the corruption, individualism, and anarchy which characterize Western-style democracies, these societies are disciplined and organized. And whether for cultural, sociological, political, or economic reasons, the workplace in these societies is characterized by a *group cohesion* – or a capacity for group loyalty – of which citizens in a democracy are utterly incapable.

This threat – namely, that an authoritarian, cohesive, organized, and disciplined society is capable of levels of economic performance that are simply impossible in a democracy – is the specter that haunts democracy. Currently, the threat is seen to come from Asian "values" as expressed most obviously in Singapore or South Korea. A few years ago, the threat was seen to emanate from Japan, and as Paul Krugman (1994) has reminded us, this threat gave rise to a slew of books with titles like *The Emerging Japanese Super State* (Herman Kahn), *Japan as Number One* (Ezra Vogel),[1] and *Looking at the Sun* (James Fallows 1994), which attributed Japan's economic success to conceptions of how to organize production that are wholly different from those practiced in the United States.

However, arguments like these are hardly confined to semipopular treatises. Indeed, a great deal of social science – especially the branch of economic theory known as game theory – has contributed, directly or indirectly, to this way of thinking. In much (not all, of course) of that work, the central problem is seen as one of finding cooperative solutions to the Prisoner's Dilemma game. In the standard analysis, rational, selfish individuals will not cooperate in a one-shot game. This lack of cooperation results in inefficiency. As a consequence, a vast effort has been put into the search for a set of conditions – and their possible interpretation through appropriate institutional design – which will lead to cooperation.

Sometimes the tendency to cooperate is attributed to mysterious cultural forces. A recent example appeared in an article by Martin

---

[1] I am indebted to Paul Krugman's "The Myth of Asia's Miracle" (1994) for these two titles.

Weitzman and Chenggang Xu (1994), who addressed the important and fascinating question of how to explain the extraordinary economic performance of the "township and village enterprises" (TVEs) started under the Chinese reform program. These enterprises are local cooperatives, managed under the aegis of Chinese local governments.[2] They evolved out of the Chinese government's free-market reform program, which began in 1978, and they have been a major factor in the economic success of that program. These enterprises have hard budget constraints, but they are not private firms, and the nature of property rights in them is not clear. The following question therefore arises: How do we explain the extraordinary growth in factor productivity in these enterprises, which compare favorably in every respect with the performance of private firms? For example, during the 1979–91 period, total factor productivity growth in TVEs averaged 12 percent annually (Weitzman and Xu 1994, p. 129). How can this performance be explained? Weitzman and Xu explain this conundrum with a mysterious variable λ, which denotes "cooperative culture." This variable represents ". . . the ability of a group of people to resolve prisoner's dilemma type free-riding problems internally, without the imposition of explicit rules of behavior, other things, including the size of the group being equal" (p. 138). Thus, they assert that "East Asia is a high–λ society relative to Europe which by comparison is more of a low–λ society" (p. 139).

Now this proposition might be surprising to many observers of China, a number of whom have documented the existence of widespread corruption there. A survey of corruption indices for forty-one countries places China second only to Indonesia in its level of corruption.[3] And the alleged cooperative nature of Chinese culture would no doubt come as a shock to the inhabitants of China's gulags, about whom we know little, but reports of which suggest a system every bit as terrifying as the one ultimately discovered and documented in the former Soviet Union.[4] Finally, this explanation is inconsistent with the one piece of evidence about property rights in the TVEs that is cited by Weitzman and Xu. "It is very common to see that the basic rights [of TVEs] are in the hands of the Party and (communal) government apparatus . . ."[5] This fact immediately suggests an alternative explanation for the superior performance of

---

[2] There are no private property rights in these firms. They are either cooperatives or government enterprises, and standard property rights theory apparently predicts inefficiency in either case.

[3] See the *New York Times* (August 20, 1995).

[4] See the review of a number of books on the Chinese gulags in the *New York Review of Books* (August 1995).

[5] Rural Policy Research Division of the Central Committee Secretariat, "A Summary of Nationwide Rural Socioeconomic Sampling Survey," in *China Agricultural Yearbook*, 1986, which was cited in Weitzman and Xu (1994), p. 132.

the TVEs – namely, that Communist party control substituted for the missing property rights.[6]

Economists are not the only social scientists searching for cooperative solutions to problems of social and economic organization. In political science, there is most recently the celebrated work of Robert Putnam (1993), who explained the differences in the effectiveness of regional governments in Italy by using trust or "social capital" (to use Coleman's 1990 term); this variable, mysteriously, is so persistent that it has survived for hundreds of years. Mention should also be made of the work of Robert Axelrod (1984), whose discovery of the "live-and-let-live system" among opposing armies in World War I suggested that it was possible even for enemies to cooperate during wartime. Of course, this is only the contemporary edge of a strand of thinking which goes back hundreds of years, perhaps as far back as Aristotle. The point I am making here is that all of it fits in with a certain way of thinking: It is possible to organize society in such a way that individuals will cooperate, even when that cooperation is inconsistent with their self-interest narrowly conceived. The basic problem of social science is to discover how to do this.

The specter that haunts the admirer of democracy who takes this point of view is the idea that the most likely form of social organization which makes this cooperation possible is some form of authoritarianism. For much of the twentieth century, it was the original specter of communism which haunted the democracies. In the 1930s the threat came from Nazi Germany. In the 1980s it was the "soft authoritarianism" of South Korea and the other Asian "tigers." In the 1990s the threat still seems to emanate from Asia, only now it seems to be the free-market communism of China that appears to have achieved the most spectacular economic success under rule by a dictatorship.

If we turn to modern economic theory for guidance on this issue – that is, for advice on how such economies might operate – we find surprisingly little which addresses this issue directly, and in a general way. The next section briefly surveys the literature on autocratic economies. Section 3 describes the basic elements of the method used here. Subsequent chapters in this part expand this general approach to explain the workings of specific autocratic institutions: Chapter 7 deals with the "capitalist au-

---

[6] Chun Chang and Yijang Wang (1994) present an excellent analysis of the "property rights" structure of TVEs, one which supports and expands on this point. They conclude that "the ownership structure of TVEs . . . is . . . a product of an environment in which an authoritarian government with monopolistic political power plays a dominant role in economic life. . . . In the case of the TVE, concentrated economic and political power under the Communist system largely explains the most important costs and benefits under alternative control arrangements" (p. 450).

thoritarianism" of South Korea or Pinochet's Chile, Chapter 8 with the labor market under *apartheid*, and Chapters 9 and 10 with communism in the former Soviet Union and in contemporary China.

2   Alternative approaches to the economy of dictatorship

As suggested in the previous chapter, there are a variety of economic systems under political dictatorship. Many of the models which have been invented were designed to illuminate the workings of a particular type. With this caveat in mind, it is nevertheless useful to classify models of autocratic economic systems under four different headings:

1. Kleptocracy (Pure Redistribution)
2. Capitalist Authoritarianism (Suppression of Redistribution)
3. The Command Economy
4. Shadow Economy.

A brief description of each of these approaches follows.

A. *Kleptocracy (pure redistribution)*

In these models dictators interfere with the economy only to affect a redistribution of resources toward themselves and loyal supporters whom the regimes wish to reward. Redistribution implies a loss of efficiency, insofar as those who are taxed work less hard, come up with fewer ideas and innovations, save less, and so forth. There may be a further loss as people waste resources in rent-seeking – that is, in trying to influence the dictator and his or her associates to include them among the favored groups. Apart from these inefficiencies, according to this approach, the economy under dictatorship works the same as capitalist economies in democratic countries. Despite its simplicity, this is actually the most common approach. It underlies the models of Herschel Grossman (1991, 1996), Herschel Grossman and Suk Jae Noh (1990), Douglass North (1981), and Mancur Olson (1993), as well as the rent-seeking approaches of Peter Boettke (1993), A.L. Hillman and A. Schnytzer (1986), and others. It has even been applied to communism (Murrell and Olson 1991; Sicular 1988).

Olson models autocracy with his well-known representation of the autocrat as a "stationary bandit" (1993, 567–9) who maximizes revenue. Stationary bandits are superior to roving bandits (e.g., Chinese warlords) because, being stationary, they have an incentive to preserve the wealth or capital of potential victims. Consequently, such bandits have some (still insufficient, from the point of view of the citizenry under their rule) incentive to provide public goods to the people. The reason is that in the model, public goods enter as factor inputs that increase the output of private goods in society. Hence, the autocrat, by providing these goods, can further increase tax revenues. Given the level of public goods, the autocrat selects the revenue-maximizing tax rate, as in G. Brennan and James Buchanan's (1980) model of Leviathan. So the model determines optimal tax rates and the optimal level of public goods from the auto-crat's point of view (i.e., both are chosen to maximize revenue).

The concept of the stationary bandit nicely explains why many among the warring factions in Zaire in 1996 actually seemed to prefer the return of the notorious kleptocrat Mobutu Sese Seko to life in his absence. This partly explains how a kleptocrat like Mobutu could have remained in power for so long. But it is obviously not a sufficient explanation or else dictators would never get deposed (and Mobutu would have stayed in power). Beyond this, however, the autocrat's survival problem is typi-cally not modeled in this literature.[7] Moreover, the autocrat does not care about power, only revenue. So it is not obvious how one can use these models to understand many of history's most important dictator-ships (e.g., Hitler in Germany or Stalin in Russia). And, as these exam-ples illustrate, the assumption of revenue maximization can result in an underestimate of the damage autocrats can do as well as a misleading idea of the benefits of stationarity if applied to some dictatorships. To put it simply and to take only the most obvious cases, we can say that the Jews under the Nazis, the blacks in South Africa, and the peasants under Stalin would all undoubtedly, were they given the choice, have preferred that their bandits were a little less stationary.

Although models of kleptocracy have certain obvious applications (the regimes of "Papa Doc" Duvalier, Ferdinand Marcos, and Manuel Noriega come most quickly to mind), they have also been applied to other regimes, including Communist ones (Murrell and Olson 1991; Sicular 1988). Sicular's model is particularly interesting in this regard, because it develops a set of conditions for the entire planning apparatus to serve no allocation function, only a redistributive one. That is, if these marginal conditions are satisfied, the entire economic planning appara-tus of communism has no effect on the allocation of resources; it just produces a set of lump sum transfers. Despite the plan, market prices guide production and the allocation of resources, and the plan only serves to redistribute income. Sicular's careful empirical work (1995)

---

[7] An exception is Grossman (e.g., 1996), who models the autocrat's survival problem in terms of deterring rival kleptocrats. The key variable in his analysis is the expected effectiveness of insurgents relative to the ruler's soldiers.

shows, however, that these conditions are not likely to be satisfied in practice, thus providing the most scientific evidence available to date that the allocation function of Communist planning has to be taken seriously.

A third approach in this category is the model of rent-seeking which is applied to autocracy in many places (see, e.g., Hillman and Schnytzer 1986; also see Anderson and Boettke 1993). These models are discussed in the next chapter. One problem with this approach as a description of reality in, say, the former Soviet Union is not that rent-seeking didn't exist there (it did and was undoubtedly widespread), but that in the rent-seeking model, the efforts made to obtain the rents were pure waste. The Party distributed rents, and the people made enormous efforts to obtain them, but the Party in no way profited from them. Now dictators, it may be presumed, dislike waste. And no one denies that the Communist party was enormously powerful for a long time in the former Soviet Union. Could it not have found a way to get something in exchange for these rents (e.g., to channel rents in exchange for compliance to its goals)? Later in this chapter and in more detail in Chapters 9 and 10, I will suggest that the Party, like other successful autocratic political organizations, was organized precisely in such a way as to be able to take advantage of rent-seeking and to get something in return for it.

One important limitation on the ruler's capacity for redistribution is described in a series of papers by North, Weingast, Root, and others (North 1981; North and Weingast 1989; Root 1994). In North's (1981) model of the monarchy, the king maximizes revenue, and the central problem is that the structure of property rights which is appropriate for this purpose is not usually that which is efficient from the economic point of view. Moreover, as mentioned in the previous chapter, the king may find that there is a tradeoff between power and revenue. As Root (1994) describes the "irony of Absolutism," absolute power gave the king the capacity to repudiate debts, but

> creditors took into account the king's reputation for repudiating debts and therefore demanded higher interest rates than would otherwise have been needed to elicit loans. Actually, *because he was above the law, the king had to pay more for loanable funds than did his wealthy subjects.* In short, the Crown had a problem asserting its credit because it had a history of reneging on commitments. (p. 177, emphasis added)

Barry Weingast (1995) and Gabriella Montinola, Yingyi Qian, and Barry Weingast (1995) used the same idea to provide another reason for the success of the TVEs in China. The fact that under China's reforms, subnational jurisdictions like provincial governments and corporations like the TVEs have hard budget constraints but that, within specified limits, their own authority has some durability frees them from both interference from and dependence on the national government. These self-imposed limitations on the power of the federal government imply a "credible commitment" on its part not to usurp the powers of the provincial governments or corporations or to bail them out. In turn, this increases the orientation of provincial governments toward efficiency and growth.

B. Capitalist authoritarianism
(suppression of redistribution)

This approach is meant to characterize the soft authoritarianism or *democraduras* (hard democracies) of Southeast Asia and Latin America, regimes which combine market economies with autocratic political systems; such systems perform in exactly the opposite fashion to the kind that has just been outlined. That is, in these systems, the regime acts to insulate the economy from the ravaging effects of pork-barrel politics or rent-seeking by *stifling* the political forces of redistribution characteristic of democratic politics. Market forces are then freed to reward effort, saving, and innovation, hence producing superior economic growth. So these models and those in the previous category are based on exactly opposite assumptions (i.e., here dictatorships redistribute *less* than democracies do). The contradiction between these two models remains unresolved. Finally, note that capitalist–authoritarian models do address the question with which we began this chapter: How can political repression have an impact on the functioning of an economy? That is, these models suggest that capitalist economic life is not independent of the political system under which it operates.

C. The command economy

This is the most common type of model used to analyze Communist economic systems, systems which replace market forces with a central planning system. In the formal structure of the system, commands to enterprise managers are issued from the center, and the managers are motivated to carry them out by explicit or implicit threats of punishment. Supplies and demands of the different sectors are reconciled through input–output tables, material balances, and other bureaucratic tools. There is of course an enormous literature on the subject of socialist planning (for surveys see Ellman 1979; also see Kornai 1992). Michael Ellman (1979) describes the basic principles of how planning was intended to work. The basic principles included "partymindedness," directive character ("instructions"), one-man management and scientific analysis:

> The principle of *partymindedness* means that the plan is a concrete expression of party policy. It must look at all problems from a party point of view. . . . Characterizing Soviet planning, Stalin long ago observed that "our plans are not forecasts but *instructions*". . . . In the USSR . . . the mark of "planning" is thought to be that economic activity proceeds in accordance with institutions from above. . . . The Leninist principle of *one-man management* is very important in Soviet planning. It means that in each economic unit decisions are made, not by a committee, but by one man. He has the authority to take decisions and is responsible to his superiors for the execution of orders . . . Soviet plans are intended to embody not the subjective decision of this or that official or organization, but a *scientific analysis* of the problems confronting society. Hence an important role in the planning process is played by scientific organizations. For example, consumption planning is partly based on scientific consumption norms worked out by the relevant organizations . . . (pp. 17–18, emphasis added)

Fifteen years later, Joseph Stiglitz (1994) provided an account of the economic failures of the planning system. He also stressed its informational requirements:

> At the heart of the *economic* failure [was] a variety of information problems which, interpreted broadly, include[d] incentive issues. . . . Perhaps the most important reason for failure was the very reason that Hayek argued that central planning would fail: The central authorities simply did not have the information required to run the entire economy. (p. 198)

Stiglitz went on to stress the specific flaws of excessive centralization: The difficulty in controlling product quality, inappropriate incentives, selection (of individuals to run the system) problems, accounting, lack of competition, and lack of innovation and adaptability. All these flaws, he suggested, could be interpreted as information problems, broadly speaking (p. 198).

On either of these accounts, the planning system itself is apolitical.[8] It follows political directions, but whether it operates well or badly is the result not of competitive political or bureaucratic forces or mechanisms, but of how well instructions can be issued and carried out. To put it another way, the command model has never been married to theories of bureaucratic behavior which go beyond Weber's (1978) authority model. But other, more modern, theories could be used, including contemporary rational-choice approaches to bureaucratic behavior. For example, one simple way to explain the "gigantism" characteristic of former Soviet enterprises and, for that matter, the whole planning apparatus itself would be along the lines of William Niskanen's (1971) theory of bureaucracy, in which bureaucrats maximize the size of the budget under their control. Planners' behavior would then be interpreted, not according to the principles of scientific socialism that had gone well or badly, but by the planners' interest in obtaining more income, prestige, or power for themselves. Other models could be used[9] by those who find the Niskanen approach too limited. Chapters 9 and 10 develop my own approach to this issue.

To sum up, the command economy model highlights a feature of the Soviet-type economy that is often neglected in other approaches to Communist economics – namely, the fact that the Soviet-type system is a bureaucratic system. From this point of view, if there are laws or generalizations about bureaucratic behavior, including this behavior in other contexts (such as large corporations or government bureaus in democratic regimes), these laws should be germane to understanding how the Soviet system itself worked. Indeed, in a context like the Soviet economy, in which markets were suppressed in the most extreme fashion, we would expect all the characteristics of bureaucratic behavior not only to be present but also to be *overwhelmingly* present. As Oskar Lange (1938/1964) foresaw long ago, "... *the real danger of socialism is bureaucratization of economic life* and not the impossibility of coping with the allocation of resources" (pp. 109–10, quoted in Shleifer and Vishny 1994, p. 167, emphasis in original).

D. The shadow economy

This approach is also mainly used to analyze Soviet-style economies and is a good antidote to the command approach. It applies as well

---

[8] Stiglitz (1994, p. 66) explicitly points out that his analysis ignores political economy elements.
[9] See the surveys by Wintrobe and Moe in Dennis Mueller (1997).

to other systems in which there is a large amount of political intervention in the economy (as in some contemporary Islamic societies). The idea is that market or marketlike incentives are the only ones which really work, so that (to illustrate with the Soviet system) the vast apparatus of central planning fails in varying degrees to solve the economic problems of the system. In fact, the system really "works" in an entirely different way – that is, by virtue of the intervention of informal and often illegal devices such as *blat* (influence), *toklachi* (expeditors), and other marketlike devices that supplement the formal system. Work in this vein began with Grossman's often cited (1977) article and continues in, for example, the books of Peter Boettke (1993), Edward Hewett (1988), Peter Rutland (1985), and Jan Winiecki (1988). Thus, Rutland's (1985) book is entitled *The Myth of the Plan*; Chapter 3 of Hewitt's (1988) text on the Soviet system, entitled "The Soviet Economic System As It Is Designed to Operate," is followed by Chapter 4, "The Soviet Economic System As It Actually Operates." In this way of thinking, the secondary supply system of black markets and *tolkachi* is the main way to obtain the supplies which may have been formally allocated by the plan but which, typically, were never received. Alternatively, *blat* is used to obtain needed inputs. *Shabashniki* (moonlighters) allow enterprises to undertake construction services (for cash) that the official system will not permit. And so on. How large a role these informal mechanisms play in repairing the "holes" in the centralized planning system is of course enormously difficult to guess. The command model takes the formal planning system seriously, and therefore it implicitly assumes that the "holes" are relatively small. At the other extreme is Boettke's (1993) view, which characterizes the Soviet system as a "pseudo-reality of a rational, hierarchical planned economy co-existing with the reality of planned failure and illicit corrective measures on both the production and consumption side of the market" (p. 69). Indeed, Boettke concludes that "the Soviet economy was not a planned economy radically different from any other economic system witnessed in history. It was over-regulated, abused and distorted, but it was, nevertheless, a market economy" (p. 69).

At the theoretical level, one problem with this idea is that while shadow mechanisms like *blat* and *shabashniki* may sometimes improve allocation and coordination, they can also obviously be used for private gain, and their use in this fashion may have the opposite effects, reducing productivity or disrupting the system. Indeed, in the planning universe, it is an article of faith that all horizontal information flows are potentially disruptive of central control (Ericson 1991, p. 19). Hewett (1988) tries to resolve this problem by distinguishing between the *shadow* economy, which supplements Gossnab (State Committee for Materials and Technical Supply) and Gosplan (State Planning Committee) in ways that allow the system to perform better than it otherwise would, and the *secondary* economy, in which the motive is private gain and in which enterprises make goods on the side which they sell for a profit (p. 179). However, the difficulty, acknowledged by Hewett, is that, as in capitalist economies, motivation does not sort out those actions which actually benefit the economy from those which do not.

3　　Overview: elements of the autocratic economy

The preceding, all-too-brief sketch of alternative approaches to the economy of dictatorship implies that there are three issues which need to be addressed. This is done in the remaining chapters in this part. The issues are:

1. *Do dictatorships tend to redistribute income or wealth more or less than democracies?* Can any generalizations be developed on this question? One thing can be said at the outset: It is obvious that there is massive redistribution in Communist economic systems. And from our modeling of the political sector in Part II, it is also clear that all dictators redistribute wealth to their cronies. The redistribution issue becomes problematic mainly in so-called capitalist–authoritarian systems like those that existed in Chile or South Korea. Chapter 7 therefore considers the general issue of whether dictators redistribute more than democracies do, with special reference to these systems, and it suggests a general principle: that all dictators *do* redistribute more than democracies and that capitalist–authoritarian regimes are no exception. So parallel to the idea developed in Part II that there is always a class of people that is repressed under dictatorship, Chapter 7 begins the substantive analysis of Part III by suggesting that there is always a second class as well – the *overpaid*.

There is a second issue which emerges from our survey: that of the workings of Communist economies.

2. *How can the command and shadow models of the Communist economy be reconciled?* Chapters 9 and 10 approach this issue by following Lange's (1938/1964) hint (cited earlier) and emphasizing a third feature of these economies – that they are bureaucracies. I use a general model of bureaucratic behavior, one that was developed previously (Breton and Wintrobe 1982), to integrate the command and shadow economy models into a single model. This model is then used to resolve a number of puzzles about the workings of these economies, such as the role of political power in the workings of the centrally planned economy,

the tendency of these economies to ossify over time, and how the Chinese were able to reform their economy along free-market lines while the Soviets could not.

One final issue must be considered.

3. *What role does the dictator's political power play in the workings of the economy?* This is the question raised at the beginning of this chapter. In our survey we saw that there has typically been little consideration of the enforcement problem in markets,[10] and there has therefore also been scant consideration of the possibility that there might be bases other than markets for making a transaction. Some of the arguments behind the shadow economy models are just extreme versions of this general point of view. So it is easy to conclude that dictators can only successfully operate the economy if they "keep their hands off it" – that is, by allowing free markets. In that case the problem outlined at the beginning of this chapter disappears. But the problem is removed by assumption: The possibility that dictatorships might be capable of supe-rior economic performance through some other means is simply not admitted, except in the command model, which is so naive on the question of incentives that it remains an easy target. Yet contemporary economic theory does provide a very simple mechanism whereby just this superior performance could be achieved: through the potential capacity of autocratic forms of organization to solve the enforcement problem.

The basic logic here is illustrated in Figure 6.1. The demand for labor is given by the D_L curve and labor supply by S_L. If contracts were costlessly enforceable, equilibrium in the free market would be at the intersection of supply and demand, with wage rate w_m and employment L_m. However, enforcement is often costly, as discussed in Chapter 2. Under these circumstances, as Carl Shapiro and Joseph Stiglitz (1984) showed, even in a free labor market, jobs are rationed, and private firms in a free market, in order to deter cheating (shirking), will pay wages higher than those which would clear the market. Equilibrium will be at the inter-section of a no-cheating condition (like *NCC* in Figure 6.1) and the demand for labor (i.e., at the intersection of the wage rate w_p with employment at L_p).

In this way of thinking, the private labor market is also characterized by information and incentive problems. Employers lack information on

---

[10] The major exception is the work of the pioneers of the "efficiency wage" model them-selves – for example, Samuel Bowles (1985) and Joseph Stiglitz (see his 1994 book for an explicit overview of the problems of Soviet-type economies from this point of view). The current work differs from theirs mainly in its explicit political economy perspective.

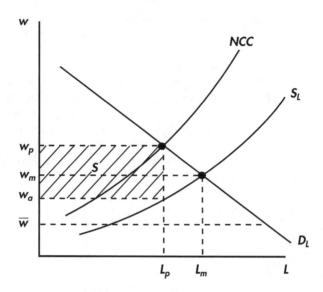

Figure 6.1. Job rationing in the labor market.

the performance of their employees, and the employees lack the correct incentive to reveal this information. One way in which private firms solve this problem is through the payment of an efficiency wage, which motivates employees to be *loyal* to the firm. Similar information and incentive problems exist in other relationships in the free-market economy (once costly enforcement is acknowledged) – for example, between managers and their shareholders, and between managers of firms and sources of capital (see Stiglitz 1994 for a good survey).

Now suppose the industry in question is controlled by a political dictatorship. Under dictatorship, jobs may also be rationed. For example, in the Soviet-type system, the government, not the market, decided on the allocation of jobs. Like the private firm, the government wanted employees who wouldn't "cheat." In this context, however, cheating could be widely interpreted to include shirking, wrongful criticism of the government, insufficient demonstrations of enthusiasm, or whatever, according to the Party, was important (as communicated in its ideology). So the government would offer a nonmarket-clearing wage like w_p (which need not be the same as the w_p that would be chosen by firms in the private market; we return to this point in a moment).

If the supply curve represents their opportunity costs, employees can earn w_a in an alternative employment. So rents in this industry are represented by the shaded area S. If Figure 6.1 is taken to represent the Soviet firm, S represents the rewards for loyalty. Alternatively, if Figure 6.1 represents a free labor market, S represents the premium necessary to deter cheating, with private loyalty to the firm replacing loyalty to a Marxist state.

Of course, so many things are left out in this oversimplified picture! For example, no mention is being made of all of the other institutions and processes which differentiate a free-market economy from a socialist one, including private ownership, competition among firms, the operation of the capital market, incentives for innovation and for maintaining product quality, relations with customers, and so on. This is so because on most analyses, all these factors explain why free markets are so efficient. But dictatorship is so common politically – and the economies of many dictatorships are so apparently successful for long periods – that the reader might think it is worth his or her while to disregard all these factors for a moment and focus on only one question: In which system will the loyalty premium be lower?

A number of variables may be expected to affect the size of the loyalty premium, including the firm's (or the state's) capacity to monitor employees, the sanctions available to punish cheating, and the individual employee's opportunities outside the firm or enterprise.[11] Consideration of them suggests the following hypothesis: *The premium necessary to deter cheating is smaller in a dictatorship than in a free society.* Several reasons justify this hypothesis. First, under dictatorship the regime typically controls many of the good jobs in the system (in the former Soviet system, virtually all of them). So the individual typically has fewer opportunities outside the system controlled by the government than an individual who is outside a capitalist firm in a market system. This makes the threat of dismissal in a dictatorship a more severe sanction than dismissal from a capitalist firm. Second, there is typically no independent legal system in a dictatorship to which an employee could go to accuse the government of such things as wrongful dismissal. So the autocrat has more freedom to optimize in the design and implementation of sanctions. Finally, the government's monitoring apparatus is typically more thorough, and (especially in the former Soviet Union) more integrated into the operations of a productive enterprise than could ever be the case inside a firm in a democratic country. These three effects reinforce each other in lowering the premium required to deter cheating inside the enterprise under dictatorship (compared with its capitalist democratic variants).

---

[11] These are only some of the variables involved. Chapter 8 develops the equations of the model and shows the role of the variables in it in greater detail.

The economic dilemma of an autocratic system is thus not at all that the regime lacks the instruments or the machinery necessary to create an effective incentive system capable of calling forth productive effort, as is often suggested. The machinery of dictatorship – rewards, sanctions, and instruments of monitoring – available for this purpose appears quite formidable. Moreover, on this interpretation, the function of this apparatus is not simply to ensure obedience to orders, but to obtain the loyalty of employees. Once that is understood, the information and incentive problems associated with the naive command model are considerably reduced: Loyal employees do not simply follow instructions; motivated by the prospect of obtaining rents and disciplined by the possibility of sanctions, they can be counted on to compete with each other to further the goals of the system.

Although the basic logic just outlined applies to most autocratic economic systems, the institutions which implement this principle differ. In the *apartheid* system in South Africa, for example, "job reservation" meant that certain jobs in the "white" manufacturing sector were reserved for white workers, who consequently earned a wage premium over what would prevail in a free labor market. Another institution used there was the "pass" system. Under that system, blacks needed a pass, without which they could not obtain a job in the manufacturing sector. Black workers who were suspected of cheating (again, broadly interpreted) and who were dismissed from their jobs also lost their passes – and therefore the right to remain in the manufacturing sector. The only alternative was to get a "bad" job in the homelands, at a lower wage ($\overline{w}$ in Figure 6.1). Again, the pass system appeared to give white employers a powerful tool to discipline black workers. Employers could threaten them with dismissal not merely from the firm but also from the entire manufacturing sector itself. The pass system can be analyzed in the same way, using Figure 6.1, except that the institutions of *apartheid* labor market regulation, rather than those of Soviet communism, determine the location of the *NCC* curve and the size of the wage premium in that figure.

These examples suggest some ways in which autocratic political power can be used to improve the efficiency of the economy. Autocratic power does this when it successfully provides incentives (in the form of rents) to the work force to adopt attitudes of loyalty and discipline. On the other hand, sometimes the mechanisms for this purpose fail. The machinery of dictatorship still grinds out rents, but they do not serve the dictator's objectives, and the economy stalls. For example, suppose that the Communist party got "corrupted" in some way, so that jobs were given out in exchange for bribes rather than political or organizational loyalty. Then the area S in Figure 6.1 would still describe the rents received by employees. (It would also describe the amount of the bribes received in exchange, as discussed further in Chapter 9.) But no political loyalty would be generated, economic efficiency would fall, and the regime would be undermined.

So what decides whether political power helps or hurts the economy? The circumstances are not at all obvious. The surprise of the economic collapse of communism in the 1989–91 period illustrates this point. The end of Soviet communism caught most observers unaware, and even those whose figures were pessimistic enough to explain it after the event could not have predicted it before it happened (unless its collapse had *always* been their prediction ever since 1917). The same could be said about the end of *apartheid* in South Africa. Chapter 8 on *apartheid* and Chapters 9 and 10 on communism develop models which address this question.

4   Conclusion

In this chapter, I have suggested that from an economic point of view, our main concern with dictatorship is the possibility that autocratic forms of economic organization might be superior to democratic ones in terms of promoting economic growth or efficiency. This belief has been a recurring nightmare, beginning in the twentieth century with the fear of communism as an economic system, followed by admiration and fear of Hitler's juggernaut in the 1930s, and extending in more recent years to the threats from "Japan, Inc.," "Asian values," South Korea and Chile, and now the free-market communism of China.

If we turn to contemporary economic theories of autocracy for illumination on the sources of this fear, we find that there is actually very little discussion of the problem from this point of view. Four kinds of models to be found in the literature were summarized – dictatorship as redistribution (kleptocracy), as suppression of redistribution (capitalist authoritarianism), as command economy, and as shadow economy. Only the second (dictatorship as suppression of redistribution) addresses this concern, and dictatorship plays virtually no economic role in that model but merely saves the economy from the ravages of pork-barrel politics alleged to be characteristic of democracy. Yet contemporary economic theory does provide at least one mechanism in which dictatorship can directly affect the workings of markets – through its potential capacity to create a loyal and disciplined labor force (as discussed in contemporary efficiency wage models). I showed how this model can be adapted to develop a political economy perspective, one which illustrates how political dictatorship and the economy affect each other.

In subsequent chapters, I will use this basic tool and I will also borrow elements from the other models outlined in this chapter to explain the economic behavior of a number of autocratic economies. The next chapter addresses the issue of redistribution, with special reference to the capitalist–authoritarian systems of Pinochet's Chile and South Korea. Chapter 8 deals with *apartheid*, and Chapters 9 and 10 with Communist economies. One way to understand the ordering of these chapters is that we proceed from lower to progressively higher levels of government intervention and the use of political power to control the economy. In other words we begin with tinpots and proceed to the economies of tyrannies and totalitarian regimes.

7 Redistribution and rent-seeking

1 Introduction

One popular explanation of how "too much" democracy can be bad for economic development involves the idea that democracy is "plagued" by redistributional impulses. Perhaps the most famous work to advance this theme is Mancur Olson's *The Rise and Decline of Nations* (1982); in this book interest groups are reclassified as "distributional coalitions" which pursue their own selfish interests at the expense of overall economic efficiency. The older and more established the democracy, the larger the number of distributional coalitions that have a chance to form, and the more the economic landscape is "rent" with inefficient laws, regulations, and other practices that hinder growth. In a similar vein, the vast literature on rent-seeking, which was originated by Gordon Tullock (1967), A.O. Krueger (1974), and R.A. Posner (1975), identified rent-seeking and its associated social costs with democratic government. This literature made it possible, by a strange twist of logic in which democracy is identified with the proliferation of economic monopolies, for monopoly to be elevated to the status of a serious problem.

Although critical of democratic processes, none of the above-named authors has embraced the notion that authoritarianism can facilitate economic development, and indeed, Olson in particular has forcefully argued the opposite (1993). However, the closely related idea that insulating economic policy from democratic processes – "a little bit"[1] of dictatorship – can be good for economic development has gained currency, especially in political science and among both economic and political science theorists of development who specifically point to the capacity of authoritarian states to resist distributional pressures as the key to successful development. One influential contemporary exponent of this view seems to be Stephen Haggard (1990), although the argument is much older. A good list of earlier references can be found in Przeworski

---

[1] The case for massive dictatorship (e.g., that Communist central planning is better able to promote economic growth than capitalism) is no longer fashionable.

and Limongi (1993). Among development economists, Pranab Bardhan (1990) is explicit on the redistributional issue. He writes "Once developmental goals are centrally involved in the issues of the legitimacy of the regime, I think it is not so much authoritarianism per se which makes a difference, but the extent of insulation that the decision makers can organize against the ravages of short-run pork-barrel politics" (p. 5).

Perhaps more important than academic fashion is the striking success in economic terms of a number of countries under authoritarian regimes – commonly known as the NICs (Newly Industrializing Countries) – especially the East Asian economies of Singapore, South Korea, Taiwan, and Hong Kong. Most dramatic has been the success of free-market communism in contemporary China, in which extensive political authoritarianism has combined with the opening of free markets to achieve dazzling economic growth. By contrast the failures of populist governments in recent years, especially in Latin America, have been only too apparent. R. Dornbusch and S. Edwards (1990) invented the derisive label "macroeconomic populism" to describe the policies of countries like Chile under Allende or Peru under Garcia, in which leftist governments attempted to respond to pressures for income redistribution through macroeconomic means. They point out that these programs usually achieved the opposite result of their objectives and ended when "foreign exchange constraints and extreme inflation forced a program of violent real wage cuts that ended in massive political instability, violence, and in the case of Chile, even in a coup" (p. 248).

Although their 1990 article uses Chile and Peru as examples of macroeconomic populism, their subsequent (1991) edited volume expands the list of "populist experiences" to include Argentina, Brazil, Mexico, and Nicaragua. The authors emphasize that they share the predilections of the policymakers who authored these episodes – that is, they believe that income is distributed unacceptably in these countries. It is just that populism is no substitute for sound economics, fiscal conservatism, and (presumably) patience while waiting for the next generation at least to improve the distribution of income.

Although controversy continues over whether the root of the success of the East Asian NICs is due to their relentless use of free markets,[2] or to the opposite,[3] the most dramatic case of turnaround is probably con-

---

[2] See Robert Wade's (1990) Chapter 3 for a survey of neo-classical economic explanations of the success of Taiwan and other NICs in these terms.

[3] The organization Freedom House gives South Korea a low ranking for economic freedom, based on its criteria, which mainly emphasize the freedom to participate in a market economy (Freedom House 1995). The Fraser Institute gives it a high ranking, based on its own criteria, which emphasize government spending as a share of GDP (Gwartney, Lawson, and Block 1995).

temporary Chile, where one of the most brutal periods of dictatorship seems to have given birth, after some false starts, to a dynamic and successful market economy, in which democracy has (mostly) returned and in which even the former enemies of the regime appear loath to abandon many of its policies.

Indeed, support for the Chilean achievement can even be found from Guillermo O'Donnell (1993), the original architect of the "bureaucratic authoritarian" model of Latin American dictatorships and one of their most important critics. He wrote,

> The sober fact is that the distributional consequences of more ambiguous and less harsh policies in countries such as Brazil, Argentina, and Peru have not been better than the ones under the Pinochet government. Furthermore, the resources presently available to the Chilean government for alleviating equity problems are relatively larger than the ones available to Brazil, Peru and Argentina. . . ." (p. 1366)

Presumably, however, Pinochet would not be pleased by the analogy O'Donnell draws between the effectiveness of some of Pinochet's policies and those of Lenin.

The argument that authoritarianism fosters growth has not gone uncriticized. In particular, scientific work on the connection between authoritarianism and growth has achieved decidedly mixed results. Przeworski and Limongi (1993) examined the statistical evidence. They reviewed eighteen studies, each of which considered a number of countries over a period of time. The countries were classified as either democratic or authoritarian, and tests were performed to see which type of regime was more favorable to economic growth. As they summarized their findings, of the twenty-one results in the eighteen studies, eight found in favor of democracy, eight found in favor of authoritarianism, and five discovered no difference (p. 60). One obvious problem with the methodology used in those studies is that the category "political regime" (democratic vs. authoritarian) is simply too coarse. Thus, such studies would end up lumping together countries like South Korea and Zaire or Haiti. Neither Zaire's Mobutu nor Haiti's Papa Doc and his successors ever evinced much interest in promoting economic growth. On the contrary such men succeeded in largely destroying their economies. Earlier, in Chapter 4, I referred to these regimes as "immiserizing" dictatorships and showed some of the conditions under which that strategy is attractive to dictators. In any case there is little doubt about the record of these regimes. Geoffrey Hawthorn (1993) described the state of the Zairian economy as of 1993:

The country's outstanding debt is widely reported to be the
same size as Mobutu's personal fortune. Half the present budget
goes to debt servicing; a quarter to Mobutu's own political
fund which he uses to pay off the politicians and officers he
constantly rotates; and the remaining quarter to internal
security. . . . Roads are 10% of what they were when the Bel-
gians left in 1960, recorded wages, in real terms, 6% . . . – it is
estimated that only about 1% of the country is now cultivated.
(p. 1305)

Another flaw in the theoretical case that capitalist–authoritarian regimes facilitate economic growth has been elaborated by Alice Amsden
(1989) and Robert Wade (1990), and recently it has been emphasized in
the economic development literature by Dani Rodrik (1993). Many of
the most prominent NICs, they say, especially Korea, Singapore, and
Taiwan, although authoritarian enough, do not fit the free-market
model. Their economies are not particularly free of trade restrictions,
and their states have been extensively involved in industrialization. According to Rodrik (1993), in Korea, "the average effective rate of protection . . . (for domestic sales only) actually rose from 30% in 1963 to 38%
in 1978, after a dip to 24% in 1970. . . . The Korean state has used trade
protection, selective credit subsidies, export targets (for individual
firms!), public ownership of [the] banking sector, export subsidies, and
price controls" (p. 22). Moreover, the policy instruments used in countries like Korea or Singapore that have been dramatically successful at
achieving economic growth are no different from those that have apparently failed so miserably in Latin America, Africa, and the rest of Asia.
The policies in question are import quotas and licenses, credit subsidies,
tax exemptions, public ownership, and so on (loc. cit.).

What is most conspicuously absent in this literature – either from those
who believe that there is a connection between dictatorship, at least in its
authoritarian–capitalist variant, and economic growth, or from those
who argue the opposite – is an adequate theoretical perspective. This
chapter tries to take some steps toward filling this gap. I ask the questions: On theoretical grounds, which type of regime can be expected to
engage in more redistribution – democracy or dictatorship? Is there any
truth to the popular idea that democratic governments inhibit growth
because of excess redistributory activity or rent-seeking? The analysis
proceeds by examining the equilibrium level of redistribution in a
number of well-known models of democracy. I look at the Allan Meltzer
and Scott Richard (1981) model, in which redistribution takes place from
the mean to the median income voter; Gary Becker's (1983) interest
group model; and the probabilistic voting model of Peter Coughlin,

Dennis Mueller, and P. Murrell (1990). I then ask what would happen to the level of redistribution in each of these models if a dictator took over the government. In all these cases, it turns out that more redistribution can be expected under dictatorship than democracy. Armed with this conclusion, I suggest an alternative explanation for the superior economic performance of capitalist–authoritarian regimes. This explanation consists of two propositions:

1. These economies perform well, not because they don't redistribute but because they *do*.
2. The redistribution in the case of these regimes happens to be toward groups that especially profit from economic growth.

2   Dictatorship, democracy, and redistribution

This section develops the general comparison of the redistributive tendencies of democratic governments and dictatorships. Although I do not present a formal proof, I develop and defend a simple proposition: *Dictatorships tend to redistribute income more than democracies do.* I conduct the analysis with reference to the standard economic theory of monopoly versus competition. In that model it is assumed that a monopoly takes over a competitive industry and that the cost curves of the firms, which now become the monopolist's plants, are unchanged. Here, I assume that a dictator "takes over" a democratic government and that this change affects neither the costs nor the preferences of the people for public goods or public policies. To illustrate, I assume that if a left-wing dictator takes over, the preferences of the population do not shift either right or left simply because a democratic government has been replaced by a dictatorship. To be sure, some right-wing citizens may be expected to shift leftward in order to obtain favors from the dictator or to avoid repression. Such changes are endogenous to the analysis. What I am ruling out by assumption is shifts in the preferences of the population in the absence of any change in public policies on the part of the government, or any change in the distribution of the benefits and burdens of the state. Note that if this assumption were dropped, it is not obvious what would happen. One can make a case that some citizens would oppose the policies of the dictator, even if they are the same as the policies of the previous democratic government, simply because the regime is a dictatorship. But others can be expected to shift in the opposite direction.[4] So I will simply assume in what follows that shifts in support or opposition

---

[4] The issue is related to whether the use of repression by a dictator generates more or less loyalty on the part of the population, as discussed in Chapter 3.

are undertaken in respect to changes in government policy, and not to the existence of dictatorship per se.

Another issue which arises in conducting an analysis like this is the "standard of comparison." If dictatorships are to be said to redistribute more than democracies, the obvious question is: "Compared to what?" One obvious standard of comparison is the free-market distribution of income, but this concept is itself ambiguous. It cannot be equated with what the distribution of income would look like in the absence of government, because in the absence of government, property rights would not exist, and the free-market distribution of income is that which would obtain by relying on purely private methods of enforcement and not on public enforcement of property rights or contracts.

Another approach to this problem is to designate the "benchmark" case as the distribution of income that would prevail under the minimal government obtaining under a constitution whose provisions are those which would be agreed to by the citizenry operating under a unanimity rule at the constitutional choice stage. In that case, even in the free-market or benchmark case, there would be redistribution of income for charity purposes of the Pareto optimal variety. But there would also be redistribution to the extent that the public provision of defense, police protection, protection of contracts, and other public goods tended to favor one group or another. One good definition of minimal government along these lines might be that provided by James Buchanan in his *Limits of Liberty* (1975).

Suppose, then, under the benchmark case just defined, the distribution of income is given by $x_1, \ldots, x_n$. Now suppose we assume a normal (not necessarily minimal) democratic government and ask what happens to this distribution. Of course, what happens depends on the model of democracy used, and there is at present no common agreement on the effect of democratic government on the distribution of income. In the standard, median-voter model, there is no solution to this problem, because under majority rule, no majority coalition is dominant and the outcome simply cycles among the alternatives available. There are, however, other models which make stronger assumptions and do obtain determinate results: in Meltzer and Richard (1981), in which income is redistributed from the mean to the median (in terms of income) voter; in Becker's (1983) model of interest group pressure; and in the probabilistic voting model of Coughlin (1986), and others. We will consider all three of these models. Each of them can be thought of as producing a vector of incomes $y_1, \ldots, y_n$.

The next step is to impose a dictatorship and to see what happens to the distribution of income. Call the resulting distribution of income

$z_1, \ldots, z_n$. Our central proposition is that the distribution of income under dictatorship $(z_1, \ldots, z_n)$ is "further away" from the benchmark free-market case $(x_1, \ldots, x_n)$ than the distribution of income under any of these three models of democracy $(y_1, \ldots, y_n)$. Alternatively, and more formally, the proposition is that dictatorship is characterized by more redistributive "activity," that is,

(1) $$\sum_{i=1}^{n}(z_i - x_i)^2 > \sum_{i=1}^{n}(y_i - x_i)^2$$

Before proceeding to a more formal analysis let us consider a couple of reasons why we should expect this result. To illustrate, let us consider one simple explanation of the redistributive tendencies of dictatorship, that which is implicit in Przeworski's (1991) analysis of "self-enforcing" democracy. Przeworski suggests that for democracy to be stable, it must be self-enforcing, and for that to be true, the competitive political process cannot result in outcomes highly adverse to any major group's interest. If it did, it would pay for that group to subvert democracy rather than to support it. The dictator faces no such constraint.

A second line of thought has to do with the origins of dictatorship. As we will show in Chapter 11, the simplest explanation of the rise of dictatorship is that in societies with polarized preferences or with low trust between the citizens and the parties – or in which there is no willingness to compromise – there are really only two possibilities: either the party which gains office in democratic voting tries to implement its preferred position, in which case large social conflict will ensue; or the society will be simply paralyzed by inaction. The allure of dictatorship under these circumstances is obvious; either the left or the right, if it takes power by force, will be able to eliminate its opposition through repression, and in this way, it will be able to implement its program. Either alternative implies a massive redistribution of income in comparison to that which is typical in a democracy.

A third and more complex line of argument concerns the rent-seeking process. To elaborate it, we first have to discuss a serious flaw in the standard model of rent-seeking. Explaining it will illustrate some of the ways in which the distribution of rents in democracies and dictatorships differ. Thus, consider the standard rent-seeking model. Citizens and interest groups compete for rents through "wasteful" activities such as lobbying, hiring lawyers, and so on. If the rent or "prize" is $10,000, and if ten groups are competing (each of which has an equal chance of getting the rent), then the expected value of the rent to each competitor is $1,000. It follows that if the competitors are risk neutral, each of them will waste up to $1,000 attempting to obtain the prize. This conclusion has been widely accepted, although debate continues on whether the total amount spent on rent-seeking exactly dissipates the rent, as it does in this example.[5] However, there is a logical problem: The process is irrational *from the point of view of politicians*. They give out a monopoly rent worth $10,000 and receive nothing in return. It is essential to the rent-seeking model that it makes no difference which of the competitors gets the prize; hence the lobbying activity is pure waste *to the politicians* as well as to society. A rational politician would organize the process differently. For example, he or she would suggest to the competitors that they should offer cash payments instead of wasting the time of politicians through their lobbying activities. But if bribes instead of lobbying are used, the $10,000 which is received in bribes by the politicians is not waste, but a pure transfer to politicians from interest groups, and in this case, the $10,000 represents no *social* waste or deadweight loss at all.

To see some other ways in which the rent-seeking process can be organized, consider what typically happens under dictatorship. Dictators, at least the more "successful" (i.e., relatively long-lived) ones, know how to organize things so that they capture a substantial return from rent-seeking efforts. To see this point, note first that under many regimes the distribution of rents reaches legendary proportions. Examples include the Marcos regime in the Philippines (for details, see Hutchcroft 1991; or for a more extensive treatment, see Wurfel 1988) and the military regimes in Latin America in the 1970s and elsewhere, whose most concrete and lasting achievement was to increase military salaries and the military budget (Nordlinger 1977; Remmer 1989). The simplest explanation for the legendary shortages characteristic of Soviet-type systems is that the shortages create rents, the distribution of which is controlled by the Communist party, which can then use them to garner political support. The South African system of *apartheid* provided both job reservation for white workers and the institution of the pass for the benefit of white capitalists.[6] In Nazi Germany rents were often created and distributed on ethnic grounds. Perhaps one example will suffice: the medical profession, whose membership was disproportionately Nazi. German doctors and medical officials took the lead (i.e., they did not wait for orders from senior party officials) in expelling Jewish doctors from the profession and taking over their practices (see Kater 1983). One might think that as highly educated professionals, they could have been

[5] See Robert Tollison's survey of the literature on rent-seeking in Mueller (1997).

[6] Black workers in the white manufacturing sector could only remain in that sector with a pass. A black worker who lost his job lost the right to work in the white sector. So the system lowered black wages in the white sector.

expected to oppose the use of such nonsensical criteria as blood, skull type, and so on as indices of human worth. Instead, they largely took the attitude that they were experts on such matters and that if these were to form the basis for regime policy, they wanted to be in the forefront of policy implementation.[7]

In all these systems, resources were not wasted bidding for the rents of the public sector. Rents were given out, and the dictator received political support or money payments in return. In other words, there was no *waste* in the economic sense. This may be due to the different ways that rents are distributed in dictatorships, on the one hand, and democracies, on the other. Dictators typically impose restrictions on entry into competition for the rents given out by the state. Sometimes the rents are reserved for specific groups (this is obviously clear from the examples we have been referring to). The Chicago Boys under Pinochet were not interested in the pleas of the old populist urban coalition (Constable and Valenzuela 1991). Blacks were not allowed to compete with whites in South Africa for privileges: the job reservation system could not have been converted into a program for overpaying blacks if only they had bid enough. Gypsies, homosexuals, Jews, and Communists could not have gained ethnic or other preferences under the Nazis. One reason for this fact is obvious: If free competition for rents were allowed, then, because rent-seeking results in net *losses*[8] and because support depends on receiving net benefits, dictators would lose support by distributing rents through an openly competitive process!

How does democracy differ? Obviously, the restrictions on entry into bidding processes for rights and privileges or goods and services distributed by the state which are characteristic of authoritarian governments are inconsistent with the very notion of democracy. In any process of allocating public resources, I suggest that a typical democracy will impose certain conditions:

1. There should be no restrictions on who can bid, except of a technical nature.
2. The winning bid should be selected on the basis of criteria involving net benefit to the public – such as the worth of the project, its costs, and so on – and not on the political connections, race, ethnicity, status, and so on of the bidders.
3. The process of bidding should be as open as possible, and it should be open to review by an independent judiciary.

[7] I owe this point to a private conversation with Michael Kater.
[8] That is, the process is economically inefficient.

The inefficiency of democracy, according to the rent-seeking model, is now exposed. All these conditions imply that more resources will be wasted under the bidding process in democracy. In short, *democracy is a much more wasteful system than dictatorship.*

Is this conclusion valid? If not, where is the flaw in the argument? One way to see the mistake is to first realize that the existence of rent-seeking losses implies gains from trade between politicians and rent seekers. If these groups can trade with each other (e.g., if a rent seeker can simply bribe a politician to give him or her a contract), the waste in the process will be eliminated. In other words, if transactions costs between these groups are low, the equilibrium level will differ from the one that was described in the rent-seeking model; it will be the "corruption" equilibrium, with no waste but with a defrauded public. On the other hand, suppose these transactions are prevented, because the rules against influence peddling, bribery, and extortion (the existence of which is characteristic of democracy everywhere) are well-enforced by alert and powerful independent authorities. This condition results in a second possible equilibrium, one in which fair competition among bidders is enforced. If this bidding results in rents being distributed to those who bid the lowest or who offer the public the most in the way of benefits, then this process produces something useful. The natural name to give this equilibrium is "strong democracy."

The rent-seeking model rules out the possibility of the strong democracy equilibrium by assuming that it makes no difference who wins the contest – no social benefits result from the bidding process. The corruption equilibrium is ruled out by the assumption that the rules against corruption and the enforcement of them are so powerful that corruption is eliminated. These two assumptions leave only the equilibrium described in the rent-seeking model: waste. A more appropriate name for this equilibrium is "irrational," because it implies that political institutions are fundamentally irrational in design: *They are there to ensure the persistence of waste.* As the Coase theorem implies, one should be skeptical of such equilibria.

At this point, the reader may be tempted to ask, "What difference does it make?" Suppose that the losses from rent-seeking are not genuine waste in the economic sense, but "merely" unauthorized (in effect, fraudulent) transfers to politicians and bureaucrats. It is true that they are not waste in the sense of economic theory, but they are certainly not what the cost–benefit analysis promised! If the proper equilibrium involves corruption, not rent-seeking, isn't that bad enough?

One reason for insisting on the distinction between corruption and rent-seeking is that the solutions to these two problems can be vastly different. In particular it is easy to imagine that a "little bit of authoritarianism" might possibly reduce rent-seeking (which after all is a form of political competition). It is much more difficult to believe that autocracy is the solution to corruption. Under autocracy, there are fewer or no constraints on the practice of rent distribution by independent courts or by an inquisitory free press. Political dictatorships also have a significantly larger capacity to organize the distribution of rents in order to maximize their own "take" in the case of bribes or to generate the most political support. Moreover, the dictator is capable of sanctioning nonrepayment directly, thus solving the enforcement problem that is inherent in rent-seeking trades in a way that no democracy is capable of. Finally, as I have suggested, dictators lack the alternative ways of creating trust or support characteristic of democracy. The distribution of rents in exchange for loyalty is therefore their major avenue of developing political support or trust. So the correct conclusion to be drawn from the rent-seeking model is simply that "democracy tends to be a less corrupt system than dictatorship."

Now let us turn to a fourth line of thought, which pursues the analysis in a bit more depth by looking at some models of redistribution under democracy. The simplest model of political redistribution under democracy is probably Becker's (1983) model of competition among interest groups. Most of the analysis there is conducted with just two homogeneous groups, s and t, that engage in political activity in order to raise the incomes of their respective members. Both groups produce political pressure, and in equilibrium, group s receives a subsidy financed by taxes on group t. The size of the tax and subsidy is determined by deadweight losses (which rise as the tax or subsidy rises) and by the fact that the "loser" in the political game (the taxed group t) need not passively accept its losses but can limit them through lobbying, threats, disobedience, migration, and other kinds of political pressure. However, no model of the political system is presented; rather, the analysis is specifically intended to apply to many different kinds of political systems, including dictatorship (p. 375).

Suppose, however, that the equilibrium described by Becker corresponds to that under democracy. How would it change if this democracy were taken over by a dictatorship? There are two main forces which would affect the outcome. The first is that the dictator has the power to repress opposition to his or her policies; the second is that the dictator is more insecure about his or her political support, because, as discussed in the previous section, among other things, the overt proffering of support from those over whom the dictator has power is necessarily less reliable than offers of support to a democratic politician. If the preferences and constellation of power relations between the two groups are unchanged (the analysis would be unchanged if many groups were assumed), the most reasonable assumption to make is that the dictator achieves power with the support of the subsidized group. The dictator, however, has the power which was unavailable to a democratic politician: to directly repress pressure by members of the taxed group by banning their political organizations, refusing to permit their views to appear in the media, refusing to allow them to meet or organize, and jailing, torturing, or even executing their leaders. In terms of Becker's analysis, the effect of political repression is the same as if the taxed group experienced a reduction in its capacity to produce pressure, as described in Becker's Proposition 1. The result is an increase in the size of the subsidy to group s and an increase in the tax on group t – that is, more redistribution than in the democratic case.

A second, widely used model of redistribution is the one developed by Meltzer and Richard (1981). In that model, the decisive voter in a democracy is the median voter, and as long as his or her income is less than the mean income, there is redistribution from the (more productive) rich to the (less productive) poor and middle-income voters. The tax rate is chosen by a "decisive voter" who, under democracy, is taken to be the median voter. The tax rate in turn determines the level of redistribution. If, on the other hand, the decisive voter were poor, he or she would choose a higher tax rate, resulting in more redistribution; but if rich, he or she would choose a lower one, resulting in less redistribution.

One problem with the model is that it simply does not allow for any mechanism by which redistribution can be effected from the poor. Thus, none of the strategies discussed in Stigler's well-known paper on Director's Law (1970) (he alleged that redistribution in a democracy was typically from both the rich and the poor to the middle classes and included such practices as tax exemptions, minimum wage laws, farm policy, regulation, licensing practices, and so on) can be introduced into the model, in which redistribution is financed by a single tax rate that applies equally to everyone. Nor can any of the practices used by dictators who have drastically redistributed from the poor to the rich be discussed within this model: practices, such as land alienation (widely practiced by colonial regimes in Africa on the endogenous black population), labor regulations (such as in the South African system of job reservation), or the ingenious schemes of Papa Doc Duvalier, who at one time "sold" workers to the neighboring Dominican Republic. So the model is not very useful for our purposes.

Nevertheless, despite these qualifications, it is simple to introduce dictatorship into the model by empowering the "decisive voter" with the capacity to repress opposition. In that case, provided only that this model permits higher taxation than is possible under democracy at any given level of productivity, the dictator would presumably repress the rich, leading again to more redistribution – in this case from the rich to the poor and the middle-income members of society.

The third widely used model of income redistribution under democratic governments is the probabilistic voting model. In simplified form (Mueller 1989), there are two candidates, each of whom maximizes expected votes. Let p_{1i} equal the probability that voter i will vote for Party 1, and consider a pure redistribution problem, one in which the government is faced simply with the problem of distributing $\$X$ among the n voters. Each party's platform is then simply a proposed allocation of the $\$X$ among the n voters. So each party maximizes

$$(2) \qquad \left[\sum_i P_{1i} = \sum_i f_i \bigl(U_i \bigl(x_{1i} - U_i (x_{2i}) \bigr) \bigr) \right] + \lambda \left[X - \sum_i x_{1i} \right].$$

Since Party 2 maximizes its expected vote total as well, the two parties propose a common platform, the equilibrium condition for which is

$$(3) \qquad f_i' U_i' = f_j' U_j'.$$

So in democratic equilibrium, each party maximizes a weighted sum of voters' utilities, in which a voter's "weight" (and therefore the sum allocated to that voter) is proportional to his or her "responsiveness" (f_i) to an increase in $U_{1i} - U_{2i}$. In a sense, then, the more "disloyal" the voter is to either party, the more that voter will receive as the result of democratic political competition.

This conclusion makes sense if voters are sensitive or responsive to changes in the utilities promised by the parties for nonpolicy reasons – that is, if a voter who is a Democrat because his or her parents were Democrats doesn't care about the policies of the democratic party, but wants to please those parents instead. Voters like that can be "exploited" by politicians, who can actually give them less than they would get if they were less loyal to the democratic party. However, if democratic voters will not easily switch to the republican side because such voters are relying on the reputation of the democratic party to take care of them by giving them a disproportionate share of the spoils, then the party which attempts this strategy of exploitation will lose its reputation. Indeed, voters who would be tempted to be loyal to a particular party will anticipate that the party will take advantage of them in this way (i.e., they will realize that loyalty does not pay and will refuse to extend it). So the political strategy unravels.

Coughlin, Mueller, and Murrell (1990) developed a model of interest group influence on democratic governments which partly solves this problem. In the model each member of an interest group has a (nonpolicy) bias b_{ij}. Thus, $b_{ij} > 0$ implies a positive bias in favor of the party on the part of the jth voter in the ith interest group. The b_{ij} are not known to the parties, but they are represented by a random variable distributed uniformly over the interval (l_i, r_i) with density a_i. Candidates are assumed to know the distribution of bias terms but not their individual values. So although each candidate cannot know with certainty how people will vote, he or she can predict that he or she will pick up a greater fraction of an interest group's vote as long as his or her platform promises more to the representative interest group member than the opponent's. Consequently, interest group influence is negatively related to the dispersion of the bias terms. In equilibrium, democratic politicians act as if they maximized a weighted sum of voters' utilities, in which the weights (f_i') are positively related to interest group influence – that is, in which they are positively related to the density (a_i) of the bias terms. In that case, a group's "weight" (capacity to receive rents) is positively related to its "influence" (number of votes it can be expected to deliver). Being known to have a certain bias is *helpful* in receiving largesse if it is also expected that there are many others with similar biases.

Now suppose that a dictator takes over this democratic polity, as before. Dictators are unlike democratic politicians in two main respects:

1. They have the power to repress opposition to their policies.
2. They do not and are not driven by competition to maximize expected "votes" (support); they are motivated by power.[9]

Consequently, the dictator makes a different calculation than the vote-maximizing democratic politician. In the post-tax and transfer distribution of income under democracy, at the margin, \$1 promised by a party to every individual raises his or her probability of voting for that party by the same amount as it does for any other recipient – that is, marginal expected support is equalized. For some, however, the absolute probability of supporting the regime still remains low. Indeed, there will be some among the recipients of largesse who actively oppose the government in power. The rents reduce their opposition to some extent, but

---

[9] More generally, the dictator maximizes utility, as discussed in Chapter 5, but the analysis here is unaffected by making this simpler assumption.

they still remain opposed after receiving them. The dictator has the option of repressing these people. If he or she represses them, his or her power increases (a) because they are silenced and (b) because the resources formerly distributed to them can now be transferred to others. Against these two sources of gain must be weighed (c) the cost of the repression itself. As long as the increase in the dictator's power from repression (plus the increased loyalty) outweighs the costs (in terms of power foregone) of the repression, his or her power is increased.

It follows that because dictators can deal with negative bias by repression, it enters their calculation directly. So there are *two* target variables of interest to the dictator – a citizen's bias (b_{ij}) and f', his or her sensitivity to a change in expected utility (where f' may depend on the density $[a_i]$ of citizens at a certain bias level, as in the Coughlin, Mueller, and Murrell model just discussed). Dictators also have two instruments at their disposal – repression and redistribution. A precise description of their optimal strategy in general is difficult. To see why, imagine that the dictator is sitting at a table and is looking at a list of the interest groups in the country. Imagine also that this list contains estimates of each group's f' and bias (b_{ij}). The dictator wants to order these groups for the purpose of deciding whom to repress and whom to buy off. The problem is that the ordering produced by the b_{ij}'s is not the same as that produced by the f_i''s. For example, some of the groups with low f''s support the dictator (positive bias), whereas others are opposed (negative bias).

One way to solve the problem – which also appears to be a reasonable strategy for the dictator to adopt – is to associate each "target" with an instrument (so repression is used to deal with negative bias, whereas rents are distributed to build support). This solution implies that those who are repressed are also subject to taxation, whereas the recipients of rents are not simultaneously repressed. Given this assumption (and with repression used against negative bias), we can see that the dictator's logic in distributing rents will be the same as that for a democratic government: The "weights" are positively related to f_i', the sensitivity of citizen i's support to an increase in the difference in utility promised to him or her by the government over that expected from the opposition (if the Coughlin-Mueller-Murrell model is used, f_i' will be related to a_i, as before).[10]

The main difference between the results under dictatorship and de-

---

[10] Of course, other factors besides those considered in this simple model might be relevant in determining the dictator's optimal choices, such as the nature of the regime's ideology or the degree of ideological "connectedness" among different groups. Axelrod (1984) finds "minimum connected winning coalition" to be superior to the minimum winning coalition concept in explaining coalition formation in democratic politics.

mocracy can then be stated simply: Under democracy, everyone – even opponents of the government – gets something in the probabilistic scheme, in which redistribution equalizes marginal expected support. The dictator, on the other hand, divides the population into two groups – those whom it is best to tax and repress, and those whom it is best to buy off. So the benefits and burdens of the public sector will be distributed more unequally under dictatorship than under democracy.

3   Redistribution in capitalist–authoritarian states

So far in this chapter, I have argued that one popular explanation for the success of many developing countries with authoritarian political systems such as South Korea or Singapore – namely, that the authoritarian governments there redistribute less or are less subject to inefficiencies caused by rent-seeking than democracies – is misguided. I have tried to show, on the contrary, that *all* dictators can be expected to redistribute more than democracies do. As far as the facts are concerned, I know of no systematic evidence on this question, but it is well known that there is massive redistribution in totalitarian dictatorships and that most left-wing dictatorships tend to be redistributive in nature. It might appear more controversial to contend that the analysis applies also to capitalist–authoritarian dictatorships, but I would not hesitate to suggest that it applies to these countries as well. The point has been missed, in my view, because of the "fallacy of the free market" – that is, the common assumption in this literature that markets operate costlessly so that to have free markets, it is only necessary for the government to get out of the way. Once the central point of the efficiency-wage literature is grasped – namely, that power relationships are central to competitive market behavior – then it is clear that how markets work depends on how property rights are specified and enforced.

Dictatorships such as that of Pinochet in Chile or South Korea under the generals essentially redistribute by altering rights in the workplace: They shift the rights of labor to a management backed by the state, they raise the cost of job loss to workers, they remove or outlaw collective bargaining rights, and in other ways they generate a labor force willing to work for low wages. Thus, in examining the success of South Korea, R. Dornbusch and Y.C. Park (1987) argued the "central point" that "Korean wages are exceptionally low by international standards, given the skill level of the labor force. . . ." (p. 391). Pinochet at first banned unions and union activity, and then he severely restricted their freedom of action with the labor code promulgated in 1979 (the first of the "Seven Modernizations"). Related reforms in health care, social security, and other areas all had the effect of raising the cost of job loss to workers.

(When democracy was restored, the area in which the government *did* make significant changes was to this labor code, and it did this shortly after it assumed office.) Other measures redistributed more directly.[11] Moreover, political measures such as the widespread planting of spies in factories and the resulting "culture of fear" (Constable and Valenzuela 1991, Chapter 6) reenforced the rights of employers over workers and linked these rights with the state. Of course, not *all* capitalists benefited; small, domestically oriented firms (part of the old, import-substitution coalition) were severely damaged by the removal of tariff and exchange-rate protection. The chief beneficiaries of the regime's policies were initially the large firms and the military.

The concentration of wealth which was produced by such policies in Chile is well known, and it is described in Oppenheim (1993, Chapter 6). Edwards and Edwards (1987) give Gini coefficients which show significantly increased inequality over the period of the dictatorship until 1983, although they do quarrel with the significance that can be attached to these numbers (pp. 167–8). However, they do not dispute the increase in unemployment over the period, and indeed they provide evidence that this occurred partly as a result of the rationing of jobs in the *grupos* (large firms).

This analysis suggests that the economic success of capitalist–authoritarian governments is not difficult to explain. It is not because they do not redistribute income, but because they *do* redistribute the capacity to earn income – in particular, by adopting measures which transfer rights over the control of labor from labor to capital. The extreme case of this type of regime is illustrated by the model of *apartheid* as a capitalist-oriented dictatorship developed in the next chapter. Of course, no institution like the pass system existed in Chile or South Korea, and no racial group was singled out for exploitation in those countries. In that sense capitalist–authoritarianism and *apartheid* are very different types of regimes. But there is also a sense in which they resemble each other: Both use the powers of the state to obtain a disciplined labor force at relatively low wages.[12]

Dictators whose support is based on capital (either domestic or inter-

---

[11] For details, see S. Edwards and Alejandra Edwards (1987), Lois Oppenheim (1993), or Pamela Constable and Arturo Valenzuela (1991).

[12] In this respect, it is worth mentioning that as of this writing (1997), nine years after the formal end of Pinochet's dictatorship and the transition to democracy, Chile still retains a "law of suspicion," one which allows police to detain people merely for appearing suspicious to them; it also has one police force (the *Carabineros*), which remains outside civilian control and which, according to Amnesty International, has been responsible for numerous violations of human rights, including torture. An attempt to reform this institution has been blocked by the Chilean Senate, which still contains numerous Pinochet appointees [*The Toronto Globe and Mail* (August 1, 1996), p. A11].

national) have an obvious reason to be future oriented, because the future returns to capital are capitalized into the price of capital, and an increased prospect of economic growth which raises those returns increases the wealth of capital owners in the present. Moreover, to the extent that these regimes successfully discipline labor and attract capital investment, the marginal product of labor is raised, possibly bringing long-run increases in real wages as well. This is a simple explanation of the economic success of these countries, but one that strikes me as superior to the idea that their success is due to an absence of redistribution. Of course, many other elements (especially their export-orientation) enter into the picture as well. But to the extent that the analysis of this chapter is correct, it raises the question of whether this kind of success is worth its price in terms of political freedom.

8   *Apartheid*

It was just too expensive.
"Pik" Botha, explaining on ABC News his
government's decision to abandon *apartheid*

1   Introduction

The system of *apartheid* in South Africa has passed into history. But
what was *apartheid*, exactly, as a political–economic system? Whose
interests did it serve, and why was it abandoned? Perhaps surprisingly,
there are no clear-cut, satisfactory answers to these questions. Moreover,
there are a number of reasons why the Apartheid Laws are of general
interest. First, they provide one of the few explicit examples of labor-
market regulations which are usually only implicit but which are generally characteristic of many dictatorships. In particular, two of the hallmarks of *apartheid* regulation – *job reservation* (in which certain kinds of
jobs were reserved for specific groups) and *influx control* (in which only
black workers with a "pass" were allowed to work in the white-
controlled manufacturing sector) – are widely, if more informally,
practiced by nondemocratic regimes, and examination of their operation
in the context of the *apartheid* system can be expected to yield insights
into how they work in general.

Second, the Apartheid Laws provide a useful illustration and testing
ground for the exploration of theories of *economic exploitation*, in which
one group uses its political power over another to appropriate its earnings. It is a commonplace that this can be done through the government's
tax and transfer system. What is striking about the *apartheid* system is
how the Apartheid Laws of job reservation and influx control were used
by whites to appropriate the earnings of blacks through the marketplace.
In that sense they provide an important, neglected, and rather subtle
illustration of how political power can be used to affect the workings of
markets.

Finally, while it is reasonably clear what group was exploited under

163

apartheid (i.e., black labor), it is much less certain who the main economic beneficiaries of this exploitation were – white labor or white capital. Exploring this issue allows us to develop general models of economic repression by labor and by capital and to ask some interesting general questions. For example, which group – capital or labor – can be expected to be more "efficient" at the economic exploitation of a minority (or majority) group? What economic conditions facilitate "successful" exploitation by either type?

A small but rich and insightful literature on the economics of *apartheid* exists, beginning with Richard Porter's seminal (1978) paper and including extensions of that model by Mats Lundahl (1982) and Ronald Findlay and Mats Lundahl (1987). Other important papers include William Kaempfer and Anton Lowenberg (1988), J. Knight and M.D. McGrath (1977), J. Knight and G. Lenta (1980), Anton Lowenberg (1989), and R.E.B. Lucas (1985). One common theme in much (but not all) of this work is that as an economic system, *apartheid* can be conceived of as a set of labor-market regulations which exploited black labor for the benefit of white labor. This economic exploitation was made possible by the political system which denied political rights to the black majority.

The truth of this view may seem obvious insofar as many of the institutions of *apartheid* – such as influx control of blacks to the white sector or the job reservation ratio (which mandated that a certain proportion of a firm's employees must be white) – appear to be nothing but restrictions on the capacity of black labor to compete with white labor. This is the typical reply of neo-classical economists (e.g. Knight and Lenta 1980; Lipton 1985) to the charge of "radical" historians (e.g., Johnstone 1976) that white capitalists were as culpable as white labor in creating and maintaining *apartheid*. What the neo-classical argument does not satisfactorily explain is why white capitalists typically supported *apartheid* until at least the late 1970s and only really began to oppose the system in the 1980s. Why would they lend their support for over thirty years to a system which forced them to buy overpriced white labor instead of cheap black labor? So one problem with the neo-classical view is that it doesn't explain the political behavior of white businesspeople and white business organizations in South Africa. Another problem is the focus, at least in the formal models of the industrial sector initiated by Porter (1978), on the job reservation ratio, to the exclusion of other, perhaps more central economic institutions of *apartheid* (such as influx control and the pass system). The literature also lends no insight into the political conflicts in the black population, which are seen as arising separately from *apartheid*. Finally, the models are either strictly economic or strictly political in character, and so they really cannot address how political changes affect the economic system.

In this chapter I try to address these issues in two ways. First, using a variant of the general model of dictatorship developed in Part II, I present a simple formal characterization of the South African polity as a racial dictatorship which exploited blacks for the benefit of white labor or white capital. This strategy makes it possible to show how political changes affect economic variables, and vice versa. It also shows what a dictatorship looks like which operates for the benefit not of a single individual, but of an economic interest group. Second, I develop an alternative model of the *apartheid* economy, focusing on the institutions of influx control and the pass law system that were more central than job reservation to the era of so-called grand *apartheid*. In this model (based on Bulow and Summers' 1986 two-sector model of labor markets), *apartheid* functioned economically as a worker discipline device, and so it benefited white capital and some elements of black labor as well as white labor. Combining this model of the economy with the model of the polity yields a novel neo-classical explanation of *apartheid* as a politico–economic institution. This provides the basis for a simple autopsy for *apartheid*.

The outline of the chapter is as follows. Section 2 develops the model of the South African polity. Section 3 shows how two central institutions of the *apartheid* economy – job reservation and the pass system – worked, and it combines this analysis with the model of the polity to show how politics and economics intertwined in *apartheid* South Africa. Section 4 shows how the operation of the system was affected by increasing black resistance, sanctions, and other variables, and why the system ultimately became unprofitable and crumbled. Section 5 concludes the chapter.

2   The polity under *apartheid*

Under the *apartheid* constitution the South African political regime was divided into two sectors – a black sector, whose members were denied political rights ("coloreds" and Asians were given limited political rights in 1985), and a white sector, whose members were free both to organize political parties and (more or less) to participate in democratic elections, and independent bureaucratic and judicial systems. However, there was severe media censorship, and beginning in 1948, politics was dominated by the Nationalist party, which was in office continuously until 1994.

A central question is the nature of the objectives of the white regime vis-à-vis the black sector. One possible objective function for the white regime was that its leaders attempted to maximize political power over the black population. This is analogous to the objective function for a totalitarian regime described in Chapter 3. The only fundamental difference between the two types of regimes would then appear to lie in the formal division of the polity in South Africa between (elected) rulers and those who were ruled – and this division was along racial lines. However, the system was unlike a totalitarian system in another crucial respect: political participation. In totalitarian systems, the population is educated, propagandized, peppered with ideology, and otherwise socialized to believe in and participate in the political system. In South Africa blacks were severely discouraged from political participation, relatively tiny amounts were spent on their education ($507 per pupil in the 1987–89 period, compared with $2,538 for whites), and the only political demand made on them was acquiescence.

There were also important conflicts within the white regime which the objective of maximizing power over blacks does not capture. White capitalists, for example, want cheap labor, but the policy of *apartheid* appeared to raise the price of labor. Moreover, accumulating power costs resources, and one would not expect the white regime to have pursued this objective at any cost.

In this chapter I will simplify drastically and assume that the objective of the white regime was to accumulate power over blacks in order to exploit them economically for the benefit of whites. Within this context I consider two possibilities. In the first, I assume the regime acted for the exclusive economic benefit of white labor. I follow Porter (1978) and Findlay and Lundahl (1987) in focusing on the job reservation ratio which mandated that employers could hire black workers in a fixed proportion only if they hired white workers as well. Thus, $C = \dfrac{N_W}{N}$ of the total labor force (N) must be white (N_W). As Findlay and Lundahl show, this policy was equivalent to granting each white worker a "license" to "import" black workers, and the white wage was a mixture of a reward for the white worker's own marginal product plus a rent equal to the difference between the black "import's" marginal product and the black wage rate. In this sense white workers exploited black workers under *apartheid*, as discussed further in Section 3A. In this model, then, I assume that the white regime maximized the profits to white workers from this exploitation.

In the second model I assume that exploitation of blacks is carried out at the margin for the benefit of white capital rather than white labor. In this analysis I focus on influx control and the pass law system, which, I suggest, benefited white capital by providing a disciplined labor force at a lower wage than would have prevailed in a free-labor market.

The objective of economic exploitation of a racial majority, in either of its variations, distinguishes the *apartheid* dictatorship from other types. I hasten to add that whereas economic exploitation of blacks was, I believe, central to *apartheid*, one need not assume that economic objectives were the sole motivation of *apartheid* policies. Furthermore, additional objectives (e.g., the utility of racial discrimination per se, as in Becker's 1971 theory of discrimination) can be introduced and their effects can be shown without greatly complicating the model.

As in the rest of this book, I will also assume that the main instruments available to the white regime for accumulating political power were repression and loyalty (or continued support). That the South African regime made extensive use of political repression against South African blacks (and against many whites and coloreds who allied themselves with black political forces) is well known. Extensive legislation – including the Suppression of Communism Act of 1950, the Riotous Assemblies Act of 1956, the General Law Amendments Acts of 1962 and 1963, and the Internal Security Act of 1976 and their amendments – gave the government, even before the implementation of the 1985 State of Emergency, extraordinary powers. According to Leonard Thompson and Andrew Prior's 1982 analysis, "[t]his mass of coercive legislation gives the government and its agents, including the police, vast powers to arrest people without trial and to hold them indefinitely in solitary confinement without revealing their identities and without granting access to anyone except government officials . . ." (p. 212).

Accordingly, they described the system as "a system of legalized tyranny comparable to that in the Soviet Union"(p. 214) and "a police state in the true sense of the phrase" (p. 217).

As widespread and systematic as repression may have been in South Africa, however, we would not expect any dictatorship to find it efficient (cost-effective) to rule by repression alone, and the white regime there did attempt to accumulate loyalty among significant groups within the nonwhite population. A particularly good discussion of policies along these lines is contained in Heribert Adam and Kogila Moodley (1986, pp. 142ff.). They suggest that three groups in particular were selected for preferential treatment: "the African bureaucratic bourgeoisie in the homelands, the colored and Indian junior partners in white control, and the permanent urban African working class with Section 10 rights"(p. 151). Thus, the relationship of the regime to the bureaucracy in the homelands was essentially a patron–client alliance, with the regime providing revenue transfers. Similarly, much of the administrative bourgeoisie of the urban community councils was "known for achieving personal enrichment through the dispensation of lucrative licenses"(p. 179). Many of these beneficiaries were commonly referred to as "stooges" of *apartheid*, and they had very little in the way of a power base among their own people. Chief Buthelezi, the leader of the Inkatha, occupied an intermediate position; he clearly did have a substantial political base among the Zulu; on the other hand, the black "homeland" of Kwazulu's "own source of revenue" was only around 18 percent of total revenue in 1981/82 (p. 89).

Another important device which was used to obtain black loyalty was direct employment. In the early 1980s 25.5 percent of the colored, 16.5 percent of the Indian, and 19.4 percent of the African employees worked directly for the state (p. 143). Adam and Moodley suggested that this "in practice removes them from active resistance" (p. 174). They added,

> [t]he Black civil servants are on the whole loyal to their employer, not only because of the security that overt loyalty promises, but also because of the status that a steady job and the authority of officialdom bestow. The harassment of Black state employees by the revolutionary forces may in fact drive the threatened dependents closer to their masters than to their opponents. After all, they have more to fear after a black takeover. (p. 174)

Given these attempts by the white regime to co-opt large sectors of the black population, it is unsurprising that there were significant conflicts and violence within the black population or that the prime targets of black political violence were often other blacks who were seen as "collaborators" with the white regime.[1] The analysis here shows that this need not be seen as the deflection of political violence away from the real enemy; it may in fact have been the most effective way to attack the power base of the white regime. In this way the large amount of black political violence which the whites deplored – and which aggravated the whites' fears about the capacity of blacks to govern – was in part the engineered outcome of white policy, which repressed most blacks and simultaneously targeted a few for co-optation (as discussed further in Section 3C).

To provide a simple formal description of the South African polity, I assume, as in previous chapters, that the relationship between the inputs of loyalty (L) and repression (R) and their output (power) can be represented by the production function

---

[1] See Adam and Moodley's (1986) discussion of the Crossroads incident (pp. 109ff.).

(1) $\pi = \pi(L, R)$.

Because *apartheid* South Africa was (more or less) democratic within the white sector, π here does not mean the same thing as π when used elsewhere in the book. In this chapter π refers to the *power of the white regime over the black population*. Similarly, R refers to the level of repression on *blacks*, and L the number of *blacks* who are loyal to the white regime. The cost of maintaining π at various levels is the regime's "*apartheid* budget" – that is, the expenditure on maintaining white power over blacks. This expenditure function may be described, as before (in Chapter 3), by the equation

(2) $B = P_L(L, R)L + \overline{P}_R R$

where P_R = the price of repression, which is assumed to be fixed at $\overline{P}_R$; B is the government's budget,[2] which is equal to its *apartheid* budget; and where P_L = the price of loyalty. I assume that

$$\frac{\partial P_L}{\partial_L} \equiv P_{LL} > 0$$

$$\frac{\partial P_L}{\partial R} \equiv P_{LR} > 0$$

$P_{LL} > 0$ if the supply of loyalty is upward-sloping and the government is a large buyer in the loyalty "market."

$P_{LR} > 0$ says that an increase in the level of repression on blacks has a cost in addition to the direct costs of repression, because it raises the price that must be paid for black loyalty, as is generally the case in tyrannies.

As in Part II (see especially Chapter 5), equations (1) and (2) may be combined into the relationship

(3) $\pi = \pi(B)$,

which shows how spending more resources on R and L yields more power. For reasons which will become apparent momentarily, we will write this relationship in inverse form, i.e.,

---

[2] In the models in this chapter, the dictator's "profits" do not come out of the government budget, but they take the form of private-sector earnings (wages or profits). Consequently, there is no variable here corresponding to the C (the dictator's consumption) in Chapter 5. In other words, C is assumed to be equal to zero. So there is no difference, in the models of this chapter, between the government's total budget and its *apartheid* budget B. Note that this assumption is made for simplicity only and to highlight the probability that a regime's rulers will receive rents in this form (private-sector earnings rather than from the government budget).

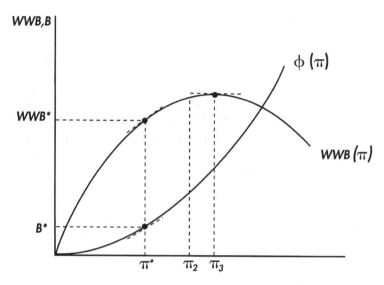

Figure 8.1. Dictatorship by labor.

(3)′ $B^{-1}(\pi) = \phi(\pi)$

where ϕ is just a function which denotes the costs (or budget B) necessary to produce and maintain each level of power π. This curve is displayed in Figure 8.1.

One difference between the *apartheid* regime and other forms of dictatorship is that the white South African regime was democratic; hence the party in power did not have the luxury of selecting levels of consumption and power to maximize utility, as in the general objective function for a dictatorship described in Chapter 5. There are several ways to model the objective function of a democratically elected political party, including expected vote maximization, median voter analysis, maximizing probability of reelection, and so on. Our concern here, as stated previously, is that the government used its power over the black population to exploit it for the benefit of whites. To sharpen the analysis, we develop two simple polar cases. In the first one, this exploitation is carried out entirely for the benefit of white labor; in the second, for white capital. The government acts merely as the agent for one of these two groups (as in the interest-group models of democracy of Becker 1983; Olson 1982; or Stigler 1970). *How* the government can use its power over blacks to increase the white wage bill or the profits of white capital is described in Section 3 on the *apartheid* economy. Here, we just assume that this is possible and develop the consequences for the *apartheid* polity.

In the first case, then, I assume the government uses its power over blacks to maximize the white wage bill, net of the costs of accumulating the power necessary to perform this exploitation. In Figure 8.1, then, the $WWB(\pi)$ curve indicates the total gross increase in white wages from this exploitation. So the $WWB(\pi)$ curve is analogous to a total revenue curve. The curve $\phi(\pi)$ shows the total *apartheid* budget needed to maintain the appropriate level of power to carry out this exploitation (i.e., it is the total cost curve).

An interesting polar case is one in which the white workers who gain from this exercise of power are required themselves to pay the taxes necessary to repress or bribe the black population to obtain its submission. In that case equilibrium is at the point where the *marginal* gain from an increase in white wages [the slope of $WWB(\pi)$] is equal to its marginal costs [the slope of $\phi(\pi)$], or at π^* in Figure 8.1. The equilibrium white wage bill is then WWB^*; total costs to maintain π at π^* are B^*. So WWB^* – B^* are the net "profits" to white workers from this redistribution.

What accounts for the difference between a regime like this and other dictatorships that we have analyzed, those in which the equilibrium is at the intersection of the *total* cost curve [$\pi(B - C)$ in Figure 5.3, which is equivalent to $\phi(\pi)$ in Figure 8.1] and benefit curve [$B(\pi)$, which is the analogue in Figure 5.3 to $WWB(\pi)$]? The difference is that when the government uses resources for purposes of redistribution to a private group and when that group pays the costs involved in effecting the redistribution, the group will of course be sensitive to those costs. For example, a redistribution which yields \$1 to white workers but which costs (and hence raises their taxes) by \$1.25 is not in their interest. On the other hand, if, as in previous models, the government were acting in the sole interests of a single dictator (i.e., it is maximizing his or her consumption or power), that government would be insensitive to marginal tax costs, as long as these costs are borne by the population, not by the dictator.

Of course, the assumption that white labor bears the entire burden of taxes to support *apartheid* is artificial and made for convenience only. It is easy to see the consequences of relaxing that assumption: If white labor were to pay one-half of these costs, equilibrium would be at the point at which marginal revenue [the slope of $WWB(\pi)$] is just one-half the slope of marginal costs [the slope of $\phi(\pi)$] – that is, at π_2 in Figure 8.1. If, at the opposite polar extreme, labor paid none of these costs but shifted all of them onto other groups, equilibrium would be at the point at which WWB is maximized (π_3 in Figure 8.1), provided that there are sufficient tax resources to support this equilibrium. This is true as long as the WWB curve cuts $\phi(\pi)$ from above, as is the case in Figure 8.1. If the WWB curve reaches its maximum beyond the point at which it cuts $\phi(\pi)$, then equilibrium is at the point of intersection of $WWB(\pi)$ and $\pi(\phi)$. This is where the white wage bill is maximized, subject to the constraint that there are sufficient tax revenues to cover the costs of obtaining the necessary power. Note that the definition of equilibrium here (where total revenues equal total costs) is exactly the same as that for an ordinary dictator (discussed in Chapter 5). This is as it should be, because that is precisely what the white labor regime would be if it could divert all of the benefits of the public sector to its own ends, while getting the rest of the population to pay the costs.

The analysis of the political sector is virtually identical if Apartheid Laws operated for the benefit of white capital rather than white labor. In this case the Apartheid Laws operate to lower black wages in the white manufacturing sector (as will be described shortly in Section 3C). The only change necessary here is that the revenue from the Apartheid Laws accrues to white capital in the form of profits rather than to white workers as increases in their wages. The curve $P(\pi)$ in Figure 8.2 shows these profits to white capital from the operation of the *apartheid* system. As before, $\phi(\pi)$ depicts the tax costs of accumulating and exercising this power. Again, there is a useful special case: where white capitalists pay all of these tax costs, in which case equilibrium is at π^* (in Figure 8.2), the point at which the marginal increase in profits to white capital is just equal to the marginal tax costs of *apartheid* enforcement. And, again, if white capitalists can divert the burden of these taxes onto other groups, the optimal level of power over the black population is larger. Finally, in the extreme case in which capital pays none of these costs, equilibrium is again at the maximum of $P(\pi)$ – that is, at π_1, if revenues there are sufficient to cover this much π – and if not, at the intersection of $P(\pi)$ and $\phi(\pi)$.

Before formally integrating this model of the polity with a model of the *apartheid* economy, let us pause to compare the two systems just described. Which system is more viable, that in which power is exercised for the benefit of capital or for the benefit of white labor? Which system tends to be more repressive?

To answer these questions, let us note first that it seems reasonable to assume that the costs of accumulating and exercising power, as summarized in the $\phi(\pi)$ curve, are the same under either system. Under job reservation the enforcement problem is to keep white employers from evading the quotas and hiring (cheaper) blacks instead of whites. Under

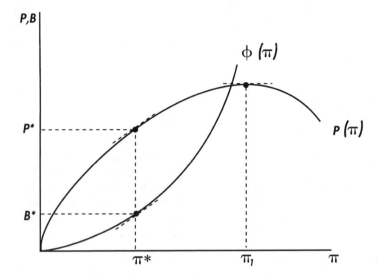

Figure 8.2. Dictatorship by capital.

the pass law system the problem is essentially the same. Indeed, the pass law system obviously is one way in which the state polices quotas on black employment by the white sector as a whole, thus controlling the entry of blacks into that sector. So as a starting point, one can postulate that the mechanisms of political domination over the black population cost the same whether they are employed by white capital or labor.

The benefit curves are not the same, however. Job reservation raises the price of labor, reducing the efficiency of firms and therefore discouraging capital investment and economic growth, on the one hand, and reducing government revenues, on the other. As we will see, the operation of the pass system *lowers* the price of labor and therefore has precisely the opposite effects, raising the return to capital, promoting economic growth, and therefore *raising* tax revenues. So at first blush, it seems that the system which favors capital is more perilous to human rights because it appears more capable of sustaining itself in the long run.

The phenomenon of "globalization" (the fall in transactions costs in international markets and the resulting increased mobility of capital) reinforces this concern, and it further suggests that labor-based regimes – in which economic and political repression is carried out for the benefit of labor – will find it increasingly difficult to survive, whereas those regimes which practice repression for the benefit of capital may have an increasingly bright future. But all of this will be better understood once we describe some of the mechanics of economic repression as used by labor and capital. This is done in Section 3.

3   The *apartheid* economy

A. Job reservation

To describe the *apartheid* economy, I first consider a special case of Porter's (1978) more general model – that is, an industrial sector only, in which, for simplicity, black labor and white labor are assumed to be equally productive, and no distinction is made between skilled and unskilled labor. Labor may be combined with white capital according to the simple well-behaved aggregate production function:

(4) $Q = f(K, N)$

where $f_K > 0$, $f_N > 0$, $f_{KN} > 0$, f_{KK}, $f_{NN} < 0$. Black labor is assumed to be available in perfectly elastic supply from the homelands at the subsistence wage rate W_B. The total supply of white labor is N_W. If the white economy and the black economy were completely segregated, so that white capital could only employ white labor, the equilibrium would be at E^S in Figure 8.3, implying a wage of W_W^S (for segregation, as in Porter 1978) for N_W workers. If the two economies were totally integrated and if the black labor supply were sufficiently large, the equilibrium would be at E^I for integration in Figure 8.3, implying a wage of W_B for both black and white workers. Because the white economy is assumed to be highly capital-intensive and the black economy labor-intensive, there are large economic gains to be realized by integrating these two economies. However, in the absence of *apartheid*-type policies, these gains (the area $A + P + V$ in Figure 8.3) would accrue entirely to white capital (in addition, the area $K + T$ would be transferred from white labor to white capital). Consequently, as Porter pointed out, if the sole aim of economic policy were to maximize total white income, all that is required is to free white capitalists to hire as much black labor as they like. No *apartheid*-style intervention would be required, but all of the gains would accrue to white capital and the white wage would fall to W_B. Such a policy would have been politically unacceptable to white labor, and a tax on white capitalists would have been required to transfer income from white capital to white labor. Such a tax, however, would have been politically infeasible.

Apartheid, seen as a set of policies which restricts the employment of

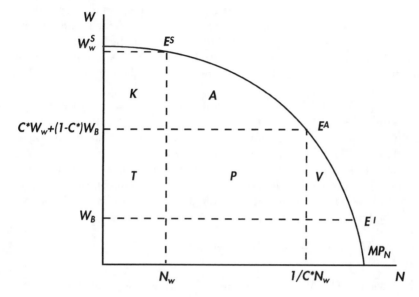

Figure 8.3. The distribution of rents under *apartheid* as job reservation (Porter). Compared with integration (E^I), white labor gains $P + T$, white capital loses $T + P + V$.

black labor, may also be seen as an (inefficient) substitute for this tax. To model these policies, Porter assumed that white labor had sufficient political power to impose a job reservation ratio: $C = \dfrac{N_W}{N}$, that is, each white employer could hire blacks only to the extent that he or she hired whites, and the proportion of whites to total employment could not fall below C.

Equilibrium under an *apartheid* regime is then at E^A in Figure 8.3, implying a total labor force of $\dfrac{1}{C}N_W$, and an average wage of $CW_W + (1 - C)W_B$.

The gain to *apartheid* (compared with segregation) is the area $A + P$ in Figure 8.3. Porter (1978) suggests that one definition (he offers four in all) of how blacks are exploited under *apartheid* is that all these gains are appropriated by whites (white capital gains $K + A$, white labor $P - K$). Alternatively, Porter compares the *apartheid* equilibrium to that under integration (E^I). In that case the only exploitation which occurs is that of white capital (which loses $T + P + V$) by white labor (which gains $P + T$).

In what follows, I will suggest that the second comparison is more appropriate, because if Apartheid Laws or their enforcement is marginally strengthened (job reservation is tightened), this implies larger gains to white labor and bigger losses for white capital. So the comparison to integration is more natural in discussing the strengthening or eroding of *apartheid*.

The equilibrium job reservation ratio is not determined in this analysis. With blacks excluded from the political process, this ratio depends on the relative political power of white labor and white capital. Findlay and Lundahl (1987), using a model similar to Porter's, described an interesting and useful special case. Suppose that white labor dominates the political process, so that the goal of the regime is to maximize the white wage bill (*WWB*). Then the equilibrium job reservation ratio C^* may be described as the solution to

$$(5) \qquad Max\ WWB = f_N N - \overline{W}_B \left(N - N_W \right),$$

which yields $f_N = W_B \left[\dfrac{1}{1-\eta} \right]$ where η is the elasticity of demand for labor. Because the black wage is fixed at W_B, and because total employment is restricted in equilibrium, the marginal product of black labor exceeds the black wage, and these gains are appropriated by white labor. If $\alpha = \dfrac{N_B}{N} = \dfrac{1-C}{C}$, as in Findlay and Lundahl, it is as if each white worker were given a license to "import" α black workers into the white industrial economy, so that white wages exceed the marginal product of white labor by

$$(6) \qquad W_W - f_N = \alpha \left(f_N - W_B \right).$$

The equilibrium white wage is then

$$(7) \qquad \hat{W}_W = \hat{f}_N + \hat{\alpha} \left(\hat{f}_N - \overline{W}_B \right).$$

In this model, then, the wage of a white worker is equal to his or her marginal product plus a multiple of the difference between a black worker's marginal productivity and that worker's wage. In this sense white workers "appropriated" the factor earnings of blacks under *apartheid*.

To integrate this model of the South African–type economy with the model of the polity elaborated in Section 2 earlier, let us begin by continuing to assume the regime acts in the interests of white workers only. However, instead of assuming that blacks have no political power, assume that by resisting or evading the regulations (in which they may be aided by white capitalists), and by other means, they can prevent white workers from imposing the monopoly level of C equal to $\hat{C}$. The equilibrium level of C then depends on the political power (π) of the white regime over black workers and hence its capacity to enforce *apartheid* – that is, $C = C(\pi)$, $C' > 0$ if $C < \hat{C}$ and $C = \hat{C}$ only if $\pi = \infty$ (i.e., in the case of "perfect" domination). A higher level of π implies a higher job reservation ratio (C) in Figure 8.3, and hence a higher white wage bill.

Now it is easy to combine the economy and the polity into a single model. For example, if white workers who benefit from the policy are also those who pay the taxes to support *apartheid*, the equilibrium level of *apartheid* (π^*) is where marginal gains equal marginal costs at π^* in Figure 8.1. The value π^* in Figure 8.1 determines the equilibrium C^* in Figure 8.3, which determines both the equilibrium size of the white wage bill, on the one hand, and the economic gains to white labor ($P + T$) and losses to white capital ($P + T + V$), on the other. Note that the equilibrium C^* is smaller than the C which maximizes the white wage bill ($\hat{C}$), because power is costly to accumulate. The fact that C and WWB are lower than that predicted by Findlay and Lundahl is of interest, but the most important aspect of the present analysis is not this point, but the fact that it permits comparative static analysis. To illustrate, let us consider the effects of an increase in black resistance.

Black resistance to white domination in South Africa grew rapidly in the late 1970s and early 1980s, resulting in the regime's declaration of the 1985 State of Emergency, and perhaps culminating in the recent liberalization of the regime. We cannot address here the important question of the sources of the increase in black resistance, but we can ask how this change affected the behavior of the white regime. This can be done with the aid of Figure 8.4.

An increase in black resistance raised the price that had to be paid for black loyalty for two reasons: First, the supply of loyalty of some blacks had presumably diminished directly. Second, to the extent that some black resistance was directed against other blacks who were seen as "collaborators" or "stooges" of the regime, blacks who were willing to supply their loyalty to the regime found this loyalty more costly than before because they were now more likely to be the victims of militant black actions. For both reasons, P_L, the price demanded for black loyalty to the white regime, increased. For any given budget, then, π would have been smaller, and the $\phi(\pi)$ curve in Figure 8.4(b) would thus shift upward, implying less π in equilibrium. The economic effects are straightforward, and they are shown in Figure 8.4(c). Because in this case the

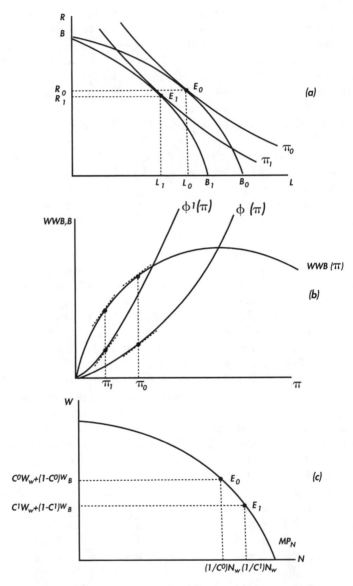

Figure 8.4. In the job reservation model, an increase in black resistance reduces job reservation and raises black employment in the white sector.

regime has less power, the job-reservation ratio (C) falls (from C^0 to C^1), as does the white wage bill. Black employment in the industrial sector rises. On almost all counts, then, black resistance benefits the black population in this model.

The political effects are shown in Figure 8.4(a) (the backward-bending L^S curve is omitted from the figure for simplicity). The rise in P_L implies an inward rotation of all budget constraints [e.g., from BB_0 to BB_1 in Figure 8.4(a)]. At the new, lower level of π (π_1 rather than π_0), L has clearly fallen. The effect on R is ambiguous – the cross-substitution effect favors an increase in R (loyalty is now a relatively more expensive instrument to produce power), but the output effect favors less unless R is an "inferior" factor of production. The latter outcome is entirely possible, because freedom tends to be income-elastic (i.e., in our terminology, less R is used as a country becomes wealthier).[3]

B. Some problems with the job reservation approach

The last section linked a simple model of the accumulation of political power with a model of how power can be used in a South African–type economy to exploit black labor for the benefit of white labor. This section suggests a number of problems with Porter's model. Section 3C suggests an alternative characterization of *apartheid* which is not vulnerable to these criticisms.

The first – and perhaps the most important – problem with this approach is that, in it, *apartheid* is represented by a single instrument [the job-reservation ratio (C)], the use of which was really limited to the early years of *apartheid*. In fact, it was never the central instrument of domination or discrimination under *apartheid*, and it was repealed altogether in the late 1970s when the general practice of *apartheid* was still very much intact. Thus, in his original formulation, Porter (1978) himself suggests that "[differential] access to education [is] the most important means of discrimination today" (p. 744). The South African economist Jill Nattrass (1981) wrote that "too much emphasis should not be put on the removal of the job reservation clauses . . . since not only did these clauses affect very few workers, but they were also never a key element in the maintenance of the dominant position of the white workers" (p. 290). Indeed, it is commonly acknowledged (see Abedian and Standish 1985, p. 141) that by the end of World War II, the South African government had largely solved the so-called poor white problem, which job reserva-

---

[3] John Bilson (1982) and Londregan and Poole (1996), for example, provide strong evidence that freedom is income-elastic.

tion was designed to ameliorate. Indeed, Lundahl's (1982) model of post–World War II *apartheid* assumed whites no longer held unskilled industrial jobs. Rather, he extended the model of *apartheid* to include the use of other instruments which were more central to *apartheid*, such as influx control. However, in these models, influx control made no *economic* sense. Thus, Lundahl concluded that "an increase in the influx (of African workers to the white economy) is beneficial for *all* white groups (p. 1177, emphasis in original), and he speculated that "it may thus very well be the case that the root cause of the segregation of blacks from whites should not be sought in economic rationality . . ." (p. 1177) but in white fears of a black political takeover.

An alternative way to think about job reservation is that although perhaps not central as a formal institution of *apartheid*, it may have been important at an informal level (e.g., through pressure on employers by white unions or by the government, as discussed extensively by Lipton 1985, p. 41; and by others). Moreover – and perhaps this is the central point – the job reservation ratio might be useful as a simple *analytic* way to represent other, historically more important techniques associated with *apartheid*, such as influx control and the pass laws, or discriminatory access to education. This representation would be useful if the economic effects of the different instruments were similar. However, in at least one important respect, they are not. Under job reservation the rents arising from restrictions on the inflow of blacks accrue to *white* workers. Indeed, as especially emphasized by Findlay and Lundahl (1987), this is how white labor exploits black labor under *apartheid*. But if the actual technique for limiting black access to jobs is either restricting black education opportunities or influx control – and if no job reservation or other form of discrimination is present – then those blacks who *do* manage to get an education and those blacks who *do* succeed in obtaining jobs in the white sector (e.g., those with Section 10 rights) should earn the same as whites! White workers may indeed gain higher wages by limiting black competition for jobs, *but there is no way that they can appropriate the rents of those blacks who do gain access to the white sector*, as they could through the job reservation technique.

Consequently, "privileged" blacks (such as those blacks with Section 10 rights), who were provided continuous access to jobs in the white sector, would have earned rents under *apartheid*. To be sure, explicit and implicit racial differences in the salary scales of private companies and government[4] were sometimes imposed, either because of a "taste" for

---

[4] See Knight and McGrath (1977) for an excellent analysis of racial wage discrimination in South Africa.

discrimination, because of pressure from white unions, or for other reasons. These differences – common until the late 1970s – ensured that black earnings were less than white earnings for the same jobs, thus limiting the size of the rents to blacks. But black rents would still have been positive as long as salaries in the white sector were greater than in the homelands, and as long as these rents were not appropriated by white labor.

The second problem with this representation of the economy results from the role of white capital. In these models *apartheid* was inimical to capitalists' interests, because they would obviously have preferred to substitute cheap black labor – available in infinitely elastic supply – for overpriced white labor. However, the assumption of an infinitely elastic supply of black labor has been challenged by Lucas (1985), whose econometric tests using data from the 1946–80 period showed that the supply of labor to gold mining, at least, was not only not infinitely elastic, but *inelastic*; and he also showed that this potential monopsony power was in fact exploited. This provides a rationale for a number of the hiring practices of the mining industry, such as the centralized system of recruiting through an employers' organization (the Chamber of Mines) and the imposition for many years of "maximum permissible average" wages (Lucas 1985, p. 1094).

Such hiring practices were long characteristic of the South African mining industry and were not necessarily central to *apartheid*. For our purposes the importance of Lucas' evidence is that if the supply of black labor is positively sloped in mining, it is probably positively sloped in other industries in the white sector as well. This fact provides a possible explanation of how *apartheid* could have served the interests of white capital as well as white labor. Such an explanation is needed because although white capitalists may not have been as strong supporters of *apartheid* as many elements of white labor (and were never in fact unanimously in favor of it), elements of *apartheid* such as influx control certainly attracted their support. As Leonard Thompson (1990) emphasizes, "[b]efore the late 1970's no powerful economic interest was fundamentally opposed to apartheid" (p. 206; see also Lipton 1985, p. 6 and Chapters 4–8). Support ultimately waned, as the economy deteriorated as a result of the influence of external sanctions, the problems and expense of administering the system, and other reasons; by the 1980s many businesses had turned against the system (Lipton 1985, p. 7; see also Lewis 1990, p. 17). But capitalists, especially Afrikaners, supported the system throughout the crucial era of so-called grand *apartheid* – the 1950s and 1960s. Moreover, as Stephen Lewis (1990) points out,

For a considerable period the Nationalist strategy of single-minded segregation, or grand apartheid . . . seemed to produce excellent economic results for its white constituents . . . the growth of real GDP was rapid by international standards averaging over 5% annually from 1950 to 1970 (pp. 15–16). . . . [Thus,] the period of most rapid economic growth, in the 1950's and 1960's coincided with the consolidation of the basic elements of the apartheid system, some of the worst political repression and an increase in white income per capita relative to black. (p. 135)

To summarize, I have identified four problems with the job reservation approach:

1. the representation of *apartheid* by a labor-market institution (the job reservation ratio), which had largely disappeared before *apartheid* began, and whose economic effects do not analytically represent those of the migrant labor/pass law system and other essential institutions of apartheid
2. the inability of the model to explain *apartheid*-induced black rents (as well as the conflicts among black groups discussed in Section 1 earlier)
3. Lucas' (1985) evidence that the supply of labor to mining is upward sloping (and even inelastic) and not infinitely elastic (as required by the Porter model), as well as his evidence that the potential for monopsony which this gave to the gold-mining cartel was in fact exploited, implying gains to capital that further contradict the model
4. the puzzling acquiescence of white capital.

C. Apartheid *as a worker discipline device*

All of the problems discussed in Section 3B can be addressed by modeling *apartheid* in a different way – specifically, by adapting the efficiency wage models of Carl Shapiro and Joseph Stiglitz (1984) or Bulow and Summers (1986). Indeed, suggestions along these lines are commonly made (but not developed) in much of the neo-classical literature on the economics of *apartheid*.[5] The idea is that from an economic viewpoint, the influx-control–pass law system was a collective means of raising the cost of job loss for each black worker, thus facilitating worker

---

[5] For example, see Knight and Lenta (1980), p. 174; Lucas (1985), p. 1096; or Lundahl (1982), p. 1178.

discipline at a lower wage than would be required if each white firm were to act individually.

To develop this point, let us consider a simple two-sector model of the labor market along the lines of Bulow and Summers (1986). Jobs in the primary sector ("good" jobs with good pay, benefits, and promotion possibilities) are costly to monitor – hence the potential for shirking there – whereas no such problem arises in the secondary sector ("bad" jobs, with none of these attributes). Equilibrium in the labor market is characterized by two conditions. First, workers in the primary sector (here called m for modern, mining, or manufacturing) are paid their marginal products:

(8) $W_m = P \cdot g(N_m),$

where P is the price of manufacturing output, W_m is the wage in the modern sector, N_m is the number of workers employed there, and g is their marginal productivity. Second, job effort in the primary sector is costly to monitor, and it is therefore always possible that some workers will shirk. Following the same logic as in our general approach to autocratic economies in Chapter 6 and illustrated in Figure 6.1, we assume that a "no-shirking condition" replaces the usual supply of labor. For workers not to shirk, the utility of shirking to a worker must be less than or equal to the expected loss from shirking. This condition, in turn, arises from the possibility of losing one's job. The no-shirking condition may be written as:

(9) $\beta \le d(PV_m - PV_h)$

where

   β = the utility to a worker from shirking
   d = the probability that a worker will be discovered (i.e., the
      level of monitoring), and
PV_m, PV_h = the present value of income earned in the primary and
      secondary sectors, respectively, which we label
      manufacturing, modern, or mining (m) and the homelands
      (h).

Thus, $PV_m - PV_h$ represents the costs of losing one's job in the manufacturing sector. Workers who shirk take the risk of losing their jobs. The right-hand side of (9), then, represents the expected cost of shirking, assuming that getting fired is the penalty if the worker is caught shirking. The main difference between this "two-sector" model and one-sector models incorporating costs of monitoring (see, e.g., Shapiro and Stiglitz 1984) is that the cost of job loss is not the possibility of becoming unemployed but of being forced to take an inferior job in the secondary sector. However, as long as (9) is satisfied, workers will not shirk, since the expected loss from doing so is greater than the gain (β).

The cost of job loss is just

$$(10) \quad PV_m - PV_h = \frac{W_m - W_h}{r + q + x}.$$

This is equivalent to the wage differential between the two sectors, $W_m - W_h$ discounted by the discount rate (r), by the rate of turnover (q) – that is, the likelihood that a worker in the primary sector will drop into the secondary sector – and by x, the likelihood that a secondary sector worker will be able to find employment in the primary sector.[6]

So (9) and (10) state that, in equilibrium, the utility of shirking to a worker in the primary sector must be less than or equal to the expected cost of job loss. The expected cost of job loss, in turn, equals the probability of being caught for shirking (d) multiplied by the difference between primary and secondary sector wages, which is discounted by the interest rate (r), the turnover rate (q), and the probability that a secondary sector worker can get a job in the primary sector (x).

It is easy to adapt this formulation in a way that shows how *apartheid* facilitates worker discipline. In the free-labor market depicted by equations (9) and (10), the opportunity cost of losing a job in the primary sector is determined by market conditions in the two sectors. *Apartheid* labor-market institutions of influx control or the pass system in effect imply collective white control over – or the attempt to control – specific variables in the no-shirking condition. For under that system, the loss of a job also implies the loss of a pass – and therefore of the right to remain in the white manufacturing sector. This gives (white) employers considerably more power over their employees than they possess in a free market. In a free market the maximum sanction available to an employer is dismissal from that *firm*. The influx-control–pass law system formally empowers the employer to dismiss an employee from the entire manufacturing *sector*, considerably raising the cost of job loss to the worker.

Of course, for this formal power to be effective, the pass law system must be enforced. Black workers clearly have an incentive to evade the

---

[6] In a free labor market,

$$x = q \frac{N_m}{N_h};$$

that is, the rate of turnover multiplied by the size of the "good jobs" sector relative to the "bad jobs" one.

regulations, as long as wages are higher in the manufacturing sector. And although the system may benefit white employers collectively, each white employer has no incentive, as far as profits are concerned, to follow the regulations. The system is not self-enforcing; rather, individually each white employer has an incentive to free ride, evade the regulations, and hire cheap black labor rather than expensive white labor. So both black workers and white capitalists will look for ways to circumvent the *apartheid* regulations. The effectiveness of the system therefore depends squarely on how rigorously it is enforced by the government.

It follows that the cost of job loss $(PV_m - PV_h)$ depends on the level of enforcement of the pass law system – and hence on the level of white power (π). We can distinguish three separate effects. First, the tighter the level of enforcement,[7] the more that workers fired for shirking are "deported" to the secondary sector (rather than being allowed to look for another job in the primary sector). Consequently, x, the probability of a dismissed worker's finding reemployment in the primary sector is not the market determined x in equation (10), but it depends instead on the level of enforcement of the pass law system and hence on the level of white power. Thus, under *apartheid*, $x = x(\pi)$, where x is the probability of a dismissed worker's evading the pass laws and being rehired in the white sector, and where $\partial x/\partial \pi < 0$. As before, π indexes the level of white power over the black population (hence the level of *apartheid* enforcement).

Second, the system of forced removals to the homelands undoubtedly lowers wages there (W_h) by increasing the supply of labor to the homeland area. In this respect *apartheid* resembles earlier measures, such as land alienation which increased the supply of cheap labor (as discussed by Lundahl 1982; and Lundahl and Ndela 1980). Again, the magnitude of this effect depends on the level of white power. Throughout the era of the Apartheid Laws, blacks attempted to evade the laws and entered the white sector illegally, locating either in the townships surrounding the white areas or living illegally in the white areas themselves. The greater the level of white power, the more whites can prevent the system from breaking down in this way. This effect (lower homeland wages W_h) also raises the cost of job loss to black workers in the manufacturing sector. That is, a lower W_h allows white capital to obtain black labor at a lower wage (W_m) in the manufacturing sector.

Finally, there is a third economic effect of the influx control system.

---

[7] Prosecutions under the pass law system varied considerably during the 1950–90 period, peaking in 1968. The Surplus People Project estimated forced removals of 3.5 million people between 1960 and 1982, a figure disputed by the government, whose own estimate was 2.1 million.

This effect arises from the fact that because workers (but not their families) were allowed into the white sector, the system either forced black workers to live away from their families or to commute many hours to work. The natural result was an increase in turnover (q) as black workers found they could only bear this for a certain period of time before ultimately quitting. So the tighter the application of the pass law system, the larger the turnover tended to be – that is, $q = q(\pi)$, $q_\pi > 0$. From (10), this effect would tend to *raise*, not lower, the manufacturing wage W_m consistent with no shirking – that is, it is *counterproductive* from the point of view of white capital. Indeed, turnover ultimately rose to very high levels, and the problems this created for business – the constant need to recruit, transport, and train huge numbers of workers – was a central element in its turning away from *apartheid* in the 1980s (Lipton 1985, p. 161), as will be discussed in more detail shortly.

In sum, influx control has three effects on the cost of black labor to white capital:

1. It reduces the probability, x, that a worker caught shirking or exhibiting other signs of disloyalty in the manufacturing sector will be able to get another job there, thus raising the cost of job loss in that sector.
2. It reduces the wages in the homeland, W_h, by increasing the supply of labor there.
3. It increases the rate of turnover, q, in the manufacturing sector, thus *reducing* the cost of job loss there.

Apartheid makes economic sense from the point of view of white capital as long as the first and second effects dominate the third.

These three effects may be incorporated into the no-shirking condition (10). They imply that each of x, q, and W_h become functions of the level of power, π, of whites over blacks:

$$(10)' \qquad \frac{W_m - W_h(\pi)}{r + q(\pi) + x(\pi)}$$

where

$$\frac{\partial W_h}{\partial \pi} < 0, \quad q_\pi > 0, \quad \text{and} \quad x_\pi < 0.$$

Equations (8), (9), and (10)$'$ now constitute a model of *apartheid* as a worker discipline device. As long as an increase in π lowers (10)$'$, it raises the cost of job loss in the manufacturing sector, implying that influx control functions successfully as a worker discipline device from the

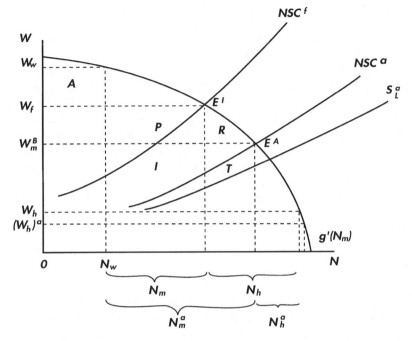

Figure 8.5. The distribution of rents under *apartheid* as "devil's bargain" between white capital, white labor, and elements of black labor. Compared with integration (E'), white labor gains A, white capital $P + R$. Black labor as a whole loses $P - T$.

point of view of white capital. Figure 8.5 shows how it works in this way, and it also displays the resulting distribution of rents. NSC^f represents the free-market/no-shirking condition which would yield a wage of W_f (equal for whites and blacks in the absence of *apartheid*, other forms of labor-market discrimination, or productivity differences). The free-market equilibrium is at E', the point at which the marginal product of labor equals the no-shirking wage. At that equilibrium, N_m black workers are employed in the "good" sector, and N_h in the homelands.

E^A is the *apartheid* equilibrium, where the marginal product of labor $[g'(N_m)]$ equals the *apartheid*-induced no-shirking condition, NSC^a. The successful operation of the pass system implies that NSC^a is below NSC^f, implying a lower level of black wages in the white manufacturing sector ($W_m^B < W_f$). Despite the lower wage, *more* blacks work in the white sector at E^A than at E' ($N_m^a > N_m$). Similarly, the wage (W_h) in the "bad" jobs sector in the homelands is lowered to (W_h)^a.

This completes the description of the black labor market under *apartheid*. These policies, by themselves, could never command the support of white labor, because they would lower white wages as well as black wages. However, the influx-control and the pass law systems are only one component of *apartheid*-style regulation of the labor market. The other is provided by a set of institutions which protect white labor: discrimination in education, job reservation, the job bar, formal and informal agreements between white employers and white unions (e.g. the quasi-legal agreements between mining corporations and white mining unions), and various other "front-of-the-line" queuing arrangements which effectively guarantee full employment to whites at artificially high wages.[8] To model these institutions in the simplest fashion possible, I assume that the support of white labor is obtained because it is treated as a separate labor force and is paid a higher wage, W_w, at which the white labor force (N_w) is fully employed:[9]

(11) $N_w \doteq \overline{N}_w$

(12) $W_w = g(\overline{N}_w)$

I also assume the total size of the manufacturing (and mining) sector is large enough to guarantee that full employment of whites does not affect marginal decisions with respect to blacks, as was true in South Africa throughout the period of grand *apartheid*.

Figure 8.5 illustrates the "devil's bargain"[10] between white capital, white labor, and some elements of black labor, which characterizes grand *apartheid*. In contrast to the integration equilibrium (E^I), capital gains $P + R - A$; white labor gains A. Black wages in both the white sector and the homelands are lower than they would be under integration ($W_m^B < W_f$), (($W_h)^a < W_h$). However, black employment in the white sector is higher. Black labor as a whole loses $P - T$ [which could be negative – i.e., a gain rather than a loss – if the demand for labor $g'(N_m)$ were elastic from E^I to E^A].

Note that this treatment of *apartheid* solves all of the difficulties that characterized the Porter model:

---

[8] See Porter (1990) for a description of the various *apartheid* constraints.

[9] An alternative way to describe the behavior of the white labor market would be to derive a white no-shirking condition, in which the probability of a dismissed white worker's being rehired in the primary sector, x, is close to 1 (because of the institutions described in the text). High wages to whites are then essential to guarantee no shirking. However, this fact would complicate the story in the text (and Figure 8.4) without materially affecting any of the conclusions drawn from it.

[10] I owe this phrase to Richard Porter.

1. At its center is the migrant-labor/pass law system central to grand *apartheid*.
2. It explains the support of white capital for the system.
3. It is consistent with an upward-sloping supply of black labor.
4. Black workers in the white sector earn rents.

The potential problems with the system – and therefore some of the reasons for its ultimate demise – are also embedded in this description, as will be demonstrated shortly.

If *apartheid* in this form were costless to implement, we could calculate the "optimal" level of *apartheid* from the point of view of white capital. This would simply put W_m as low as possible, consistent with the satisfaction of the no-shirking condition – that is, where

$$(13) \qquad \frac{\partial W_m}{\partial \pi} = \frac{\partial W_h}{\partial \pi} + \frac{\beta}{d} \left[q_\pi + x_\pi \right] = 0.$$

At the optimum in this sense, the marginal reduction in the black wage in the white sector (due to *apartheid*'s effect in reducing W_h and x) is just equal to its marginal increase (due to the effects of *apartheid* in raising q).

However, whereas *apartheid*-style regulations can be passed in a white legislature at low cost, such regulations are very costly to implement and enforce because although it may be in the *collective* interest of white capital and of loyal blacks to support the regulations politically, it is in the private interests of white capitalists as individual businessmen to evade regulations when hiring, and of black workers to evade the controls and enter the white sector illegally. To derive the optimum level from the point of view of white capital, which takes into account the costs of policing the system, we need to integrate this model of the economy with a model of the political sector developed earlier.

We first restrict our attention to the "rational" range of *apartheid* for capitalists, which is where

$$(13)' \qquad \frac{\partial W_m}{\partial \pi} = \frac{\partial W_h}{\partial \pi} + \frac{\beta}{d} \left[q_\pi + x_\pi \right] < 0.$$

In this range, an increase in π shifts the black *NSC* downward, lowering W_m and benefiting capitalists. Figure 8.5, with this property, can then be combined with Figure 8.2, which shows the optimal level of π from the viewpoint of white capital. The optimal level of power of whites over blacks determines the position of the *NSC* in Figure 8.5 (more power implying a lower *NSC*) – and hence the black wage, level of black

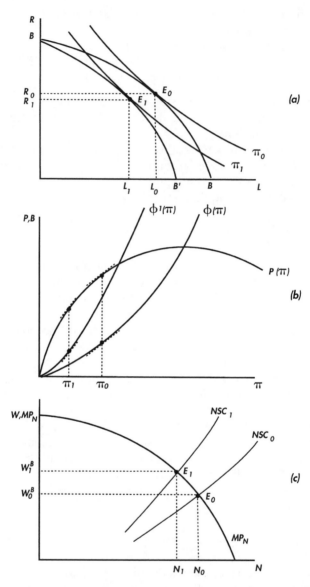

Figure 8.6. In the efficiency wage model, an increase in black resistance shifts *NSC* upward and reduces black employment in the white sector.

employment, rents to white capital, and earnings of blacks employed in the white sector. The complete model, incorporating Figures 8.2 and 8.5, and incorporating the repression–loyalty diagram from Chapter 3 or 5 (Figure 3.1 or 5.2), is shown in Figure 8.6.

4   Comparative statics and the fall of *apartheid*

A. Changes in black resistance

As we found in the analysis of job reservation, we discover that the initial effect of increased black resistance is that P_L, the price demanded for black loyalty to the white regime, will increase; π will be smaller in Figure 8.6(a), and the $\phi(\pi)$ in Figure 8.6(b) curve will shift upward, implying lower profits (P) to white capitalists. The political effects, which are shown in Figure 8.6(a), are the same as before: a fall in π and L, and an ambiguous effect on R.

The economic effects on the labor market, however, are very different. Since the regime has less power, the *NSC* curve in Figure 8.6(c) shifts upward, hence *increasing* the equilibrium black wage in the white sector from W_0^B to W_1^B, and *decreasing* black employment in that sector. So although the political effects of the two models are the same, the labor-market effects are very different. Black resistance *raises* employment of blacks in the white sector in the job reservation model, but *lowers* it in the efficiency wage model.

B. Economic variables

With the present model, we can also derive the effects that changes in the variables in the *NSC* (β, r, d, q, and x) have on all of the endogenous political and economic variables (π, R, L, N_m, and W_B^m). For example, one important factor affecting the profitability of *apartheid* for white capitalists is the level of turnover (q). The effects of an increase in q are illustrated in Figure 8.7. The *NSC* curve shifts upward for any given level of π (as depicted in the shift from NSC_0 to NSC_1 in Figure 8.7(c)), thus increasing the wage that must be paid (W_m). Consequently, the profits to capital from *apartheid* (P) shift downward, implying a lower optimal level of *apartheid* (π_1 rather than π_0) and a lower *apartheid* budget (B_1 rather than B_0) in Figure 8.7(b) – and hence lower repression and loyalty as shown in Figure 8.7(a). Finally, the fall in π implies a further upward shift in the *NSC* (to NSC_2) in Figure 8.7(c), implying, in final equilibrium, lower employment in manufacturing (N_{m_2}) and higher black wages W_{B_2}.

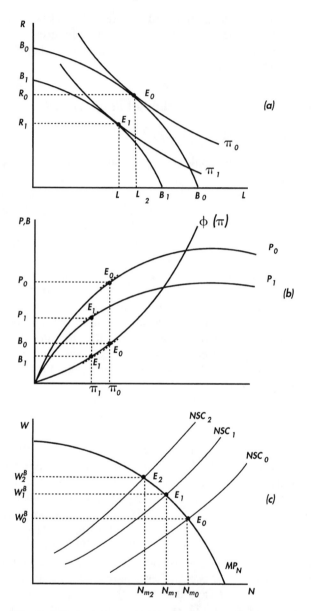

Figure 8.7. An increase in labor turnover shifts *NSC* upward, leading to the erosion of *apartheid* (fall in *B* and *P*).

The model thus predicts that higher turnover rates reduce profits; hence, they can be expected to reduce white capital's demand for *apartheid* policies. Indeed, the increase in turnover rates in South Africa in the 1970s and 1980s is often cited as one of the key elements in the erosion of *apartheid* over that period. Lipton provides some data on turnover for the mining sector. They reveal that "Absconders" – workers who broke their contracts from Chamber-affiliated mines – increased from about 10,000 annually in the early 1970s to 50,000 in 1977 (1 in 8 of the workforce) despite improvements in wages and working conditions. Other changes reduced the attractiveness of the discipline model as well. Lipton (1985) notes that "the more educated Africans entering the mines were also less amenable to the old style military discipline, barking out orders and wielding the *sjambok* (stick or whip)" (p. 131). Moreover, the great shortage of *white* skilled laborers by the late 1970s also led to an erosion of discipline among these workers. All these factors led to an increased desire on the part of business for a stable labor force in the late 1970s, as noted by many observers, including Knight and Lenta (1980, p. 174) and Lucas (1985, p. 1096).

An increase in the relative size of the white manufacturing sector $\left[\dfrac{N_m}{N_h}\right]$ has the same effects on the *NSC* as an increase in q, because the larger the relative size of the white manufacturing sector, the higher is x (the probability that a worker who loses a "good" job will be able to find another good job).[11] So the *NSC* shifts upward as $\dfrac{N_m}{N_h}$ rises, leading to a rise in the equilibrium black wage rate W_m^B. The effects on the *apartheid* system are identical to those from an increase in turnover (i.e., they lead to the erosion of *apartheid*). Employment in the manufacturing and mining sectors did increase substantially under *apartheid* until the late 1970s. Employment in manufacturing, for example, rose from 536,275 in 1951 to 1,362,079 in 1976 (Lundahl 1982). Growth was particularly rapid during the 1964–75 period (see Nattrass 1981, Table 8.1, p. 165). So the growth of the economy under *apartheid* is, oddly enough, part of the explanation for the ultimate demise of the system. A related factor is the increased size and bureaucratization of the typical South African firm in

---

[11] Recall from footnote 5 that

$$x = q\frac{N_m}{N_h}.$$

the white sector over this period (Table 8.1 in Nattrass 1981, p. 165),[12] which increased the possibilities of substituting internal promotion ladders or more comprehensive internal monitoring for the collective worker discipline device of *apartheid*. Finally, the "privatization" of the worker discipline problem was also favored by the enormous costs of policing the system as resistance mounted (including the costs of forced removals themselves) and of policing both employers and employees to ensure their adherence.[13]

C. Sanctions

The basic effect of an increase in the level of international sanctions (e.g., on exports, imports, or capital investment), which effectively denied South Africa access to international trade, was to lower the marginal revenue product of labor. This was because

1. South African labor had less capital to work with.
2. Productivity fell as imported inputs became less available than before.
3. There was a fall in the demand for South Africa's products.

The MP_N curve would shift inward in Figure 8.7(c) (not shown), thus implying a smaller manufacturing sector and fewer "good" jobs. At every level of π, profits P would be lower, leading to a lower optimal level of π (e.g., π_1 in Figure 8.7(b) rather than π_0), a lower *apartheid* budget B, and lower R and L.

The economic effects are straightforward in this case. As π falls, the NSC shifts upward, thus reinforcing the fall in the MP_N in lowering black employment in the white sector. The effect on black wages is uncertain: The fall in the MP_N tends to lower them, but the upward shift in the NSC has the opposite effect. So although black employment in the white sector necessarily falls, black wages may either rise or fall.

These conclusions differ from those obtained in the job reservation model. In that model reductions in the *apartheid* budget and in white power imply a fall in the equilibrium job reservation ratio (C) and hence an *increase* in black employment in the white sector at an unchanged black wage there. The common argument of opponents of sanctions that

---

[12] Large firms tend to have formal methods of job evaluation for setting relative pay scales. According to Lewis (1990, p. 170) the introduction of these practices in South Africa in the 1970s undermined the practice of setting wage rates based on race.

[13] Even when businessmen supported influx controls collectively, it was still in the interests of any *individual* businessman to evade the policy (as with any collective policy). This problem became so serious that in 1979 penalties on illegal workers were reinforced by heavy fines on their employers (Lipton 1985, p. 152).

they hurt black employment thus receives support from the efficiency wage model – but not from the Porter model. This result is paradoxical, because it says that sanctions hurt black employment in a model in which *apartheid* furthers the interests of white capital, not white labor, and yet the main argument usually made against sanctions was that capitalist-driven economic growth is the most effective way to get rid of *apartheid*!

The worker discipline model suggests, then, that sanctions also contributed to the decline of *apartheid*, and they worked in concert with the factors already mentioned (increased turnover, the growth of the manufacturing sector, and increased black resistance). By the late 1980s, as the costs of the system mounted and its benefits declined, business became strongly opposed to the *apartheid* system. White labor no longer needed its protection. Perhaps for these reasons, in 1991 the South African government formally abandoned *apartheid*.

5   Conclusion

In this chapter I have presented a simple model of the South African polity as a racial dictatorship, and I linked this model to two models of the *apartheid* industrial economic system. The first model expands the neo-classical view of *apartheid*, which originated in Porter's (1978) article (and which is now widely held), as essentially a system by which white labor used its political power and the disenfranchisement of the black majority to exploit black labor in the industrial sector. In the second model, *apartheid* is seen as the result of a more complex political coalition that benefited white capital and some elements of the black community as well as white labor. The two models are not necessarily mutually exclusive. If skill levels were distinguished (as they have not been in this chapter), the job reservation model might be more appropriate for unskilled labor and the worker discipline model developed here might be more appropriate for semiskilled or skilled labor. Alternatively, the models may be viewed as concerned with different institutions: The Porter model analyzes job reservation, whereas the worker discipline model analyzes influx control and the pass system. One strength of the worker discipline model is that it provides a more satisfactory economic rationale for *apartheid* because it can account for both the "successes" (for whites) of *apartheid* in the 1950s and 1960s and its decline in the 1980s (as mirrored in the initial support for and later opposition to *apartheid* by white capital). It also yields some insights into the conflicts among black groups in South Africa, on which the Porter model is silent.

Of course, which view of *apartheid* is (more) correct rests on the accuracy of its empirical implications. Although the two models yield similar predictions in many respects, they diverge crucially in others. The most important of these differences is that black resistance (or sanctions) tends to *increase* black employment in the white sector in the first model, but to *decrease* it (and to increase black wages) in the second one. Consequently, it makes a difference which model is used with respect to our understanding of how *apartheid* itself worked and how institutions such as influx control work in other societies. Most important, this choice also affects our ability to predict how the South African economy will develop without *apartheid*.

The models have other applications, because job reservation is commonly practiced in many nondemocratic countries (and in some democratic ones); so too is influx control (especially with respect to the toleration of illegal immigration; see Hillman and Weiss 1996). Finally, the models show what a dictatorship which exploits one economic group for the sole benefit of another looks like, and they suggest that this exploitation is more viable when it is done more for the sake of capital than labor.

9 The bureaucratic economy I: the model

1 The Soviet experience

This chapter and the next one are devoted to the economics of communism. In an attempt to understand how these systems work, one good place to start is with the fact that within the planning sector (comprising, for example, roughly 80 percent of the 46,000 industrial enterprises located throughout the former Soviet Union in the mid-1980s[1]), the use of money is severely circumscribed. Thus, "in the Soviet banking system the absolute order to pay is unknown; payments from any account are made only if in agreement with the applicable rules and authorizations."[2] Similarly, in China prior to 1979, only currency in circulation was considered by the authorities to be money, and monetary policy consisted primarily of regulating the amount of currency in circulation. Individual households could hold savings and time deposits in banks, but not checkable deposits. The "transfer balances" of government agencies and enterprises were transferable only with explicit hierarchical approval. Before giving approval, the banks in each case had to ensure both that the transaction had received prior authorization by the proper authorities in accordance with the economic plan and that all papers relating to the transaction were in order (see Cheng 1987 for details).

Consequently, a distinction became popular between "active money" and "passive money" (Wiles 1962). Passive money (the transfer balances of enterprises) may be a decision-making criterion for the planners but not for the enterprises. As Grossman (1966) defines the distinction, it "hinges on whether magnitudes expressed in monetary terms directly influence economic decisions or whether such magnitudes are employed for controlling compliance with directives only. The spheres of circulation of the two kinds of money correspond respectively to the domains of

---

[1] See Paul Joskow, Richard Schmalansee, and Natalia Tsukanova (1994) for details on Soviet industrial structure.
[2] George Garvy, "The Role of the State Bank in Soviet Planning," in J. Degras and A. Nove (eds.), *Soviet Planning: Essays in Honor of Naum Jasny*, Blackwell: Oxford, 1964. Cited in Gregory Grossman (1966), p. 214.

the market mechanism and the command principle" (p. 216). To under-stand the distinction, consider the case (discussed by Kroll 1987) of a Soviet firm which sued another firm in court for nondelivery of input. The firm won its suit, but it never bothered to pick up the money! What value would it have? The firm could not spend the money without the prior authorization of the authorities for spending it that way. If it had been capable of receiving that authorization, the authorities would also have been willing to provide the money balances. As Grossman explains it precisely, money in the production sector of the Soviet economy was *rendered* passive in order not to challenge the regime's political authority (1966, p. 234). Alternatively and most simply, the planning sector may simply be thought of as *demonetized*.

Of course, consumers used money to some extent, but as is well known, markets did not clear in the former Soviet Union. Rather, the distribution system was characterized by pervasive shortages. Indeed, a fundamental characteristic of the Soviet-style economy was the extent and persistence of shortages throughout the system. There has been much speculation and theorizing about the causes of these shortages in the former Soviet Union, most famously by Janos Kornai both in his 1980 book and in his latest (1992) comprehensive treatise on Communist economics. Kornai explained shortages with his concept of a "soft budget constraint" – the fact that the state will make up for the losses of as well as extract the profits from the enterprise. Consequently, there is no economic limitation on a firm's demands for inputs – it can always get the money to pay for them. So firms always want more inputs than are available. Undoubtedly, this is an important part of the explanation. However, this still does not explain shortages in consumer markets, which were equally legendary in the former Soviet Union. So one central question for any theory of the system is this one: How can the prevalence and persistence of shortages be explained?

Another characteristic feature of Soviet-style systems is the explicit *political control and direction* of the growth process. Growth was organized in five-year plans. The society was explicitly "mobilized" for growth, which was extensively promoted by "tasks" and "campaigns." A third feature, partially related to the second, was the institution known as the Party *Purge*. At periodic intervals, the suitability of large numbers of individuals for membership in the Party and participation in its decision making was explicitly called into question. Often, a number of individu-als' memberships were not renewed. Sometimes, much more dramatic steps were taken, as in the famous great purges of the Soviet Party under Stalin in the 1930s or in the Anti-Rightist Movement and the Cultural Revolution in China under Mao. But lesser purges – which could simply take the form of a general calling in of Party cards, a number of which were then not sent back – were a regular feature of the system.

A fourth feature, and a most important contemporary issue, is the dynamics of the *reform* of such systems. From its inception the former Soviet Union was characterized by the periodic introduction of important and fundamental changes in the production system. There was the early period of "War Communism," followed by the New Economic Policy, the Stalin industrialization drive, the Khruschev reforms, and finally the period of Perestroika and Glasnost under Gorbachev, which ended by virtue of the fact that it reformed the system out of existence. The Chinese system was subject to a dramatic reform beginning in 1978, and it has been steadily evolving on a more gradual and experimental basis ever since. One important issue to which a good deal of attention has been paid is the spectacular success of the Chinese reforms, on the one hand, and the failure of reforms which appeared very similar in a number of respects under Gorbachev in the former Soviet Union, on the other. Is this difference due to the adoption of a "gradualist" policy in China compared with the "big bang" approach adopted in the former Soviet Union and Eastern Europe, as some (e.g., Jefferson and Rawski, 1994; McMillan and Naughton 1992) contend? Or is it due to the fact that China maintained political repression while the Soviet Union relaxed it, as others (Murphy, Shleifer, and Vishny, 1992; Sachs and Woo, 1994) suggest?

A fifth feature is the peculiar pattern of Soviet growth. The best Western scholarship on Soviet affairs – including the pathbreaking and important work on the Soviet economy by noted specialists such as Abram Bergson (e.g., 1978, 1987) and Raymond Powell (1968), followed by Gur Ofer (1987) and others – all painted an impressive picture of Soviet growth from the 1920s to at least the 1960s. It is worth briefly reviewing the evidence on the growth rate of the GNP and on the growth of factor productivity to see the solid grounds on which this belief was based. Once this is understood, the question becomes not one of the perpetual flaws in the Soviet system but why it could not continue to replicate its early success.

Consider first of all the evidence on the growth of Soviet GNP. As late as 1987 Ofer estimated the annual average growth rate of GNP during the fifty-seven years from 1928 to 1985 to be 4.2 percent per year. Comparing this experience with that of other countries, he declared Soviet performance to be "among the best for such an extended period" (1987, p. 1777). GNP per capita grew over the same period at the rate of 3.1 percent. During the postwar period (1950–80) GNP per capita in the Soviet Union grew at a 3.3 percent rate, but compare this to the

1.9 percent rate for the United States (Table 2, p. 1780). Ofer also points out that most other Western estimates were close enough to these figures.

On the growth of factor productivity, Abram Bergson (1978) summarized his findings as of 1978:

> Soviet Net National Product per unit of factor input grew over the period 1928–1958 by 1.4 to 1.9 percent yearly, with output valued at base-year prices, and by 3.5 to 4.1 percent yearly, with output valued at given-year prices. The United States during 1929–1957 must have nearly matched the foregoing Soviet performance with valuation for both countries in base-year prices. With valuation for both countries in given-year prices, the USSR must have appreciably surpassed us. (p. 144)

He then compares Soviet growth during the 1928–58 period with U.S. growth from 1869 to 1908 (i.e., at a time when the United States was at a comparable state of development). He says, "Consider now the period 1869–78 to 1899–1908 in the United States. With output in both countries valued in base-year prices, we should have at least matched the Soviet 1928–1958 rate. With output in both countries in given-year prices, the Russians during 1928–1958 may possibly have outdistanced us" (p. 144).

For the postwar period – from 1955 to 1970 – Bergson estimated average annual rate of growth of Real National Income per employed worker in the USSR at 4.2 percent. The corresponding figure for the United States is 2.1 percent (p. 153).[3] Martin Weitzman (1983) looks at the growth of Soviet *industrial* output for the 1950–78 period using a synthetic series constructed by the Office of Economic Research of the CIA. The average annual rate of growth over that period is 7.4 percent, which, he concludes, is "more than respectable by world standards"

---

[3] Bergson (1987) compares the absolute level of productivity in 1975 in several Eastern Bloc countries with that of several highly developed countries in the West, and he finds a considerable shortfall (25%–34%), which he attributes to the differences in economic systems. However, the richest Eastern Bloc countries (East Germany and Czechoslovakia) were excluded from the comparison. In addition, a major difference in technique in the 1987 book distinguished it from the previous work: Rather than comparing countries at similar levels of development or using the share of the labor force in agriculture to adjust for this fact, he adjusted for the level of development using capital per worker. Because capital accumulation was very rapid in the USSR (see, e.g., Easterly and Fischer 1994) and because misallocation of capital is probably more characteristic of Soviet-type economies, using this measure probably overstates the level of development of Soviet-type economies at that time relative to Western ones. It is also well known that the huge Soviet investment in agriculture did not pay off. (One reason for this failure, I would argue, is the historical exploitation of – rather than the development of trust links with – the Soviet peasantry.)

(p. 81). A similar conclusion is reached for the growth of labor productivity in industry.

So in the late 1970s and even into the 1980s, the Soviet system did not appear at all like the bumbling behemoth it had apparently become by the late 1980s. Indeed, in 1988, Edward Hewett (1988) suggested that "the Soviet economic system 'works' reasonably well by world standards and has done so for over half a century" (p. 158). Earlier, of course, the scare caused by the USSR's apparent achievements was much more vivid. Barrington Moore, Jr. (1950), described the Soviet system as "an organizational weapon"; Grossman (1966) described the Soviet system as the "union of a particular authoritarian ideology and the logic of hasty industrialization" (p. 228). Peter Rutland (1985) approvingly quotes John Fischer's (1947) description of the Communist party as "the most efficient machine ever devised for the governing of men" (Rutland, p. 174). One lesson of all this, as if the reader needs any reminding, is that statistics should be handled with care, especially statistics that emanate from dictatorships. That this lesson has not been learned is amply shown by the fact that contemporary observers treat the figures on Chinese growth with the same respect as figures from other, more reliable sources.[4]

Of course, considerable revision of the statistics on Soviet economic performance is now under way on the basis of new evidence emanating from the now mostly democratic Republics of the former Soviet Union (see, e.g., the evidence discussed in Easterly and Fischer 1994). But although the new evidence will undoubtedly lower the estimates of growth, it is doubtful that the progress of the system at least up to the 1960s will ever be able to be dismissed.[5]

Moreover, there are two more positive lessons that emerge from these studies. One is the widely accepted proposition that growth in the USSR was peculiar because it was almost all extensive growth (i.e., it was almost completely accounted for by growth in factor inputs – mainly capital accumulation). This fact suggests that there was little or no technological progress under the system. Thus, according to Ofer (1987), "During the entire period but more so with time, Soviet growth is generated by high rises in inputs and declining growth of overall input produc-

---

[4] Alwyn Young's (1996) careful analysis does suggest that Chinese growth rates have been considerably overstated.

[5] Official statistics provided either by the Soviet Union or by the CIA are estimates not of growth rates but of levels of national income. Therefore, it is not sufficient to dismiss these statistics simply as the biased products of Cold War mentality (on both sides). The constant upward bias in the figures does not change estimates of growth *rates*; the bias would have to be increasing every year in order to do this. This point is made by William Nordhaus (1990).

tivity. . . . During the entire period 1928–1985 inputs grew at 3.2 percent and contributed 76% of the total GNP growth while factor productivity grew 1.1% a year, accounting for only 24% of total growth" (p. 1782). G.B. Powell (1986) in a much earlier study estimated that capital accumulation in the USSR had averaged 16.5 percent a year for thirty-eight years, and he concluded that "More than half and perhaps upwards of three-quarters of Soviet growth has been achieved by the essentially mechanical and ruthless process of forcing out of the economy ever-greater supplies of productive resources" (p. 23).

These figures show a systematic difference between the pattern of growth in the Soviet Union, which is based almost entirely on growth in factor inputs, and growth in the United States and other Western democracies, in which most of the growth is growth in factor productivity and is attributed to technological progress. However, Alwyn Young (1992, 1995) and others (Krugman 1994 provides additional references to this work) present surprising evidence that documents a pattern in the growth of the East Asian NICs that is similar to that of the former Soviet Union! The extraordinary growth in those countries is also due to their capacity to mobilize resources for the accumulation of capital and for the reallocation of inputs from less productive to more productive uses. Once these sources of growth are removed, the growth rates of total factor productivity in these countries appear, on this analysis, to be entirely "normal" – that is, well within the range experienced by other Western countries.

The second point about Soviet growth on which all the main analysts seem to agree is that it has declined over time. Ofer (1987) shows Soviet growth rates declining from 4.7 percent during the 1950–80 period, to 4.2 percent during the 1960–80 period, and to 3.1 percent during the 1970–80 period. By comparison the United States grew at 3.3 percent per year from 1950 to 1980 and at 3 percent from 1970 to 1980 (p. 1780).

Soviet growth continued to decline, and by the late 1980s it appeared to many to have largely stopped. According to Ofer, "The relative contribution of inputs to growth grew to 80% in the post-war period and became its sole component from 1970 on, when productivity completely stagnated or even retreated" (loc. cit.). Easterly and Fischer (1994) attempt to explain the decline. The general story they tell is one of limits to extensive growth aggravated in the USSR by the low elasticity of substitution between capital and labor. The basic question which remains in this framework seems to be whether it is negative total factor productivity growth or falling returns to capital which explain the dramatic decline in performance after 1970. But a more basic question is this one: What feature of the Soviet growth process is it that limited extensive growth? Easterly and Fischer speculate that it was due to the fact that the Soviets accumulated a narrow (rather than a broad) range of capital goods – for example, no marketing skills, entrepreneurship, distribution, or information-intensive physical capital. Ofer points out that one reason for the low elasticity has to be that research and development in such a society doesn't work properly to make capital a better substitute for labor.

The more general problem with approaches like these is that they do not explain very much. The growth accounting approach is useful in isolating the sources of growth or decline, and the general story that it tells about the pattern of growth in Soviet and other authoritarian societies (which are based on extensive growth of inputs rather than technological progress) is an important contribution. But it is limited. Although not inherently unmeasurable, many "inputs" to the growth process – most important, the pattern of political decision making, the nature of property rights and their evolution, and changes in organizational structure – are hard to quantify, and they do not make any appearance in the growth accounting framework. They are buried, along with technological progress, in the "residual."

Turning to the various approaches to the economy of autocracy which were reviewed in Chapter 6, we see that the command model can easily explain the ultimate collapse of the Soviet Union; but taken literally, this model implies that the Soviet Union should have collapsed much earlier! That is, it cannot explain the pattern of above-average growth which persisted from the 1920s right through to the 1950s. Similar problems bedevil the "shadow" economy approach as a general explanation of the workings of the system. The kleptocracy model is accurate in pointing to the enormous redistributive impact of Communist economics. However, the redistribution seems to have been a fairly broad one, which is not what the kleptocracy model is about. On the other hand, if, as is postulated in the model, the kleptocrats were "really" simply the ruler and his cronies (the Party elite), what allowed the Soviet regime to survive so much longer than other kleptocracies? What was the source of its undoubted ideological appeal? And after the revolution, why have (reformed!) Communist parties been returned to power everywhere in Eastern Europe? Are their members reformed kleptocrats? If so, how do kleptocrats reform, and how do they do so with such credibility that their former victims choose to vote for them and their party in a reasonably free election? And why would those who were presumably the most victimized (the older generation) be their strongest supporters?

So each of these explanations appears flawed as a general account of the workings of Communist economics. Nevertheless, each contains important insights. A good theory would incorporate them and also explain all the facts about the system discussed in this section. In Sections 2 and 3, I approach these issues with a model which assumes front and center that there is a logic to Communist economics, a logic which is basically similar to that of any bureaucratic organization. The purpose of demonetizing the production system was to make it possible to politicize the economy. Given political control of the economy, the system, like any bureaucracy, does not run primarily by command but through exchange. The difference between it and a market economy is that exchanges under communism are supported by Party loyalty rather than by law-based property rights and money. However, the system contained a central flaw that ultimately destroyed it – namely, the tendency for relations of loyalty of the "wrong" or "unproductive" sort to ultimately clog the system and undermine control from the top. Section 2 describes the working of the system in both its productive and unproductive phases. Section 3 shows how each of these phases can be generated from a single model of the Communist system.

2   Rents, shortages, and bribes

In Chapter 6 I suggested one simple explanation for shortages and rents in the former Soviet Union – namely, that they were an excellent device for building Party loyalty. By creating shortages the Party created a difference between the value of the goods, services, jobs, apartments, and so on (which were distributed) and the official price charged for such goods and services. Because the demand for these goods and services exceeded the supply, the Party could extract a political price on top of their money price. One way it did this, for example was by giving out the rationed goods and services in return for investments in loyalty by the recipient, a system which was described in our basic model of autocratic economics outlined in Chapter 6. As suggested there and as depicted in Figure 6.1 (or in Figure 8.5 on the *apartheid* system), shortages and rationing of jobs in the labor market implied a wage premium that could be used to deter "cheating." Cheating included shirking, lack of discipline, disloyalty, drunkenness, or any other form of behavior disapproved of by the Party. Other features of the Soviet system, such as "tasks" and "campaigns" (analyzed by Ferrero 1994) served the function of "screening" applicants. Those who demonstrated the most loyalty – for example, through productive effort – were entitled to a premium. This premium was exactly analogous to the market premiums that were analyzed in the reputation models discussed in Chapters 2 and 3; it

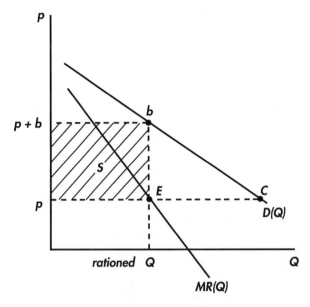

Figure 9.1. Rents and shortages in Soviet industry.

cements loyalty provided the present value of the premium stream is larger than the potential gains from "cheating" the Party.

The same model can be used to explain shortages of consumer goods, as depicted in Figure 9.1. Because the good (Q in Figure 9.1) is rationed, its marginal value ($p + b$) exceeds its official price (p). Those who actually obtain the good at its official price earn rents equal to the shaded area S. By creating these shortages and then distributing goods in exchange for loyalty to the regime, the government creates a powerful economic lever which can be used to enforce compliance with its goals.

So this model explains how an autocrat might rationally create shortages of jobs or of goods and services. But another explanation of shortages, one put forth by Andrei Shleifer and Robert Vishny (1992), interprets shortages as a symptom of precisely the opposite phenomenon – a lack of central control. In their model, shortages are created by enterprise managers in order to collect bribes from customers. Shleifer and Vishny assume that the bureaucrats in the supervising ministry and the managers collude to maximize their "take" at the expense of both their customers and the state treasury (p. 239). In our terms this assumption is equivalent to the idea that the government's mechanisms of control over officials in the supervising ministry and the enterprise have broken down. Free from any hierarchical constraint, the ministry and enterprise can pursue a different objective. So this model also illustrates the power of the regime to affect the workings of markets; only here it illustrates the power of the bureaucracy instead of the dictator. The model provides a particularly useful way to think about Soviet enterprise in its final, degenerate phase, when the political apparatus had largely lost control of the bureaucracy. The rest of this section describes the Shleifer–Vishny model. Section 3 shows how these two alternative visions of the Soviet system can be combined into a single model.

In the Shleifer–Vishny model, prices of goods are set centrally, so the colluding enterprise manager and ministry do not control the official price at which products can be sold. They can, however, control the quantity sold at that price. In Figure 9.1 (adapted from Shleifer and Vishny 1992, Figure 3, p. 243), the official price is given by p. The value of the good to consumers is given by the $D(Q)$ curve, which is equivalent to an ordinary demand curve. Shleifer and Vishny assume that the industry acts as a monopoly, so $MR(Q)$ is the monopolist's (i.e., the colluding officials and managers of the state enterprise who are acting as a single entity) marginal revenue curve. The peculiar nature of the state firm under these conditions is the cost curve. To see the central point, assume that the firm has a soft budget constraint. It effectively need not worry about its costs of inputs, which are paid for by the state. Nor is it concerned with its profits, because all profit is turned over to the state and all losses are made up for by the state. Under these assumptions, from the point of view of the firm manager who wants to maximize personal income, *the firm's costs are in fact its official revenues!* Why? If the firm charges a bribe which is the difference between the value of the good to consumers and its official price $[D(Q) - p]$, the total amount of bribes collected is the area S (for surplus), and the total price of the good is equal to its official price plus the bribe $(p + b)$. The barrier to collecting more in bribes, apart from the constraint of the demand curve $D(Q)$, is thus the firm's price p. This is because whatever the firm receives in official revenues (pQ) belongs to the state and not to the officials in the firm – and it is therefore a *cost* to the firm's manager because it diminishes the total amount of bribes that could be collected. So the total costs to the firm are its total revenues. Similarly, the marginal cost of production to the firm is p, the official price of its output. Therefore, the firm maximizes profits (bribes collected) by setting marginal revenue equal to marginal cost (or p), as depicted by point E in Figure 9.1.

A special case of the model is one in which the firm is free to set its price as well as its output level. In that case the firm will set a price of zero, and it will simply produce the revenue-maximizing output level (where marginal revenue equals zero). Output expands to the point at which the marginal revenue curve cuts the horizontal axis and at which the bribe price is the full value of $D(Q)$ above this point.

The model is not just a theory of the Soviet firm; it can also be applied to any manager of a public enterprise – and indeed to managers of private firms as well. The model is relevant to their behavior if

1. individual managers have some freedom to set the quantity of output that the firm produces
2. at the margin, bribes are worth more to these managers than the official revenues of the firm
3. monitoring is sufficiently lax that they can get away with taking a bribe.

These three conditions imply that even a manager of a private firm, one which is not 100 percent owner-controlled, for example, will be tempted to create a shortage and collect a bribe. Indeed, if managers of private enterprises are less closely monitored than those in public ones, it might appear that private managers would be more likely, *ceteris paribus,* to engage in bribe-taking. However, to a private firm, there is an additional cost in collecting a bribe. This cost is the possible effect of this action on bankruptcy. This cost is obviously smaller, the "softer" the budget constraint. Budget constraints are typically softest in socialist enterprises and hardest in purely private enterprises. So this fourth condition – (4) the budget constraint is soft – implies that the model applies more closely to socialist enterprises than to public enterprises, as well as more closely to public enterprises than to private ones.

One way to extend the theory would be to apply it to the theory of regulation. I will only sketch this possibility here. Presumably, regulators of firms are also interested in collecting bribes, and they are capable of collecting them under the corrupt circumstances described by Shleifer and Vishny (i.e., perfect collusion between the manager and his supervisors). The difference is that regulators can collect bribes by granting *exemptions* from regulations, not by producing more of them. The same logic that suggests that producers of goods and services will create shortages in order to extract bribes implies that "producers" of regulations will produce *surpluses* – that is, *overregulation*. The reason is simply that the larger the "quantity" of regulations, the greater the value of the bribe which can be extracted in exchange for exemptions from them.

In summary, this section has looked at two alternative models of shortages. In the first, the government created shortages of jobs or goods and distributed them in exchange for political loyalty. In the second, shortages were created by enterprise managers in order to collect bribes. Both models illustrate the power of autocratic governments to affect the working of the economy; in the first model, they behaved this way to further the ends of the political leadership; in the second, to further the aims of the bureaucracy. Section 3, which follows, uses bureaucratic theory to determine which of these outcomes occurs.

3   The Soviet system as a bureaucracy

A. *The general approach*

The peculiar feature of the Soviet system (compared with other totalitarian societies) is that production in it was organized within a single bureaucracy. This organization was to a considerable extent driven by the ideology of communism, which dictated the abolition of private property. Without capitalists or their agents to manage enterprises, some other institution had to be found to perform this task, and the solution chosen was the system of central planning, meaning, in practice, management by a giant bureaucracy under the control of the Party. Joskow, Schmalansee, and Tsukanova (1994) speculate that the origins of the system are also to be found in a conception of the optimal structure of the production system that is modeled on the early Ford factories of the 1920s. The most important requisites for growth and efficiency were, at that time, conceived to be economies of scale and specialization. Accordingly, the industrial organization of the USSR was modeled on the principle of "gigantism" to take advantage of this conception. By the same token, the firms in the USSR were unusual because they were monopolies – again, presumably on the notion that this was the most efficient way to organize production.

It follows that one way to understand how the Soviet system worked is to use bureaucratic theory. But there are many models of bureaucracy. In economic theory one example is the model of William Niskanen (1971), which stresses the incentive for bureaus to maximize the size of the budget under their control. However, this model is best thought of as a special case, as discussed elsewhere.[6] In sociology and organization theory, stress is often put on the importance of the bureaucracy's formal structure, along the classical lines invented by Max Weber.[7] Indeed, the "command" model commonly used by economists is just a variant of the

---

[6] For more details on this and other economic approaches to bureaucratic behavior, see my recent (1997) survey of economic models of bureaucracy.

[7] Organization theory and sociological models of bureaucracy are discussed in Wintrobe (1982).

Weberian model of bureaucracy. The sway which Weberian thinking still holds may also be illustrated by the fact that the preeminent historian of the Soviet Communist party in the West, Leonard Schapiro, found it necessary to reject the bureaucratic model as applying to the Soviet Union, on the grounds that the system was clearly *not* a bureaucracy in Weber's sense. Schapiro (1971) stated, "In place of officials with clearly-defined and enforceable rights [and duties] within the hierarchy, office is dependent on favour, in place of competence and efficiency, the prime qualification for office becomes loyalty. Never, at any stage in Soviet history, have these distinctive features been absent from the party machine" (p. 623).

However, as I have discussed in many other works (e.g., Breton and Wintrobe 1982; Mckee and Wintrobe 1993; Wintrobe 1982; Wintrobe 1997; Wintrobe and Breton 1986), few bureaucracies behave the way the Weberian model predicts. Private enterprises, state enterprises, political parties, unions, and governments are all bureaucracies that can be better understood by using the concepts of exchange and competition rather than of command. Like other forms of nonmarket exchange, bureaucratic exchange is based not on legally enforceable property rights but on networks or loyalty. So the observation that the Soviet system depended on loyalty rather than rigid Weberian rules does not mean that it was not bureaucratic; quite the contrary. Few bureaucracies work by command or rigid rules. Section 3B, which follows, shows why.

B. Networks

The importance of exchange within bureaucracy derives from the fact that rules and regulations which can be formally or contractually specified are inherently rigid, so that a bureaucracy which actually operated according to its formal structure would be extremely inefficient. The goals of superiors would be drowned in red tape, "control loss," administrative overload, inflexibility, and so forth. Because formal rules and authority are limited, there are always numerous ways in which subordinates (S) could be induced to perform their tasks with greater efficiency (e.g., knowing that they would be rewarded for doing so). Thus, a subordinate S could offer extra effort – more accurate information, more inventiveness at getting the job done, and so on. S's superior, B (for boss), typically also has many things to offer in exchange – more rapid promotion, bigger bonuses, a larger budget, travel privileges, and so on. Such trades between S and B may increase organizational productivity, in which case they are *efficient* trades – that is, they raise organizational productivity. Alternatively, subordinates may attempt to collude to obtain resources by deception (information distortion), trickery (e.g., agenda manipulation), sabotage – or through formal collective actions such as strikes or slowdowns. This class of behavior was studied by Niskanen (1971) and in other models which emphasize the pathology or the inefficiency of organizational behavior. In these latter cases the agreements or trades are obviously *inefficient* from the organization's point of view.

Whether the agreements are efficient or inefficient, they are not contractually enforceable, so either party faces the prospect that the other could cheat or renege on his or her (possibly implicit) obligations; hence, the demand for some guarantee that the parties be repaid. Albert Breton and Ronald Wintrobe (1982) posited that *trust* or organizational *networks* are capital assets accumulated by subordinates with each other (as well as by subordinates and superiors) to fill this gap and allow exchange. He and I suggested that this asset may be accumulated by forgoing opportunities to cheat – hence, making an investment in the future relationship. Salmon (1988) described an alternative process based on conjectures and refutations.

The next step is to derive a link between the level of these investments and organizational productivity. Breton and Wintrobe (1982; see also Wintrobe and Breton 1986) assumed that superior–subordinate ("vertical") trust links tend to enhance productivity, whereas subordinate–subordinate ("horizontal") links tended to diminish it. This assumption permitted the development of a number of comparative static implications. It may be difficult to measure trust, but one can derive a theoretical link between various aspects of organizational *structure* (e.g., levels of turnover, monitoring, "perks," supply of promotions, and so on) and productivity if these variables can be shown to affect the incentives to accumulate vertical and horizontal trust in plausible ways. For example, an increase in promotion possibilities increases vertical and decreases horizontal trust. An increase in demand for the organization's output increases the supply of promotions within the organization; hence, the model predicts a positive relationship, *ceteris paribus*, between demand and productivity. So this model provides a simple explanation for the well-known procyclical behavior of productivity.

Some evidence of the existence and importance of bureaucratic networks was provided by McKee and Wintrobe (1993) in support of "Parkinson's Law" – that is, the observation that the administrative component of an organization (A) sometimes expands at the same time as the organization itself is contracting and as its direct labor force (L) is declining. The law is a simple implication of the existence of vertical networks, combined with the assumption that the organization is sufficiently large so that cuts in personnel are made according to formal criteria such as seniority. Thus, when the organization declines, subordinates who are in vertical networks with their superiors will demand protection from dismissal. This "protection" can be provided only by promoting them to a rank (e.g., administrators) from which they can't be dismissed. Because subordinates demand this protection and because superiors want to provide it (to protect both the capital value of their networks and their reputations for rewarding loyalty), the result is an increase in A at the same time as L declines. McKee and Wintrobe (1993) tested both the law and this explanation of it on two rather different sets of organizations – the U.S. steel industry and the Canadian school system. They found that the law held in both cases, and in one case (the steel industry), they were able to show that the decline in L and the increase in A were *strictly contemporaneous* – an implication of the Breton–Wintrobe version of Parkinson's Law, not of other possible versions related to budget maximization.

In the former Soviet Union, for example, one institution which facilitated the development of trust links among officials was the *nomenklatura*. This is the name originally invented to describe the "lists" of Party members considered reliable enough and fit enough to fill the positions in every walk of life controlled by the Party: government officials, managers in industry and commerce, publishers, army officers, judges, union leaders, headmasters, and so on. The name eventually expanded to describe all those who had access to the special privileges available in the Soviet system, such as special hospitals, special shops in which foreign goods could be bought, apartments, and so on. The *nomenklatura* trade favors among one another, and to the extent that the group formed a closed clique, many of the exchanges among them should be classified as corrupt or "inefficient" exchanges.

C. Competition

The other principle emphasized in the Breton–Wintrobe model is bureaucratic competition, the most neglected aspect of bureaucratic behavior in command models of bureaucracy. In general, competition within any bureaucracy takes several forms. There is competition between bureaus for resources as well as competition among bureaucrats for jobs and for membership in bureaucratic networks. Much of this competition is likely to take the form of coming up with new ideas, new initiatives, new policies or projects, or what is sometimes called Schumpeterian competition or entrepreneurship.

To see the importance of competition within the bureaucracy, we will consider the Shleifer–Vishny analysis of bribes once again. Recall that in their model, enterprise managers and bureaucrats in the supervising ministry collude to maximize bribe collection. Implicitly, the model also assumes that bureaucrats and managers do not compete with each other (otherwise, the rents received through bribes would be bid down). Yet this assumption hardly describes the Soviet production system, which was for much of its history (as described in the next chapter) the locus of fierce competition for plum managerial posts and for the special privileges that went with them, including access to special shops and to special schools and hospitals, travel privileges, the right to a car and chauffeur, and so on. A Soviet manager faced competition for his or her job, not only from underlings, but also from managers in other enterprises. It follows that even in cases in which monitoring of managers broke down and in which there was collusion between the minister and the enterprise manager, as assumed by Shleifer and Vishny, this is insufficient to demonstrate that managers there received rents at the expense of the Party. The Shleifer–Vishny equilibrium for the Soviet industry, in which the manager received all the rents, represents a special case not only in which these two conditions hold but also in which it is necessary to postulate that enterprise managers did not compete among themselves but colluded in some fashion. In other words they made agreements with each other, based on horizontal networks.

D. A simple formal model

To describe the Soviet-style production system formally in terms of this model, we will let T_V denote vertical or Party networks and T_H represent horizontal networks that, on balance, reduced productivity. The collusion among managers which lies behind the Shleifer–Vishny model is then simply an illustration of a particular use of horizontal networks to obtain non–Party sanctioned goals (bribes in this case). Assume further that there are diminishing marginal productivity gains to vertical trust and increasing marginal productivity damages to horizontal trust (see Wintrobe and Breton 1986). This last assumption implies that firms and other organizations have an inherent tendency to decline, as suggested by writers as diverse as Marshall (1961, with respect to firms), Robert Michels (1959, with respect to political parties – the so-called Iron Law of Oligarchy), and, more recently, Mancur Olson (1982, with respect to nation states). The reason for this decline is that as an organization ages, its members come to know each other better, and therefore both T_V and T_H continue to rise (where T_V and T_H are the aggregate quantities of vertical and horizontal trust, respectively). As T_V and T_H

continue to rise, diminishing returns to T_V eventually set in; so too do increasing damages from T_H. Eventually, the loss in output from the change in T_H outweighs the gain from T_V.

This completes the theory of the relationship between trust-and productivity. Productivity tends to be positively related to T_V and negatively related to T_H. The growth rate of productivity tends to be related to the growth rates of these variables (positively related to T_V and negatively related to T_H), but it will also be related to their *levels*, because a high level of T_V and a low level of T_H tend to permit a relatively rapid accumulation of conventional inputs such as physical and human capital. It also permits more rapid technical change. For example, the higher the amount of T_V, the greater the willingness of employees to absorb changes in machinery and methods for using it. The smaller the amount of T_H, the smaller their capacity to disrupt or block them if they choose to do so.

It follows that an organization's rate of growth of output will tend to be higher as vertical trust is higher and lower as horizontal trust is higher, as in

(1) $\dot{Q} = Q\big(T_V, T_H\big)$

where $\dot{Q}$ is the rate of growth of output of the firm, and $\partial\dot{Q}/\partial T_V > 0$, $\partial\dot{Q}/\partial T_H < 0$. The levels of T_V and T_H, in turn, tend to be related to various characteristics of organizational structure: organizations can encourage subordinates to invest in more vertical and less horizontal trust by

1. providing bonuses, perquisites, and opportunities for rapid advancement within the organization.
2. monitoring or policing or otherwise (e.g., by transfers or reorganization) discouraging horizontal associations (collusion) among subordinates.

We would also expect political dictatorships to use these instruments. In addition political dictatorships possess a larger variety of sanctions to deal with horizontal associations, and they are of course much less restricted in their capacity to use them. Finally, the destruction of alternative opportunities for advancement in competing organizations, which is characteristic of one-party states, is obviously a powerful weapon that encourages subordinates to further their careers by investing in loyalty to the regime.[8]

Applying this theory of bureaucratic production to the former Soviet Union is straightforward: If T_V is high and T_H is low, exchanges within the

---

[8] For further discussion of this model of bureaucracy, extensions and some evidence of it, as well as of alternative approaches to modeling bureaucracy, see Wintrobe (1997).

enterprise and the ministry are primarily based on vertical trust (or loyalty to the Party), the system tends to operate relatively efficiently, and its rate of growth, *ceteris paribus*, will be relatively high. If T_H is high, exchanges tend to be inefficient or corrupt, as in the Shleifer–Vishny model, and growth is accordingly low. The command model applies when there is little trust of either kind within the system. In that case efficiency – and the rate of growth of output – presumably lies in between the two cases just mentioned.

These considerations also reveal the basic contradiction of Communist rule. The ideological basis of communism is solidarity. In order to promote that solidarity, markets and private ownership are suppressed. But in order to make the system work, it has to function as a bureaucracy that is under political control. But in any bureaucratic system, vertical control is paramount, and solidarity among the work force interrupts this control and lowers output or productivity. This result is especially likely when the whole society is organized as a single bureaucratic system, such as in the former Soviet Union and other Communist countries. The more the system operated as any bureaucracy must, the more the contradiction between its reality and its promises, as embedded in its ideology, became apparent.

We can complete the theory of the Soviet production system by introducing these ideas into our general model of the relationship between power and economic growth, as outlined in Chapter 5. For this purpose it seems reasonable to assume that the greater the power (π) of the Party, the greater its capacity to discourage horizontal associations and to reward vertical trust through the use of bonuses and monitoring, as just described. So $T_V = T_V(\pi), \partial T_V/\partial \pi > 0$, and $T_H = T_H(\pi), \partial T_H/\partial \pi < 0$, implying simply that, for the classic Soviet system

$$(2) \qquad \dot{Q} = \dot{Q}(\pi)$$

where

$$\partial \dot{Q}/\partial \pi > 0$$

as depicted in Figure 9.2.[9]

Equation (2) is simply a variation on the general model developed in Chapter 5 (with the government budget B replaced by economic growth $\dot{Q}$). Recall from our discussion in that chapter that a relationship like (2)

---

[9] Note that equation (2) can also be derived from Figure 6.1 of Chapter 6, in which an increase in the power of the Party shifts the no-cheating condition (*NCC*) downward, as the Party's capacity to monitor and sanction cheating within firms is presumably related to its power (π). A similar relationship was posited for the *apartheid* regime in the preceding chapter (see Figure 8.5).

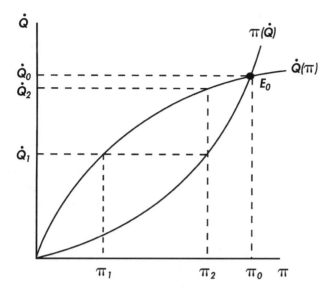

Figure 9.2. Equilibrium growth and power in the classic Soviet system.

describes a system in which, as in the former Soviet case, the vast majority of production was organized through a plan. In a system like the
current Chinese system, which combines both plan and market, it is easy
to imagine that this relationship could be reversed. When the government is the sole producer of goods and services, an increase in the power
of the government implies that the government is more capable of making its wishes effective on the bureaucracy. If part of production is
organized through markets, then it is easily possible that an increase in
government power can *reduce* the rate of growth of aggregate output.
This can happen either if there is an overregulation of the market sector
or if the increase in government power causes a substitution of plan for
market and the market is more productive than the plan. So the upward
slope of the $\dot{Q}(\pi)$ curve only pertains to a system in which, effectively, all
production is organized through the government bureaucracy, as in the
classic Soviet system. That this relationship can be reversed in a system
that is partially based on markets is of considerable importance, as
we shall see in the next chapter when we turn to our discussion of
the reforms of the system. But first, let us turn briefly to the other
relationship in Figure 9.2, the $\pi(\dot{Q})$ curve.

The upward slope of the curve $\pi(\dot{Q})$ may be derived along the same
lines as those discussed in Chapter 5. First, increased economic growth

obviously raises the government budget B. The larger the government's budget, the more that can be spent on either repression (R) or loyalty (L) to increase π (as also described there). Second, increased economic growth may be expected to increase the level of loyalty to the system. This result lowers the price of loyalty (P_L) and raises the level of π which can be purchased with any given budget B. Both effects therefore imply

(3) $\pi = \pi(\dot{Q})$,

with $\partial \pi / \partial \dot{Q} > 0$. Once again, it seems reasonable to suppose that both curves display diminishing returns (as shown in Figure 9.2). Equilibrium is at E_0, with economic growth $\dot{Q}_0$ and power π_0. That E_0 is an equilibrium can be demonstrated with an argument like the one used in Chapter 5. Thus, at a lower level of π (e.g., π_1), economic growth is $\dot{Q}_1$. But $\dot{Q}_1$ yields a higher level of power (π_2), which in turn yields more growth ($\dot{Q}_2$), and so on until E_0 is approached. Similarly, any point to the right of E_0 (implying higher levels of π and Q than π_0 and Q_0) is unsustainable (there is not enough growth to generate the power needed to sustain that growth), and the system returns to E_0.

The complete model of the Soviet system is easily summarized. The power of the Party determines the balance between Party networks and non-Party networks (vertical versus horizontal trust) in the system. This, in turn, determines the extent to which a typical firm behaves according to the loyalty model or the bribes model – and therefore the rate of growth of the system's output. On the other hand, how much power the Party has itself depends on the rate of growth of output [as described by the $\pi(\dot{Q})$ curve in Figure 9.2]. So $\dot{Q}$ and π are simultaneously determined.

In the next chapter we will put some flesh on this abstract model by using it to explain the classic features of Communist party organization: central control, the prohibition against factions, exclusive membership, and the Party purge. I also use the model there in an effort to understand a number of events in Soviet and contemporary Chinese history.

4   Conclusion

The approach to the Communist economic system taken here is based on the notion that what distinguishes this system is the replacement of money and monetary incentives (as a means of allocating resources) by a single bureaucratic system under the control of the Communist party. This idea is not uncommon in the literature. What distinguishes this approach from others is the conception or model of bureaucracy used here. The most common approach in the literature is the central planning or command economy model, in which orders are given from the top and filter down to the bottom, where instructions are carried out. This model easily explains why the system collapsed, since any bureaucracy which operated in this way would obviously be drowned in red tape, would lack information and incentives to innovate, and so on. What it cannot explain is why the system did not collapse much earlier but managed to survive for more than sixty years and to prosper for a good part of that time. The same problem bedevils other points of view, such as the rent-seeking model or the Shleifer–Vishny model. These models prove useful in trying to understand the operation of the system in its final or degenerate phase. They cannot explain the appeal of the system in many parts of the world in its first fifty years or so of operation – or just what it was about it that so frightened the citizens of democratic countries for so long.

In this chapter I have suggested that the classic Soviet system, like any bureaucracy, did not run primarily on orders or commands but on exchange. The basic difference between a bureaucratic and a market system is that exchanges within bureaucracy are based not on laws but on trust or loyalty. Under communism, loyalty to the Party combined with the Party's capacity to repress opposition became the source of its power. Consequently, when the Party was strong, either because it was ruthless in its use of repression or because it was believed to be capable of fulfilling its promises, the system was capable of good economic performance. The fundamental prediction of this model is therefore that in a Soviet-style system, there is a positive correlation between the power of the Party and measures of economic performance such as economic growth.

The basic problems with such a system as an *economic* system lie in the conditions for running any large bureaucracy efficiently; bureaucracies require vertical or hierarchical loyalty and not horizontal solidarity among co-workers, which can be used to escape Party control and therefore tend to lower productivity. In turn, this implies that there is a fundamental contradiction between the promises of communism – essentially, equality and solidarity – and efficiency. As we will see in the next chapter, over time, this contradiction became more and more apparent, and the system could only maintain itself, Stalin-style, through the use of the purge and other techniques for breaking up the horizontal networks and other nonsanctioned alliances which tended to grow up within it. The next chapter also describes the period of Soviet decline after Stalin's death, Gorbachev's attempts at reform, and how and why the Chinese were able to reform this system successfully while the Soviets could not.

10 The bureaucratic economy II: rise and fall

1   The working of the system

We will now apply the model of the preceding chapter. The basic conception of the way the classic Soviet system is intended to work that will be
advanced here is that the entire Soviet system of production may be
likened to a giant bureaucracy. Within this bureaucracy the Communist
party serves a function which is analogous to private property rights in a
capitalist economy (insofar as it enforces trades). When the system functions as it is supposed to, subordinates within it compete with each other
to advance the goals of their superiors by showing initiative, enterprise,
dedication, and flexibility, just as they do within any successful large firm,
government bureau, or other form of bureaucratic organization. Successful performance (not obedience to orders) is rewarded with (exchanged
for) bonuses, more rapid promotion, and so forth, all of which are
ultimately under the control of the Party in the classic Soviet system. The
Party leadership sets the goals of the system, and through its vertical
network, it "enforces" trades which advance those goals. In this sense,
commentators such as Alec Nove (1964) are correct in saying that "it is,
most of all, the *Party* which, by its decisions at all levels, replaces the
operation of economic forces" (p. 61). But they are, in our way of
thinking, wrong to conclude that this primacy of political decision is
necessarily "inconsistent with economic rationality" (p. 62). The political
articulation of economic goals and the replacement of economic by
political forces through the mechanism of Party control is the basic
modus operandi of the system. Within this framework, this or that decision may surely be irrational or inconsistent with the leaders' goals, but
to criticize the *system* on this ground is to miss its basic logic. Property
rights are not free. Spending resources to maintain political networks in
the Soviet-style system – trust-based property rights – is, in principle, no
more irrational than spending resources on the courts and on the enforcement of laws which maintain exclusivity of ownership in a capitalist
economy. It is possible that trust- or loyalty-based property rights are

218

less efficient than law-based property rights. But first we have to understand how they worked. This is the task of Section 1, which describes the workings of the system, its central dilemma, and Stalin's solution to that dilemma (the Party purge). Section 2 describes the decline of the system between Stalin's death and the era of Brezhnev. Section 3 describes the attempts to resuscitate the system in the Soviet Union and China, and that section explains why the Chinese attempt succeeded while the Soviet one failed.

A. The Communist party as an enforcement mechanism

How does the Communist party operate as a vertical network? As discussed briefly in Chapter 2, it has three basic features:

1. exclusive membership
2. centralized control and internal discipline (the prohibition against "factions" and other horizontal associations)
3. an exclusive ideology.

We explain the role of each of these in turn.

i. Exclusive membership. Although any political party may be fruitfully viewed as a trust network in some respects (this view is developed in Galeotti and Breton 1986), certain features of the Communist party of the former Soviet Union (henceforth, CPSU) make this interpretation especially useful. Foremost among them is the fact that unlike membership requirements in democratic political parties, membership in the CPSU has always been an exclusive privilege (see Friedrich and Brzezinski 1965). The principle dated from Lenin (Schapiro 1971, p. 50). Under the last set of rules (in the 1980s), for example, membership required that the individual "works actively for the construction of communism, works inside one of the Party organizations, carries out the decisions of the Party, and pays his dues" (Schapiro 1978, p. 70). New members had to pass through a probationary stage of one year. A candidate had to be recommended by three CPSU members of not less than five years' standing, who knew the candidate and his or her work for at least a year, and the admission of the candidate required the approval both of the primary meeting and of the appropriate city or district CPSU organization (Schapiro 1978, p. 71).

Exclusivity of membership makes expulsion possible, and the threat of expulsion, whether on an individual or a mass (the Party purge) basis, was obviously a powerful weapon in the hands of the leadership to encourage loyalty. Again, the principle dated from Lenin, who in 1921 demanded a widespread purge of the "rascals, bureaucrats, dishonest or wavering communists, and of Mensheviks who have repainted their facade but who have remained Mensheviks at heart" (V.I. Lenin, quoted in Hough and Fainsod 1979, pp. 323–4).

Making political opposition by communists inside the CPSU the subject of an open *criminal* charge (punishable by death) was, of course, Stalin's invention (Schapiro 1971, p. 406). Though their violence diminished, Party purges continued as long as the system survived. More than 500,000 members were expelled between 1951 and 1956, more than 400,000 between 1956 and 1964. A calling-in of Party cards was ordered by the CPSU in 1971, and 347,000 were not renewed as a result of this operation (Schaprio 1978, p. 71).

The principle of exclusivity, the demand for participation on the part of members, and the use of expulsion all imply that the CPSU was a trust network in the classic sense of that term. What about its "vertical" character? That is established next.

ii. Central control and internal discipline. The principle of central control and internal discipline was the cardinal one in the Leninist theory of organization, and perhaps it was his most important departure from Marx. Lenin understood the logic of collective action not from the point of view of an economic theorist but from that of a revolutionary actor:

> The committee should lead all aspects of the local movement and direct all local institutions, forces and resources . . . Discussion of all party questions, of course, will also take place in the local circles, but *the deciding of all questions of the local movement should be done only by the committee.* The independence of local groups will be permitted only in questions of the technique of transmitting and distributing. The composition of the local group should be determined by the committee which designates delegates to such-and-such a district and entrusts these delegates with setting up a district group, *all the members of which must in turn be confirmed in their positions by the committee.* The district group is a local branch of the committee which receives its powers only from the latter. (Wolfe 1969, p. 171, emphasis added)

These principles remained a feature of Soviet political organization up to its collapse. Thus, the Party organizations of the union republics were in no sense national parties but branches of the all-union party, and they were subject to central discipline and direction like any other subordinate party organization. Decisions of the higher organs of the Party were unconditionally binding on lower organs. All factions and groups within the CPSU were officially prohibited in the Party's statutes. The prohibition against factions, the vertical control of appointments, and the vertical control over resources were ways of ensuring that vertical network links, not horizontal ones, predominated throughout the system. In simple terms they increased the attractiveness of investments in vertical as opposed to horizontal trust.

iii. An exclusive ideology. It is a commonplace that ideology played a very important role in the former Soviet Union. Just what that role was, however, is very difficult to determine. Concepts such as "brainwashing" are not easy to fit into the theory of rational choice. Friedrich and Brzezinski (1965, p. 22) list "an elaborate ideology, one that consists of an official body of doctrine covering all vital aspects of man's existence ..." as the first in their six characteristics of totalitarian government, yet the role that ideology plays in the model is not at all clear. On their view the population does not believe in the ideology. Indeed, one of their central propositions is that a vacuum increasingly surrounds the leadership because the monopolistic control of the media creates in the general public a profound distrust of what it is told. But if the ideology is not believed, what purpose does it serve? We have already mentioned (in Chapter 3, Section 3) the basic and important notion that ideology serves as a set of promises, which codify the goals of the regime and against which performance could conceivably be measured. Ideology also promotes exchange in the same way that commercial advertising does – through repetition. The more the message is repeated, the greater the "stake" the state has in fulfilling the promises implied by it. Consequently, when the performance of the system declined in the 1970s and 1980s, and the gap between promises and reality widened steadily, the regime was stuck. As Gianfranco Poggi (1990) nicely put it, "the promises had been made for too long to be believed, and for too long to be surrendered" (pp. 168–9).

Other aspects of ideology are less easy to explain. To illustrate the magnitude of the problem, let us listen to Milovan Djilas, the former vice president of Yugoslavia, speaking in a radio interview before his fall from power:

> Can there be any greater honour and happiness than to feel that one's closest and most beloved friend is Stalin? ... Stalin is the bitterest enemy of all that is inhumane, he is deeply concerned, he is the wisest person, he nurtures human kindness ... Stalin is the only statesman with a pure conscience and an unselfish heart. Stalin is Marxism–Leninism revitalized and enriched. He

is a man who never wavers, a man before whose eyes are unrav-
elled future events, entire centuries . . . He knows all and sees
everything; nothing human is alien to him . . . There are no rid-
dles in the world Stalin cannot solve. . . . Stalin – he is an epoch,
the most crucial epoch in the history of mankind . . . (Milovan
Djilas, in Urban 1982, p. 214)

The interviewer then inquired whether Djilas really believed this at the
time, seeing that some twenty years later he wrote that Stalin was "the
greatest criminal of all time, 'for in him was joined the criminal senseless-
ness of Caligula with the refinement of a Borgia and the brutality of Czar
Ivan the Terrible' . . ." (loc. cit.). Djilas replied that, broadly speaking, he
did believe it, but he qualified this by saying that one had to conceive "of
this praise at a higher level of political consciousness" (p. 215).

What does that mean? Perhaps the role of ideology may be clarified
with the aid of our conception of the CPSU as a vertical trading network.
For one thing, network links are easier to establish – and the transactions
costs of trade are reduced – when members of a network or potential
network share a common language, ethnicity, kinship, or other trait. In
the terminology of Breton and Wintrobe (1982), such traits are called
"indicators." These indicators make the signals and responses which are
part of the process of trust formation more precise, thus reducing the
cost of communication and therefore of forming trust. Ideology is clearly
an indicator of this type. Moreover, in the former Soviet Union, in China,
and in similar types of societies, ideology has the special property that it
is controlled from the center, hence Gianluigi Galeotti's (1987) useful
definition of ideology as a "set of opinions controlled by a party apparatus" (p. 125). From these two points, the importance of obedience to the
"party line" is immediately apparent: dissidence threatens exchanges –
and therefore the efficiency of the system – in the same way that crime
threatens property rights and efficiency in a capitalist economy.

Changes in the content of ideology therefore play a role analogous to
prices in a market system in communicating information, because they
signal the direction which investments in loyalty should take. When the
ideology of equality was de-emphasized by the CPSU in the course of
industrialization in the 1930s and replaced by the encouragement of
inequality that was accompanied by "a multiplication of ranks, titles,
uniforms, and other visible accouterments of status" (Bialer 1980, pp.
23–4), it was plain that different types of behavior were henceforth to be
rewarded by the state. Similarly, when Stalin began the deification of
Lenin in the 1920s, this was a prelude to the later deification of himself

and a fundamental part of his takeover of the CPSU. The object of loyalty was henceforth to be not the Bolshevik party, nor the ideology of Marxism–Leninism, but Stalin himself.

Ideology is, finally, a way of framing the goals and actions of the state in order to build support for them. It is a form of what Milan Kundera (1995) calls "lyrical" talk. He explains the peculiar conjunction of terror and lyricism under Communist rule in his native Czechoslovakia this way:

> After 1948, through the years of Communist revolution in my native country, I saw the eminent role played by lyrical blindness in a time of terror, which for me was the period when "the poet reigned along with the executioner . . ." [quoted from his novel *Life Is Elsewhere* (1986)]. I would think about Mayakovsky then; his genius was as indispensable to the Russian revolution as Dzherzhinsky's police. Lyricism, lyricization, lyrical talk, lyrical enthusiasm are an integrating part of what is called the totalitarian world; *that world is not the gulag as such; it's a gulag that has poems plastering its outside walls and people dancing before them.* (1995, p. 157, emphasis added)

B. Competition

Although most existing models of the Soviet system form one variant or another of the directed society paradigm, it has not been uncommon among scholars to take note of a great deal of competition within the Soviet state. According to Barrington Moore (1950), "the spurs and checks found in a capitalist democracy which are largely the product of the division of authority and economic competition are replaced in the Soviet system by pitting the various sections of the bureaucracy against one another" (p. 286).

Similarly, the former dean of American Sovietologists, Merle Fainsod (1967), wrote:

> By pitting the competitive hierarchies of administration, Party, and secret police against each other at lower levels of the government structure, the leadership frees itself from exclusive dependence on any single channel of fact gathering and encourages rivalries among the various agencies to correct distortion and prevent concealment. In this fashion, it mobilizes the cumulative resources which competition sometimes generates. (p. 341)

This system of overlapping multiple control – of "checks and balances," one might say – was one of the basic features of Soviet organization. Like other features we have examined, it also dates from Lenin (Moore 1950, p. 170). In its final form it implied that a factory director, say, is responsible not only to his or her ministry but also to the regional party (*Oblast*); this regional party was charged with responsibility for everything in its area, including industrial undertakings, but it also answered to the primary Party organization – the Party unit within the factory itself – which was charged with the duty of exercising control over the enterprise in which it was formed (Schapiro 1978, p. 68). A similar system of multiple control existed in the various government offices (see Moore 1950, pp. 289–90; Hough 1977, p. 65).

So the Soviet state may have been a "directed society," but the directions came from many directions at once. The various agencies tried to form "protective alliances" (horizontal networks) in response to this competition. The Party officially discouraged this, branding it as the sin of "familyness" (Moore 1950, pp. 290–1). Thus, instead of the single chain of command which the command model would have predicted, at least four separate hierarchies with (to a greater or lesser degree) overlapping responsibilities can be distinguished:

1. the economic hierarchy
2. the Soviets
3. the Party
4. the Party control commission.

Another important form of competition in the Soviet system was what was often called "centralized pluralism," the "fierce competition" (Hough 1977, p. 84) among ministries for resources from the center. This competition was exactly analogous to competition among bureaus for resources within any bureaucracy, such as those in the U.S. or Canadian federal governments or in any private business firm. This process, in which bureaus competed by inventing new projects and policies, resembles nothing more than a process of Schumpeterian competition or entrepreneurship. A more common view is that the ministries acted like interest groups, pressing for the allocation of scarce funds to projects originating within their individual ministries. A similar form of competition prevailed among the *Oblasts* (regions) and *Obkom* (districts).

As long as this competition was conducted within the framework of loyalty-based property rights established by the CPSU, it was reasonable to assume (see Wintrobe and Breton 1986 for justification) that this competition was efficient in meeting the goals of the Soviet leadership. I suggest that it was this system – competition based on vertical loyalty – which essentially characterized the Soviet system of production when it functioned well, and that it was the efficiency of such a system which up to the 1970s accounted for the strength of Soviet economic performance. The system, however, had one central flaw. That is examined in Section C, which follows.

C. The central dilemma

The central problem of any bureaucratic system, as pointed out in the summary of the theory in the preceding chapter, is that over time, horizontal trust (as well as vertical trust) tends to accumulate and the accumulation of horizontal trust is ultimately very damaging to the efficiency of the system from the point of view of its leaders. We would predict that this problem was particularly acute in the Soviet system, with its intertwining of the Communist party and the state, as well as the consequent absence of an institutionalized takeover mechanism (such as general elections in politics or hostile takeovers in business) or any other mechanism which could "shake up" the loyalties which tend to accumulate within such a system. Consequently, the only weapon available for this purpose was the purge. The most infamous example of the use of this technique in Soviet history is, of course, the Great Purge of the Party launched by Stalin in the late 1930s. The purge was undertaken *after* the decision to industrialize, the introduction of five-year plans, and the liquidation of the kulaks. It is the momentous events of this period for which Stalin is widely "credited" for fully turning the USSR into a command economy. This is odd, for as we shall contend in this section, the experience of the USSR in its most "authoritarian" or "totalitarian" period shows precisely the opposite conclusion: the importance of competition and loyalty.

First of all, the bureaucracy under Stalin was competitively organized. Bialer (1980) writes,

> The proper picture [of the Stalinist bureaucracy] would encompass a number of major and lesser bureaucracies encroaching on each other's territory, fighting for their share of the bureaucratic empire, and duplicating each other's efforts. If the Party apparatus was empowered to organize and supervise political indoctrination, it competed not only with the military's separate political department [which, although formerly a branch of the Party bureaucracy, was certainly run for the most part independently under Mekhlis and Shcherbakov] . . . It also competed with the

police and even the ministry of railroads. The prerogatives of the planners were constantly challenged by the ambitions of the police [authorities] to expand their own economic empire. The rights of local Party secretaries to control local Party enterprises were effectively countered by the managers' recourse to the influence of their respective ministries. The extent of the control by industrial ministries over their key enterprises was undermined in turn by the rights and actions of the Party's central committee organizers . . . and so on. (pp. 16–17)

This picture of interagency competition applies as well to the Great Purge, as discussed in Chapter 3. The extent of Stalin's attack on the CPSU in the 1936–38 period was enormous. Out of the 139 full and candidate members of the central committee elected in 1934, at least 98 were arrested and shot. Of the total of 1,961 voting and nonvoting delegates to the seventeenth Party Congress, no fewer than 1,108 – or more than half – were arrested on charges of counterrevolutionary crimes. The turnover of CPSU and Soviet officials during the main years of Stalin's campaign against the CPSU (1937–38) can probably be reckoned in the hundreds of thousands (Schapiro 1971, pp. 420–1).

Many explanations have been offered for the Great Purge. Without dwelling on them, there is one point which should be made clear: No explanation is possible using the command model. No evidence has ever been adduced of any major "disobedience" among the accused or to substantiate the existence of any of the plots and conspiracies of which they were accused. The bulk of the evidence consisted solely of the admissions of the accused made under interrogation during their confinement in the hands of the NKVD. As Adam Ulam points out, "99 percent of the people liquidated in the Great Terror were totally innocent of any opposition to the Soviet system and, a fortiori, of the charges brought against them" (Urban 1982, p. 119). This yields a simple explanation for the infamous confessions of the accused, in which Stalin in effect demanded adulation from his victims before shooting them. "Stalin needed these people's confessions and adulation precisely because they were innocent" (loc. cit.).

There is obviously no place for any of this behavior in the command model. In that model, orders are given and carried out. Sanctions may be imposed for disobedience. There is no need to sanction those who do not disobey, and indeed it is probably counterproductive to do so. If one is to be shot for obedience as well as disobedience, there is little point in choosing the former over the latter. Accordingly, there has been much speculation about Stalin's behavior, including the characterization of it as "pathological" behavior.[1]

Stalin may have been extraordinarily ruthless, but he was not irrational if we look at the effects of the terror from his point of view. First, he transformed the CPSU, especially its upper echelons, from an organization dominated mainly by Old Bolsheviks whose loyalties were primarily to the CPSU itself (or to each other) into an elite which was entirely of Stalin's own making. Thus, "tens and hundreds of thousands of new elite members from predominantly low-class origins ... acquired positions of power during and as a result of the Great Purge of 1936–1938 ... They owed to Stalin, directly or indirectly, their meteoric rise into the middle and upper levels of the power structure from almost total obscurity ..." (Bialer 1980, p. 44). So the purge opened up vast new opportunities within the system, and it allowed Stalin to fill these ranks with those who were loyal to him and not to the CPSU. Thus, it is not uncommon to refer to the events of the late 1930s as "Stalin's victory over the Party" (see Schapiro 1971, Chapter 22) or to declare that "under mature Stalinism the Communist Party became extinct as a political movement" (Bialer 1980, p. 14); henceforth, it was simply Stalin's Party. I suggest that the depth of the purge reflected not merely the extent of Stalin's ruthlessness but also the strength of the loyalties which had evolved among the Old Bolsheviks (horizontal trust) and which could only be eradicated by Stalinist means. Finally, as Schapiro (1971) points out,

> [The terror] broke up, effectively and for a long time to come, all possibility of cohesion or solidarity. For the purge of the party was accompanied by much more extensive terror against all important sections of society. No one, in any walk of life, that had for some time past become entrenched in a position of authority and had surrounded himself with compliant subordinates or congenial colleagues remained unscathed. In the wave of panic, denunciation, hypocrisy and intrigue which was unleashed, no one could trust his fellow or feel secure in the protection of any institution or individual on whom he had hitherto relied. The "atomization" of society, which some have seen as the most characteristic feature of totalitarian rule, was completed in the years of the terror. (pp. 434–5)

---

[1] See the discussion of these in Roy Medvedev (1973, pp. 305ff.), who rejects this view, and in Hough and Fainsod (1979, pp. 177ff.), who appear to accept it.

To sum up, the central dilemma in any bureaucracy is the tendency for loyalties to accumulate which reduce the control of the leadership over the bureaucracy. This dilemma is obviously particularly acute in the one-party state, which forecloses the possibility of rejuvenation by means of the takeover of the state by a different party or by means of the shifting of the functions of the state bureaucracy to the private sector. The bizarre and grotesque events of the late 1930s are therefore at least in part explainable within the framework of our model of bureaucracy. Whether the degree of violence used by Stalin was really "necessary"[2] for the performance of the system is not a question which could ever be definitively answered. But, however cruel, the destruction wreaked on the Party and the country was not necessarily irrational from Stalin's point of view.

2   The decline of the system

The USSR changed a great deal between Stalin's time and the era of Brezhnev and his successors. However, the main features of the system – exclusive membership, centralism, ideology, and the multiplicity of control systems – were still in place up to the 1980s. The major change after Stalin's death was the reduction in the degree of repression, both against the general population and especially within the higher ranks of the CPSU. The last point can be strikingly illustrated by the fall in the turnover of leading personnel from the 1950s to the 1970s. Thus, turnover among Politburo members in the 1956–61 period was 70 percent; the corresponding figure for the 1971–76 period is 27 percent. Turnover among full members of the Central Committee fell over the same period from 50 percent to 16 percent; among secretaries of the Central Committee, from 75 percent to 20 percent; among members of the USSR Council of Ministers, from 67 percent to 17 percent, among republic first secretaries, from 79 percent to 29 percent; and among *Obkom* first secretaries, from 86 percent to 21 percent (Hough 1977, p. 29).

The reduction in repression against the population is harder to document precisely, but mass political terror had been abolished, and the role of the secret police had certainly been considerably reduced even before the advent of Glasnost and Perestroika. This reduction in the level of repression implies the withdrawal of a major instrument for encouraging the accumulation of vertical trust and for discouraging horizontal trust accumulation. And it is obvious that by the 1980s the time for a major

[2] Alec Nove argues that Stalinism may have been necessary for the industrialization program but not for the functioning of the political system, as argued here. See his "Was Stalin Really Necessary?" in Nove (1964), pp. 17–40.

purge, especially among the members of the aging leadership, had come and gone. Perhaps one reason for the purge's loss of appeal, even for those who might have had the stomach for it, was its essential *unpredictability*: It can never be clear *ex ante* just who will end up being caught in the web of accusations once the process has been unleashed. And both the great purges under Stalin and the great Cultural Revolution in China suggested that the bigger the purge, the more likely it was that many of the perpetrators themselves would have to be counted among its victims for the slate to be wiped clean at the end of the process. In any case no purge took place. So it is no surprise that the performance of the system deteriorated. The rate of growth of output and of productivity began to fall off in the late 1970s and continued to decline in the 1980s (as discussed earlier).

In the absence of the purge and with the concomitant reduction in turnover among managers at higher levels came a steady decline in promotion possibilities. As David Granick (1983) suggests,

> The political purges of the second half of the 1930s brought into office a generation of young executives who were to grow old in their posts, thoroughly clogging the lines of promotion during the entire third period . . . The previous practice of widespread and rapid demotion for failure was abandoned, and managers were provided with a degree of security in their current job never granted in large American companies. (p. 242)

As a consequence, perhaps the greatest achievement of the Soviet system over the period from about the 1960s onward was to provide security, not only for its managers but for its entire workforce. Anders Aslund (1989) echoed the views of many when he wrote, "The one achievement a majority of Soviet citizens seem [*sic*] to appreciate is the high degree of *economic security*. Jobs are easily found and maintained. You are paid approximately the same whether you actually work or not . . ." (p. 20).

With the increase in economic security, the absence of upward and downward mobility, and the withdrawal of political repression in the form of the purge and other sanctions, the natural result was an increased tendency to collude – that is, to form, strengthen, deepen, and solidify horizontal network links at all levels of the hierarchy. For example, the *nomenklatura* increasingly turned into a closed elite. Perhaps the most detailed account of the privileges available to the *nomenklatura* is contained in Mervyn Matthews (1978). These privileges included "the 13th month, [which was] an extra month's pay for a year's work sometimes described as 'hospital or cure' money reportedly received by Party functionaries in Central Committee apparatuses in Moscow and the Union Republican capitals and others" (p. 36); the "Party packet," which was a sealed envelope containing sums of money delivered monthly; access to restricted consumer outlets, foreign currency, or certificate shops, which sold a wide range of Western and superior Soviet goods that were sold at prices which were a quarter or fifth of Soviet prices at the official rate of exchange (p. 41); special housing, access to private transport in the form of an official vehicle with a chauffeur; a closed system of hospitals, clinics, and dispensaries (the fourth directorate of the ministry); special educational facilities; and holiday facilities and foreign travel. All of these privileges were obtainable only through *blat* – the use of personal contacts, influence, or even bribery to make life easier (p. 52).

Timothy Garton Ash (1983, 1991) describes the situation of the *nomenklatura* in Poland on the eve of the 1980 Solidarity revolt:

> The *nomenklatura* can accurately be described as a client ruling class. Its members enjoy power, status and privileges (in varying degrees) by virtue simply of belonging to it. They may not individually own the means of production but they do collectively control them. In the 1970s they were popularly known as "the owners of People's Poland." By contrast with other class systems, economic and political power [is] concentrated permanently in the same hands. Neither is this a purely functional elite. The children of the *nomenklatura* enjoy automatic advantages, so long as they remain loyal to the system. In the 1970s these advantages were comparable with heredity privileges in the West: If you were the son of a senior apparatchik you had a much higher standard of living, better education and career chances than your contemporary, the son of a worker. If one includes families, perhaps one-half million people depend directly on the continuance of Party monopolies for their jobs, power or privileges. (p. 9)

The difficulty for the Party posed by the growth of these networks at every level of the hierarchy was that it brought with it a steady loss in Party power. This point can be seen with the aid of Figure 10.1. The restriction of privilege to a few contradicted the CPSU's basic promises of equal opportunity and rewards. The result of these broken promises was a rise in the marginal costs of accumulating loyalty, as depicted by the leftward shift of $\pi(\dot{Q})$ in Figure 10.1. Second, the efficiency of enterprises declined because of the increased importance of horizontal as opposed to vertical network links. This implies that any given level of

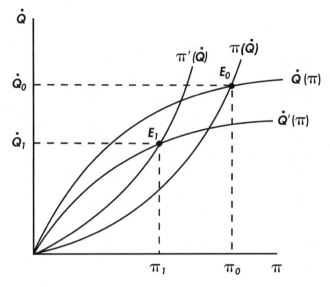

Figure 10.1. The decline of the Soviet system.

power translated into a smaller rate of economic growth, as shown by the downward shift of the curve $\dot{Q}(\pi)$ in Figure 10.1. Both of these shifts reinforce each other in lowering equilibrium power (π) and the rate of economic growth $\dot{Q}$. Thus, in Figure 10.1 the decline of the Soviet system is depicted by the downward shift in equilibrium power and economic growth from a point like E_0 to a point like E_1.

The symptoms and results of this decline in Party economic and political power were:

1. increased shortages as more and more firms escaped the control of the leadership and moved from a mixture of command, Party-induced shortages and corruption-induced shortages to an all-bribe equilibrium.
2. increased overregulation, for the same reason.
3. softer budget constraints as the *nomenklatura* in the ministries more and more often traded extensions of credit to the firms in exchange for bribes.
4. budget deficits, because of the fall in productivity and the loss in revenues to the center, a result which was exacerbated by the growth of the second economy (another symptom of declining CPSU power).

5. monetary overhang, because there was nothing to buy.
6. declining growth, for all the reasons already discussed.

Although official Soviet statistics do not suggest it, a number of economists – including Abel Aganbegyan, Alec Nove, and Michael Ellman – maintain that there was no growth in the Soviet Union after 1978.[3] Aslund suggested, shortages [by the mid-1980s] "permeate[d] Soviet life to such an extent that the words 'buy' and 'sell' have largely been replaced by 'give' and 'take' in every day parlance" (p. 18). The most startling symptom was that Soviet male life expectancy actually declined in the 1970s (cited in Easterly and Fischer 1994, p. 9). Aslund quotes the Soviet economist Mikhail Shmelev on the possible reasons:

> Apathy and indifference became mass phenomena, theft, disrespect for honest work and a simultaneous aggressive jealousy against those who earn a lot even if they earn honestly; signs appeared of almost physical degradation of a sizeable part of the population on the ground of drinking and idleness. (Shmelev, quoted in Aslund 1989, p. 18)

Into this sea of totalitarian torpor stepped comrade Gorbachev, who was bent on reform. What was his reform strategy, and why did it result not in reform, but in the demise of the system? The next section takes up these subjects.

3   Soviet versus Chinese reform strategies, or the totalitarian twist

In the mid-1980s, faced with all the problems alluded to at the end of the preceding section, Gorbachev launched his well-known Perestroika and Glasnost campaign. As will be discussed in more detail shortly, the twin pillars of the campaign were a loosening of central control over state enterprises and a considerable relaxation of restrictions on freedom of speech in order to allow for feedback, criticism, and discussion. The strategy raises a major problem for our analysis of totalitarian rule: Why would a totalitarian leader, who is assumed to be maximizing power, react to a loss in power by giving up more of it? To understand the strategy, we should find it useful to look first at the Chinese model. The Chinese reforms began in 1978. Broadly speaking, the strategy there was strictly economic, and it has been variously characterized as the introduction of product market competition while retaining "socialist" ownership (McMillan and Naughton 1992), or a strategy of "marketization without

[3] See the citations in Aslund (1989, p. 15).

privatization" (Berliner 1994). There were four basic elements of the strategy:

1. New forms of *independent enterprises* were allowed, which could operate outside the plan. The strategy began with the decollectivization of agriculture, beginning in 1979 with the introduction of the "household responsibility system," in which peasants were given multiyear leases, wide latitude over their own operations, authorization to sell portions of their output on the market, and the right to retain profits after the payment of taxes and crop delivery obligations to the state (Berliner 1994; Perkins 1994). Subsequently, a category of nonagricultural enterprises began to be organized by lower-level units of government (town and village governments, or TVGs). These enterprises – known as "town and village enterprises" (TVEs) are nominally owned by the citizens of the township or village, but they are controlled by the township or village government (Chang and Wang 1994). As mentioned in Chapter 6, they have been spectacularly successful. The annual average rate of growth of output in TVEs was 25.3 percent per year over the 1979–91 period (Weitzman and Xu 1994). One reason may be that they operate under a budget constraint that is "as hard as that faced by the typical capitalist enterprise" (Berliner 1994, p. 251). But they are not private enterprises, and privatization has not been a central element in the Chinese strategy (Perkins 1994).
2. The second component of this strategy was greater *autonomy* for state-owned enterprises (SOEs). Thus, managers of these enterprises acquired the right to sell over-plan output on the market, production quotas were reduced, and managers were allowed to retain a substantial portion of their profits (sometimes as high as 100 percent) after making a fixed payment to the state.
3. There was a *dual pricing* system, in which products produced for the plan were sold at officially determined state prices, whereas over-plan output could be sold at market prices.
4. Finally, the Chinese economy was *opened up to the world market*. Enterprise rights to export and import without having to get permission from the authorities were introduced and foreign investment was encouraged.

Why would a totalitarian government relinquish its powers in this way? One obvious rationalization of the strategy is that a partial but not complete withdrawal of central control will induce greater efficiency on the part of the SOEs and other enterprises, thus spurring economic growth. This idea is depicted in Figure 10.2(a). The reduction in state powers is shown by the shift to the left of the $\pi(\dot{Q})$ curve – that is, any given level of economic growth $\dot{Q}$ yields a smaller level of the government budget B (hence, there is less which can be spent to produce π than before, and there is therefore less π). This seems a reasonable description of fewer legal powers. The strategy presumably is to prevent the regime's collapse by inducing greater efficiency and causing economic growth to increase, thus ending up at a point like E_2 rather than E_3 in Figure 10.2(a), and it should accomplish this goal with a smaller decline in power than would have happened in the absence of these measures. Figure 10.2 shows that for the strategy to work, it is essential that the $\dot{Q}(\pi)$ curve be downward sloping [as in Figure 10.2(a)] and not upward sloping over the reform range [as in Figure 10.2(b)]. The introduction of marketization (product–market competition) in order to deal with the twist in the $\dot{Q}(\pi)$ curve is what I refer to here as the "totalitarian twist." Note finally that if the reforms worked well and stimulated enough economic growth, it is possible that the supply of loyalty to the regime would rise, reducing the price of loyalty and shifting the $\pi(\dot{Q})$ curve back in the direction of E_4 [in Figure 10.2(a)]. Even if this doesn't occur, the general idea is that by giving up state powers (in this case, control over enterprises), the regime may end up with more *power* than it would otherwise have had without the reform. This explains how a power-maximizing totalitarian regime can pursue a "reformist" strategy like this.[4]

In the former Soviet Union, the strategies pursued by Gorbachev during the Glasnost and Perestroika period were, as has been forcefully pointed out by Berliner (1994), basically the same as those pursued by the Chinese. Like the Chinese, the Soviets provided for the introduction of a sector of independent enterprises that operated outside the state plan, and these enterprises could sell over-plan output on the market. The Enterprise Law allowed firms to keep their own profits after the payment of taxes and other obligations to the state. A dual price system was introduced, state enterprises were given the right to export and import directly, and they were encouraged to form joint ventures with foreign firms (Berliner 1994, pp. 253–5; Sachs and Woo 1994, pp. 120–1). Thus, as Berliner emphasizes, the difference between the reform strategies adopted by the Soviets and the Chinese was not a difference be-

---

[4] Note the similarity of the strategy (power is given up in order to raise revenue) to that pursued by the English monarchy in the Glorious Revolution of 1688 (as analyzed by North and Weingast 1989; and discussed in Chapter 5 [p. 133]).

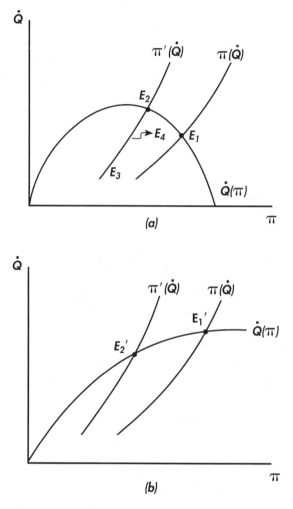

Figure 10.2. Reform, or the totalitarian twist.

tween gradualism and the "big bang" approach. A gradualist approach was tried in the Soviet Union for several years, presumably for the same reasons as those that were discussed above for the Chinese case – namely, that more power would be achievable in the long run if formal controls over state and other enterprises were partially relaxed and if product competition were allowed than would be obtainable if powers of central direction and control were clung to.

In the Soviet Union there was an additional rationale behind the reforms: By the 1980s the powers of the CPSU to create shortages and to distribute rents had increasingly been abused due to the growth of collusion or horizontal network trading. Consequently, the rents arising from the shortages were increasingly diverted into bribes and horizontal trades and were not contributing to the goals of the state as such. The situation was different in China, which had experienced the Cultural Revolution for a decade or so prior to the onset of reform in 1978. During that period 60 percent of Chinese Party officials were purged (Fairbank 1992; cited in Sachs and Woo 1994, p. 111). Although this is usually interpreted as meaning that Party control had been undermined in China, the interpretation suggested here is very different. As a result of the purge, everybody was suspicious of everybody else, and network links not tied to the Party apparatus in China were weak and fragile, thus making it easier, not harder, for the Chinese Party apparatus to maintain control during the reform process. Perhaps it was for this reason that Gorbachev launched Glasnost along with Perestroika while the Chinese didn't. They had already had their Glasnost, in terms of the desired effects of weakening non-Party links that could support bribes, corruption, and other forms of trade which did not advance the goals of the Party.

However, although the reform programs under Gorbachev in the Soviet Union and Deng in China may have been similar, the effects were very different. From the economic point of view, in China the result was a long period (which persists to the present) of sustained economic growth at very high levels [over 8 percent annually for the fourteen years from 1978 to 1992 (Perkins 1994, p. 24)]. Total official budgetary revenues grew at rates of 10 percent a year. Extra-budgetary revenues grew even faster (Sicular 1992, p. 10).[5] In the Soviet Union the ultimate effects (by 1991) were a macroeconomic breakdown, the breakdown of the planning system, an explosion of government deficits and inflation, and the collapse of communism after more than seventy years in power. In terms of Figure 10.2, the Chinese performed the totalitarian twist successfully, moving from a point like E_1 in Figure 10.2(a) to a point like E_2. In the Soviet Union, budgetary revenues collapsed after the onset of reform, and the regime traveled down the $\dot{Q}(\pi)$ curve in Figure 10.2(b) from a point like E_1' to a point like E_2'.

---

[5] During the 1980s SOE earnings and outlays were largely shifted from within-budget to extra-budget accounts. Sicular (1992) shows that when those extra-budgetary revenues are included, the central government's deficit is much smaller and the proportion of total revenues and expenditures of the central government which go to the provinces is much larger than is commonly thought.

What explains the difference? Although many factors undoubtedly contributed, some of which will be discussed briefly in a moment, there is one difference in strategy which stands out: The Chinese authorities maintained a high level of repression throughout the reform process, and indeed they still maintain it today (mid-1997). The Soviets relaxed political control. Put another way, although the Chinese relaxed detailed control over firm operations, the state remained as a substitute for property rights and the legal system necessary to enforce them, both of which were necessarily underdeveloped during the transition process. The Soviets introduced Glasnost and in other ways undermined Party control. To buttress the assertion that this was the crucial difference, let us consider three specific areas widely considered critical to successful reform:

1. managerial discretion
2. the supply diversion problem (the diversion of supplies from plan to market output)
3. inflation.

In each of these cases, I will show that a loosening of central control does not solve the problem and that "marketization" cannot be counted on to solve it either; instead, this loosening and marketization typically aggravates the problem in the absence of a highly developed property rights system. Developed property rights existed neither in China nor in the former Soviet Union. Whether the two countries recognized the problem consciously or not, the maintenance of state control in the Chinese case in effect provided a substitute for the missing property rights; this substitute was lacking in the Soviet reform program.

To see this point more precisely, let us consider each of these problems in more detail.

1. *Managerial discretion, or underdeveloped mechanisms of managerial control.* If managers are freed from central control over their decisions (such as investment policy, wage policy, and so on), what guarantees that their behavior will be in the interests of the firm? In U.S.-style corporations, where the shares in corporations are widely held and the managers themselves have small equity stakes in the firm, there are certain well-known devices which impose some discipline on managers: a well-developed capital market to evaluate share prices, including possibly the existence of some shareholders with a substantial equity stake in the firm; executive compensation mechanisms which tie managerial pay to the firm's performance; and the possibility of a takeover by well-heeled outsiders with substantial access to the capital necessary to finance it (see Jensen and Meckling 1976; Wintrobe 1987). The absence or extreme

weakness of financial markets in both the Soviet Union and in China meant that no managerial discipline was possible from these sources. Accordingly, the increased autonomy in the former Soviet Union after 1987 effectively gave managers the freedom to grant themselves and their workers large increases in remuneration at the expense of tax payments to the state. The maintenance of soft-budget constraints into the reform period aggravated this problem, because this meant that in effect the state stood by to make up for any increased losses experienced by the firms as a result of wage increases! Thus, Soviet average industrial real wages rose 79 percent from 1985 to 1991 – that is, during a period in which prices were largely constant and supplies of goods hardly grew at all (Boycko 1992; Lipton and Sachs 1992, p. 220). The result of liberalization was therefore an intensification of shortages (Boycko 1992; Lipton and Sachs 1992, pp. 220–1). The phenomenon which took place is sometimes referred to as the "plundering" of the firms or "spontaneous privatization." From the state's point of view, another result was the plummeting of state revenues, aggravating a preexisting budget deficit. Similar problems appeared in China with the onset of reform, but they were arrested through a tightening up of state monitoring of managerial behavior (McMillan and Naughton 1992, p. 135). Thus, as McMillan and Naughton correctly insist, "the state must monitor the firms during the transition" (p. 135).

2. *Supply diversion.* The second major problem with a partial reform is the possibility that with two different prices for the same good (the official price and the market price), the greater the difference between the official and the market price, the greater the incentive for any firm to divert output intended for the state to the free market (Sicular 1988; Murphy, Shleifer, and Vishny 1992). The two-track (plan and market) system presents numerous other opportunities and incentives for sellers to try to evade the plan. For example, as Sicular (1988) suggests,

> the system created an incentive to switch from planting crops with relatively high quotas to those with low or no quotas. Fields subject to grain quotas were converted to cotton or other economic crops, and vice versa. Another evasion tactic was to save output for one or two years and then deliver it all at once, or for several families to transfer their output to one family for delivery to the state. Finally, local officials, under pressure from their neighbors, occasionally succumbed to the temptation of carrying out unauthorized reductions in quota levels. Such sorts of behavior resulted in under-fulfillment of quotas at the same time

that deliveries at above-quota and negotiated prices increased ... (p. 289)

It is not obvious how market mechanisms can be used to circumvent these problems. As Sicular (1993) points out, if market prices are lowered to official prices, marketization is incomplete, output will tend to fall, and the reform process is stalled. If market prices are raised, the temptation to evade the quota obviously increases as the divergence between official and market prices increases. Finally, if the state responds to the shortage in quotas by buying on the market, the action entails a budgetary deficit, and this tends to have inflationary consequences.

In the absence of a feasible market-type mechanism to control the supply diversion problem, there is always recourse to the repressive state apparatus. The Chinese responded to these problems by periodically reimposing price controls, by narrowing the gap between official and market prices, by heavily policing quota evasion and delivery shortfalls, and by other means (Sicular, 1993, 1995). Indeed, on a number of occasions, the state's reimposition of its will essentially resulted in a stalling of the reform process in particular areas. Thus, according to Sicular (1995),

> in [the] 1986–87 [period] the central government announced that grain and cotton procurement contracts were no longer voluntary. In ensuing years the government reinstated its monopsony on rice and cotton, and it prohibited grain trade on free markets unless local (county) quotas had been met. Mandatory production targets, which had been abolished in 1985, were revived so as to ensure contract fulfilment.
>
> The need to reassert controls over prices and markets was a major theme of Li Peng's government work report ... in March 1985. Emphasis on enforcement of mandatory procurement quotas was renewed, and by early 1985, 29 of China's 35 largest cities had reintroduced grain rationing. (pp. 5, 7)

On the other hand, according to Murphy, Shleifer, and Vishny (1992), in the Soviet Union after 1988,

> traditional suppliers to many of these state firms *broke their ties* and sold or bartered their supplies to private or state enterprises [that] were able to offer better deals. The chief of a large oil distribution concern, for example, complained that refineries sold the oil to cooperatives [that] were then reselling it to con-

sumers at triple the state price ... At the same time, state firms were unable to replace the diverted inputs because they had no access to markets. As a result, state firms often cut output, broke contracts themselves, and by doing so created further bottlenecks downstream. (pp. 890–1, emphasis added)

3. *Inflation.* The third critical problem which arises during the transition process is inflation. Fundamentally, this is due to the "remonetization" of relationships among firms, because they are now allowed to make independent contracts with each other and to buy and sell on the market. The introduction of a dual pricing system allows the suppressed inflation typical of the shortage economy to appear openly. The potential for inflation is compounded by the fact that prices are liberalized in the absence of experience with or an adequate framework for monetary and fiscal management. These problems were exacerbated in the Soviet Union by the fact that reform began in the presence of a large monetary overhang and budget deficit. Even in China, however, major mistakes were made. For example, in 1988 the government announced a series of price reforms that would eliminate price controls entirely on most commodities. According to Berliner (1994), "the announcement set off a chain of inflationary expectations causing large withdrawals of bank deposits in response to panic buying. Between August 1 and 15 the banks issued an amount of money equal to about one-third of the entire U.S. targeted amount" (p. 263). However, in China, again, even though the central government was steadily losing power to the provinces, it retained enough power to control the process. Extensive price controls were reintroduced, deep cuts were made in state spending, and a severe austerity program was introduced which succeeded in controlling inflationary pressures. Berliner (1994) nicely summarizes the difference between the capacity of the two governments to control the inflation problem. He writes,

> The Chinese government was no doubt better able to impose its will on local government than was the Soviet, for it continued to maintain its power while the Soviet government steadily lost its power. The difference is apparent in the ability of the Chinese government to raise consumer goods prices on various occasions in the 1980s, which contributed in many ways to the control of inflationary pressures: by reducing subsidies and therefore the size of the budget deficit, and by narrowing the gap between controlled and market prices, which reduced the gains from arbitrage and fostered the development of productive independent enterprises. In contrast, when Gorbachev was advised to

raise consumer goods prices, he responded that any Soviet government that did that would be out of office in two weeks. (pp. 270–1)

Of course, there are many other factors which contributed to the divergent outcomes of partial reform in China and in the Soviet Union. Perhaps the most important is that production in China had never been as centralized as in the Soviet Union, and so there were very few products in China that were produced in only one or two plants in the country (the typical situation in the former Soviet Union). This made it easier to devolve power to the provinces and to other lower-level governments in China. Thus, it was easier to "de-bureaucratize" the Chinese system, with the central government maintaining its hold on the repressive apparatus while control over many economic functions was devolved to the provinces. This shift of power to lower-level governments is particularly emphasized by Gabriella Montinola, Yingyi Qian, and Barry Weingast (1995), who trace much of the dynamism of the system to the resulting competition among provincial and local governments.[6]

Another important difference is that there was no pressure for reform from below in the Soviet Union, where an extensive system of social protection, much of the benefits of which were linked to the site of employment (Sachs and Woo 1994, pp. 108–9; Aslund 1989, p. 20), gave managers and workers a great deal of economic security, even though they were neither very productive nor very well paid. Finally, in China, communes had largely been left to themselves in managing their economic activities as long as their production quotas were met. Thus, rural reform was relatively easy to achieve there, and the spontaneous decollectivization and rapid economic development in agriculture which resulted provided an important cushion of economic growth against which the more difficult task of reforming urban enterprises could proceed. Comparable developments did not take place – and could not have taken place – in the former Soviet Union.

Despite these caveats, it still appears that the Soviet attempt at simultaneous economic and political liberalization was a mistake from the point of view of the Party wishing to keep its hold on power. Although the Chinese reform succeeded from this point of view, the Russian attempt disintegrated into hyperinflation, and the regime collapsed.

From another point of view, of course, matters are not so clear. Com-

---

[6] While Montinola, Qian, and Weingast (1995) see the resulting system which they term "market-preserving federalism" as conducive to economic growth, Alwyh Young's (1996) evidence suggests that there is considerable waste and duplication in this jurisdictional competition.

munism as an integrated politico–economic system is dead in Russia, democratic political structures are being erected there, and democratic politics is progressing. In China it is worth emphasizing that although the Chinese reform strategy has often been described as one of implementing economic reforms prior to the implementation of political reforms, after nineteen years of reform there is not a trace of civil liberties, competition among political parties, free elections, or any of the other attributes of democracy.

4   Conclusion

In the preceding chapter and in this one I have used bureaucratic theory to model the Soviet system of production. Applying that model makes it easy to see that the characteristics of Communist economics – central control by the Party over the distribution of economic rents, intensive monitoring of individual behavior, and the threat of expulsion from the Party (the purge) – give the Party tools to discipline workers which are well beyond that available to the typical firm in a market economy. Hence the basic characteristics of the system: shortages (to create rents), demonetization (to allow political control), extensive promotion of loyalty to the Party through ideological indoctrination and forced political participation (to facilitate loyalty), and so on. So the system was not deficient because it lacked incentives, as is often claimed. The basic problem with it was the same one that is faced by any large bureaucratic organization as it ages – the tendency for loyalty to the top to erode over time. Stalin "solved" this problem with the Great Purge, but after his death, the arbitrariness and uncontrollability of the process was revealed, no leader arose with the necessary courage and ruthlessness to repeat the operation, and the system declined. This chapter examined the decline of the Soviet system and showed that its problems were magnified by a fundamental contradiction between its promises – essentially, equality and solidarity – and the conditions necessary for running any large bureaucratic system efficiently, which dictates vertical or hierarchical loyalty and not horizontal solidarity among co-workers. Over time, the discrepancy between the promises and the reality of the system, combined with these problems, continued to erode the loyalty within it (which is the basis of Party power).

As the system deteriorated, pressures for reform grew. Why would a totalitarian government, bent on maximizing power, be interested in reform? The basic difference between the former Soviet Union and China is not that reform was gradual in one case and precipitous in the other. Gradual reform was tried in both the USSR under Gorbachev and in China under Deng. The basic difference is that reforms in China were accompanied by the maintenance and possibly the intensification of political repression, whereas repression was relaxed in the Soviet Union. Moreover, China had undertaken a large-scale purge of the Party prior to the initiation of market reforms. I analyzed three critical problems accompanying the transition process – the control of managers, supply diversion, and inflation – and I showed that tight political control is necessary to solve all three. Through the use of repression, China performed what I have dubbed "the totalitarian twist" successfully – that is, by giving up formal controls over enterprises, its leaders made it possible for these enterprises to become more efficient, and as a result growth resumed and the revenues of the state increased. In the former Soviet Union, the attempt to perform the same delicate operation without the anaesthesia of repression resulted in the collapse of government revenue, a descent into hyperinflation, and the breakdown of the regime.

Part IV

The dynamics of dictatorship

11   Democracy in the inaction zone

1   Introduction

This part of the book looks at some aspects of the dynamics of dictatorship – that is, its origins and some of its consequences.[1] This chapter is
concerned with political inaction – the conditions under which democratic politicians may fail to respond to or provide leadership on important political issues, thus effectively suppressing the demands of their
constituents to "do something" about them. The inertia or powerlessness
of democracy under certain conditions is one of the seeds of dictatorship,
since dictators can act under many circumstances in which democratic
politicians cannot. I show the forms of social structure which are particularly likely to result in this pathology – for example, polarized political
parties, rigid political preferences, and lack of trust in politicians and in
the political system.

Another germ of dictatorship is ethnic conflict and nationalism. These
phenomena are modeled in Chapter 12. Ethnicity is modeled as a capital
good which reduces the transaction costs of market and political exchange within the group. Investments in ethnicity have two peculiar
features:

1. Much of the investment is done by parents for the benefit of
   their children
2. The payoff to an individual depends on investments made by
   others in the group and on the group's collective (political)
   choices.

Hence the potential for conflicts of various sorts, both between groups
and between generations. I show that neither market nor democratic
political mechanisms can easily resolve these conflicts.

The analysis in both chapters is illustrated by the breakdown of the
Weimar Republic, in which these seeds or germs were present in particu-

---

[1] Much of the material in this chapter originally appeared in P. Howitt and Ronald
Wintrobe (1993) and (1995).

larly virulent form. The regime proved itself unable (or unwilling) to respond to demands for action on unemployment, which rose to particularly high levels in Germany during the Great Depression, or to curb political violence in the streets (on both the left and the right), a violence which apparently terrified many voters. Ethnic and intergenerational conflicts exacerbated these difficulties.

From these weaknesses, conflicts, and distempers of Weimar, Hitler and the Nazi party forged the machinery of an extraordinarily powerful dictatorship. How this machinery worked – how policy was made and carried out – is discussed in Chapter 13, with special reference to its most terrible and incomprehensible feature: the Nazi solution to the Jewish question. Once the operation of this bureaucratic machinery is understood, it becomes easy to answer one important question related to the fall of dictatorship: Who was and should be held responsible for the crimes against humanity committed by the regime?

Although the specific application in much of what follows is to the Nazi regime, much of the material is abstract, especially in this chapter, in which a new analytical tool is introduced to explain the allure of dictatorship. So the models developed are quite general. And perhaps it is unnecessary to emphasize that the themes of this part – democratic political inaction, ethnic conflict, and the responsibility of bureaucrats for crimes committed by an authoritarian regime (of which they are a part) – seem to be as prominent in the world at the end of the twentieth century as they were in the 1930s and 1940s.

2   Political inaction

In any democracy it is easy to think of particular issues on which people have very strong political views – such as government deficits or abortion – but about which politicians are often loathe to do anything despite the demands of their constituents. The result is that the political preferences of the constituents are suppressed. The issue just never appears on the political agenda. Since political parties only compete when issues are raised, this constitutes a limitation on the effectiveness of democratic politics. Under some circumstances this problem may become particularly severe, thus contributing to the breakdown of democracy. This is the basic argument of this chapter. This result illustrates the fundamental attraction – what I like to call the "allure" – of dictatorship: Dictators can easily solve the conflicts which give rise to inaction (and other problems) by simply repressing those elements in the population that oppose their solutions. The result is that there is a fundamental tradeoff between the capacity of a political system to represent different points of view and its capacity for political action.

To illustrate how one might think about the problem of inaction in theoretical terms, it is useful to ask whether this suppression of political preferences can occur in the standard two-party convergence or median voter model. In that model it is easy to see that although only one political *viewpoint* (that of the median voter) is ever expressed, all *issues* are raised. This is so simply because unless the status quo on some issue or public policy is exactly at the median, the issue will be raised by either party, because both prefer the median to the status quo. So this kind of preference suppression cannot occur in the median voter model. To model it, I therefore follow the tradition initiated by Donald Wittman (1973, 1983) and recently developed further by Alberto Alesina (e.g., 1988a and 1988b) and others, in which parties are policy-oriented and do not converge but offer distinct policy platforms in equilibrium. This section shows how political inaction can occur in this type of model. Section 3 examines both the precise costs imposed on citizens by this behavior of political parties and who (i.e., what kind of political preferences) are particularly likely to get suppressed. Section 4 applies the model to the fall of the Weimar Republic and, more briefly, to other classic instances of democratic breakdown. Section 5 shows the circumstances under which inaction is inefficient. Section 6 relaxes some of the assumptions of the model. Section 7 describes the tradeoff between inaction and representation and concludes. More formal parts related to the argument of this section and Section 5 can be found in the appendix.

To proceed, let us assume that the political system contains only two parties. They face an election, in which an issue x may or may not be raised by either party. The parties offer distinct platforms in equilibrium, as in the class of models developed by Douglas Hibbs (1977), Wittman (1973, 1983), I. Hansson and C. Stuart (1984), Randall Calvert (1985), and Alesina (1988a). Assume that party R is the right-wing party, party L is the left-wing party, and x_R and x_L are their respective platforms on some issue x. Higher values of x are preferred by the right (think of x as the level of defense spending, for example).

Suppose that a policy is already in place on some issue x, which will be referred to as s, the status quo. Either party can then "raise" the issue by proposing a different level of x as part of its platform. If it does so, the other party will also propose a policy. Alternatively, both parties can choose to do nothing about issue x. If neither party raises the issue, the existing level or status quo s is then its position on that issue. A party may prefer not to raise the issue because doing so carries risk. The risk is that the party will not end up with the policy it desires on that issue. The most obvious way this can happen is that when one party raises an issue, the other party will also propose a policy on that issue which, in the end, could prove more popular with the voters. However, there are other possible risks. The attempt to change any policy in a democratic system usually galvanizes opposition by interest groups, legislators, bureaucrats and others who would be adversely affected by that change. The possible risks then include the failure to change the policy and the resulting loss of credibility or reputation – or even the possibility of losing an election over that issue. For simplicity, assume to begin with that there are only two possibilities:

1. Party R wins the election and implements its preferred platform if the issue is raised, with probability p.
2. Party L wins and implements its platform, with probability $1-p$.

Assume further, for the moment, that each party has complete credibility with voters. Each party can then compete for votes by

1. raising an issue or not.
2. devising platforms which deviate from the preferences of its own members in order to appeal to centrist voters.

Assume the two platforms satisfy the conditions of Nash equilibrium – that is, each party chooses that platform which maximizes its expected utility, given the position of the other party. Conditions for the existence of equilibrium platforms, assuming all issues are raised, are given in Alesina (1988a). However, parties also have the option of not raising an issue, which voters will interpret as a binding promise to leave the status quo unchanged if elected. If $\hat{x}_R$ and $\hat{x}_L$ would be the equilibrium platforms if the issue is raised, it follows that party R will prefer not to raise the issue if:

(1) $U_R(S) > pU_R(\hat{x}_R) + (1-p)U_R(\hat{x}_L)$.

Similarly, party L will not want to raise the issue if

(2) $U_L(S) > pU_L(\hat{x}_R) + (1-p)U_L(\hat{x}_L)$.

If both inequalities are satisfied, then neither party will raise the issue during the campaign, and whichever party is elected will maintain its implicit promise to do nothing in that policy area to disturb the status quo. However, some voters, including members of both political parties, would prefer that action be taken on that issue. The desires of these voters are suppressed, not in the overt sense that they are not allowed to speak, to make demands, to organize protests, and so forth, but in the sense that although they are free to speak, there is no one listening who is willing to put their demands on the political agenda. Neither party wishes to raise the issue during the election campaign, and neither party will do anything to disturb the status quo if elected. Consequently, although the means of suppression are different, the policy outcome is the same as if the voters were never allowed to utter their demands in the first place.

To depict the magnitude of suppression in this sense, consult Figure 11.1. The area labeled DNZ (the "do nothing zone") is the zone in which, if the status quo s were located there, neither party would want to raise issue x. To interpret the figure, consider party L's inaction threshold first. Along the threshold line, party L is indifferent between raising and not raising the issue. The threshold line slopes upward, because for a given status quo s (measured along the horizontal axis), an increase in p implies that party R's probability of election victory increases. Consequently, so does the likelihood of $\hat{x}_R$ occurring rather than $\hat{x}_L$. If party R was just at the threshold of inaction at the initial p, an increase in p with s unchanged implies that the loss from the status quo is greater than that from raising the issue, and the party will thus prefer action to inaction. For the party to remain indifferent between acting and not acting, therefore, s will have to increase as p increases. So party R's threshold of inaction is upward-sloping in (p, s) space. The same argument implies that party L's threshold is also upward-sloping. Moreover, since party L's platform ($\hat{x}_L$) is to the left of party R's, its threshold must generally lie to the *right* of that of party R: For a given p, the left-wing party will only wish to act when the status quo is sufficiently far away and to the right of its platform (e.g., at y in Figure 11.1), and the right-wing party will only prefer action when s is sufficiently to the left of its platform (e.g., w in Figure 11.1).

To see the shape of the DNZ, note that the two thresholds intersect at $(p = 1, s = \hat{x}_R)$ *and* $(p = 0, s = \hat{x}_L)$. At $(1, \hat{x}_R)$ the status quo is located just at party R's platform, and party R is guaranteed election, so the same outcome $\hat{x}_R$ will obtain whether the issue is raised or not. Hence both parties must be indifferent between action and the status quo and so must be on their threshold of inaction at that point. A similar argument shows that the two threshold lines must also intersect at $(p = 0, s = \hat{x}_L)$.

This argument proves that there is an area in which both parties prefer not to raise the issue – the DNZ in Figure 11.1. Inside the DNZ are all the combinations of p and s at which both parties prefer to live with the status quo rather than announce a policy.

How big is the DNZ? We will see that it will be larger, the smaller the degree of credibility of the parties' platforms (the less that voters trust

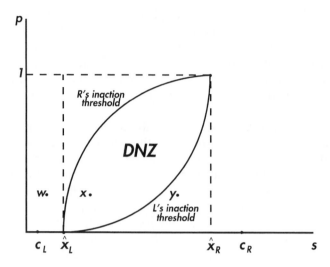

Figure 11.1. The inaction zone.

politicians), the smaller the willingness of the parties to compromise (hence making the *DNZ* larger for divisive issues like abortion or capital punishment), and generally (but not always) larger, the greater the level of polarization of the parties' platforms.

To see these points, let us first restate conditions (1) and (2) in more precise language. Each party's utility function is

$$(3) \qquad U_i = -\left(x - c_i\right)^a$$

where c_i gives the ideological position of party i (i.e., c_i is the value of x which maximizes the party's utility function). Assume only two parties and $c_L < c_R$ (i.e., party R is the right-wing party and party L is the left-wing party), as before. The parameter of the utility function (a) measures each party's willingness to compromise; formally, $a - 1$ is the elasticity of marginal utility or the Arrow–Pratt measure of relative risk aversion. Assume that $a - 1 > 0$; each party is risk averse.

How the parties compete in the election (i.e., what kind of platform each party will want to offer to the voters) depends crucially on the credibility or the capacity of a party to get voters to believe its promises. To illustrate, let us suppose that neither party is trusted by voters or has any hope of building trust. Suppose also that voters are rational and that they are unbiased in their forecasts of party behavior once a party is in office. Then $x_i^e = c_i$ – that is, the parties' platforms (expected policies x^e) are simply their ideological positions (c_i), and there is no point for either party to try to devise a platform which pretends otherwise. Moreover, there is no sense in which parties can raise an issue or not, because voters know each party's preferences on all issues, and they also know that they will be implemented when one of them is elected.

Now allow for the possibility that a party can try to appeal to voters by

1. raising an issue or not
2. devising a platform which deviates from its own preferences, in order to appeal to centrist voters.

Assume for simplicity that each party has complete credibility with voters. Each party then proposes a platform consisting of promises to implement policies on a vector of issues $x^1, \ldots, x^n$. Moreover, it can choose not to raise any issue, which implies that if elected, the party will not implement a new policy in that area. The existing level or status quo (s) is then its position on that issue. Voters believe the parties, so that if party R proposes a policy x_R on any issue x, voters believe it will implement that policy. If no proposal is made, voters correctly believe that no policy will be implemented, and so the status quo s on that issue will be maintained. If either party, once in office, deviates from these rules, it loses credibility with voters and will be expected in the future to simply implement its ideal policy c_i.

Assume that each party chooses that platform which maximizes its utility, given the position of the other party. Alesina (1988a) presents conditions under which Nash equilibrium platforms $(\hat{x}_R, \hat{x}_L)$ exist, where $c_L < \hat{x}_L < \hat{x}_R < c_R$. Part 1 of the appendix to this chapter describes this optimization, and it develops the conditions describing each party's threshold of inaction – the two borders of the DNZ in Figure 11.1. Here, we simply assume these results (i.e., the DNZ exists).

Now let us investigate how the size of the DNZ changes in response to exogenous changes. We consider three parameters:

1. the level of polarization – that is, the distance between either the parties' platforms $(\hat{x}_R - \hat{x}_L)$ or their ideological positions $(c_R - c_L)$
2. the willingness of the parties to compromise, as measured by the parameter a
3. the degree of credibility of the parties with the electorate.

Credibility is defined here as a party's capacity to promise a move away from its ideological center and be believed by voters. It is indexed by a new parameter λ. The larger λ, the greater is $\hat{x}_R - c_R$ or $\hat{x}_L - c_L$.

Consider first the effect on the DNZ of an increase in polarization. Figure 11.2 shows the effect of an increase in polarization of party

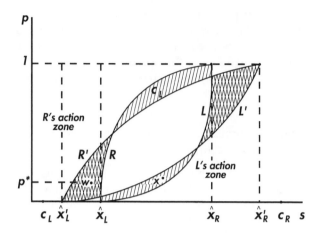

Figure 11.2. Effects of increased party polarization on the *DNZ*.

platforms $(\hat{x}_R - \hat{x}_L)$. The original *DNZ* is given by the area bounded by $\hat{x}_R$, $\hat{x}_L$. The new *DNZ* is enclosed by $\hat{x}'_R$, $\hat{x}'_L$. If polarization increases from $\hat{x}_R$, $\hat{x}_L$ to $\hat{x}'_R$, $\hat{x}'_L$, and if the parties' fortunes are affected symmetrically so that p remains the same, it is clear that the *DNZ* must widen, because its endpoints are always the same as the party platforms. The crosshatched areas in Figure 11.2 show the corresponding expansion of the *DNZ*. However, it is equally clear from the figure that some points in the original *DNZ* will represent circumstances in which one of the parties will now wish to announce a policy. These points are given by the shaded areas in Figure 11.2. From the figure, then, it is unclear whether the *DNZ* expands or contracts as a result of the increase in polarization of the party platforms.

To understand the factors at work, consider two possible status quo points such as w and x in the figure. A status quo x is in party L's *DNZ* when the platforms are $(\hat{x}_R, \hat{x}_L)$. A change in platforms to $(\hat{x}'_R, \hat{x}'_L)$ means that a status quo at x is farther away from L's platform than before; hence it is less satisfactory. Consequently, when L becomes more extreme, it becomes more eager to act on a "moderate" status quo such as x. The same argument holds for party R's attitude toward "centrist" status quos, as shown by the disappearance from the *DNZ* of the set of points in the upper shaded area of the original *DNZ*.

Now consider why the *DNZ* expands to include points like w. At $(\hat{x}_R, \hat{x}_R)$, w is to the left of both party platforms. The right-wing party therefore has nothing to lose by raising this issue, even though its probability of victory p is low, because whichever party is victorious promises to implement a more right-wing policy than w. But at $(\hat{x}'_R, \hat{x}'_L)$, party L (the likely victor at p) promises $\hat{x}'_L$, a more *left*-wing policy than w. Hence, even though w is less satisfactory to party R at $\hat{x}'_R$ than at $\hat{x}_R$, it will be even worse off if it raises the issue and party L wins the election. Consequently, party R prefers the status quo to raising the issue. (As far as party L is concerned, because w is close enough to its own platform at either $\hat{x}_L$ or $\hat{x}'_L$, there is insufficient reason to raise the issue.) An analogous argument explains the expansion of the *DNZ* into the upper right-hand corner of Figure 11.2.

To summarize, we can say that when the parties become more polarized and adopt more extreme platforms, centrist status quos become less satisfactory. If one of the parties has a high chance of winning the election, it may want action, whereas before it was content to do nothing. On the other hand, the *DNZ* expands to include status quo points at the extremes (i.e. which were previously to the right or the left of both party platforms).

To get an idea as to whether the forces of expansion generally counteract those of contraction on the *DNZ* as polarization increases, we need to calculate the area of the *DNZ*. We have not performed this calculation in general, but we have done so for a special case – namely, where the parties' utility functions are quadratic and the polity is symmetric (see Part 2 of the appendix). In that case, the area of the *DNZ* is

(4)
$$\frac{\left(\hat{x}_R - \hat{x}_L\right)^2}{3\left(c_R - c_L\right)}.$$

Equation (4) shows, first, that in general, polarization tends to increase the do-nothing zone; and, second, that the level of polarization of platforms must be measured relative to the polarization of the party's ideological positions (although a proportional expansion of both platforms and ideological positions does increase the *DNZ*).

To illustrate, let us suppose that as in Canada today, there is no law restricting the right of women to have abortions, the previous set of legal restrictions having been struck down by the Supreme Court of Canada. Suppose that this policy appeals most to extremists on the left of the abortion debate. Formally, let x = the level of restrictions on abortions, so that a movement to the right along the x-axis in Figure 11.2 implies greater restrictions. Suppose further that the two major Canadian parties were to become more polarized prior to the next election. We would predict that the abortion issue is *less* likely to be raised than before. The surprising part of the analysis is that this is so despite the fact that as a result of the polarization, both parties are more extreme, hence more pro- or anti-abortion than before. The resolution of the paradox is that raising the issue is now too dangerous for the conservatives, and it is still relatively uninteresting for the liberals, who are reasonably satisfied with the status quo.

Another important influence on the size of the DNZ is how much voters can trust politicians – as measured by their credibility parameter λ. The greater the parties' credibility with the electorate (λ), the more they are capable of moving to the center from their ideological positions.[2] The greater the parties' ability to credibly promise to implement centrist policies if elected (despite their right or left ideologies), the smaller the area of the DNZ. So in a sense, *the area of the DNZ is an index of the mistrust of politicians by voters* (holding the ideological distance $c_R - c_L$ constant).

This explains the great lamentation and hand-wringing in the United States and elsewhere over "dirty politics" or "negative campaigning." When each party's campaign attempts to destroy the other party's credibility (and when both succeed!), the result is that both parties will be less willing to raise or act on important political issues (i.e., the capacity of the public sector for action is reduced).

Finally, the size of the DNZ is affected by the relative willingness of the two parties to compromise (as measured by the parameter a). Part 1 of the appendix shows that a rise in a increases the loss from gambling by raising the issue (relative to maintaining the status quo). It follows that for divisive issues (like abortion or capital punishment), in which parties (like individuals) feel that allowing the preferred policy of the other side to be implemented would be disastrous, the DNZ will be relatively large. (Diagrammatically, as a increases, the DNZ fattens around unchanged end points.) The parties will either try to avoid the issue entirely, or, if that is impossible, they will try to raise it in some fashion that does not really commit the party to a specific position on that issue.

It follows that the inaction zone will be relatively large when:

1. the parties are relatively polarized.
2. issues are divisive.
3. the parties have relatively little credibility with the electorate.

Under these circumstances the inaction problem can be particularly serious. The consequences are examined in Sections 3 and 4.

---

[2] Recall that credibility is measured not as the probability that the party will implement its promised platform if elected, but by how far away from its ideological center a party can move and still credibly (i.e., with probability equal to 1) promise to implement that platform.

3   Who gets harmed, and why?

The preceding section described the *DNZ*, showed the factors which tend to make it larger or smaller, and suggested its potential burden on society. This section addresses the question of the distribution of the burden on different groups in the society and the ways in which those groups are affected.

To begin, let us note first that every individual in the polity has his or her own preferred *DNZ* (i.e., a range over which, if the status quo is located there, that individual prefers that the issue not be raised by either party). For voter i, this is simply the range over which[3]

(5) $U_i(s) > pU_i(\hat{x}_R) + (1-p)U_i(\hat{x}_L).$

Equation (5) just states that i prefers the status quo when the loss from the status quo to i is less than the expected loss if the issue is raised and if the parties implement their Nash equilibrium platforms $(\hat{x}_R, \hat{x}_L)$.

The size of the *DNZ* for a number of different individual types is illustrated in Figure 11.3. For each left-wing type, the *DNZ* is the zone to the left of the line indicated (i.e., that person only wants the issue raised if the status quo is to the right of the threshold line indicated). The argument for citizens on the right of the spectrum is symmetrical (i.e., their *DNZs* would all lie to the *right* of their inaction threshold lines).

Consider first a left-wing extremist – that is, an individual whose ideal point (c_{le} in Figure 11.3) is to the left of the left-wing party's ideological position (c_L in Figure 11.3). At any given p, the extremist wishes to raise all the issues that the left party does (i.e., all points to the right of the left party's *DNZ*). In addition, because he or she is to the left of the party, there are some issues in which, for the party, the utility loss from the status quo is less than that from the Nash equilibrium platforms that would be announced if the party raised the issue; but for the left extremist, this inequality is reversed. For example, a status quo at x in Figure 11.3 is within the party's *DNZ* but not the extremist's. The status quo is to the right of center, but it is close enough to the ideological position c_L to be "good enough" for the party, given the risks of raising the issue. But x is relatively far from the extremist's ideal point c_{le}, and it is just not good enough for him or her. At x, he or she prefers to raise the issue. Consequently, the characteristic situation of the extremist in a two-party

[3] In the special case of the utility function described in (3), equation (5) becomes

(5') $-(s-c_i)^{a_i} > -p(\hat{x}_R - c_i)^{a_i} - (1-p)(\hat{x}_L - c_i)^{a_i}$

where c_i = voter i's ideal point, $a_i - 1 = i$'s elasticity of marginal utility, and the other terms have the same interpretation as in the appendix.

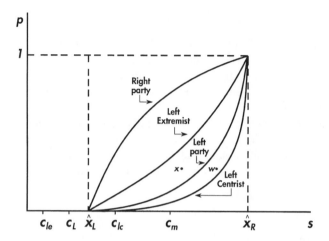

Figure 11.3. The burden of inaction on different individuals.

democracy is frustration: Extremists always want the party to take *more* stands on issues. Right-wing extremists are in a similar position with respect to the party of the right; the party is too cautious for them. In this sense extremists of both parties have something in common: They are both characteristically frustrated by the lack of action on many issues, and, if the political agenda were left up to them, they would agree to raise a much larger number of issues (on which they would then take opposite stands) than their parties would.

If extremists tend to be frustrated by the lack of political activity on many issues, centrists in either party tend to believe that there is *too much* political activity. The *DNZ* of a left centrist (whose ideal point is c_{lc}, which is to the right of $\hat{x}_L$) is the area to the left of the centrist's inaction threshold in Figure 11.3. Centrists agree completely with their party; they think that all issues in which the status quo lies to the left of the party's threshold should be left alone. But there are also a number of issues which the party wants to raise (such as the status quo w in Figure 11.3) but which the centrist prefers to leave alone. Centrists of both parties are in agreement on this; if they controlled their parties' agendas, the *DNZ* would be larger.

The extreme case of a centrist is the median voter (whose ideal point is at c_m, which, in the case of a symmetric polity as illustrated in Figure 11.3, lies exactly halfway between $\hat{x}_R$ and $\hat{x}_L$). Irrespective of p, if the status quo were to lie anywhere between $\hat{x}_R$ and $\hat{x}_L$, the median voter would obviously prefer that point to either $\hat{x}_R$ or $\hat{x}_L$. Consequently, the median voter's preferred *DNZ* is the entire rectangular area between $\hat{x}_R$ and $\hat{x}_L$ in Figure 11.3.

Note that if the degree of polarization of party positions $\hat{x}_R - \hat{x}_L$ were fairly large, equilibrium on an issue could be quite distant from that desired by centrist voters. Yet although unhappy with the status quo, they would not demand action by either political party, whose actions could only make matters worse from their point of view. Their characteristic attitude toward political institutions is resignation or cynicism – that is, the situation is bad, but they do not wish politicians to do anything about it, because their intervention invariably makes it worse.

Why do the median voters, ringmasters of the democratic political process in the standard theory, end up in this pickle in our model? Their strength in the usual convergence models – the relative ease with which they can switch from one party to the other – is precisely their weakness in our analysis. Parties need continued loyal support in order to function effectively. They cannot count on the loyalty of the median voter, who, of all citizens, has the most opportunities to switch to a different party. So the median voter pays a price for his or her disloyalty: No party wants to take the risk of being his or her representative.

4   Dynamics of instability and democratic breakdown

The argument so far demonstrates three points:

1. An equilibrium of political inaction is possible in a two-party democratic system.
2. Inaction is more likely when parties' platforms are relatively polarized, when the issues are divisive, and when the parties have relatively little credibility with the electorate.
3. Under these circumstances, the people most frustrated by the lack of action are the extremists in both (left and right) parties.

The formal analysis in this chapter is static, not dynamic. However, the frustration among voters caused by continued political inaction is obviously not conducive to political stability, and a number of dynamic sequences are possible in which such inaction leads to a breakdown of the system. For example, continued political inaction by both parties may be expected to erode their credibility. This erosion of credibility in our analysis simply reduces further the capacity of the system for action. The parties may become polarized, or in a multiparty system (analyzed shortly), voters may switch to more radical or extremist parties. In either case the result is a further loss in trust in the regime, greater frustration, and so on, which produces a destructive amplifying process.

There is a large literature in political science which associates the historical breakdown of democracy in various countries with precisely these variables: inaction, lack of credibility, and their mutually reinforcing effects (see, e.g., Huntington 1976; Sartori 1976).[4] Alan Cassels (1975, p. 37) cites the "inactivity" and "lack of leadership" of the post–World War I central government in Italy as instrumental to the rise of Mussolini. Karl Bracher (1970, 1995), Harold James (in Kershaw 1990; see especially pp. 46ff.), and Carl-Ludwig Holtfrerich (1990), among many, many others, analyze the breakdown of the Weimar regime in these terms. Bracher's influential concepts of the "power vacuum" (see, e.g., 1995, p. 7) and the "paralysis" of party democracy (loc. cit.)[5] under Weimar in its final years are particularly noteworthy. Juan Linz (in Linz and Stepan 1978) summarizes the findings of a large, multi-author project on the breakdown of competitive democracies in Europe and Latin America. He wrote,

> In the last analysis, breakdown is a result of processes initiated by the government's incapacity to solve problems for which disloyal oppositions offer themselves as a solution. That incapacity occurs when the parties supporting the regime cannot compromise on an issue and one or the other of them attempts a solution with the support of forces that the opposition within the system perceives as disloyal. This instigates polarization within the society that creates distrust among those who in other circumstances would have supported the regime. (p. 50)

Of course, many of the classic historical examples of democratic breakdown are multiparty systems. Although it is difficult precisely to generalize the model developed here to the multiparty case, it is easy to explain why the problem of inaction persists in that situation. With a larger number of parties, any issue is more likely to appear on the political "agenda." The larger the number of parties, the more likely it is that one or more of them will raise any particular issue. But in these

[4] Wintrobe (1991) provides an alternative explanation of the rise of dictatorship through "illegitimate" methods of political competition which often accompany polarization. G.B. Powell, Jr. (1986), sheds some doubt on the general thesis. Using empirical data from Western European democracies in the 1970s, he suggested that it is alienation from the political system rather than political polarization, which is associated with political turmoil.

[5] Originally developed in his study *The Dissolution of the Weimar Republic*. They are discussed more recently in Bracher (1995).

systems, it appears that it is less rather than more likely to be acted upon. The reason is that in multiparty systems (which usually result from electoral systems based to some extent on proportional representation), it is highly unusual for any single party to command a majority, and it usually takes negotiation and agreement to initiate any action.[6] So more problems may be on the political agenda in a multiparty system, but they are not acted upon unless the different parties in the governing coalition can agree on what to do. So the inaction problem is merely transferred from the electoral arena to the parliament. Most analysts expect more paralysis in multiparty than in two-party systems. Thus Gianluigi Galeotti (1991) suggests – and he provides some evidence to demonstrate – that political competition tends to decrease with the number of parties competing. V. Grilli, D. Masciandaro, and G. Tabbelini (1991) look at inaction on the public debt and find that "in almost all instances explosive public debts are found in countries governed by highly proportional electoral systems" (p. 345).

Indeed, in an influential contribution Giovanni Sartori (1976, pp. 160–5) emphasized that the number of political parties is the crucial determinant of whether party competition is "centripetal" or "centrifugal." He suggested that a large number of parties (five or more) is crucial to the shift to "polarized pluralism," a political system which often, but not always, results in dictatorship and which he used to characterize a number of countries over certain periods: Weimar Germany 1928–33, Italy 1946–72, France 1945–56 and 1958–73, Chile 1945–73, Finland 1945–75, and Spain 1931–36. In each case the shift of voters toward extremist parties (on both the right and the left) was notable over the period.

The classic case of centrifugal competition (polarization) is undoubtedly Weimar Germany. Carl-Ludwig Holtfrerich (1990) emphasizes the role of political inaction on the unemployment problem:

> There can be no doubt that in 1931/2 there was a strong popular demand for government action to stimulate the economy, which Bruning and – until the final agreement on reparations in June/July 1932 – practically all non-Nazi parties were loath to satisfy. [There was] an avoidable failure in political leadership, defined

[6] Mueller (1989) surveys the work on proportional representation. Of course, one can think of examples in which large left-wing or right-wing parties are prevented from acting on their "radical" platforms because they need the support of small "center" parties in order not to be voted out of power. If voters' opinions were more polarized, this inertia might be avoided. Since pure-strategy equilibria are difficult to derive with more than two parties, the point in the text cannot be demonstrated theoretically. However, it has a common-sense rationale insofar as proportional systems are often, though not always, characterized by short-lived coalitions or minority governments, as has been typically the case, for example, in Italy and Israel.

as a situation in which democratic parties pursue goals of some power elites, but disrespect the electorate's primary concerns. They thus drive voters into the arms of extremists who are clever enough to lure them by offering radical solutions to the public's most pressing needs. (p. 73)

J.M. Enelow and M.J. Hinich (1982) model the rise of extremist candidates or parties as the consequence of voter cynicism. However, their analysis is different from the one presented here. Voter cynicism in their model implies that voters essentially don't believe what politicians say, so when voters become more cynical, they are more likely to vote for extremist candidates, because they believe the extremists to be less extreme than their statements imply. Enelow and Hinich suggest that this accounts for the rise of extremism under some circumstances. As an illustration, they cite the case of Germany in the early 1930s. However, the key factor they point to in explaining the rise of Nazism was government inaction. They wrote, ". . . it was widely thought that the inability of government to solve the society's basic problems was so deep-seated that only a candidate of the extreme right could do anything to bring about a desired charge in the status quo" (p. 499).

The analysis of this phenomenon offered here appears more satisfactory. Voters switched to extremist candidates not because they didn't believe any of the parties, as Enelow and Hinich suggest, but because they believed the extremists would act and centrist parties wouldn't, and they preferred extremist action to no action at all. For example, the parties in power were unable to curb political violence on both the left and the right, a violence which terrified many voters. We have already emphasized the strong popular demand for government action to stimulate the economy, which Chancellor Bruning and practically all non-Nazi parties were loath to satisfy. Hitler, on the other hand, promised a job for every German (Holtfrerich 1990, p. 73).

Why would voters prefer extremist action to no action at all? The next section addresses this question. To do so, we return to our (static) model of inaction and extend it to show the *inefficiency* of inaction.

5   The inefficiency of inaction

This section extends the analysis of political inaction to cover the case in which the status quo is regarded by many voters as not just unsatisfactory but as actually Pareto-inefficient. In that case the suppression of demands for action represents not just the imposition of a minority viewpoint in favor of the status quo but also a failure of the political system to take advantage of an opportunity to improve everyone's lot.

To deal with the inefficiency of inaction, we have to extend our analysis to two dimensions. With one dimension one can have either more or less of a policy x, but at least two dimensions are needed (a production possibility curve) to show inefficiency. So we will consider an issue to which there are two dimensions that concern voters: x_1 and x_2. For example, the issue might be abortion, with x_1 the rights of the unborn and x_2 the rights of women. Government policy can be used to select any combination of (x_1, x_2) from a compact, convex feasible set whose northeast frontier (henceforth "the efficiency frontier") is strictly concave to the origin, as shown in Figure 11.4. All voters' preferences are strictly increasing in both dimensions. Thus, any point inside the efficiency frontier, like s in Figure 11.1, represents an inefficient policy in the sense that all voters could feasibly be made better off.

As before, the two political parties, L and R, are each motivated by a concern for the actual policy (x_1, x_2) that will be implemented according to a utility function $u^j(x_1, x_2), j = L,R$. This function represents the policy preferences of the activists (those who join parties) in each party. The functions u^j are assumed to be smooth, strictly concave, and strictly increasing in each dimension. Party L has a comparative preference for x_2, in the sense that its indifference curve at any point in Figure 11.4 is less steep than party R's. It follows that within the feasible set, party L's most preferred policy (c^L) lies to the northwest of party R's (c^R).

Again, electoral competition between the parties can be seen as a game in three stages. First, each party chooses whether or not to raise the issue. Then both parties prepare platforms and fight an election on the issue if it has been raised. Then the winner implements the policy to which it is committed.

Now consider the payoffs to each party prior to the election. If neither party has raised the issue, then each party j will attain the utility level $u^j(s)$ with certainty. If the issue has been raised, then the party will attain the expected utility:

$$Pu^j\left(x^R\right)+\left(1-P\right)u^j\left(x^L\right)$$

where P is the probability that R wins the election and x^R, x^L are the parties' respective platforms. Part 3 of the appendix shows that, in equilibrium, these platforms remain divergent. Will either party choose to raise the issue? Consider the situation of party j. If the other party has raised the issue, j will have no choice but to go into an election over the question. If the other party has not raised the matter, j can choose

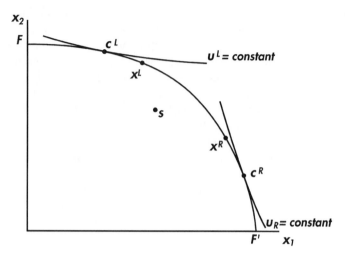

Figure 11.4. Inaction in two dimensions (the feasible set is the subset contained in OFF').

between the status quo and an election over the issue by deciding whether or not to raise the issue. It will not raise the matter if its expected utility is greater under the status quo than under an election over the issue:

$$(6) \qquad u^j(s) > Pu^j(x^R) + (1 - P)u^j(x^L).$$

If (6) holds for both $j = L$ and $j = R$, then the issue will not be raised. On the other hand, if the inequality in (6) is reversed for either party, then the issue will be raised.

Define the "inaction zone" as the set of feasible policies s such that (6) holds for both parties. This zone is depicted by the shaded area in Figure 11.5. If the status quo lies in the inaction zone, then it will remain even if the status quo is inefficient, because neither party will raise the issue. The central result of this section is this theorem: *The inaction zone contains inefficient policies.*

The proof of this theorem is straightforward and can be given geometrically in terms of Figure 11.5.

Point $\bar{x}$ represents the expected policy if the issue is raised. If this were the status quo, then (6) would hold for both parties because of strict concavity of utility. That is, both parties would strictly prefer to have the status quo $\bar{x}$ with certainty than to have the same expected outcome with a risk of something worse. Because the feasible set is convex, therefore,

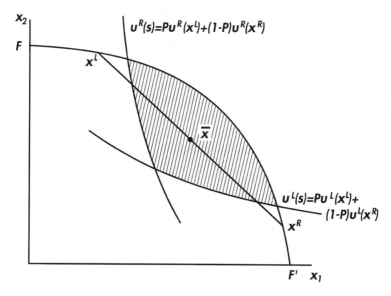

Figure 11.5. The inefficiency of inaction. [The inaction zone is the shaded area. It contains $\bar{x} = Px^L + (1 - P)x^R$, which is inside the efficiency frontier.]

$\bar{x}$ is feasible. Hence, $\bar{x}$ lies in the inaction zone. But because the efficiency frontier is strictly concave, $\bar{x}$ is inefficient.

6   Relaxing the assumptions

It may be worthwhile to discuss in some detail the precise nature of the forces which lead to these results and to see what happens if some of our assumptions are relaxed.[7] Several issues are considered, including

1. the role of multidimensionality in generating inaction.
2. why a new party doesn't arise to fill the policy gap between the parties and eliminate inaction.
3. the relationship between political inaction and political ambiguity.

[7] The explanation of a bias in favor of the status quo given here is entirely different from – and possibly complementary to – that offered by R. Fernandez and D. Rodrik (1991). Their status quo bias refers to the forgone benefits from not embracing an uncertain but, on average, beneficial policy. Our model is more directed at a situation in which there is a festering social or economic problem of which everyone may be aware but on which nothing is done. Theirs is a model of economic uncertainty, with a political system guaranteed to deliver the median voter's preferred policy. Ours is a model of (possible) political paralysis, with no necessary role for economic uncertainty.

4. the consequences of relaxing the electoral rules assumed in Sections 2 and 5.
5. the effects of cooperation versus competition between political parties.

Note first that the analysis assumes that neither party has the ability to unbundle the different dimensions of the issue. That is, there is no instrument available to either party which is capable of increasing x_1 without at the same time decreasing x_2 (or vice versa). Otherwise, it would be in each party's interest to raise the subissue of increasing x_1 whenever the status quo was inefficient; with the sub-issue of x_2 not raised, political competition would cause each party to promise to increase x_1 right up to the efficiency frontier. This result would obviously yield higher expected utility to both parties than the status quo.

To illustrate this point, let us consider the abortion issue in some more detail. The two dimensions are the rights of the mother and the rights of the unborn child (as shown in Figure 11.6). There are many possible instruments which can be used to deal with this issue, including the accessibility of abortion clinics, the level of public subsidy given to them, how much police protection is offered to protect women who are entering them and doctors who are working in them from anti-abortion activists, the nature of the examination a woman has to submit to before she can legally have an abortion, the number of doctors whose agreement is required, whether the father's consent is also required, the maximum number of weeks a woman can be pregnant and still be allowed to go through with one, and so on. Consider just two of these instruments – for example, the accessibility of clinics (l_1 in Figure 11.6) and the maximum number of weeks of pregnancy within which abortion is allowed (l_2). As in the figure, assume that increasing accessibility increases the rights of women (x_2) but reduces those of the unborn (x_1). Reducing the number of weeks has the opposite effects (i.e., it reduces x_2 and raises x_1).

Note that as depicted, the tradeoff between x_1 and x_2 differs between the two instruments. As long as this is the case, the status quo is inefficient, because by using both instruments, it is possible to "tack" up to a point like B, at which both target variables are raised, implying Pareto improvement.[8] However, political competition between two parties, one of which is relatively more sensitive to x_1, and the other to x_2, may easily

---

[8] For some purposes, of course, it is useful to represent the abortion issue as a one-dimensional problem (e.g., the level of restrictions). Efficiency issues, however, cannot be discussed in the one-dimensional case. Nor is it easy to explain, using one dimension, why restrictions typically are greater on abortions later in the term. With two dimensions – the rights of the mother and of the child – the explanation is obvious: The child presumably is accorded more rights as it progresses from conception to birth.

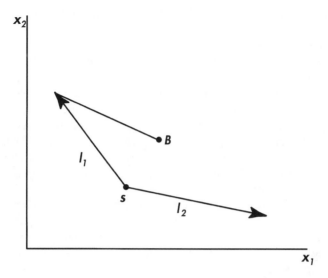

Figure 11.6. The necessary condition for inaction. [The status quo s is inefficient if by using l_1 (increased accessibility) and l_2 (tighter limit on maximum fetal age), the rights of both women (X_1) and the unborn (X_2) can be increased.]

yield the result that both parties prefer the status quo s to raising the issue. This is possible as long as no instrument is available which is capable of increasing one of the target dimensions without lowering the other.

The necessary condition for inaction is simply this: There is no instrument which can improve matters from one party's point of view without making it worse for the other. What emerges from considering the multidimensional case is not the possibility of inaction, but the possibility of inefficient inaction, since the issue of efficiency cannot be discussed in the one-dimensional case.

A second question is why a new party doesn't enter to fill the gap between the two nonconvergent platforms of the existing parties, thus breaking the political deadlock. Here, one can refer to J.H. Aldrich's (1983) argument that each party must offer distinct platforms in order to attract the activists needed to carry out its campaigning and other activities. Without a gap no one would care which party won the election, and hence no one would be motivated to incur the cost of joining – let alone campaigning for – a political party. Furthermore, the evidence of Douglas Hibbs (1977) Alesina (1988b and 1992), and Wittman (1983) shows that in fact the gap does remain unfilled in many political systems, including that of the United States, in all of which the policies actually implemented are affected systematically by which party wins the election.

A. Alesina and H. Rosenthal (1989) and M. Fiorina (1988) developed models in which centrist voters could compensate for the nonexistence of centrist candidates through midterm balancing (Alesina and Rosenthal) or "split ticket" voting (Fiorina). Thus, although no median candidate is available, voters can nevertheless obtain median *policies* by voting one way (e.g., Democratic) in presidential elections and the other way (Republican) in midterm congressional elections, or by splitting their vote between parties in either election. The present model's stress on the possibility of inaction exposes a flaw in either strategy: voters' attempts to obtain centrist policies in these ways may simply result in inaction on important issues rather than in the hoped-for compromise action. Indeed, stalemates and deadlocks are commonly observed in the United States whenever the president and a majority of either House or Senate are from opposing parties.

Third, note that the concept of political *inaction* used in this chapter is different from the concept of political *ambiguity*, which is discussed in a number of papers, including those by A. Alesina and C. Cukierman (1990), A. Glazer (1990), and K. Shepsle (1972). In these models, parties or candidates either adopt vague or fuzzy positions on an issue (Shepsle, Glazer) or choose policy procedures which increase the variance or the "noise" between policy instruments and policy outcomes (Alesina and Cukierman). The purpose in all cases is to increase uncertainty in the minds of voters as to the party's true position.

In Shepsle's model, parties would do this only if voters preferred risk (an unsure or ambiguous outcome relative to a certain outcome). In Alesina and Cukierman, on the other hand, ambiguous policies may improve the tradeoff between a party's true preferences and the policies it adopts in order to get reelected by confusing (even risk averse) voters about its true policy. In Glazer's model, candidates are unsure about *voters'* preferences, and they thus select ambiguity in order to avoid committing themselves to a precise position which may be disliked by the median voter.

In this model, parties are also concerned with the risks of defeat due to the adoption of an unpopular position on some issue. One difference between this conception of how politicians deal with this problem and that suggested in the literature on ambiguity is that in this model, parties do not choose between more or less ambiguity; but instead they try to decide whether to adopt a (precise) position or not to adopt a position at all. However, the main difference is that in this model, if no position is declared, no policy will be implemented. In the ambiguity models, policies are in fact adopted on every issue. So the phenomenon examined here is different from that discussed in the ambiguity literature. In this model, voters are frustrated because politicians refuse to do anything to alter the status quo. In the ambiguity models, they do something (i.e., they implement policies on every issue) once in office, and what frustrates voters is they don't know what those policies are going to be.

Fourth, an objection may be raised with respect to the assumption that if an issue has not been raised during the election campaign, the party which wins is bound to the status quo once in office. Why can't a party raise an issue once in office and simply implement its preferred policy, even though the issue was not raised during the election campaign? Indeed, party platforms are often vague, sometimes can hardly be interpreted as constituting a binding commitment, and are often ignored in the implemention of policy. However, in most – if not all – democratic systems, the simple fact of election does not give the winning party an absolutely free hand to implement its preferred policies. This is most obvious in the United States, where power is divided and presidents still have to fight to get their programs through; and in federal systems, in which policy implemented at the federal level can be undone by the states or provinces. But all democratic systems – even parliamentary systems – feature an array of legislative, judicial, bureaucratic, and political checks and balances.[9] And in all systems the attempt to implement a policy galvanizes opposition to that policy by opposition parties, interest groups who are adversely affected, bureaucrats who might stand to lose in some way from it, and so on. Thus, opposition will tend to be larger and it is more likely to succeed if the government has earned no mandate to implement the policy in an election fought on the issue.

In short, raising an issue always carries the risk that a party will not necessarily obtain the policy it desires, even if that party holds office. And the risks are clearly greater as the importance of the issue increases. Recent examples are too numerous to list here, but perhaps we could simply note the U.S. government's attempt at health reform in Clinton's first term or the Canadian government's failures to reform the Constitution in 1989 and again in 1992.

To put it differently, suppose we relax the electoral rules described here and discard all references to elections, commitments, and so on. Instead, suppose p simply represents the probability that if a party raises

---

[9] For an elaboration of these checks and balances, especially with respect to parliamentary systems, see the papers in A. Breton, G. Galeotti, P. Salmon, and R. Wintrobe (1991).

an issue, it will be able to successfully implement its preferred policy x_R. Then $1 - p$ obviously covers many possibilities, including failure and maintenance of the status quo, getting the policy of the opposition (x_L), and so on rather than simply the probability of getting x_L. However, the essence of the problem remains the same: A party – whether in or out of office and facing an election or not – may prefer inaction to raising the issue and taking the risk of ending up with a policy very much worse from its point of view than the status quo.

Finally, it is important to emphasize that the failure to change an inefficient status quo in the inaction zone does not result from collusive behavior among politicians. The equilibrium in each of the first two stages of the political game is a noncooperative Nash equilibrium. At stage 1 each party makes a dichotomous choice – to raise the issue or not – taking the other's choice as given. At stage 2 it chooses its platform, taking the other's platform, as given, with no commitment from stage 1.

Indeed, if the parties could make binding agreements with each other at stage 1 concerning what platforms they will propose to the voters in stage 2, then as Alesina (1988a) has shown in a similar context, they would agree to a common platform. Otherwise, they could each receive a higher expected utility from agreeing to adopt the expected outcome as a common platform, which would eliminate risk. Furthermore, this common platform would have to lie on the efficiency frontier, because otherwise the parties could each benefit from agreeing to move their common platform to the northeast. Inefficient status quos would therefore never remain, because the parties could each benefit from agreeing to raise the issue and adopt a common platform to the northeast of the status quo.

Implicit in the model developed here is the assumption that parties do not have the power to make such binding commitments to each other, whereas they can make binding commitments to voters. These two assumptions would seem to characterize a well-functioning democracy. The ability of parties to commit to voters is what allows them to compete for votes in stage 2 by promising credibly that once elected, they will implement their platforms instead of their preferred policies. Their inability to promise to each other in stage 1 not to compete for votes in stage 2 also precludes the kind of cooperative outcome that might theoretically eliminate an inefficient status quo in the inaction zone.

Before concluding that this kind of cooperation is desirable, let us note that if the parties could make binding agreements with each other, what would prevent them from acting as a monopoly seller of public policies to the voters and extracting all the rents that accrue to this monopoly of political power? It is interesting in this context that in Italy, where the parties apparently make deals with each other all the time (see, e.g., LaPalombara, 1987), the derisive term *partyocracy* has been invented to describe a system in which elections are used only to decide how to divide the spoils of office among the parties (see Ferrero and Brosio forthcoming, who adopt the label *nomenklatura* for Italian party officials). What is even more interesting, however, is the well-known fact that the Italian system is plagued with inaction (e.g., its debt-to-GNP ratio in 1992 exceeded 100 percent). The parties easily compromise on dividing up the spoils of office – but they do not compromise as easily on policy – just as one would expect in a system in which the role of party activists is paramount.

By contrast, the assumption that, in general, parties are capable of building trust with voters but not with other parties characterizes a well-functioning democracy, the essence of which is that parties are forced to compete with each other for the votes of citizens. This assumption parallels analogous assumptions in the theory of industrial organization that markets in which contractual enforceability is weak work well when consumers trust firms (firms are capable of building "reputations") but firms don't trust each other (see for example Shapiro 1983). In one sense, therefore, the fact that political inaction *could* be eliminated by a reduction in political competition does illustrate the classical attraction of dictatorial rule: Authoritarian governments are capable of giving "strong leadership" and of "acting on important issues" in circumstances in which democracies would be unable to act, simply because of their capacity to repress alternatives to their policies. From this point of view, the inaction zone is part of the price citizens pay for democracy.

However, it can also be argued that the existence of the inaction zone is the result of *too little* competition. If each party were to compete harder to attract each others' voters, presumably the two parties would move toward each other and converge on a common platform, as in the median voter model (or in probabilistic models of convergence). In those models all issues are raised, unless the status quo on some issue is exactly at the median. Otherwise, the issue will be raised by either party, because both prefer the median to the status quo.

This point neglects the role of party activists in political competition. But it does show that the fundamental source of political inaction is not competition or collusion, but the existence of a diversity of viewpoints (equilibrium platforms) among political parties. As long as the parties espouse different policies on an issue, circumstances will arise when both are afraid to raise that issue out of the fear that they may end up with the opponent's policies, which they dislike more than the status quo. The tradeoff suggested by the model, then, is one between political action and political representation, the capacity of the political system to represent different points of view and to expose these alternatives to electoral competition. In the median voter model and in notions of dictatorship, this tradeoff disappears because only one point of view is represented by the political system.[10]

7   Conclusion: the tradeoff between action and representation

The analysis in this chapter appears to point to a fundamental tradeoff characteristic of any political system: between political action and representation. We can illustrate this tradeoff by considering the limiting case in which party platforms converge on a single policy, as in the median voter model. This case eliminates the inaction zone, as we have seen, thus maximizing the system's capacity for action. But it also minimizes the capacity for representation. Parties do not offer voters a real choice, because they represent only one point of view – that of the voter whose preferred policy coincides with the common platform of the two parties.

The cost of inaction can be represented using the standard tools of welfare economics – that is, it is the difference between the maximum of a social welfare function over the feasible set and the value of the same welfare function under two-party competition when the status quo is in the inaction zone. This cost will almost always be positive.

The cost of nonrepresentation is less amenable to conventional welfare analysis, especially since we have assumed up to now that individual utility functions depend upon policy outcomes, not upon representation. Nevertheless, it seems clear that most people would feel better off if some political party were giving active voice to a point of view similar to their own, even taking as given the policy outcome. They might also believe that having a point of view expressed by one of the parties during the current campaign might change the direction of political debate and hence alter the outcome of future elections. Thus, the cost of nonrepresentation might be represented as a weighted average across voters of the distance in utils between the voter's most preferred policy

---

[10] Perhaps this analysis also explains why in wartime, politicians and citizens who are opposed but not too opposed to the war effort might mute their opposition in order to avoid weakening the capacity of the political system for (military) action. On the other hand, other (equally patriotic) citizens might see the associated weakening of democracy as too high a price to pay for effective military action.

and the nearest party platform – that is, for voter j, the difference between the maximum of $u_j(x)$ over the feasible set and $max \; \{u_j(x^R), u_j(x^L)\}$.

Clearly, a pair of platforms that minimizes the sum of these two costs will generally involve a positive degree of polarization – that is, a difference between the two platforms. Zero polarization would maximize the cost of nonrepresentation, whereas too much polarization could reduce both representation and action. For example, if the two platforms are located at either extreme of the political spectrum, with most voters between these extremes, the inaction zone will be maximal, and most voters will feel themselves poorly represented by existing parties. Thus, some positive – but not too extreme – degree of polarization will be optimal.

Extreme polarization, on the other hand, tends to be associated with the breakdown of democracy. The model developed here provides a simple explanation of this association. Extreme polarization caused by the radicalization of parties, by their increasingly ideological motivation, or by a breakdown of trust in politicians would raise the costs of both inaction and nonrepresentation. Presumably, citizens would get increasingly fed up with a system that was both increasingly unrepresentative and at the same time unable to act on the important issues of the day, and they might thus be tempted to support an authoritarian alternative. The model thus also provides some theoretical foundation for the idea that democracies are more likely to work and therefore to survive when a substantial middle class has emerged, an outcome which will tend to limit excessive polarization of opinions.

MATHEMATICAL APPENDIX

Part 1

This part of the appendix describes the equilibrium platforms of the parties when issues are unidimensional (as in Figures 11.1 and 11.2 of the text), and it derives the conditions corresponding to each party's threshold of inaction as depicted in those figures.

To proceed, let us assume that the two platforms must satisfy the conditions of Nash equilibrium (i.e., each party chooses that platform which maximizes its expected utility, given the position of the other party). So party R maximizes

$$(A.1) \quad w^R(x_R, x_L) = p\left[-(x_R - c_R)^a\right] + (1-p)\left[-(x_L - c_R)^a\right] + pk$$

where the first term on the right-hand side gives the utility to party R of its platform if it wins office (the probability of which is p); the second term gives the utility to party R if party L wins office (with probability $1 - p$); finally, the third term gives the expected value to party R of being in office per se. Similarly, party L chooses a platform which maximizes its expected utility, given the platform of party R:

$$(A.2) \quad w^L(x_R, x_L) = (1 - p)\left[-(x_L - c_L)^a\right] + p\left[(x_R - c_L)^a\right] + (1 - p)k.$$

Alesina (1988a) presents conditions under which equilibrium platforms exist with $c_L < \hat{x}_L < \hat{x}_R < c_R$. Assume that whenever an issue is raised, we will observe equilibrium platforms which satisfy this condition. However, parties also have the option of not raising an issue, which voters will interpret as a binding promise to leave the status quo unchanged if they are elected. If neither party takes a stand on an issue, they are indistinguishable (both are implicitly promising the status quo s); in that case, the probability that party R wins is given by p^s.

The gain to party R from raising the issue is then the difference between its expected utility going into an election over the issue and its expected utility going into an election in which the issue isn't raised. So the gain to party R from raising the issue, g_R, is:

$$(A.3) \quad g_R = p\left[k - (\hat{x}_R - c_R)^a + (\hat{x}_L - c_R)^a\right] - (\hat{x}_L - c_R)^a - p^s k + (s - c_R)^a$$

The right-hand side of (A.3), except for the last two terms, may be interpreted in the same way as equation (5) – that is, as the expected utility to party R if the issue is raised. The last two terms $- -p^s k + (s - c_R)^a$ – give the negative of party R's utility if the issue is not raised. A similar equation may be written for party L:

$$(A.4) \quad g_L = (1 - p)\left[k - (\hat{x}_L - c_L)^a + (\hat{x}_R - c_L)^a\right]$$
$$- (\hat{x}_R - c_L)^a - (1 - p^s)k + (s - c_L)^a$$

The conditions under which party R will be indifferent between raising and not raising an issue is simply that $g_R = 0$, or

$$(A.5) \quad p = \frac{(x_L - c_R)^a - (s - c_R)^a - (p - p^s)k}{(\hat{x}_L - c_R)^a - (\hat{x}_R - c_R)^a}$$

Similarly, for party L the condition that $g_L = 0$ may be written as

(A.6) $1 - p = \dfrac{\left(x_R - c_L\right)^a - \left(s - c_L\right)^a - \left(p - p^s\right)k}{\left(\hat{x}_R - c_L\right)^a - \left(\hat{x}_L - c_L\right)^a}.$

These two equations define each party's "threshold of inaction," as illustrated in Figure 11.1 under the simplifying assumption that $(p - p^s)k = 0$.

The area where both parties prefer not to raise the issue is the *DNZ* in Figure 11.1. Note that in this analysis, the policies x_i do not depend on p. Rather, the figure simply displays all the possible values of x_i and p, where inaction would be preferred to action, assuming the two variables can be varied separately. Put simply, the *DNZ* answers the question: For any status quo s, how high does p have to be ($1 - p$ for the left party) before action (a platform proposing $x = \hat{x}$) is preferred to the status quo? Alternatively, for any given p, the *DNZ* shows how large the distance $\hat{x}_i - s$ has to be before a party is willing to announce a policy rather than stick with the status quo.

Let us briefly note the consequences of relaxing the assumption that $\sigma \equiv (p - p^s)k = 0$. If σ were > 0, party R clearly would have an additional incentive (higher likelihood of election victory) to raise the issue, so its threshold would shift downward. However, party L would have *less* incentive to raise the issue, so its threshold also would shift downward. In general, then, the effect of σ on the size of the *DNZ* is ambiguous. But in the limit, as $\sigma \to \infty$, it is clear that the *DNZ* would disappear. In other words, sufficiently high spoils of office or a high enough popularity to be gained from raising an issue will cause the issue to be raised by one party or the other.

The size of the *DNZ* is affected by the relative willingness of the two parties to compromise, as measured by the parameter a. Higher values of a imply, formally, that utility decreases more rapidly as the platform becomes more distant from the party's ideological position. Rewrite equation (A.5) as

(A.7) $-\left(s - c_R\right)^a = -p\left(\hat{x}_R - c_R\right)^a - \left(1 - p\right)\left(\hat{x}_L - c_R\right)^a + \left(p - p^s\right)k,$

and (A.6) as

(A.8) $-\left(s - c_L\right)^a = -\left(1 - p\right)\left(\hat{x}_L - c_L\right)^a - p\left(\hat{x}_R - c_L\right)^a + \left(p^s - p\right)k.$

Assuming the platforms themselves are unchanged as the result of the increase in a, we find that an increase in a reduces the right-hand side of each equation relative to the left-hand side – that is, it increases the loss from gambling by raising the issue, relative to maintaining the status quo.

In general, we would also expect the platforms themselves to change as a result of an increase in a, becoming more polarized as each side's unwillingness to compromise reduces the utility of any movement away from its ideological center. This increased polarization would likely further increase the size of the *DNZ*, as shown in Section 2. (I am indebted to an anonymous referee for this last point.)

Part 2

This appendix demonstrates that if

1. preferences are quadratic ($a = 2$),
2. there is no value to winning per se ($k = 0$), and
3. the polity is symmetric ($c_R - \hat{x}_R = \hat{x}_L - c_L$)

then the area A of the *DNZ* equals $\dfrac{\left(\hat{x}_R - \hat{x}_L\right)^2}{3\left(c_R - c_L\right)}$.

Demonstration: From (5) and (6) in the text, we get

$$
A = \int_{\hat{x}_L}^{\hat{x}_R} \left[\frac{\left(s - c_R\right)^2 - \left(\hat{x}_L - c_R\right)^2}{\left(\hat{x}_R - c_R\right)^2 - \left(\hat{x}_L - c_R\right)^2} - \frac{\left(\hat{x}_L - c_L\right)^2 - \left(s - c_L\right)^2}{\left(\hat{x}_L - c_L\right)^2 - \left(\hat{x}_R - c_L\right)^2} \right] ds.
$$

By symmetry (iii): $(\hat{x}_R - c_R)^2 = (\hat{x}_L - c_L)^2$ and $(\hat{x}_L - c_R)^2 = (\hat{x}_R - c_L)^2$. Therefore,

$$
A = \int_{\hat{x}_L}^{\hat{x}_R} \left[\frac{\left(s - c_R\right)^2 - \left(\hat{x}_L - c_R\right)^2 - \left(\hat{x}_L - c_L\right)^2 + \left(s - c_L\right)^2}{\left(\hat{x}_R - c_R\right)^2 - \left(\hat{x}_L - c_R\right)^2} \right] ds
$$

$$
= \frac{1}{\Delta} \left[\frac{\left(\hat{x}_R - c_R\right)^3 - \left(\hat{x}_L - c_R\right)^3}{3} - \left(\hat{x}_R - \hat{x}_L\right)\left(\hat{x}_L - c_R\right)^2 \right.
$$

$$
\left. - \left(\hat{x}_L - \hat{x}_R\right)\left(\hat{x}_L - c_L\right)^2 + \frac{\left(\hat{x}_R - c_R\right)^3 - \left(\hat{x}_L - c_L\right)^3}{3} \right]
$$

$$
= \frac{1}{\Delta} \left[\frac{2}{3}\left(\left[\hat{x}_R - c_R\right]^3 - \left[\hat{x}_L - c_R\right]^3\right) \right.
$$

$$
\left. - \left(\hat{x}_R - \hat{x}_L\right)\left[\left(\hat{x}_L - c_R\right)^2 + \left(\hat{x}_R - c_R\right)^2\right] \right]
$$

where $\Delta = (\hat{x}_R - c_R)^2 - (\hat{x}_L - c_R)^2$. Since $x^3 - y^3 \equiv (x - y)(x^2 + y^2 + xy)$, therefore,

$$
\begin{aligned}
A &= \frac{1}{\Delta}\left[\frac{2}{3}\left(\hat{x}_R - \hat{x}_L\right)\right. \\
&\quad \left(\left[\hat{x}_R - c_R\right]^2 + \left[\hat{x}_L - c_R\right]^2 + \left[\hat{x}_R - c_R\right]\left[\hat{x}_L - c_R\right]\right) \\
&\quad \left.- \left(\hat{x}_R - \hat{x}_L\right)\left[\left(\hat{x}_L - c_R\right)^2 + \left(\hat{x}_R - c_L\right)^2\right]\right] \\
&= \frac{-1}{3\Delta}\left[\left(\hat{x}_R - c_R\right)^2 + \left(\hat{x}_L - c_R\right)^2\right. \\
&\quad \left.- 2\left(\hat{x}_R - c_R\right)\left(\hat{x}_L - c_R\right)\right]\left(\hat{x}_R - \hat{x}_L\right) \\
&= \frac{-1}{3\Delta}\left[\left(\left[\hat{x}_R - c_R\right] - \left[\hat{x}_L - c_R\right]\right)^2\right]\left(\hat{x}_R - \hat{x}_L\right) \\
&= \frac{1}{3\Delta}\left(\hat{x}_R - \hat{x}_L\right)^3.
\end{aligned}
$$

Since $x^2 - y^2 \equiv (x + y)(x - y)$, therefore,

$$
\begin{aligned}
\Delta &= \left(\hat{x}_R + \hat{x}_L - 2c_R\right)\left(\hat{x}_R - \hat{x}_L\right) \\
&= \left[\left(\hat{x}_R - c_R\right) + \left(\hat{x}_L - c_R\right)\right]\left(\hat{x}_R - \hat{x}_L\right) \\
&= \left[\left(c_L - \hat{x}_L\right) + \left(\hat{x}_L - c_R\right)\right]\left(\hat{x}_R - \hat{x}_L\right) \quad \text{(by symmetry)} \\
&= \left(c_L - c_R\right)\left(\hat{x}_R - \hat{x}_L\right)
\end{aligned}
$$

Therefore,

$$
A = -\frac{1}{3\left(c_L - c_R\right)\left(\hat{x}_R - \hat{x}_L\right)}\left(\hat{x}_R - \hat{x}_L\right)^3 = \frac{\left(\hat{x}_R - \hat{x}_L\right)^2}{3\left(c_R - c_L\right)}.
$$

Part 3

This part describes the two parties' equilibrium choices of nonconvergent equilibrium platforms (x^L, x^R) in the two-dimensional policy space as depicted in Figure 11.4. Using the same notation as in Section 5 of the text, assume that the probability P depends upon the two platforms according to the smooth function $P(x^L, x^R)$, which satisfies for all feasible x^R, x^L:

(A.9) $0 < P\left(x^R, x^L\right) < 1$,

(A.10) P is concave in x^R, convex in x^L,

(A.11) $\partial P/\partial x_j^L < 0 < \partial P/\partial x_j^R; j = 1, 2$,

(A.12)   If x^R and x^L are efficient and policy x lies on the efficiency
         frontier strictly between x^R and x^L, then $P(x^R, x) < P(x^R, x^L)$
         $< P(x, x^L)$.

Assumptions (A.9) and (A.10) are made for technical convenience. Assumption (A.11) states merely that a party will be more likely to win if it unambiguously improves its platform. This assures that if the issue is raised, each party will propose an efficient policy. Assumption (A.12), the probabilistic analogue to the result in one-dimensional deterministic spatial models, can be interpreted to mean that moving closer to its competitor allows a party to capture some of the voters in between without losing any on its other side. Although the policy space is two-dimensional, competition in this model occurs on the one-dimensional efficiency frontier.

If the issue has been raised, each party chooses its platform so as to maximize its expected utility given the other party's platform. That is, (x^R, x^L) must satisfy the Nash-equilibrium conditions:

(A.13) $\pi^R\left(x^R, x^L\right) \le \pi^R\left(x_1, x_2\right)$ for all feasible x

         $\pi^L\left(x^R, x^L\right) \le \pi^L\left(x_1, x_2\right)$ for all feasible x,

where π^j denotes party j's payoff function:

$$\pi^j\left(x^R, x^L\right) = P\left(x^R, x^L\right)u^j\left(x^R\right) + \left[1 - P\left(x^R, x^L\right)\right]u^j\left(x^L\right).$$

Assume that the two preferred policies c^R and c^L are in the interior of the efficiency frontier as shown in Figure 11.4. Then it can be shown by standard methods that a pair of platforms (x^R, x^L) exists on the efficiency frontier, which satisfies the equilibrium conditions (18) and:

(A.14) x^R lies strictly between c^R and x^L
         x^L lies strictly between x^R and c^L.

Assume that such a pair of platforms will be announced if the issue has been raised.

As shown in Figure 11.4, result (A.14) implies that each party will be induced by electoral competition to compromise, moving away from its preferred position in the direction of the opposition. This is because a party that was contemplating proposing its preferred policy could raise its probability of winning by compromising [Assumption (A.12)]. The cost of utility in the event that it wins, given that it is starting at its most preferred policy, would be second order.

As Figure 11.4 also shows, result (A.14) implies furthermore that electoral competition will not lead to convergence of platforms as in other spatial models of competition; x^R will lie to the left of x^L. This is because if the two policies were identical, then either party could gain utility in the event it wins by moving its platform in its preferred direction. The cost of such a move would be a reduced probability of winning. But this is a second-order cost, because assumption (A.12) implies that, given the other party's platform, each party's probability of winning is maximized when it offers the same platform.

12   Ethnic conflict and nationalism: from expressionism and futurism to *kitsch*

1.   Introduction

The preceding chapter examined one important element in the break-down of democracy and the rise of dictatorship – the possibility that democracy will become trapped in inaction. This chapter examines a second historically important element in the rise of many autocracies – ethnic conflict and nationalism. Again, the classic example is Nazi Germany, and again the analysis is conducted with special reference to it. Although the word is much bandied about, the concept of nationalism remains largely shrouded in mystery and it is little understood, especially from the point of view of rational choice.[1] In this chapter I will therefore proceed step by step. I begin with an analysis of the economic value of ethnicity (explaining why people form ethnic groups), and I will then proceed from there to the connection between ethnicity and nationalism, and finally to that between nationalism and Fascism. I then try to analyze the origins of prejudice and hatred of other ethnic groups. Finally, I begin to address the most difficult question of all – how these attitudes could result in a willingness to take part in "crimes against humanity" or genocidal actions against minority ethnic groups – in this chapter, and to explore it further in the next one.

The next section of this chapter suggests that in both public and private life, one particularly cost-effective way to provide a foundation for exchange under many circumstances is to invest in ethnic networks or "ethnic capital." The central feature of ethnic capital is the peculiarity of blood as a basis for network "membership." To the extent that this criterion is used, entry and exit from the network (within a generation) are blocked. I argue that this criterion provides a number of advantages to ethnic networks as a support for exchange, and it partly explains the persistence of ethnicity in modern societies. But if ethnic capital cannot be "moved" from one group to another, it also follows that competition

---

[1] A recent collection which does apply rational choice methods to the understanding of nationalism is A. Breton, G. Galeotti, R. Salmon, and R. Wintrobe (1996).

among ethnic groups does not equalize returns among them. Consequently, differences in returns and therefore in incomes will persist. The result is that successful ethnic groups tend to engender fear and jealousy in outsiders, whereas members of ethnic groups with low returns tend to become stigmatized. These disparities, combined with the zero-sum nature of economic rents, imply that there is an inevitable potential for conflict among ethnic groups ("if you can't join them, beat them"), one which is not regulated or reduced by market forces. This analysis is the focus of Section 2.

I also look inside the ethnic group (in Section 3) – and, in particular, at the process of formation of ethnic capital, investments which are largely made by parents for their children. I assume for the purpose of analysis that parents are selfish and that they invest in their children in the hope of being repaid in later life. I show that a second peculiar feature of ethnic investments (in contrast to other kinds of investments in children, such as general human capital) is that they are *self-enforcing*, because the children cannot get the benefits of the capital without exposing themselves to "ethnic pressure" to repay their parents for their sacrifices. This self-enforcing feature makes ethnic investments very attractive to the parents, but not necessarily to the children. Consequently, parents will tend to overinvest in their children's ethnic capital (from the children's point of view). I then speculate on the circumstances under which this intergenerational conflict can lead to "authoritarian" attitudes in the children, as originally described in the classic work on the "Authoritarian Personality" syndrome by Theodor Adorno, Else Fenkel-Brunswick, Daniel Levinson, and R. Nevitt Sanford (1950), and as extended in more recent work, notably by Bob Altemeyer (1981, 1988, 1996). Finally, I apply these concepts (in Section 4) to the collapse of Weimar Germany (expressionism) and the emergence of Nazism (*Kitsch*) in the 1930s.

2   The value of ethnic capital

The starting point for our analysis consists of two assumptions, which will be maintained throughout this chapter (except in Section 3B, where, as noted there, assumption 1 is relaxed). They are:

1. All individuals are rational, in the standard sense of that term in neo-classical economic theory – that is, faced with any two alternatives, the individual is capable of making a choice between them, and his or her choices are consistent.
2. Property rights or contracts are not costlessly enforceable, and sometimes they may not even exist.

As has been repeatedly emphasized, the second assumption implies that in any exchange there is the possibility that one of the parties will cheat or renege on his or her commitments. Earlier, we looked at the solutions put forward initially by Benjamin Klein and Keith Leffler (1981), Carl Shapiro and Joseph Stiglitz (1984), and Carl Shapiro (1983), which involved a price or wage premium. The existence of the price premium provides the consumer with a reason to *trust* the firm. In this way, markets can solve the trust or contractual enforcement problem even in the absence of legally enforceable property rights.

One problem with this solution from the buyer's point of view is that it is expensive. For example, in consumer markets buyers are forced to pay a premium. In order to deter the firm from cheating, this present discounted value is at least as large as the gains to the firm from cheating. Consumers willing to pay this premium are not cheated, but they do not get good value for their money. Such people stay at Holiday Inn, buy Bayer Aspirin, IBM computers, Sony stereo equipment, and so on. An alternative solution for the consumer is to establish a trust relationship with a local seller – the local drugstore, computer hack, and so on. The costs of "signaling" or building trust on a one-on-one basis may be reduced considerably when there is genuine interaction between the parties, as opposed to when impersonal market signals prevail. In these cases trust can describe a relationship which is, at the limit, completely private; it exists between a seller and only one buyer – a "network."

The same choices apply in other markets, such as labor markets or political markets. It follows therefore that a typical individual who wants to buy goods and services at reasonable prices and not be cheated, who wants or wishes to keep a "good" job, and who wishes to get his or her share of the largesse being distributed by politicians – or even to have his or her views reflected in public policy – has a very complex pattern of network investments to make. For each good or service or political service that such consumers wish to purchase – namely, in situations in which there is some prospect of being cheated – they may wish to invest in a specific trust relationship. Some goods and services will be bought so infrequently that such investments will not be worth their cost. In many cases, also, the individual has to calculate that investments in these relationships will be lost if the person moves to another jurisdiction. In these situations the individual is stuck with the market – and market premiums. In others the individual may try the networking strategy just discussed. So the optimal investment strategy (distribution of investments in trust among all the different possible relationships involved) can be complex, and what many individuals really want is a mutual fund. These funds exist in the form of ethnic networks.

The central feature of ethnic networks is that "membership" is held to be determined by blood,[2] making it very difficult for outsiders to enter and, often, for insiders to truly exit (within a generation), a characteristic that I will refer to as "Blocked Entry and Exit." This method solves one of the problems characteristic of networks – namely, the fact that if the returns turn out to be substantial, others will want to enter, and hence it will lower the yield on the initial investments of "insiders." Moreover, since membership is to some extent at least not subject to choice, part of the difficulties normally encountered in establishing a trust relationship is resolved. Thus, a German, say, who meets another German and contemplates a transaction with him or her, one that requires trust, does not have to worry that the other party is only German *temporarily*, because the yield on German capital is temporarily high. The *level* of Germanness exhibited – the extent to which the other person uses German phrases, pretends to like potatoes with whipped cream,[3] goes to German social events, and so on – may be precisely subject to such calculations, but, fundamentally, either he or she is German (or French, or Jewish, or Italian), or not. In part, this is because one's ethnicity is not completely subject to choice but is also determined by the attitudes of others (as members of minority ethnic groups – e.g., the Jews under the Nazi regime – tend to discover).

Just as it is difficult – if not impossible – for an outsider to enter an ethnic group, it may also be difficult – if not impossible – for insiders to exit. A black man can marry a white woman, live in a white suburb, work for an all-white firm, and so on; but he can still find himself greeted by shouts of "Hey, brother!" when he finds himself in the "wrong" neighborhood. And he may also find, to his surprise, that whereas other connections come and go, the permanence of the ethnic connection can sometimes come in handy. This is particularly likely to happen if he discovers that just as insiders would never completely let him go, so outsiders never really let him in, and he is passed over for promotion or turned down in romance because he "is" black.

To be sure, any individual is free to foreswear association with other members of his or her ethnic group; such individuals can tell their friends and family to get lost, they can move to another city and refuse to give out their addresses, they may never phone their mothers again (even on their birthday), they can change their names to Smith, and so on. Even if they did all these things, however, they will still not be in the same position vis-à-vis their ethnic group as outsiders. Their ethnic networks

[2] Of course, how much blood is required for admission is, in general, an open question, and we expect standards to vary in accordance with economic forces.
[3] I am indebted to my friend Hans Scheel for this illustration.

will depreciate through lack of use, *but they will not depreciate to zero.* This "zeroing out" takes a generation or more. And should such individuals have a change of heart later on in life and decide to recontact the old network, they will be able to rebuild their capital at less cost than outsiders would incur. It is in this sense that exit from ethnic networks is blocked – an individual is free to reduce his or her gross investment in this form of capital to zero, but he or she cannot sell, transfer, or dispose of the "sunk" capital which has been accumulated through upbringing, socialization, and ascription by others.

Of course, in reality it is easier to enter and exit some types of ethnic groups than others. Moreover, ethnicity is subject to manipulation, as is *nationalism*, its sister concept, which is usually defined (e.g., by Rogowski 1985) as "the striving of members [of a culturally distinct group] for territorial autonomy, unity or independence . . ." (p. 8). In the present context, nationalism is naturally interpretable as the claim that the return to ethnic capital can be raised if the group in question were to form a sovereign state or, more generally, to acquire more territory. Ernest Gellner (1983) emphasizes that nationalism is essentially deceptive. As he puts it, "A modern, streamlined, on-wheels high culture celebrates itself in song and dance, which it borrows (stylizing itself in the process) from a folk culture which it fondly believes itself to be perpetuating, defending and affirming" (p. 158).

Michael Hechter (1987) suggests ways in which groups can manipulate exit barriers to encourage loyalty; so too does Lawrence Iannaccone (1992), who explains the often bizarre practices of cults as ways in which the cult tries to lower the marginal rate of substitution of ordinary goods and services to cult members, hence making it more difficult to leave the cult. From our point of view, what matters is only that people *believe* that there is something special about blood or ethnicity. If they do, the barriers are generated, whether real or not. A more general analysis than that offered here would allow the level of barriers to entry and exit to vary and to develop into an "industrial organization" of ethnic groups. In this chapter I will simply assume blocked entry and exit in order to bring out the implications of this assumption.

Indeed, several other characteristics of ethnic networks follow from the property of blocked entry and exit. Thus, ethnic networks are *multipurpose*, and they can be used for finding a job or an apartment, a good plumber, a mate, and so on (not necessarily in that order). Ethnic networks also have an *infinite life* – indeed, they go backward as well as forward in time. This means that ethnic networks solve the "Hangman's Paradox" often discussed in game theoretic analyses of the cheating problem. Thus, if a game is finite, cheating is guaranteed on the last play (because there is no possible sanction after the end of the game); if the second party (who has the last move) is going to cheat the first party on the last move, the first party should obviously cheat the second one on the next-to-last move; hence, the game unravels and cheating takes place on the first move. Whatever importance this analysis has in real life – and there are many who believe it to have some – the problem raised is solved by ethnic networks, because blood ties may thin out but they never disappear. Because of this longevity, there is always the prospect of punishment if one ethnic member cheats another in the same group, and there is always the prospect that members of one ethnic group will punish the descendants of another for some transgression or other. In these and other ways, ethnic networks often have a superior capacity to sanction transgressors, both by insiders and outsiders. Thus, the Serb leader Slobodan Milosevic was able to raise genuine fears of conquest and occupation by reminding the Serbs of what the Ottomans did to them at the Battle of Kosovo in 1389. The tactic was apparently effective in building his power base (Ramet 1992, p. 228).

A fourth property of ethnic networks is (*relative*) *homogeneity of tastes*. "Jews like Chinese food, tend to be in favor of human rights, and feel comfortable in big cities." "Germans and Asians are more willing to work hard than Americans." Of course, such ethnic stereotypes are often invalid, but to the extent that tastes do tend to be relatively more homogeneous within ethnic groups than between randomly chosen individuals, collective decision making within the group is made easier, and the capacity of the group for collective action is enhanced. Finally, the costs of forming trust will be lower if signaling and communication are easier, as it often is between members of the same ethnic group (Landa 1981; Breton and Wintrobe 1982).

Finally, ethnic capital investments are *subsidized* through inheritance and upbringing. An individual whose parents are members of an ethnic group will, by the time he or she becomes an adult, have already accumulated a substantial amount of ethnic capital. Some of it is "in the genes," some will have been accumulated through education and forced socialization with other members of his or her ethnic group. Of course, at some point the individual is free to choose a different ethnic identity, but in that case he or she will have to accumulate all of the costs at his or her own expense. A French man who decides that he really wants to be a Korean can of course try to be, but his parents are unlikely to help him, and he will be throwing away all of those French connections.

There are also of course disadvantages to ethnic networks. The most important of them also follow from the central assumption of blocked entry and exit. In the standard economic theory of markets, two broadly conceived assumptions are necessary to ensure the efficiency or (Pareto) optimality of competition:

1. the absence of externalities, "publicness," or other factors which would lead to the systematic under- or overpricing of economic costs or benefits
2. free entry and exit of capital.

As is well known, the second assumption implies that capital will flow out of those industries from which its yield is relatively low and into those industries in which its yield is relatively high. So rents will not persist in long-run equilibrium but will be eliminated as capital flows to those industries in which it is most valuable and as the supply of goods and services from those industries expands, thus driving down prices and reducing economic rents. This mechanism assures the efficiency of competition in economic markets. As discussed earlier, entry to or exit from ethnic networks is blocked. Consequently, if one ethnic group experiences abnormally high returns (e.g., U.S. Jews) and another group abnormally low returns (e.g., U.S. blacks), there is no mechanism whereby the returns to ethnic capital can be equalized across ethnic groups.

To illustrate this point with a simple model, let us suppose that there are only two ethnic groups, the Grails and the Snails. Assume that all individuals of either type are identical. However, although the individuals are identical, the yield to forming network capital need not be. Suppose that the returns to network capital formation are higher among the Grails than the Snails. The Grails might have a superior capacity to sanction deviant or nonparticipating members, or they may be able to communicate better with each other, or they may be more isolated from the rest of society and therefore interact with each other more, and so on. Finally, assume that for either group there are diminishing returns to aggregate ethnic capital.

To derive the simplest possible model of the optimal formation of ethnic capital, let C' = the marginal cost of this capital's formation. The benefits are the increased likelihood of obtaining a rent (p) multiplied by its value (R). The return to ethnic capital is the sum of these rents $\Sigma p_i R_i$, where i denotes all the "uses" of ethnic capital (jobs, apartments, plumbers, mates, investment counselors, political patronage, and so on). Each member of the Grails will invest in ethnic capital to the point at which the marginal return just equals its cost – that is,

(1) $$\left(\sum_i p_i R_i \right)_G = C'_G (r + d_G),$$

where G indexes variables for the Grails, r is the interest rate, and d is the depreciation rate for ethnic capital. The same equation holds for the Snails. Individuals in either group will invest until their *marginal* yields are equal to their costs (and therefore to each other's costs). However, if inframarginal yields were high for the Grails and low for the Snails, the total amount invested would be high for the Grails and low for the Snails.

In equilibrium, therefore, the average yield is high for the Grails and low for the Snails. Grails will get more of the good jobs, good apartments, and so on than the Snails. If mobility were possible between groups, Snails would enter the Grail network and average yields would fall there and rise among the Snails. However, blocked entry and exit prevents this mechanism from operating. Returns could be equalized by differential rates of population growth, if the high yield to Grail ethnic capital resulted in high population growth rates there and if the low yield to Snail ethnic capital resulted in low rates of population growth for that group. However, if anything, this mechanism appears to work in reverse: High-income groups appear to have low rates of population growth, and low-income groups high rates of growth. Consequently, high yields among some ethnic groups will persist, giving rise to fear, envy, and possibly hatred among other groups who will never share those yields. Low returns among other groups will result in stigmatization or statistical discrimination (Arrow 1972) as individuals within an ethnic group are judged on the basis of the performance of the average for that group.[4]

In short, the phenomenon of blocked entry and exit explains why market mechanisms do not eliminate ethnic conflict and why competition among ethnic groups has the potential to breed conflict. Individualism is devalued as the characteristics of the group become more important as determinants of individual welfare. The absence of the market-regulating mechanism implies its replacement by evolutionary or conflict mechanisms, as groups either prosper or decline as a whole. And there is a natural demand for leadership in the management of ethnic capital. In *extreme* form, all these characteristics – the importance of the group over the individual, the Leader and evolutionary principles, and the stress on struggle and the inevitability of conflict – are precisely the characteristics of Fascism, in both its Italian and German manifestations.

To illustrate this point, let us consider A. James Gregor's (1969) description of the intellectual roots of Fascism in the thinking of early

---

[4] George Borjas (1992) presents highly suggestive evidence of the persistence of differential earning capacity among ethnic groups across generations.

twentieth-century sociologists like Gumplowicz, Mosca, and Pareto. He quotes Mosca:

> Human beings have a natural inclination towards struggle. ... [but] even when he fights, man remains primarily a social animal. Ordinarily, therefore we see men forming into groups, each group made up of leaders and followers. The individuals who make up a group are conscious of a special brotherhood and oneness with each other and vent their pugnacious instincts on members of other groups. (Mosca, quoted in Gregor 1969, pp. 42–3)

Similar ideas can be found in the work of Pareto and Gumplowicz – and later in the work of Roberto Michels and, of course, Mussolini (see Gregor for an extensive discussion). Although anti-Semitism was not important in the formation of Italian Fascism, *ethnocentrism* was, as was the idea that ethnocentric dispositions had a high survival value because they facilitated the survival of the group.

Now the central problem with such "group survival" explanations is the "free-rider" problem (see Becker 1976 for a good exposition). In biology this means that even though a gene (e.g., one for altruism) might contribute to the survival of the group as a whole, such a gene will nevertheless be selected against *within* the group if it reduces the *individual's* fitness. This is the central problem in explaining altruistic preferences, which increase the welfare or fitness of the group at the expense of the individual altruist. Those who possess "selfish" genes do not give to others in the group, but they *will* free ride on altruistic genes. As a result the selfish genes will tend to be selected for, and the altruism genes will be selected against and disappear. The same problem arises with any other trait which contributes to group survival while reducing these chances for an individual.

The (biological) free-rider problem was not identified in Fascist thinking; however, the related idea that the masses were incapable of mobilizing themselves but required a vanguard or an elite leadership to mobilize them was a central theme, as, of course, it had been earlier in the thought of Lenin and was to be in Hitler's thinking.[5] For all these twentieth-century revolutionaries, the Leader principle was central: The majority was the fodder – rather than the conscious agent – of social revolution.

The most important idea in Fascism of course was nationalism. As

---

[5] See Aldous Huxley's (1994) Chapter 5 for an insightful description of Hitler's views of the masses and the use of propaganda to deal with them.

Linz (1980 in Larsen, Hagtuet, and Mykelbust 1980) points out, "If there is one characteristic of Fascism on which all analysts agree it is the central place of nationalism in its ideology, particularly the type of nationalism that goes as far as placing loyalty to the nation ahead of the state" (p. 161). How does nationalism arise out of ethnicity? In part, nationalism arises naturally out of a framework which stresses the competition among ethnic groups, in which ethnic groups are divided into states, and in which the "leadership" of the ethnic group is institutionalized in the political leadership of the state. Thus, E. Hobsbawm (1990) defines the "principle of nationality" as the idea that the boundaries of the state should be linked to those of the "nation" or ethnic group (p. 15).

But there is a further link between the concepts of ethnicity, nationalism, and the free-rider problem, one which arises wherever the boundaries of the nation are not those of the state, and which can sometimes give rise to a more virulent form of nationalism. For whenever these boundaries do not coincide, groups that are not part of the nation but exist within the state are easy to single out as the poison *within* the state. "They" (like the selfish individual who decreases the fitness of an otherwise altruistic group) are the source of many of the nation's difficulties and its inability to compete against other nations. This notion is central, I believe, to explaining the extremity or the viciousness of ethnic conflicts, such as the one under the Nazi regime or the contemporary conflict between the Serbs and the Croatians. In order to explore it further, we will have to look more deeply inside the ethnic group and to investigate in more detail how ethnic capital is formed.

3   Intra- and intergroup ethnic conflict

A. *Overinvestment in ethnicity*

So far, I have suggested that ethnic investments can yield a positive return, and I assumed in the last section that individuals accumulate the optimal level of this form of capital. Intergenerational harmony was thus assured, despite the fact that much of the investment in ethnic capital is performed by parents for their children. I also assumed that entry to and exit from the network are blocked. In this section I want to elaborate a more complicated model, one in which parents make investments in their children in exchange for control over the behavior of their children in later life, and in which this exchange is "enforced" by the pressure that can be brought upon the children by other members of the ethnic group.

Thus, suppose that parents invest in the ethnic capital of their children by sending them to ethnic schools; inculcating ethnic customs and rituals, language, and other communication techniques; restricting their socialization while young to other members of the ethnic group; and so on. Parents expect to be repaid for these sacrifices through the obedience of the children in later life to the norms of the ethnic group, which presumably include support and attention to their parents in their old age, but which may also encompass other aspects of their children's behavior (e.g., that they will marry within the group and raise children who will continue to participate within it; that they will participate in ethnic cultural activities, rites, and rituals; that they will respect and/or worship ancestral heroes, take credit as members of the group for the accomplishments of their forefathers, assume the debts of previous generations; and so on). In short, children may repay their parents not only directly with support, but also indirectly by making decisions based on their parents' wishes or utility functions and by participating in the activities or adhering to the norms of the ethnic group.

But what mechanism can parents count on to enforce the implicit contract between them and their children? The children can't be sued in court if they don't repay. There are obvious reasons for this. One reason is surely that the contract may not be voluntarily entered into by the children, or, even if it is, the children may be too young to be deemed capable of "credible" or enforceable commitments. Another is that the preferred form of repayment can take subtle forms – for example, that the children's career or marriage choices are those that their parents would have liked them to make. With these forms of repayment, it may be difficult for an outsider to ascertain whether repayment has in fact occurred and to adjudicate disputes between parents and their children over this matter. Yet both parents and children might prefer these forms of repayment to, say, cash repayments.

So how can parents be confident that their children will in fact repay them for the sacrifices they have made on their behalf? Clearly, the problem is a general one – that is, it applies to all forms of parental investment (e.g., to investments in general human capital, such as the children's education or occupational training, and to "gifts" of land, houses, cash, and so on).

I can think of at least five mechanisms which can act as substitutes for legal enforcement:

1. altruism
2. bequests
3. trust

4. guilt
5. shame.

Gary Becker (1974, 1976), Robert Frank (1988), and others have argued that altruism is a powerful force in family life. As discussed earlier (in Chapter 4), when talking about the famous "Rotten Kid Theorem", I cited Becker's (1974, 1976) argument that under certain conditions one-sided altruism (i.e., the parent loves the child but not vice versa) is sufficient to motivate the child's cooperation. But sometimes altruism within the family is insufficient. Gary Becker and Kevin Murphy (1988) explicitly acknowledge this fact and suggest that state intervention (compulsory schooling, pension plans, and so on) often mimics the kinds of contracts that the family would have entered into if legally enforceable contracting were possible. However, they do not inquire into the private behavior that ensues when love is insufficient – that is, there is no analysis of alternative bases for exchange within the family. Yet even when love is plentiful, as long as it is not complete – that is, when the children do not care for the parents as much as they do for themselves (Becker 1974 calls this "full caring") – interaction will sometimes occur between parent and children on the basis of self-interest. For all these reasons, it is necessary to look beyond altruism in discussing family interaction.

B. Bernheim, A. Shleifer, and L. Summers (1985) suggested that in addition to caring for their children, parents want attention from them, especially when they get older. Children may not mind visiting their parents at first, but after awhile, they get tired of it, and additional visits bring disutility. Parents never tire of seeing their children (at least, never before their children tire of visiting them), and so at the margin, parents are willing to trade larger bequests for more visits. So the strategic threat to withdraw the bequest is used by parents to enforce their wishes on their children, as discussed in Chapter 4. Note that the bequest mechanism does not precisely mimic legal enforcement, since with legal enforcement, it would not always be necessary to give all the bargaining power to the parent. Perhaps it is this problem which explains why in some countries (Germany, France) a parent is legally proscribed from depriving a child of the parent's estate beyond a certain point (e.g., in a two-child German family, each child is entitled to a minimum of one-fourth of the estate).

Both the analysis and the evidence on bequests show that family relations can be illuminated using the model of exchange. However, it still appears that poor parents with no planned bequest have nothing with which to protect themselves in their old age. One other possibility is that the parents might simply trust their children to look after them.

However, if we rule out the altruistic and economic motives already discussed, and if we also assume that the children are rational, then there must be some explanation of why the children would behave in this way (i.e., visit their parents). The most obvious motives are shame and guilt. The two are commonly distinguished (see, e.g., Freud 1929/1991; Kandel and Lazear 1992) on the basis that shame ("external pressure") requires external observability, whereas guilt ("internal pressure") does not. Freud interprets much of the advance of civilization to this economy of guilt as a mechanism in enforcing behavioral codes and norms. I will not attempt a comprehensive analysis of the operation of these two motives here, but I will suggest that ethnic capital is an investment vehicle for which they are particularly suited, and I will discuss their operation in this context.

In brief the argument is that parents can partly "bind" their children to them by ethnic capital investments in them while they are young. The children are bound not just because the yield on this form of capital is specific to the ethnic group in question and not just because it cannot be sold or otherwise transferred. The reason is that in order to obtain the yield on this form of capital, the (grown) children will have to associate with other members of the ethnic group. They, in turn, can be counted on, in the course of normal association, to pressure or shame each other into repaying debts to the parents and to adhere to the other norms of the group. So the "contract" is "self-enforcing" from the parents' point of view – the children can only obtain the benefits from this form of capital to the extent that they use ethnic networks and therefore subject themselves to ethnic pressure to repay their parents for the investments made.

To illustrate, let us imagine a mythical ethnic group, the Harriets. Two Harriets, Harry and Larry, are discussing a business deal over lunch. Because they are both Harriets, it is easy for them to communicate,[6] and they feel free to ask personal questions. Here are some standard ones (Harry is the interlocutor, Larry is the respondent who would be answering the questions): "Of course, Larry, your wife is also a Harriet?" "How many little Harriet children do you have?" "Your mother lives with you, or did you put her in a home?" If the answer to questions like these create a negative impression, the respondent may find the deal coming unstuck, as the interlocutor discovers that he is not maintaining his ethnic capital.

Why does the interlocutor (Harry) want to enforce the norms? Even if

---

[6] I would argue that two members of an ethnic group do not necessarily like or trust one another, but they should find it easier to communicate with one another, thus making it easier to establish whether or not they can trust or like each other.

they are beneficial to the group, why doesn't Harry free-ride and leave it to other members of the group to police behavior? Although I will not give a comprehensive analysis of this problem here,[7] I will suggest three reasons why other members of the ethnic group can often be counted on to apply the required pressure:

1. *Ordinary self-interest.* If the respondent (in this case, Larry) didn't honor his implicit contract to repay his parents, there is, ipso facto, some reason to believe that he is more likely to renege on his current obligations. Hence, it is worthwhile to get this information.

2. *Guilt.* By pressuring other members of the group to honor their obligations, a group member (in this case, Harry) in part fulfills his own obligations and thus lessens his sense of guilt.

3. *Sanctions for not enforcing the group norm.* Ethnic groups may have a particularly powerful capacity to use sanctions effectively. The reasons are implicit in their value as exchange networks, as discussed earlier – namely, subsidized early socialization with other members (hence facilitating mutual monitoring), infinite life (therefore, implying common ancestry and descent and, therefore, a long period over which transgressions can be punished), multipurposeness, and so on.

To the extent that members of the ethnic group, for these reasons, can be counted on to encourage, pressure, or police each other's obedience to group norms, parents who invest in the ethnic capital of their children can count on them to repay. Hence ethnic investments are self-enforcing.[8] In this respect ethnic networks differ from other forms of parental investment (e.g., general human capital), for which parents may have to rely entirely on the affection of their children – or on internal pressure (guilt) – to be repaid.

It follows immediately that, in contrast to other types of capital, there will be "overinvestment" by parents in the ethnic capital of their children. Because no other form of capital has this self-enforcing aspect,[9]

---

[7] A more general analysis would derive the level of enforcement both from the characteristics of the ethnic group and from its environment. Here, I will just assume general obedience to the norm, and I will suggest why this could be the case. On some conditions for the persistence of codes, see Ronald Wintrobe (1983).

[8] Indeed, the self-enforcing nature of ethnic capital provides a further reason for the persistence of ethnicity.

[9] The statement in the text is obviously too strong. Other parental gifts, interpreted here as loans, may be partially self-enforcing (e.g., the gift of a house next door to one's parents keeps the children next door, and it therefore encourages attention, as long as the house is illiquid).

parents are guaranteed a return on ethnic capital investments; but for other forms of investment in their children, they are forced to rely either on their children's affection for them or on guilt or trustworthiness to be repaid for their sacrifices. Consequently, this biases their investments in the direction of ethnic capital investments: Given two investments of equal yield to their children, parents will strictly prefer the ethnic over the nonethnic investment. Indeed, they will prefer an ethnic investment of lower yield and the potential differential will be larger, the more militant and committed are members of the ethnic group (i.e., the more that members are willing to act to enforce the repayments of debt).[10]

Of course, to the extent that the parents love their children, they will take their children's welfare into account in deciding on their investments. Here, we have assumed that the parents are entirely selfish and that they decide on the level of investment which is optimal from their point of view alone. It is worth noting, however, that the overinvestment theorem will still hold in the case of altruistic parents, although the level of overinvestment will presumably be smaller as the degree of genuine altruism (concern for the welfare of the child)[11] gets larger.

In any case, at some point the children will reach maturity, and at that point they will find that they have involuntarily been made a partner to these contracts with their parents (and perhaps with other relatives). Unless the child's preferences are identical to those of the parents, the

[10] To demonstrate this point, let p = the level of ethnic pressure which the parents can anticipate can be brought to bear on the next generation – i.e., p = the estimated probability that the children will be forced to repay their debts by pressure from their fellow ethnics; t = the extent to which parents, in the absence of pressure, trust their children to repay out of a sense of moral obligation (guilt); and A_k = the probability that the children will want to repay out of a sense of affection or altruism toward their parents. Suppose the parents invest $\$X$ in their children, which yields $\$X(1 + \pi_e)$ in the case of ethnic capital, and $\$X(1 + \pi_g)$ in the case of general human capital. Suppose for simplicity that the fraction k of it must be repaid in either case. Then the parent will be indifferent between two investments – one ethnic and one general – where $kX(1 + \pi_e)(t + A_k + p) = kX(1 + \pi_g)(t + A_k)$. The required ratio between the yield on general versus that on ethnic capital is

$$\frac{(1 + \pi_c)}{(t + A_k)} = \frac{(1 + \pi_g)}{(t + A_k + p)},$$

that is, investments in general human capital will be "artificially" discounted by the factor $1/1 + p$.

[11] Note that for altruism to reduce overinvestment, the altruism must take the form of concern for the child's own welfare or utility and not for the child's consumption pattern – that is, the parent's utility function must have the form $U_p = U_p(c_p, U_k)$, where p = parent, k = kid, c = a vector of consumption goods, and not $U_p = U_p(c_p, c_k)$. Increased altruism of the latter variety can lead to *more* ethnic investment if the parent believes that ethnic capital is particularly good for the kid.

mature child will find that he or she is "out of equilibrium" – his or her desired level of ethnic capital is different from the stock which has been accumulated for him or her. From the overinvestment theorem, it follows that typically the individual will want to allow some of his or her ethnic capital to depreciate, although those children whose tastes or opportunities lie heavily in the direction of the ethnic group may want to invest more (the overinvestment theorem only holds on the average). Perhaps it is for this reason that many ethnic groups have institutionalized "rites of passage" that signal the onset of maturity. At this point the individual, by participating in the ritual, indicates his or her acceptance of the responsibility for the debts that have been incurred on his or her behalf. It is peculiar (and it deserves further exploration) that although these rites are common to many ethnic groups, the age at which they take place appears to vary enormously among different groups. Thus, for some Chinese groups, it only takes place just before marriage (hence never at all for those who don't marry), whereas for Jews, it happens at the age of thirteen. The strategic aspects are obvious enough. In the Chinese case, the pressure to marry (and perpetuate the group) is increased, as the individual who never marries is in effect considered never to have grown up; in the Jewish one, "maturity" (and the onset of responsibility for debt) is deemed to have taken place at an age when the individual is too young to resist.

Note that the overinvestment theorem obviously neglects possible external effects due to ethnic capital. Thus, if, as de Tocqueville suggested and as Hechter (1992) has recently reemphasized, ethnic groups impart useful social values to their members, which contribute to the creation and maintenance of social order, overinvestment from the viewpoint of the children who are invested in might be an underinvestment from the social point of view. On the other hand, to the extent that ethnic investments create prejudice and hostility among groups – thus raising tensions, creating hostility, and leading to wasteful expenses on rent-seeking – the criterion of optimal investment used here [equation (1)] could easily be an overestimate of the socially optimal level. In that case the level of overinvestment would be even larger from the social viewpoint than from the children's.

B. A speculation on the "authoritarian personality"

So far throughout this book, I have held to the principle of rationality in explaining behavior. However, the extremity of some ethnic conflicts – such as the behavior of the Nazis toward the Jews and perhaps the contemporary conflict between Serbians and Croatians – is difficult to explain with a strictly rational approach. The fundamental problem in explaining these conflicts is that the ethnic group which is the object of conscious hatred is, to an outside observer, obviously not the real enemy. Indeed, this is one reason why acts of hatred and destruction toward the conscious enemy are inherently unsatisfying and result only in frustration, thus breeding further hatred and violence.[12]

In what follows, therefore, I accept this element of irrationality, and I introduce it into an otherwise straightforward economic model. My purpose is to explain a prejudicial syndrome, as initially described in the classic work by the research team headed by Nevitt Sanford and published as *The Authoritarian Personality*, the now-classic work by Adorno, Fenkel-Brunswik, Levinson, and Sanford (1950).

The authoritarian personality is a personality structure or constellation of attitudes which is believed to show, as one of the concept's inventors later described it, a *potential* for Fascism, a *susceptibility* to anti-Semitic propaganda, and a *readiness* to participate in antidemocratic social movements (Sanford in Adorno *et al.* 1950, p. 142). The essential technique used in the original work was to discover, on the basis of interviews, attitudes that linked, in a nonobvious way, with general prejudice, anti-Semitism, or Fascism; these "discovered" attitudes gave rise to the "*E*" (Ethnocentrism), "*A-S*" (anti-Semitism), and "*F*" (Fascism) scales. As might be expected, the scales are highly correlated with one another.

To proceed, let us first express the model of parental investment in ethnic capital described in the preceding section with a simple equation, in which π = the gross yield of ethnic capital to individual i at his or her maturity (subscripts are suppressed for notational simplicity), r = the rate of interest on the debt which must be repaid to the parents, and K = i's stock of ethnic capital. Let p = the level of ethnic peer pressure on i to repay his/her parents for their investments in ethnic capital, so $r = r(p)$. To derive a very simple picture, assume that marginal and average yields are equal and that rates of interest are also constant, so that π and r are constant (given p). Then the marginal net yield to i's ethnic capital is $\pi - r$, and total net profits are $(\pi - r)K$.[13]

---

[12] In other respects the implications of the present approach accord with those which might be predicted from completely rational models – that is, ethnic conflict would appear more likely, *ceteris paribus*, the greater the difference in wages or other factor returns between groups, the smaller the complementarity between their factors (hence, the less they "need" each other), and the more similar they are in terms of tastes or resource utilization (hence, the more they are in direct competition with each other for scarce resources).

[13] A more complete model would also specify the sanction f for nonrepayment, so that at maturity an individual would have the choice between repayment (and earning $\pi - r$) and nonrepayment [yielding expected profits of $(1 - p)\pi - p(\pi - f)$].

Because ethnic capital is a sunk investment which cannot be sold or transferred whose value is specific to ethnic networks, the gross yield on this capital is a quasi-rent (in the sense of Klein, Crawford, and Alchian 1978). Its main value is to permit trade with other members of the ethnic group. Consequently, the yield on this capital (π) will be high when other mechanisms which can enforce trade (such as legal enforcement) are weak, and vice versa. Space prohibits consideration of all the possibilities, but one interesting case is that in which:

1. K is relatively high
2. π is low
3. p is high

so that $\pi - r < 0$ and (since K is high) the individual is incurring substantial losses. The problem is compounded if exit is difficult. What can the individual do? I suggest that individuals in this position are particularly likely to develop prejudices against members of other ethnic groups, and they thus have the potential to engage in conflict with them, to encourage antidemocratic forces (in order to raise the yield on ethnic capital), and to display the characteristic personality traits described in the Authoritarian Personality Syndrome.

Thus, one item on the scale, to which respondents were asked to express agreement or disagreement, was: "He is indeed contemptible who does not feel an undying love, gratitude, and respect for his parents." Because of the way it was expressed, agreement with this statement was held to mask an underlying or unconscious hostility toward the parents. The overt glorification and unconscious hostility toward one's parents (other evidence of which became apparent during the interviews) was held to be a distinguishing feature of the highly ethnocentric person.

A second characteristic was an exaggerated, emotional need to submit to authority, again springing, according to theory, from an underlying hostility to in-group authorities, originally the parents (Sanford, 1973, p. 144). Other characteristics were superstition (a tendency to shift responsibility from within the individual to forces outside his or her control), stereotyping (a tendency to think in rigid, oversimplified categories), and a narrow range of consciousness.

Adorno, Fenkel-Brunswik, Levinson, and Sanford found no specific relationship between the scales and socioeconomic factors. But they did find that people who scored high on the E-scale tended to express political and religious preferences that were similar to those of their parents. Subsequent work on the correlates of the F-scale found a correlation between an emphasis in upbringing on obedience and strict control, on the one hand, and low education, on the other. Although some believe that subsequent work has discredited much of the original psychoanalytical framework, new and similar scales have been developed and intensively tested for their reliability, notably the "Right Wing Authoritarianism Scale" developed by Altemeyer (1981, 1988, 1996). The term "right wing" is not used in the political or economic sense, but in a psychological one. The right-wing authoritarian is one who aggressively defends the *established* authorities in his or her life. So, for example, defenders of communism in the former Soviet Union in the late 1980s would tend to score highly on the scale. The scale is a unidimensional measure of three attitude clusters:

1. submission to established authority
2. authoritarian aggression (i.e., aggression which is believed to be sanctioned by established authorities and which is directed at various persons whose activities are frowned upon)
3. conventionalism (i.e., a high degree of adherence to the social conventions which are perceived to be endorsed by society and its established authorities).

High scorers on the scale tend to accept government injustices such as illegal wiretapping; to believe that "strong medicine" is necessary to straighten out troublemakers, criminals, and perverts; to believe in traditional family structures, obedience, and respect for authority; and so on. And they are highly prejudiced against minority groups.

One explanation of authoritarian aggression offered by the Adorno group was the one advanced by Fenkel-Brunswik, which postulated that authoritarianism arose in people raised by rigid, threatening, rule-driven, and status-conscious parents who had only recently ascended to the middle class and who punished unconventional responses heavily. Altemeyer (1988) contends (although not everyone agrees[14]) that there is little evidence for this. He prefers a "social learning" explanation. People acquire these attitudes, he believes, from their parents and peer groups during adolescence. Scores are lowered as a result of education, raised from having children, and raised during social crises, especially if a violent left-wing movement appears.

The foregoing is a very brief summary of some of the main themes of *The Authoritarian Personality* and subsequent work in that vein. Its purpose is to illuminate my conjecture that hostility toward other ethnic groups can be predicted on the basis of a particular constellation of returns to ethnic capital – that is, relatively high K and p combined with

[14] Brewster-Smith, in his Foreword to Altemeyer (1988), suggests that the evidence is more favorable to the psychoanalytic theory than Altemeyer admits.

low net yield, or $\pi - r$. Thus, consider the likely attitudes of a person in such a position, who is rational in every respect save one: He or she must follow the norm of honoring one's parents. So the person is unlike *homo economicus* because he or she is capable of repressing unpleasant emotions. I assume that the more the parents have invested, the more unpleasant it would be to think negative thoughts about them. Now suppose that the investments are low-yielding and that K and p are high. Individuals in this position are awash in debt to their parents (and possibly to other ethnic group members), but the yield on the capital investments that the parents have sacrificed so hard to give to their children is low, too low to cover the debts to them. Because the children have substantial ethnic capital, they venerate their parents and forefathers, and these ancestors cannot be overtly blamed for the pickle they are in. (But unconsciously, they know that these ancestors have plied them with excess ethnic capital). The children have very little space to exercise their own choices in life, because in order to repay the debts, their behavior is largely dictated by the parents' wishes and the norms of the ethnic group. So the children's political and religious choices are the parents' choices, and the children's range of consciousness and capacity for conscious choice is narrow. In a sense the children are quite rightly superstitious (their behavior *is* largely outside their control, given their adherence to the norm). Thus the authoritarian personality can be made sense of as a response to this constellation of returns to ethnic capital. I do not claim that this is the *only* way this syndrome can arise. No doubt other sets of circumstances can generate it. However, this is one account which springs naturally from the theoretical approach used here.

Why is the child prejudiced? To the individual in question, his or her problem is not that the parents invested too much in his or her well-being, but that through no fault of theirs, the yield on this capital is low. Whose fault is that? In Nazi Germany it was "the Jews," of course, with their tight, high-yielding international network and their connections with the state and to international markets[15] (the development of which lowered the yield on other ethnic capital). What to do about it?

1. Get rid of them.
2. Engage in other collective actions to raise the yield on ethnic capital.

The Nazi ideology of blood and ethnic purity as a means of organizing society was certainly an extreme response, but it is one which fits this pattern.

---

[15] Hannah Arendt (1951/1973), in Part One ("Antisemitism"), discusses these factors in the context of antisemitism in the nineteenth century.

Why can't the individuals simply renegotiate their debts with their parents? Because the assets they bequeathed their children are low-yielding, the simplest solution would appear to be to renegotiate the debts downward. In this context it is worthwhile to recall the original, psychoanalytic explanation of authoritarian aggression, the one advanced by Fenkel-Brunswik (in Adorno et al. 1950), which postulated that authoritarianism arose in people raised by rigid, threatening, rule-driven, status-conscious parents, who had only recently ascended to the middle class and who punished unconventional responses heavily. In our terminology, what this suggests is simply that a contributing factor is the inability to bargain or renegotiate matters within the family (i.e., that authoritarian aggression is more likely to arise in family structures in which "transactions costs" are high).

Why can't the individuals affected act collectively to exert political pressure to change the norms or to solve the problems created directly? If the family is unresponsive to their demands, the children could still be accommodated through the political system if it were responsive to them. However, under some circumstances, the political system may be unwilling to act (as discussed in detail in the preceding chapter).

In summary, individuals find themselves in a position of conflict with their parents – that is, in a conflict generated by the difference between the yield on the assets they have bequeathed their children and the size of the debts which have to be repaid. The conflict could, in principle, be resolved through renegotiation (within the family) of the debts owed or through political action to increase the yield on the assets. When all these avenues of trade are foreclosed, the individuals involved in such conflicts are likely to develop a tendency toward authoritarian aggression.

Note that the analysis developed here draws on both the classic work of the Adorno (1950) group and the more recent work of Altemeyer and others. Like the Adorno group, it emphasizes (what I refer to as) "transactions costs" within the family and a repressed hostility toward one's parents as the generating factor of authoritarian attitudes. But it differs from the Adorno group's analysis in emphasizing ethnic capital, a factor which does not appear in that group's analysis (or in Altemeyer's); in seeing adolescence as the main period during which these attitudes are crystallized (as does Altemeyer); and in visualizing a role for social learning. Its main contribution is to try to generate these attitudes with the minimum possible departure from rationality (not a typical concern of psychology), as well as with more precise modeling which makes the drawing of comparative static implications possible (again, not typical in psychology). Thus, Altemeyer (1996) has data on the recent evolution of authoritarianism (it has been going up). But the social learning explanation adapted from the work of Bandura (e.g., 1977), which he favors, does not lend itself easily to explaining changes in the level of authoritarianism over time or across countries.

Of course, the theory advanced here is itself primitive and could be greatly refined and extended. But the main point is to show that models incorporating variables such as those discussed here – transactions costs within the family and the yield on investments made by parents for their children – are capable of yielding insight into and predictions about psychosocial human behavior in a way that can complement the research of social psychologists. The next section expands the model in another way by applying it to the historical experience of the decline of the Weimar Republic.

4   Weimar and the decline in the yield on ethnic capital

To apply our analysis of ethnic conflict to the rise of Nazism, let us note first that a number of historical factors that are often cited to explain the collapse of the Weimar Republic can be interpreted as lowering and threatening to lower further the yield on German ethnic capital. However, what James Coleman (1990) might have called the "microfoundations" of the explanation are usually missing. I claim that the concepts of "ethnic capital" and "equilibrium political inaction" provide the missing links. The preceding chapter showed how political inaction on unemployment and violence in the streets caused the population to turn away from Weimar. Here, we focus on the fall in the yield of ethnic capital and the resulting intergenerational conflict, a conflict which, again, the paralyzed political system was incapable of resolving.

The fall in the yield of ethnic capital was the result of several factors. First, the hyperinflation of the 1920s largely destroyed the savings of the German middle class (Kühnl, in Larsen, Hagtvet, and Mykelbust 1980). In terms of our model, this means that middle class German parents lacked the power to enforce repayment of their children's debts which strategic bequests typically confer. And it also implies a considerable reduction in the level of financial assets ultimately passed on to their children, thus reducing the children's capacity to repay. In this context, perhaps, it is worth digressing to note that according to Martin Paldam's (1987) study of the causes of dictatorship in Latin American countries, few regimes survived a hyperinflation.

Second, the youth of the 1930s inherited substantial debts, further magnified by the reduction in its capacity to repay caused by the Great Depression. These debts included the substantial reparations payments imposed on Germany by the Treaty of Versailles at the end of World War I. In addition, the so-called war guilt clause of the treaty required Germany to turn over its war criminals (including the former emperor) for trial for atrocities, to accept responsibility for causing losses and damages, to cap the German Army at 100,000, and to put an end to the General Staff (Gay 1968/1974, p. 157). The effect of these provisions was that in postwar Germany the sons were forced to accept a position of permanent weakness in return for the sins of the fathers in leading Europe into war.

Third, although Germany had surpassed the other European countries both in GNP and in population by 1913, after the war German capital was prevented from investing in African, Asian, and Australian colonies (Kühnl, in Larsen, Hagtvet, and Mykelbust – 1980, pp. 127–8). The treaty deprived Germany of what few colonies it had, as well as of other territories such as Alsace-Lorraine (which was returned to France) and Upper Silesia, West Prussia, and Posen (which were turned over to Poland (Gay 1974, p. 157). By depriving Germany of *Lebensraum*, the victors ensured that the ratio of ethnic capital to land was raised, hence lowering the yield to ethnic capital.

Fourth, a constellation of factors further threatened, or appeared to threaten, the usefulness of German ethnic capital in the future: "the Jews," international socialism, and international capitalism. Thus, the rapid development of markets, modernization and bureaucratization, and the enormous growth of trusts over this period meant that, on the one hand, impersonal bureaucratic criteria were increasingly replacing ethnic connections and background as criteria by which loans might be granted, promotions decided, and so on. (In this sense, the "Fascism as modernization" school can be given a rational interpretation within the context of our model. The threat posed by "scientific socialism" can, at least in part, be interpreted similarly.) On the other hand, the Jewish "threat" can be interpreted as meaning that underneath the rationalist face (in which jobs, privileges, and promotions were lost) lurked another ethnic group with powerful connections to both international capitalism and international socialism, a group which was secretly monopolizing all the rents which good Germans were being deprived of in the name of one or the other of these abstract principles. The two were nicely combined in the resonating Nazi propaganda theme of the "chain stores," a theme which was discussed by the historian Michael Kater (1983), who suggests that "To the small craftsman and shopkeeper the Jew was the instigator (and owner) of a system of factories and chain stores that threatened their livelihood" (p. 26).

Arendt (1951/1973) points out the Jews were historically involved in financing the wars of the European states, a role which the development of modern capital markets had rendered obsolete. She suggests that this involvement left them particularly vulnerable when they were believed to be no longer needed. An alternative point of view is that this historical involvement made them an especially appropriate target under circumstances in which the two institutions that had failed most badly were the state and the financial system. Trust in them had collapsed as a result of the war and the Versailles peace settlement, the 1920s hyperinflation, and the weakness or the unwillingness of Weimar to deal with the Depression, which hit Germany particularly hard.

Although the evidence on various theses concerning Nazi membership is still muddled (see Larsen, Hagtvet, and Mykelbust 1980; Kater 1983), there do seem to be matters on which there is a consensus and which are relevant to the model proposed here. One concerns the thesis of "classes-into-masses" or the "atomization" of German society originally propounded by Arendt in her book *The Origins of Totalitarianism* (1951), which gave rise to a vast literature. To simplify drastically, we can say that the basic idea was that totalitarian dictatorships arose because of the rise in the twentieth century of "atomized" masses – that is, individuals with few or no social ties, who were unorganized in interest groups. In democracies these interest groups served as intermediary links between individuals and political parties (as de Tocqueville emphasized), and they helped to promote responsive government and democratic stability. In modern guise a related thesis has been put forward by Robert Putnam (1993), who argues that differences in "social capital" (essentially, the density of interest group association) among the various regions of Italy account for the variations in effective government to be found there. (As mentioned in Chapter 6, he also argues that these differences are amazingly stable, but that controversial contention does not concern us here.)

If the thesis that it was the atomization of the German people which effectively left them vulnerable to the Nazi propaganda machine and helped to account for the rise of Hitler were true, it would suggest that there are serious problems with the model in this chapter, which is based on the idea that it is those with *high* levels of ethnic capital (a form of social capital) who are likely to engage in authoritarian aggression. However, Bernt Hagtvet (1980) provides convincing evidence that

1. there was no paucity of intermediary links between individuals and political parties. On the contrary, Weimar Germany appeared to be densely permeated by a network of intermediary organizations.

2. the Nazis' most conspicuous success came in the regions with the greatest cohesion. As Hagtvet says, "it was not the people with the fewest social ties who were most receptive to mass appeals, as Kornhauser asserted, but those most thoroughly integrated" (in Larsen, Hagtvet, and Mykelbust 1980, p. 90).
3. the interest groups themselves facilitated the rise of Nazism. For example, as Hagtvet says, "when the rural producers joined the Nazi party, they did so as members of precisely the same intermediary network which, in theory, is presumed to establish social defense against extremism" (p. 91).

On this line of analysis, the mass society theorists simply confuse cause and effect; the mass society was not the cause of the Nazis' rise to power but an outcome of it (see, e.g., Broszat 1981 on the systematic destruction of alternative centers of power once the Nazis took over).

The model developed here also suggests an alternative interpretation of much of the atomization literature, one which is consistent with the evidence presented by Hagtvet and others. It was not that the level of social or ethnic capital was low, but that it was *low-yielding*. This result would naturally give rise either to atomization (as people would drift away from networks that yielded little return), to a demand for radical new leadership, or to a shift to alternative political groupings by the leaders of the existing networks.

The second piece of evidence which is now, I believe, well established is that the Nazis were disproportionately young. Thus, for example, approximately half of the 1933 Nazis and the vast majority of the stormtroopers were born after 1901. Peter Merkl (1980) summarizes the evidence comparing Fascist movements in a large number of countries. He concludes that "... Pending further research, the evidence for generational revolt as the one great motivating force all these diverse fascist movements have in common appears to be strong and persuasive indeed" (quoted in Larsen, Hagtvet, and Mykelbust 1980, p. 781). Gay's well-known book, *Weimar Culture* (1968/1974), describes the central theme of Expressionist culture as the son's revolt against the father (p. 119). And he describes the change in the atmosphere as Weimar crumbled:

> ... from 1918 to 1924. ... Expressionism dominated politics as much as painting or the stage. ... [but] between 1929 and 1933, the years of disastrously rising unemployment, government by decree, decay of middle-class parties and resumption of violence, culture became less the critic than the mirror of events; the newspaper and film industries ground out right-wing propa-

ganda; the best among architects, novelists or playwrights were subdued or silent; and the country was inundated by the rising tide of *Kitsch*, much of it politically inspired. (p. 126)

Whence the title of this chapter. Note that the revolt against the parents and the desire to raise the yield on ethnicity can be made sense of in perfectly rational terms as a response to the decline in the yield on ethnic capital which was instigated by defeat, by inflation, and by the secularism of the Weimar Republic, which was too weak to deal with the Depression and organized violence. Moreover, the Nazi movement appealed to the young in many other ways; in its futuristic outlook (the thousand-year Reich); in its programs, which promised to deal with problems that no other party was willing to address directly (unemployment, reparations); and in the structure of the party, which by its fluidity and dynamism offered unusual scope and opportunity to those among the young who were willing to swear allegiance to its goals.[16] Finally, the totalitarian solution was appealing not least because of its claim, as Karl Bracher (1995) puts it, "that there is total trust and complete agreement, that the people and the leader, rulers and ruled, the party and the state are identical" (p. 73). Consequently, what Gay (1968/1974), for example, refers to as the "strange connexion" among the young in revolutionary mutiny (toward their parents as well as the Weimar regime) – combined with blind obedience toward the Führer (p. 31) – is not, on this interpretation, necessarily irrational, but it is in part a simple instance of what Coleman (1990) would call a "transfer of authority" from one group to the other, motivated, on the present analysis, by the fall in the yield on ethnic or trust capital.[17]

Indeed, the only irrational element in the present approach is the upsurge in prejudice and ethnic hatred: the projection of blame onto minority groups for problems which even the elimination of these groups will obviously not do much (if anything) to resolve. Anti-Semitism was common in Germany, as well as in much of the rest of Europe, in the nineteenth century (Bracher 1970; Goldhagen 1996). The phenomenon to be explained here is not the existence of anti-Semitism and other racial animosities, but their violent upsurge in the 1930s. I attribute this to a single irrational element: The children could not break with the norm of honoring their parents, and so they therefore transferred their anger elsewhere for the problems their parents bequeathed to them, including the consequences of defeat in World War I, the Versailles Treaty and reparations agreements, and many of the costs of

---

[16] Some details on the Nazi party structure are provided in the next chapter.
[17] Coleman's concept of authority is discussed in more detail in the next chapter.

hyperinflation and the Great Depression. And even this irrational element combines with a rational one – namely, the youth of Weimar, perhaps correctly, saw the success of these minority groups as the precise mirror image of the failure of their own.[18]

---

[18] If the present way of thinking about ethnicity and nationalism has any value, it could be extended to the analysis of upsurges in ethnicity and authoritarianism in other societies. In Wintrobe (1995), I applied a similar framework to the rise of nationalism in the former Soviet bloc. Another possibility is the upsurge in ethnicity in the United Stated in the 1970s, which caught all observers by surprise (see, e.g., Glazer and Moynihan (1975) and which is easily explained here as a rational response on the part of the baby-boom generation (upon reaching maturity) to the widely anticipated difficulties of the U.S. pension system, which, in all likelihood, will not be able to provide adequately for them when they reach old age. By passing on ethnic values to their children, the parents may be hoping to create an enforceable mechanism which will oblige their children to take care of them in their dotage! Possibly, a similar line of thought can explain the extraordinary rise in recent years of authoritarianism among elements of the Republican right. But analysis of that problem must be left to another occasion.

13 The simple economics of criminal bureaucratic responsibility

1 Introduction

Should Adolf Eichmann have been found guilty of the crimes with which he was charged and for which he was condemned in 1962 by the court in Jerusalem?[1] Were the eighteen Nazi leaders condemned by the International Military Tribunal in Nuremberg similarly guilty? Were the three defendants – Fritzsche, von Papen, and Schacht – who were acquitted by that tribunal innocent? Seventeen minor subordinates from Auschwitz were pronounced guilty at the Frankfurt trial, while others were acquitted. On what logical or legal principle were those and other verdicts based?

This question persists because in every case the accused made and continue to make what appears to be a perfectly sound defense: They are not guilty because they were merely subordinates in large organizations (bureaucracies) – "cogs in a machine" – who were obeying "superior orders." In all the trials noted above, the defendants repeatedly made this point.

Perhaps even more interesting, the bureaucratic status of the defendants has often been acknowledged by the judges presiding over the trials, by the prosecuting and defense lawyers, by the jurors (when they were used), as well as by the scholars and reporters writing on the trials.[2] All these people struggled with the problem they thought was posed by that subordinate status. They did so because they all more or less explicitly based their reasoning on a common theory of bureaucracy. That theory states that in large organizations, orders typically emanate from the top

[1] Some of the material in this chapter is reprinted, with minor changes, from A. Breton and R. Wintrobe (1986).

[2] A prime case is Hannah Arendt (1976). To illustrate, let us consider her 1964 postscript to the New York articles reprinted as *Eichmann in Jerusalem*. She wrote, "Of course it is important to the political and social sciences that the essence of totalitarian government, and perhaps the nature of every bureaucracy, is to make functionaries and mere cogs in the administrative machinery out of men, and thus to dehumanize them. And one can debate long and profitably on the rule of Nobody, which is what the political form known as bureaucracy truly is" (p. 289). See also William Shirer (1960) and Karl Bracher (1970).

and are implemented through a chain of command by subordinates at lower echelons of the organization. In such a context, even though the crimes perpetrated by the organization itself may be enormous, it is deemed difficult to assign individual responsibility for the crimes to anyone except the one or the few at the very top. Everyone else, it is assumed, simply obeyed orders.

The classic and perhaps the most provocative analysis of this issue is the one presented by Hannah Arendt (1976) in her famous book on Adolf Eichmann's trial and on the Nazi bureaucracy, *Eichmann in Jerusalem*. In it, she so forcefully addressed the question of guilt within the framework of the commonly accepted theory of bureaucracy that the book can be used as the basic reference point on the subject.

But the question has arisen repeatedly since then. Who is responsible for the deeds committed by the Stasi in East Germany and by secret police everywhere in Eastern Europe and the former Soviet Republics? Who should be prosecuted for the "disappearances" in Argentina or for the killings in Chile? Should the government of the newly enfranchised majority in South Africa prosecute the perpetrators of government violence under *apartheid*? If so, is the defense "I only acted under orders" credible? In all these cases the issue is identical to the one which arose in the Eichmann case: Who in the regime is and should be held responsible for the crimes against humanity committed under the dictatorship?

To recall that case, we know from Arendt and from others that for a good part of his career, Eichmann was Chief of Jewish Affairs who occupied desk IV–B–4 in the SS (*Schutzstaffel*, or guard detachment). From 1933 to 1939, he organized the expulsion of Jews from Germany and Austria. After that, he had the administrative responsibility for organizing their deportation to the concentration camps. He was the transport coordinator of the Final Solution to the Jewish question. Arendt portrayed him as "the perfect bureaucrat," and indeed he presented himself that way at his trial. His basic defense was that he only acted under superior orders. At one point, in what according to Harold Rosenberg (1961) was one of the climactic moments of the trial, he "stepped out of his glass cage to defend himself with – an organization chart" (p. 380 n.*)! He would say things like "officialese is my only language"; he argued that he could not be responsible for the deaths of the Jews because his office did not deliver the Zyklon B cyanide gas to the camps. He said that he was not an anti-Semite and that he would send his own father to death if ordered to do so.

The prosecution tried to paint him as an archfiend – a sadistic and vicious Jew-hater who enjoyed sending millions to their deaths. The problem, at least as Arendt saw it, was that he simply did not appear that way – not at the trial, not at his interrogations, and not in the historical record. He appeared to be "normal" and was pronounced normal by six psychiatrists (as one of them put it: "He is more normal than I am after examining him"). Arendt coined the phrase "the banality of evil" to describe a system in which normal people could be induced to perform hideous acts under orders. This idea was subsequently taken up by the social psychologist Stanley Milgram (1974) in his famous "obedience" experiments. These experiments offered compelling scientific evidence that a high percentage of normal people would in fact become agents in a destructive process, even when the consequences of their actions were entirely apparent and even when they had nothing to gain by doing so.

Was Eichmann guilty? Arendt argued that he was. She argued that it was true, broadly speaking, that he only followed orders – that he was, indeed, a mere "cog in a wheel" – but that a cog in a machine that is perpetrating monstrous acts is responsible for those acts. In her view it was essentially the monstrosity of the acts that produced the responsibility.

A not dissimilar argument was developed by the judges at Nuremberg, although the criterion of guilt in their case was derived from a "knowledge test." This can be appreciated, to some extent, by reference to a fragment of the final verdict read to the International Military Tribunal by judge Francis Biddle:[3] "Hitler could not make aggressive war by himself. He had to have the cooperation of statesmen, military leaders, diplomats, and businessmen. When they, *with knowledge of his aims*, gave him their cooperation, they made themselves party to the plan he had initiated. They are not to be deemed innocent because Hitler made use of them *if they knew what they were doing*" (Conot 1983, p. 493; emphasis added).

It is therefore not much of a surprise that all the defendants, in addition to claiming that they were obeying superior orders, asserted that they were ignorant of anything going on in Germany and in the East, in their bureaucratic organizations, or even in their own bureaus.[4] They obeyed orders "blindly," as the saying goes.

---

[3] The statement is in respect to the first indictment formulated in the charter for the tribunal, and it pertains to crimes against peace, including the launching of an aggressive war, but it can easily be applied to the other indictments.

[4] Even "Mulka and others" from Auschwitz pleaded ignorance (see Naumann 1966). Naumann points out that Mulka – although he was an SS Obersturmführer (first lieutenant) and the adjutant to the commandant of Auschwitz – claimed that "he had seen nothing and had not issued any orders. Moreover, he was careful not to question the legality of the killing of prisoners, of which he had heard rumors, for that would have meant signing his own death warrant: 'I had a responsibility toward myself' " (p. 20).

Ignorance, in turn, tends to be accepted by all who are involved in these matters (judges, lawyers, writers, and so on) to be a natural outcome of the formal hierarchical character of bureaucracies in which a subordinate's behavior and activity are formally defined only within the confines of his or her department or bureau. This belief is succinctly encapsulated in the archetypal exchange between Avner Less (a captain in the Israeli police appointed to conduct the pretrial interrogation) and Eichmann:

> LESS: Very well, but in all your statements you keep hiding behind "it wasn't in my department," "it wasn't in my province," "the regulations". . . .
>
> EICHMANN: Yes, Herr Hauptmann [Mr. Captain], I have to do that, because as head of Bureau IV–B–4 I was really not answerable for everything, but only for my rather narrowly circumscribed department. (von Lang 1983, p. 105)

A profound difficulty with either of these lines of reasoning – that of Arendt and that of the Nuremberg judges – is that they cannot draw a line between the perpetrators of the crime and their victims. As is well known and was pointed out by Arendt, in every country they occupied, the Germans set up Jewish councils. These councils, *under orders backed by threats*, actively participated in rounding up and selecting Jews for deportation; moreover, in the camps, some of the actual killing was done by Jews. Although Arendt (1976) absolved the Jews of any guilt in their own destruction, noting the extreme threats to which they were subjected and claiming that "no non-Jewish group or people had [ever] behaved differently" (p. 11), the problem remains that, given her conception of how the Nazi regime functioned, there simply is no obvious criterion on which to distinguish the behavior of Eichmann and other criminals from that of their victims. *Both acted "under orders."*

At this point the reader should note that this dilemma arises only because the Nazi bureaucracy is modeled as an authoritarian or command system. So the question must be asked: Does the authoritarian model provide a good explanation for the behavior of the SS? Is this conception of Nazi Germany useful? And, by extension, are such intellectual constructions as Orwell's *1984* or "Japan Inc." helpful in understanding how these and other societies actually operated? In the command model, superiors are assumed to give all orders and to direct (coordinate) all operations, whereas subordinates are assumed to obey. It may be objected that this conception of authority is too simple. So the next section presents two more sophisticated analyses of authority, those of James Coleman (1990) and George Akerlof (1991). I then suggest that the model of bureaucracy used in this book[5] provides a simple and attractive alternative to these analyses based on authority. Sections 3 and 4 of this chapter then show, on the basis both of evidence presented by Arendt (1976) herself in *Eichmann in Jerusalem* and of evidence from standard historical sources, that the conundrums of responsibility which have arisen around the Nazi regime – the Nazi "bureaucracy of murder" in Arendt's words (p. 172) – are easily resolved using this model of bureaucracy.

2   Authority and power

We can begin a discussion of recent developments in the analysis of authority relationships by examining Coleman's (1990) work on this subject. In Coleman's model, authority is defined as "the right to control another's actions" (p. 66) over a limited domain and possibly restricted in various other ways. An individual *a* could acquire authority over *b* either because *b* vests or transfers that control over to *a*, or because *a* holds these rights at the outset in the way that either a parent holds them over a child or the state holds them over its citizenry with respect to the obedience of laws. This definition of authority is standard. R.H. Coase (1937), for example, defined the employer–employee relationship (which he viewed as an authority relationship) as a contract in which the employer acquires the right to direct ("order") the actions of the employee in exchange for which he or she agrees to pay the employee an agreed upon wage. The difference between authority and power is not clearly drawn. For example, in the behaviorist view of power (see, e.g., Coleman 1990), *a* has power over *b* to the extent to which the former can get the latter to do something that he or she would not otherwise do. Presumably, the difference is that power is broader than authority, because it may be exercised by *a* over *b* even where *a* has not acquired the right to do so.

Coleman's analysis of authority is most illuminating when he turns to the description of different kinds of authority systems. One useful distinction is between simple and complex authority systems. In a simple authority system, *a* transfers the right to control his or her actions to *b*. In the complex system, *a* transfers the right of control and also the right to transfer (delegate) that right (e.g., to a lieutenant). In short, in a simple authority system, authority is and can only be exercised by the actor in whom it has been vested. One example is charismatic authority.

---

[5] See the outline of this theory of bureaucracy in Chapter 9 on the Soviet system or in Albert Breton and Ronald Wintrobe (1982) for its original exposition.

At the other extreme is the authority relationship typical in modern society, in which authority is identified not with a person but with the office or position from which it is to be exercised. Coleman suggests that this development of transferability of authority is similar to the change which occurred in economic transactions when personal notes came to be acceptable as transferable.

One difficulty with Coleman's approach is that he does not draw a clear line between authority and exchange. Indeed, authority relations are often seen in exchange terms. For example, he suggests that "even coercion can be regarded as a transaction . . . [because] if a despot accompanies an order by a threat of punishment or an offer of reward, this indicates that the despot is willing to be bound by the results" (1990, p. 71). Again, he suggests that the concept of exchange can also be used to characterize phenomena that are ordinarily conceived of as coercion – for example, a parent threatening a child with spanking (p. 38). Coleman's attempt to encapsulate authority into exchange is reminiscent of Armen Alchian and Harold Demsetz's (1972) discussion of authority relations within the firm. They asserted that the firm "has no power of fiat, no authority, no disciplinary action any different in the slightest degree from ordinary market contracting between any two people . . . [t]elling an employee to type this letter rather than to file that document is like my telling my grocer to sell me this brand of tuna rather than that brand of bread . . ." (p. 777).

The problem with this way of thinking is that all it really shows is that almost any exercise of authority can be described in the language of exchange. If an SS officer in a concentration camp commands a (male) inmate to enter the gas chamber, the inmate always has a choice: He can refuse. If he accepts, there is "exchange": He enters and the SS officer reciprocates by not shooting him immediately. Defining relations that are obviously authority relations in exchange terms does not, in my view, extend the usefulness of the economic concept of exchange; it contracts it, for if authority relations can be viewed in exchange terms, then exchange relations can just as usefully be viewed in command terms (the consumer "instructs" his grocer to sell him a particular brand of tuna), and it is no longer possible to speak of either type of relation with any clarity.

A strikingly different picture of authority relationships can be found in a recent paper by Akerlof (1991). Akerlof begins by discussing various forms of individual behavior which are commonly observed but which are, to varying degrees, "pathological" (e.g., procrastination, excessive obedience to authority, membership in cults or youth gangs, and escalation of commitment to courses that are truly unwise). In each case a "near-rational" individual is engaged in making a sequence of decisions over time. At each moment the individual is close to being rational in his or her decision making, but the cumulative effect of these decisions is an outcome which he or she clearly would have liked to avoid. In procrastination, for example, this comes about because the costs of doing something *now* can have an undue salience. To illustrate, let us suppose a woman academic is certain that the benefits to her exceed the costs of writing up her current research and submitting the paper for publication. On each day, however, she faces a choice between beginning this activity and watching reruns of old movies on television. For example, the painfulness of beginning the task of writing or the ecstasy to be experienced from watching Rock Hudson and Doris Day in *Pillow Talk* may acquire an undue salience. Moreover, the costs of delay by one more day are small. Consequently, on each day the academic watches TV, comforted by her decision to begin writing tomorrow. The inconsistency arises because the individual does not foresee that tomorrow she will make exactly the same calculation; the only change is the substitution of the undue salience of *Bad Day at Black Rock* for that of *Pillow Talk*. At the end of the week, the academic has still not begun the paper, and her mind has been poisoned with phrases such as "I won't marry you until you say those three little words" and "I've been focusing on the wrong thing, Emma: You and the kids – that's all that counts."

All of this seems a sensible enough analysis of the little pathologies of everyday life. The model becomes much more interesting in Akerlof's analysis of authority. The behavior to be explained is provided by Stanley Milgram's (1974) famous experiments on obedience. In the experiment the experimenter posed as a scientist conducting experiments in learning. The scientist conducted the subject into a room where there was both a large machine for administering shocks and a fake "learner" (who was actually an actor), who was visible to the subject through a glass window. The subject was instructed to administer shocks to the learner when he or she gave wrong answers. (The learner was actually not connected to the shock machine.) The subjects were told to administer ever larger shocks as the learner gave wrong answers to the questions that were asked. The general, and surprising, result was that most subjects would go along with the scientist to a considerable degree, administering ever larger shocks to the "victim." At fairly high dosages, the victims would cry out that the experiment must be terminated and that they must be set free and so on. At very high dosages, the victims screamed in pain. Despite this apparent result, the scientist continued to admonish the subject to continue the experiment. A significant fraction of the population administered the maximum dosage.

Akerlof (1991) emphasizes that the results of this experiment are significant for two reasons:

1. the apparent tendency of the subjects toward excessive obedience;
2. the contradiction between this finding and the result from surveys that most individuals believe that neither they nor others would behave in this fashion.

For example, he cites a survey of psychiatrists, conducted by Milgram, at a major medical school, who predicted that "most subjects would not administer shocks in excess of 150 volts, and virtually no subjects would administer the maximum 450 volts" (p. 8).

The behavior observed by Milgram is modeled with a slight variation of the procrastination model. Again, the key is that the decision is made in a series of small steps. Presumably, most subjects invited to administer a very large and dangerous shock to the learner right at the beginning of the experiment would not do so. At each step, however, the cost of disobedience to the scientist presumably acquires undue salience, whereas the extra disutility of administering a shock of, say, 300 volts (compared with 280, which the subject has already committed himself or herself to) is small. So the individual compares the disutility (to him or her) of the *escalation* (from 280 to 300) rather than the disutility of administering a shock of 300, on the one hand, to the disutility of disobedience, on the other, and he or she agrees to escalate. In this way the near-rational individual is led, in a series of steps (on each one of which he or she is close to utility maximizing), to the point at which he or she is performing an action which is totally irrational. Indeed, many of the subjects were extremely distressed at their behavior after the fact. Akerlof uses variations on this model to analyze group decision making (such as the decision, now regretted by most of the participants [for example, Robert McNamara], to escalate American intervention in Vietnam by a series of small steps) or the bizarre collective behavior of youth gangs and cults. In these cases there is an additional factor at work, one which contributes to group irrationality: Some of those who are least committed to the course of action tend to drop out as the action proceeds, leaving further escalation in the hands of a more and more radical group.

One way to interpret Akerlof's paper is to say that it shows how it is possible for "normal" (near-rational) people to get drawn into a system in which they end up behaving in an entirely pathological way. But it is worth pointing out that the process he models need not always be pathological at all in its results. Thus, one could model the decision of many people who choose to stay in a university and complete a Ph.D. along similar lines: Before each academic year, a student calculates that the benefits of a Ph.D. are not worth its costs. However, the disutility of quitting and looking for a job may acquire undue salience. The student compares this "result" with the disutility of suffering through one more year of lectures, exams, and so forth, and he or she decides to continue, vowing that next year he or she will get a job. But next year, the student makes exactly the same (near-rational) calculation. In the end, he or she gets a Ph.D., becomes a successful academic (instead of a bank teller), and rationalizes that this was his or her plan all along!

From this angle the contribution of Akerlof's analysis is different. Basically, he shows that there is an alternative way to interpret a lot of human behavior that is similar to rational behavior; this alternative method allows us to understand and empathize with the process by which decisions are made but which is totally unlike the rationality criterion because it does not imply that the outcome of individual choices is always what was intended and desired to begin with.

To summarize, I have outlined two new approaches to understanding authority in terms of rational choice. Coleman sees authority in terms of an exchange of rights: A man *a* gives *b* the right to control his actions in exchange for some (unspecified) price. Akerlof sees the individual as being embedded in a process by which he or she is induced, in a series of small steps, to surrender more power over his or her actions than he or she intended. In Coleman's analysis responsibility clearly remains in the hands of the individual, because authority is *voluntarily* given up. In Akerlof's analysis the responsibility for one's actions is not at all clear.

In contrast to both of these interpretations, the analysis of Breton and Wintrobe (1986) emphasized that *any* model of authority is inappropriate for analyzing the operation of one archetypal illustration of authority: the Eichmann case. We employed the same model of bureaucracy outlined in Chapter 9 on the Soviet system: The bureaucracy in a dictatorship is composed of competing bureaus as well as competition among individual bureaucrats and bureaucratic networks. This competition for rewards will benefit the system when vertical trust is maintained at a high level, as it will tend to be when the organization is expanding and prospering. In that case the actions of individuals in the organization are best understood in terms of vertical-trust–based exchange rather than in terms of the authority model. On the other hand, the relationship of the organization's agents of destruction (Eichmann and other SS officers, heads of concentration camps, and other participants) to their *victims* is entirely different. Here is pure authority (orders backed by threats), enforced by the repeated application of the ultimate sanction.

Note that Breton and Wintrobe's analysis in terms of trust instead of authority is also applicable to the Milgram experiments. After all, it is a fact that the subject tends to trust the scientist's expertise, which leads him or her to cooperate, and it is the disutility of the loss of trust which makes the subject reluctant to cease cooperating (no sanction is imposed on the subject who discontinues the experiment). And the accumulation of trust is usually slow and takes place in small, sequential steps, as noted by both Breton and Wintrobe (1982), and Coleman (1990).

Which interpretation (trust or authority) of Eichmann's behavior is correct? Let us consult the evidence.

3   Competition in the Nazi state

> It must be remembered that all these organs, wielding enormous power, were in fierce competition with one another – which was no help to their victims, since their ambition was always the same: to kill as many Jews as possible. This competitive spirit . . . inspired in each man a great loyalty to his own outfit. (Arendt 1976, p. 71)

How did the bureaucracy of murder work? It is true that Eichmann carried the formal responsibility for Jewish affairs, as his title implied, but that did not mean that his desk had a monopoly in the area. In fact there was fierce competition on the part of many to deal with the Jewish question. The reason is simple: It was widely appreciated throughout the Nazi bureaucracy that in the eyes of the political leadership, "solving" the Jewish question had a priority that was second only to the war – and possibly not even second to that. Otherwise, it is difficult to explain the fact that as late as 1942/43, when trains were desperately needed to transport materials to the various fronts, the Final Solution, rather than being scaled down, was speeded up (Dawidowicz 1975, pp. 191–6). One reason why it was so well known that the Jewish question was a priority of the leaders is that abundant resources were put at the disposal of those who chose to take the initiative and to show enterprise in the pursuit of the Final Solution – in particular, they were put at the disposal of the SS.

The fact that the political demand on the part of the top echelons in the hierarchy was strong and that a number of agencies competed for a larger role in the Nazi solution to the Jewish question is explicitly recognized by Arendt (1976) herself:

> [Eichmann's] chief competitors were the Higher S.S. and Police Leaders, who were under the direct command of Himmler, had

easy access to him, and always outranked Eichmann. There was also the Foreign Office, which, under its new Undersecretary of State, Dr. Martin Luther, a protégé of Ribbentrop, had become very active in Jewish affairs. . . . It occasionally issued deportation orders to be carried out by its representatives abroad, who for reasons of prestige preferred to work through the Higher S.S. and Police Leaders. There were, furthermore, the Army commanders in the Eastern occupied territories, who liked to solve problems "on the spot," which meant shooting; the military men in Western countries were, on the other hand, always reluctant to cooperate and to lend their troops for the rounding up and seizure of Jews. Finally, there were the Gauleiters, the regional leaders, each of whom wanted to be the first to declare his territory judenrein, and who occasionally started deportation proceedings on their own. (pp. 151–2)

The competition among the many agencies and bureaus reflected the general operation of the Nazi bureaucracy. Schemes were constantly being put forward by rival power centers or rival entrepreneurs, and Hitler would choose among them. Some were "successful," others not. The latter included Gottfried Feder (the economics ideologue), who was given a post as undersecretary in the Ministry of Economics but who was rapidly ejected by the more orthodox Schacht (Shirer 1960, p. 261); Alfred Rosenberg (commissioner for the central control of questions connected with the East-European region), who was given the responsibility for the East, but who found himself unable to compete with Himmler's SS and other agencies in the area and who was eventually ridiculed by Hitler himself (Holborn 1969, p. 809; Bracher 1970, p. 411; Dawidowicz 1975, p. 19); and Hans Frank (Reich commissar for the coordination of justice in the states and for the renewal of jurisprudence), who was not successful in persuading Hitler to draw up a new legal code (Broszat 1981). These failures, and many others like them, are one measure of the existence and strength of competition.

Organizational charts are unable to tell us much, at least at first blush, about the networks of trust in bureaucracies. As a rule, they are not capable of telling much about the extent of competition between bureaus and bureaucrats because, by their very nature, they are designed to show the "orderly" lines of authority. But in the case of the Nazi bureaucracy of murder, the overlapping lines of command, the confusion of jurisdictions, and the duplication of responsibilities are, to some extent, apparent only in formal organizational charts, which, it must be insisted, were not produced by the Nazi authorities but by historians and analysts.[6] If the reader consults such a chart (e.g., in Conot 1983, p. 223), the overlapping jurisdictions of Himmler, Goering, Heydrich, and (after Heydrich's assassination) Kaltenbrunner and Muller will be readily apparent.

Even those who, like Eugen Kogon (1980), appear to place considerable importance on the formal structure of the bureaucracy – which he would most surely have called the bureaucracy of hell – acknowledge that "the many diversified branches of [the whole machine] enjoyed considerable degrees of independence" (p. 7). The independence of the various bureaus and bureaucrats is also recognized by Broszat (1981). Conot (1983) remarks that "Himmler was free to undertake whatever tasks he saw fit" and that, even though Heydrich was accountable to both Himmler and Goering, "neither took an active interest in his operations [so that] he could play them off against each other when necessary, and in practice act virtually independently" (p. 131).

The lines of command were so imprecise that contradictory testimony as to who was responsible for what could easily be given. For example, one of the witnesses at Nuremberg declared that "even in Heydrich's lifetime, Eichmann occupied a dominant, not to say absolute, position, which increased steadily in scope. At Reich Security he handled the whole Jewish sector independently. From Heydrich's death to the end, he was directly responsible to Himmler. This was generally known at Reich Security" (von Lang 1983, p. 120). Eichmann, who was not at Nuremberg, vehemently protested this description, arguing that it was surely self-serving on the part of the witness because by placing the responsibility for crimes on an absentee, it was hoped that the person present could be exonerated.

The overlapping competitive structure of the Nazi state is well described by Shirer (1960):

> Old party comrades such as Goering, Goebbels, Himmler, Ley and Schirach were given free rein to carve out their own empires of power – and usually profit. Schacht was given a free hand at first to raise the money for expanding government expenditures by whatever sleight of hand he could think up. Whenever these men clashed over the division of power or spoils, Hitler intervened. He did not mind these quarrels. . . . Thus he seemed to take delight at the spectacle of three men competing with each

---

[6] "For the judges and other participants in the Nuremberg trial, the comprehension of the Nazi's governmental structure proved a major challenge; and Lawrence [the British judge], to a certain extent, remained puzzled by the snarls, overlapping, and confusion until the end" (Conot 1983, p. 131).

other in foreign affairs: Neurath, the Foreign Minister, Rosenberg, the head of the party's Foreign Affairs Department, and Ribbentrop, who had his own "Ribbentrop Bureau" which dabbled in foreign policy. (pp. 275–6)

That description of foreign policy formulation and implementation could be repeated for many other areas of policy, including the one involving the Final Solution to the Jewish question.

In addition to the loose formal organizational lines of command, about which more evidence could easily be cited if space permitted (see, e.g., the discussion in Bracher 1970, pp. 277–8), another indicator of competition among bureaus in the Nazi state is the imprecision of the orders emanating from the top. When orders do not have specific content and when they are not directed at anyone in particular, they will elicit a large response from diverse quarters. In other words, they will lead to competitive behavior.

At his trial in Jerusalem, Eichmann explained how things were done in the Third Reich. He stated, "Whenever Hitler made a speech in which he was particularly violent about the Jews, we knew something would come from Himmler" (von Lang 1983, p. 98). Or also, he said, "No sooner had Hitler made a speech – and he invariably touched on the Jewish question – than every party or government department felt that it was up to them to do something" (p. 59).

The imprecision in the orders is one of the reasons why, as time went on, the number of bureaus that wanted and sought to participate in the Final Solution grew almost without bound. Arendt (1976) writes descriptively that "the inexhaustible source of trouble, as he [Eichmann] saw it, was that he and his men were never left alone, that all these other State and Party offices wanted their share in the 'solution,' with the result that a veritable army of 'Jewish experts' had cropped up everywhere and were falling over themselves in their efforts to be first in a field of which they knew nothing" (pp. 72–3). Eichmann himself declared to Avner Less, "You can't imagine the difficulties I ran into, the tedious, tooth-and-nail negotiations, the thousands of objections raised by the various agencies. They all felt it was their business" (von Lang 1983, p. 67). The duplication and overlap of responsibility characteristic of Nazi policy in this area are well summarized in Gordon (1984):

> How did Hitler delegate authority over racial issues? He did not authorize one central agency to handle the "Jewish Question." Instead, he encouraged a multitude of agencies in both party and state to dabble in racial politics. This structural fragmentation

created anarchy among competing agencies and resulted in contradictory policies. Hitler chose from among these contradictory
policies; his choices depended on his estimate of domestic opinion, party unity, and foreign affairs. He then allowed his many
agencies to compete in implementing the approved policy. This
resulted in further power struggles, after which Hitler acknowledged the emerging victor as the "primary authority" in racial
matters. Between 1933 and 1938 party agencies were "primary
authorities"; between 1938 and 1939 the SS and party contested
for power; and after 1939 the SS was the "primary authority."
Agencies that lost out in these struggles for power were not
eliminated, however; they were allowed to meddle in their role
as second- and third-rate powers. (pp. 144–5)

Another indicator of competition is provided by historical evidence of
entrepreneurship within the bureaucracy on the racial issue. Suggestions
for a final solution to the Jewish question were often voiced in the
bureaucracy. For example, a top civilian official (Friedrich Ubelhor) in
the district of Lodz in 1939 suggested that the ghetto being planned there
should be only a temporary measure toward a more "permanent" solution. Governor Hans Frank also put this same idea forward a year later
in 1940. In July 1941, another official by the name of Hoppner sent
Eichmann the official minutes of a discussion on the Jewish question in
the Wartheland that proposed extermination. Hoppner asked Eichmann
for his comments, adding "these things sound to some extent fantastic,
but in my view absolutely practicable" (Dawidowicz 1975, p. 218).

Eichmann himself had, for a time, played a fairly prominent role in the
bureaucracy, especially with respect to the deportation of Jews from
Germany and from the Western occupied countries. He obtained that
position not because he was good at following orders, but through entrepreneurship. He accumulated more power into his hands in the same way
that a competitive firm accumulates more customers: by being better
than his competitors. In the very early years of his career, Eichmann was
in charge of the Jewish desk in the SS office in Munich, but there was
another desk for Jewish affairs in the Berlin Gestapo (Dawidowicz 1975,
p. 107). Eichmann learned a little Hebrew and read books by Zionist
leaders; he was commended for this initiative. In 1938, the authorities
decided on the policy of forced emigration for the Jews; Eichmann was
sent to Vienna to organize their expulsion from Austria. Many of the
Jews there were eager to leave (most of the prominent ones had already
been put in prison), but a bottleneck was created by the number of
papers every emigrant had to assemble to get out. Eichmann invented an

assembly line system that integrated all the offices concerned: The Ministry of Finance, the income tax people, the police, and the Jewish leaders were all housed under one roof. He also sent Jewish functionaries abroad to solicit foreign exchange from Jewish organizations so that the Jews could buy the visas needed for emigration.

As Arendt (1976) put it, in the end it was like an automatic factory: "At one end you put in a Jew who still has some property, a factory, or a shop, or a bank account, and he goes through the building from counter to counter, from office to office, and comes out at the other end without any money, without any rights, with only a passport on which it says: 'You must leave the country within a fortnight. Otherwise you will go to a concentration camp'" (pp. 44–5). As a result of the assembly line system, in eight months 45,000 Jews left Austria, whereas no more than 16,000 left Germany. Eichmann was promoted to the rank of *Obersturmbannführer* (lieutenant colonel).

Later, when the war broke out, forced emigration was no longer possible, and it looked to Eichmann as if he might be out of a job. He hatched or resurrected a number of schemes, including the establishment of separate Jewish states in Madagascar and in German-occupied Poland, where he went on his own initiative to reconnoiter the territory. Despite this impressive entrepreneurship, events moved too fast for him, and in 1941 Hitler ordered the Final Solution, in which Eichmann was to act only as a transportation man.

Although this was a big assignment, it was not as important as Eichmann had hoped for. A bureau different from Eichmann's was put in charge; the Final Solution was officially given not to Heydrich's Office for Reich Security (the RSHA), which included Eichmann's Jewish affairs desk, but to a rival agency within the SS, the Economics and Administration Affairs Office (the WVHA) under Oswald Pohl. Eichmann was never to rise as high in the hierarchy as he felt he deserved. But as discussed in the next section, he continued to behave as an energetic bureaucratic entrepreneur.

4   The efficiency of competition in the bureaucracy of murder

> On the other hand he [Hitler] remained loyal to his old comrades from the fighting days of the party. To be sure, whoever opposed him could be certain of the dictator's ruthless vengeance. But if a man merely proved ineffective in his job, Hitler was unlikely to remove him. In general, Hitler cherished faith more than expertness. (Holborn 1969, p. 750)

Earlier (see Section 2 of this chapter or Chapter 9, Section 3), it was suggested that from the point of view of superiors, competition between bureaus and bureaucrats is efficient – that is, it furthers and promotes their interests and objectives – if loyalty or trust between superiors and subordinates is such that subordinates feel that they can supply informal services (noncodified, noncontractual, or informal services) and, as a result, be rewarded for them. In the absence of such loyalty, subordinates would presumably perform the tasks they are formally required to do, but they would – especially if there exists considerable trust between them – engage in actions that, even if they were not outright sabotage, would be geared to the direct interests of subordinates and not to those of superiors. From the point of view of the latter, then, competition would be inefficient – that is, the initiative and enterprise instigated by competition would be counterproductive.

The preceding section sought to demonstrate that the Nazi state was intensely competitive. What to many appeared to be confusion, duplication, overlap, and even disorder was the outward manifestation of an extremely competitive social structure. In this section evidence is presented to show that the rank and file of the bureaucracy of murder was very loyal to the Nazi leadership – that, in other words, the SS slogan "My honor is my loyalty" (Kogon 1980, p. 199) was not an empty one but, at least to some extent, a reflection of a true state of affairs.

It must be insisted at the outset that it is not easy to document the existence of loyalty or trust from standard historical sources. One reason for this is surely the fascination of students of the regime for the formal relationship between members of the organization. It is true that one sometimes encounters affirmations such as the following (emphasis added throughout): "This *close confidant* [Rudolf Diels] of Goering", or "his [Himmler's] *closest intimate*, Reinhard Heydrich" (Kogon 1980, p. 9); or "He [Ribbentrop] . . . quickly proved his *devotion* to him [Hitler]" (Holborn 1969, p. 773); or "His [Hess's] career was that of a follower . . . with well-nigh religious *faith* in the Fuhrer" (Bracher 1970, p. 280); or again "Wilhelm Frick, the Minister of the Interior and one of Hitler's most *faithful* followers" (Shirer 1960, p. 219). There are many others, such as the quotation at the beginning of this section, all of which suggest the existence of loyalty. But reasonable knowledge of the full network of trust relationships in the Nazi regime does not, to our knowledge, exist.

Because of this state of affairs, one is left with the necessity of inferring the existence of trust networks indirectly from particular behavior and activities. In the case of Hitler's Germany, it is widely known that the building of trust assumed enormous importance. Indeed, according to

Arendt (1951/1973) herself, the central characteristic of totalitarian movements, "compared with all other parties and movements . . . [,] is their demand for [the] total, unrestricted, unconditional, and unalterable loyalty of the individual member" (1951/1973, p. 323). She also describes one organizational device by which the movement created loyalty: its carefully graduated and fluctuating hierarchy of militancy. Thus, the masses who were part of the movement were divided into two categories: sympathizers and members. Moreover, Hitler "was the first to devise a conscious policy of constantly enlarging the ranks of sympathizers while at the same time keeping the number of party members strictly limited" (p. 366). And "this relationship . . . is repeated on different levels within the movement itself. As party members are related to and separated from the fellow-travelers, so are the elite formations of the movement related to and separated from the ordinary members" (p. 367). This pattern is analyzed with particular reference to the SS. Arendt writes,

> Another advantage of the totalitarian pattern is that it can be repeated indefinitely and keeps the organization in a state of fluidity which permits it constantly to insert new layers and define new degrees of militancy. The whole history of the Nazi party can be told in terms of new formations within the Nazi movement. The SA, the stormtroopers (founded in 1922), [was] the first Nazi formation which was supposed to be more militant than the party itself; in 1926, the SS was founded as the elite formation of the SA; after three years, the SS was separated from the SA and put under Himmler's command; it took Himmler only a few more years to repeat the same game within the SS. One after the other, and each more militant than its predecessor, there now came into being, first, the Shock Troops, then the Death Head units (the "guard units for the concentration camps"), which later were merged to form the Armed SS (Waffen-SS), finally the Security Service (the "ideological intelligence service of the Party," and its executive arm for the "negative population policy") and the Office for Questions of Race and Resettlement (Rasse- und Siedlungswesen), whose tasks were of a "positive kind" – all of them developing out of the General SS, whose members, except for the higher Fuehrer Corps, remained in their civilian occupations. To all these new formations the member of the General SS now stood in the same relationship as the SA-man to the SS-man, or the party member to the SA-man, or the member of a front organization to a party member. (p. 368)

The incentives that this system gives to accumulate vertical loyalty (and to prevent the accumulation of horizontal trust) are obvious. In contrast to the opportunities provided by a conventional hierarchy, the possibilities of advancement in this system are almost never-ending, and a paramount criterion for advancement is loyalty. Arendt writes that "the fluctuating hierarchy, similar to that of secret services, makes it possible, even without actual power, to degrade any rank or group that wavers or shows signs of decreasing radicalism by the mere insertion of a new more radical layer, hence driving the older group automatically in the direction of the front organization and away from the center of the movement" (p. 369).

How much more sophisticated is this analysis from *The Origins of Totalitarianism*, compared with the simple-minded command image of the Nazi hierarchy to be found in her later book, *Eichmann in Jerusalem*! Indeed, in the earlier (1951) book, Arendt explicitly disavows the command model. She wrote,

> [in] the organization of an army and the military dictatorship established after its model . . . absolute power of command from the top down and absolute obedience from the bottom up correspond to the situation of extreme danger in combat, *which is precisely why they are not totalitarian*. . . . Every hierarchy, no matter how authoritarian in its direction, and every chain of command, no matter how arbitrary or dictatorial the content of [its] orders, tends [*sic*] to stabilize and would have restricted the total power of the leader of a totalitarian movement. (pp. 364–5; emphasis added)

The leader's (in this case, the Führer's) power in the totalitarian movement is analyzed in terms of his capacity to keep his subordinates from trusting each other. "His position within this intimate circle depends upon his ability to spin intrigues among its members and upon his skill in constantly changing its personnel. He owes his rise to leadership to an extreme ability to handle inner-party struggles for power" (p. 373).

The other major device used by the Nazis to encourage loyalty to the regime was the systematic neutralization or destruction of alternative centers of power (competing organizations), such as the *lander* (regional governments), the unions, other "horizontal" associations, and, of course, the other political parties. The facts are well known (see, e.g., Broszat 1981, Chaps. 3–5); it would serve no purpose to recount them anew here. Of particular interest, however, was the policy of the Nazis toward the civil service.

After Hitler's accession to power in 1933, he had to govern as well as to hold onto power. He could have governed through the existing bureaucratic machinery of the German state which he had inherited from the Weimar Republic, and indeed, if the conventional theory of bureaucracy, which assumes that subordinates in large organizations are neutral individuals obeying orders from above, is correct, then Hitler would simply have had to take that bureaucracy over, issue orders, and observe them being carried out.

But the evidence goes in the opposite direction. Indeed, it shows that in many bureaus and, more particularly, in the bureaus that were the most important for the implementation of Nazi objectives, Hitler and the National Socialist leadership proceeded to displace the established civil service (see Broszat 1981). The general drift is well described in a sad letter to Hitler from Wilhelm Frick around 1940. Frick wrote,

> I have, my Führer, always seen it as my duty as your civil service Minister since 1933 [he was then Reich Minister of the Interior] . . . to make available to you for the great tasks of state policy a highly qualified professional civil service and to develop in it the old Prussian conception of duty as well as the National Socialist character, as is the case with the German armed forces. The course of the last years makes me doubt, however, whether my efforts can in any way be regarded as successful. To an ever growing degree, according to the agreed observations of my department and all other departments, bitter feelings are spreading in the professional civil service about the lack of appreciation of their abilities and services as well as of unjustified neglect. The feeling of being left defenceless is beginning to cripple the best creative forces. . . . There can no longer be any talk whatever of the professional civil service being preferred as a body *enjoying the special trust of the state leadership.* . . . The civil service is also suffering badly from the fact that new tasks are not being entrusted to it, but to the Party organizations, although this often concerns genuine administrative duties. (Quoted in Broszat 1981, pp. 257–8; emphasis added)

What seems to have been the case throughout the bureaucracy was particularly marked in respect to the War Ministry, the conduct of diplomacy and foreign affairs, the police, and, of course, the extermination of the Jews (for which there was, obviously, no pre-Hitler bureaucratic organization).

A final measure of the extent of the trust between the Nazi leadership and subordinates in the organization is provided by what happened when it became obvious that the Third Reich was collapsing. This episode provides a good illustration of one of the basic contentions about trust in the Breton–Wintrobe model: However extreme (large) it might be, such trust is not necessarily "blind" and it is never, as Arendt (1951/1973) suggests, the kind of "total, unrestricted, unconditional, and unalterable" (p. 323) trust that the regime demanded and (as Arendt sometimes implies) that its members supplied. Instead, we suggested that loyalty rises or falls depending on a number of things, especially the anticipated future prospects of the regime. What happened was that competition within the bureaucracy continued, but now it was "inefficient" because it was not geared to the objectives of superiors.

As early as 1944, Himmler had come to the view that the war was lost, and in defiance of Hitler's wishes, he asked Eichmann to stop killing Jews. He assumed that the Allies, in their gratitude for this act, would make him prime minister of postwar Germany! According to Arendt, Eichmann sabotaged his orders as much as he felt he could. When there were no trains available for transporting Jews from Hungary in 1944, Eichmann organized foot marches; and when Himmler ordered him to desist, he threatened to obtain a decision from Hitler himself. As a result, in January 1945, Eichmann's old enemy Kurt Becker (who was cooperating with Himmler's plan to sell Jews) was promoted to colonel and Eichmann was transferred out of his desk on Jewish affairs to the insignificant one dealing with the fight against churches.

Later, Himmler "deserted the sinking ship of state. The Reuter dispatch told of his secret negotiations with Count Bernadotte and his offer to surrender the German armies in the West to Eisenhower. To Hitler, who had never doubted Himmler's absolute loyalty, this was the heaviest blow of all" (Shirer 1960, p. 1122).

When Goering, in April 1945, sought to reactivate the 1941 decree that made him deputy führer by sending a telegram to Hitler that was signed "Your loyal, Hermann Goering," Hitler sighed, "Goering has betrayed and deserted both me and his Fatherland," and then he added, "No allegiances are kept, no honor lived up to, no disappointments that I have not had, no betrayals that I have not experienced" (p. 1119).

In addition to the Himmler and Goering actions, there were others, such as the ones by Ribbentrop, who was negotiating in Sweden, and Speer, who was "urging commanders such as Manteuffel to disobey orders to destroy bridges, dams and factories rather than leave them to the enemy" (Toland 1976, p. 1174). Bormann was right to declare that "treachery seems to have replaced loyalty" (Shirer 1960, p. 1121). And Hitler was also right to say that "I am lied [to] on all sides" and to add that "those arrogant, tedious, indecisive SS are no good to me any more" (Toland 1976, pp. 1172, 1198).

5   Bureaucratic responsibility

In a bureaucracy which was characterized by rigorous and unflagging competition between its personnel and agencies – and in which, at least until the closing days of the war, that competition furthered the interests of the rulers (because trust between these rulers and their subordinates was strong) – what can be said about the responsibilities of the subordinates for the actions of the regime? More specifically, what responsibility does an individual SS officer like Eichmann bear for the crimes perpetrated by the regime and by the agency he was heading?

To answer these questions, let us consider two hypothetical situations. Suppose first that Eichmann, rather than being employed by the SS, had been self-employed – that is, he had owned a transportation company – and rather than a rank, a salary, and a prospect for promotions *within* the system, he had been an outsider who was given the opportunity to bid against other companies for a contract that involved transporting millions of people to their deaths. If he had been the lowest bidder or the one who promised to move the maximum number of persons to their deaths for a fixed sum, he would have been given the contract. If he had lost out in the bidding, he might have received other contracts or nothing at all. Nothing else would have happened to him.

In such a circumstance we suggest that no one would have any difficulty in assigning responsibility and that everybody would convict Eichmann of guilt. Indeed, on canonical principles of responsibility, whether as a principal or as an accessory, no new issue is raised by that case. We suggest that the incentives facing Eichmann – and other subordinates like him – were no different from those assumed in our hypothetical situation. Eichmann did not obey *orders* any more than a self-employed entrepreneur does when he or she responds to the *demands* of the marketplace in order to make money. His rewards took the form of promotions, perquisites, and power rather than negotiated contractual sums – but that fact makes no difference when it comes to the question of his guilt or innocence.

Furthermore, as successful entrepreneurs in a competitive environment, Eichmann and all others like him must be assumed to have had knowledge of existing opportunities as well as of the possibilities of new opportunities. Aggressive entrepreneurs are always on the lookout for ways to improve their positions. Guilt and responsibility derive from entrepreneurship in a criminal venture, not from a claimed bureaucratic ignorance of the facts.

Turning to the second hypothetical situation, let us suppose instead that a gun had been held to Eichmann's head and that he had been told to carry out orders or face execution for disobedience. In that case it would appear to be hard to hold him responsible for carrying out the orders he received. There is considerable evidence (Robinson 1965; Dawidowicz 1975, 1981) that these were in fact the incentives facing members of the *Judenrate* (the Jewish councils) and the Jewish commandos in the concentration camps. The argument of Arendt that "it was undeniable that he [Eichmann] had always acted upon 'superior orders'" (1976, p. 294) but that "all the cogs in the machinery, no matter how insignificant, are in court forthwith transformed back into perpetrators, that is to say, into human beings" (p. 289) is logically invalid and raises a false issue. It is invalid for the following reason: If Eichmann merely followed orders because they were backed by possible sanctions, he could not be found guilty for the reasons already indicated. It is a false issue because Eichmann did not merely follow orders and, furthermore, would in all likelihood not even have been sanctioned, let alone executed, if he had pursued the Nazi solution to the Jewish question with less zeal. He would simply have participated less in the informal rewards that would then have gone to the more ardent entrepreneurs.

Eichmann – like innumerable other Nazi subordinates – was a competitive entrepreneurial bureaucrat in a very competitive bureaucracy. It was this fact, combined with his loyalty, that explains his efficiency. And it is the fact that there were thousands of Eichmanns, all entrepreneurial and competitive and all fiercely loyal to their superiors, that explains the terrible efficiency of the Nazi bureaucracy of murder. There is little to be feared from the standard picture of a totalitarian society in which "cogs," who are watched by Big Brother or his equivalent, carry out orders emanating from the top. Such a society would collapse in inefficiency. What is infinitely more fearsome is the capacity of a dictatorship to use the principle of competition to organize terror and murder.

6   Conclusion

The question addressed in this chapter is one that was posed with particular force by the events that took place in Nazi Germany: Should subordinates in large organizations be held responsible for criminal acts that they do not deny having committed but that they claim to have perpetrated under orders? A number of answers have been provided to this question, but all, to our knowledge, accept the defense as reflecting reality in an exact way.

So many find this defense compelling simply because the image or theory of bureaucracy that is almost universally held is one that is developed from the idea that in large organizations subordinates are given orders from above and, as long as they remain subordinates, have no choice but to obey. Saddled with such a theory, serious people, convinced of the guilt of the subordinates, have sought rationales for their conviction in different directions. The rationales of Hannah Arendt and the Nuremberg judges were outlined earlier. They do not appear very robust.

The basic point of this chapter is that subordinates in large organizations do not "obey orders." They are placed in a competitive framework in which they are rewarded for entrepreneurial initiatives that promote the interests and objectives of their superiors. The more useful they are to their superiors, the larger the rewards. The bureaucratic structure of Nazi Germany itself was extremely competitive, and the bureaucrats (the SS officers, the heads of concentration camps, and so forth) who were active in the bureaucracy were energetic, entrepreneurial, and competitive – and, except toward the end, they were intensely loyal to their superiors.

If, as the evidence presented in this chapter suggests, that model of bureaucracy, which is based on competition and exchange, describes well the Nazi regime, then the question with which we began this chapter is easily answered, and that answer is: *guilty*.

Part V

Conclusion

14   The machinery of dictatorship

1   Introduction

Much of the world still lives, today, as always, under dictatorship.[1] Yet we know very little about the behavior of these regimes. One reason for our ignorance is simply that dictatorships tend to be closed societies, and information on them is hard to obtain. Another reason is that they are typically feared and disliked, so that most research on them has focused on how they arise (with the view that once this is understood we can prevent further instances) and comparatively little work has been done trying to understand how these regimes actually function. Finally, when their behavior has been researched, the point of view taken has often been that they operate by repression and command. Policies are decided at the top – by the dictator, with the help of a small group of advisers – and then imposed on a hapless population. The population acquiesces either as a result of fear, on the one hand, or brainwashing, indoctrination, and thought control, on the other. However, the explanatory power of these concepts – their capacity to explain changes in the level of repression, for example, or to explain why regimes rise and fall – is not very large. In this study I have tried to understand and explain the working of dictatorship from a different point of view – namely, that of an economist. This means that I assume that the people within such systems – the ruler and the ruled – operate no differently from people in democratic societies: They are self-interested and rational in the economic sense – that is, whatever their goals are, they try to achieve them as best they can, and they are always alert to opportunities to do better.

Although I have assumed that dictators are rational, I have not assumed they are exclusively materialistic; their quest for *power* – either

[1] Freedom House has prepared annual estimates of the levels of political freedom and civil liberties for many countries around the world since 1978, and other estimates are sometimes made for earlier periods (for the behavior of these variables over the last fifty years or so, see Huntington 1991). In 1996, according to Freedom House (1997), only 22 percent of the world's population lived in "free" societies. Another 39 percent were classified as "partly free," and the remaining 39 percent were "not free."

for itself or for instrumental reasons (e.g., the capacity to impose their own preferences on society) – has been a central theme of this book. In general, dictators are interested in both consumption and power, and the relative weights of these factors in the dictator's utility function are important in the classification of dictatorships and in understanding their behavior.

This gives us two dimensions of the behavior of dictatorship. In total, five dimensions of behavior have been modeled formally: the dictator's personal consumption (C), power (π), level of repression (R), extent of loyal support (L), and the size of the government as measured by its budget (B). I derived them all as functions of more basic aspects of the political and economic structure of the regimes, as well as of the dictator's preferences. Other aspects of the behavior of dictatorships have been discussed less formally: their proclivity for nationalism and war, their tendency to redistribute wealth, their emphasis on ideology, and their implementation of a competitive social and bureaucratic structure.

Apart from the intrinsic interest and importance of studying dictatorship itself, there are a couple of byproducts of this study that are worth mentioning. One is that once the reader understands a bit more about dictatorship, he or she will see that democracy, despite all of its flaws, looks more attractive than before, because a number of the alleged flaws of democratic politics are even more characteristic of dictatorship. Another is a more nuanced view of democracy. Observing the conditions under which democracy breaks down and slides into dictatorship makes us aware of the fact that democracy comes in all kinds of forms: strong and weak, corrupt or not, representative or not, and so on. Consideration of these conditions leads naturally to the question of how to improve the workings of democratic institutions and of how to modify economic prescriptions to take account of the goal of better governance as well as goals like economic efficiency. In this conclusion I won't try to summarize everything in the book, but I will try to highlight some of its major themes with this point of view in mind. I will look at a number of issues, and I will try to summarize the arguments on them in this book in simple English:

1. How do dictators stay in power?
2. Is dictatorship good for economic growth and efficiency?
3. What foreign policies should the democracies adopt to deal with dictatorships if they are interested in promoting freedom?
4. Who inside the dictatorship is responsible for the crimes committed by the regime?

At the end I offer a brief speculation about the future of dictatorship.

2   The Dictator's Dilemma and the machinery of dictatorship

Our starting point was what I like to call the Dictator's Dilemma – the problem facing any ruler, who wants to know how much support he or she has among the general population, as well as among those smaller groups with the power to depose him or her. It is true that dictators have power over their subjects, much more so than do democratic rulers. But this very power over them breeds a reluctance among the citizenry to signal displeasure with the dictator's policies. The problem is magnified when the dictator rules by the most basic instrument in the dictator's arsenal: political repression. The more the repressive apparatus stifles dissent and criticism, the less the dictator knows about how much support he or she really has among the people.

Another way to see this point is to compare the situation of the dictator with that of a leader in a democratic country. Democratic institutions (such as freedom of speech, freedom of information, elections, a free press, organized opposition parties, and an independent judiciary) all provide means whereby dissatisfaction with public policies may be communicated between citizens and their political leaders. The dictator typically dispenses with these institutions and thus gains a freedom of action unknown in democracy. But there is a cost: the loss of the capacity to find out just how popular the ruler's policies are (and therefore how safe he or she really is). The Chinese Communists found out how unpopular the collectivization of agriculture was only when they abandoned it. The Chilean dictator Pinochet was assured by his advisers that he could win the free (more or less) 1988 referendum on his rule, and he was deeply shocked when he lost it. As a consequence, the most likely personality characteristic possessed by dictators is *paranoia*, and many of the "great dictators" of human history have in fact been consumed by this form of anxiety, including the Roman emperors Tiberius and Commodus, and, in our own time, Stalin and Mao Zedong. Many lesser dictators are afflicted as well. The diaries of Ferdinand Marcos, for example, are shot through with these symptoms (see Rempel 1993). The point is that there is a real basis for the paranoia. Ironically, the typical dictator is less secure in office than is a democratic leader.

From a theoretical point of view, the Dictator's Dilemma originates in the lack of a mechanism in politics that permits rulers to enforce promises or commitments. It would be advantageous for dictators to "buy off" some of their constituents, especially both those who may be too powerful to repress and those whose demands are easily satisfied. So a simple trade of rents or policies in exchange for support would solve the Dictator's Dilemma, and it would also allow the subjects to rest easy. But there is no mechanism that is analogous to legal contractual enforcement which would enforce this trade.

The Dictator's Dilemma is not insoluble. Dictatorships with any permanence are those that discover and institutionalize programs or mechanisms

1. that promote competition among the agencies of the bureaucracy and among other powerful groups in the country.
2. that "automatically" both reward their supporters and monitor their support.
3. that fund these "reward" and "monitoring" programs through taxation and systematic repression of the opposition.

These institutions of repression, competition, and redistribution – the machinery of dictatorship – solve the dilemma in one way or another and define the character of the dictatorship. A number of such systems were examined in the book, including Caesarism (in which the machinery functions by virtue of gifts and external conquest), communism (Party direction and control of the economic system), *apartheid* (job reservations and the pass system), and Nazism (war and ethnic cleansing). Other dictatorships are more temporary. In this category, generally called *tinpots*, I have placed military dictatorships, kleptocrats, and other regimes with more limited purposes.

From an economic point of view, the essence of the problem of obtaining support is to "overpay" supporters – that is, to distribute rents in the form of a wage, price, or capital value premium. Dictators "buy" the loyalty of a group when they give those who belong to that group more than they can expect to obtain under a different regime. The support of workers can be obtained by paying them excessive wages, of capitalists by giving them monopoly privileges, of particular regions by locating manufacturing facilities in places where they don't really belong but where they are politically valuable, of ethnic groups by giving them special privileges, and so on. Similar practices are widely practiced in democracy – in the United States the word invented to describe them is "pork-barrel politics." These practices are often decried as a failure of democracy. But if democracy may be likened to a pork barrel, the typical dictatorship is a warehouse or temple of pork! These practices appear to be much more widespread under dictatorship than under democracy.

So although there is always a class of people who are repressed under a dictatorship, there is also always another class – the overpaid. As far as the people in the middle are concerned, the sad thing is that they can side with either group. The general population may be repressed (insofar as its civil liberties may be taken away), but other policies of the regime may compensate for this loss as far as the people are concerned.

Indeed, as has been emphasized throughout this study, *the use of repression doesn't mean that dictators aren't popular*. Indeed, it sometimes appears from the historical record that the more repressive they were, the more popular they became![2] All the evidence indicates that Hitler was very popular. Communism's current comeback in Eastern Europe is an illustration of how *popular* it was at one time; when it became unpopular, the regimes fell.

The other tool used by dictators to stay in power is repression, the use of which is the hallmark of dictatorships of all stripes. However, although repression is a constant under autocratic regimes, its level is not, and explaining changes in the level of repression is fundamental to any explanation regarding the behavior of dictatorship. To do this, it is necessary to distinguish between different kinds of regimes, and I defined four types in the book: tinpots (low repression and loyalty), tyrants (high repression, low loyalty), totalitarians (high levels of both), and timocrats (low repression, high loyalty). The regimes differ in their response to economic change. Suppose, for example, that there is an increase in economic growth which raises the dictator's popularity. Tinpots and timocrats both respond to an increase in popularity by lowering the level of repression; tyrants and totalitarians, by raising it. This fact also provides the key to establishing a policy toward these regimes, as described in Section 4 below. But before turning to policy issues, let us briefly summarize our results with respect to an important question.

3   Is dictatorship good for the economy?

A lot of research has been conducted that has tried to answer the question: Which is better for the economy – democracy or dictatorship? One reason for the interest in this question is the fact that there always seem to be some autocratic regimes which appear to outperform the democracies: in the 1930s, Hitler's Germany and Stalin's Russia; in our own time, Pinochet's Chile, South Korea under the generals, and, most spectacularly, China and its "free-market communism." However, the answer is complex, mainly because the economic systems under autocracies vary so much. Those who believe there is some simple formula for distinguishing the economy of dictatorship from that of democracy should compare,

---

[2] The reader will find this proposition less counterintuitive as soon as he or she realizes that one of the most important targets of the autocrat's repressive apparatus is negative information about the regime and its policies.

for example, the economies of Nazi Germany, *apartheid* South Africa, "Papa Doc" Duvalier's Haiti, Pinochet's Chile, and the former Soviet Union.

One thing, however, does seem clear, and it provides our starting point in addressing this question – that is, dictators have a greater capacity for *action*, good or bad. Dictators who wish to raise taxes, declare war, or take tough measures against crime may have to deal with some opposition to these policies among their advisers, but by and large they can do so. Democracies, on the other hand, are often mired in *inaction*. The basic reason is that democratic leaders can only act when they can build support for their policies, but there may be no consensus as to what to do. Even on problems on which there is agreement that something should be done, there may be no agreement on *what* should be done. In extreme cases the political system of a democratic country may become paralyzed by conflicts or opposing viewpoints. In these circumstances politicians often prefer to do nothing, to shroud their positions in ambiguity, or to pretend to be on all sides of an issue. The result is that the population can become cynical and lose trust in the promises of any politician, and this in turn can set in motion a downward spiral, because the more this happens and trust is lost, the harder it becomes for politicians to do something by forging a compromise. This result is more likely when the pressures for political action on an issue are particularly conflicting, when positions are far apart, when issues are particularly divisive, when the population is divided along racial or ethnic lines, and when there is relatively little trust in politicians by the citizens.

To put it another way, although there may be freedom to speak in democracies, sometimes no one is listening. And, in general, there is a tradeoff: The more points of view that are represented by the political system, the smaller the system's capacity for action. This is one source of the allure of dictatorship. Dictators possess the capacity to repress opposition to their policies, and this means they can act in circumstances in which democratic rulers cannot. The classic example is the Weimar Republic, in which the democratic leadership did nothing about political violence in the streets or about the unemployment problem caused by the Great Depression. Hitler promised to do something about unauthorized political violence; he promised a job for every German; and he promised a way for the young to rid themselves of the sins of the old, for both groups to rid themselves of the menace of communism, and for many Germans to become proud of being German again.

But if dictators are more capable of action than democracies, who benefits from these actions? This question leads naturally to a second proposition: There tends to be greater *redistribution* (of income, wealth, or the means to earn it) under dictatorship than under democracy. To see why, let us ask the following question: In a democracy, what is it that stops the majority – or a minority which gains hold of the reins of government – from picking out some minority and expropriating all its wealth? This is an old question, and many things could be mentioned to answer it, but certainly among the most important is the resistance which the taxed group will put up against such treatment. Now dictators have ways to deal with that resistance – there are far fewer constraints on their ability to stamp it out – and they are much more capable of hiding what they do while the operation is in progress and after it is over. So, the dictator's capacity for repression also entails a greater tendency to redistribute income or wealth, in contrast to democracies. The benefits to the group that wins power are a second, more obvious, source of the allure of dictatorship.

Who the redistribution is for – and what the consequences for economic growth and efficiency are – depends partly on who controls the regime. In this book I considered a few different possibilities. For example, some historical regimes can be thought of as serving labor's interests. Many think the *apartheid* regime in South Africa was a regime which exploited black labor for the benefit of white labor, and some institutions of the regime – job reservation in particular – undoubtedly worked this way. Another possibility is communism in the former Soviet Union, which removed private property from the productive system and took power in the name of workers. The Party substituted for legally enforceable property rights by rewarding those who worked for the system's goals and by punishing those who didn't. However, without markets there was no way of finding out what people's wants or economic needs were. In addition there was the question of who would manage enterprises if capital's rights were expropriated. The solution adopted under Communist regimes was the substitution of a massive central bureaucracy for management by capital owners or their agents. Bureaucracies are not inherently inefficient (after all, there have been and are today many giant firms and other organizations which are superbly managed). But they have a central flaw: Over time loyalty to the top tends to deteriorate and to be replaced by alliances among the bureaucrats themselves, alliances which bureaucrats use to line their own pockets, to do favors for friends, to distort information traveling up the hierarchy to make themselves look better, and in other ways to benefit themselves at the expense of the goals of the organization. So to remain effective, bureaucracies need to be "shaken up" periodically, as happens in businesses when they are taken over and in democratic governments when a new party takes office.

The only mechanism possessed by the Communist party for this purpose was the Party Purge, most famously employed by Stalin to gain dominance over the Party and to ensure loyalty from the bureaucracy. However, it turned out that this technique was itself flawed. Its flaw lay in its *uncertainty*. For example, under Stalin (and under Mao during the Great Cultural Revolution) the process was only completed when those who did the purging were themselves purged, so that the perpetrators of the process ended up being counted among its victims, something which is not uncommon in societies that operate without the rule of law. After the death of Stalin, no successor arose with the same confidence and with the same capacity for ruthlessness needed to carry out this operation, resulting in a generation of bureaucrats who were to grow old in their posts until Gorbachev came along and tried to shake up the system with Glasnost and Perestroika. In the end Gorbachev too had to count himself among the victims of the process he initiated, along with the Communist system itself. So although communism was capable of substituting for private property rights in underpinning the economy in some ways, it lacked the self-renewing capacity provided by democratic elections (in the political sphere) and by the capital market, by takeover bids, and by other institutions associated with transferable, legally enforceable property rights (in private markets).

The alliance or networks among bureaucrats which contributed to the ossification of the Soviet regime also possessed implications for the transition. In Russia, for example, enterprise managers had become so powerful that even after the Soviet Union collapsed, it was felt that their interests had to be taken into account in the design of the privatization program under Yeltsin; and the upshot was that they acquired those firms at rock-bottom prices ("Sale of the Century," according to *The Economist* magazine [1994]), both effectively consolidating huge rents in their hands more firmly than had been the case under communism and hobbling the transition to a genuine market economy.[3]

In general, labor-dominated regimes appear to be at a disadvantage from the economic point of view, because they tend to raise the price of labor, hence driving away capital investment in one way or another and therefore reducing the capacity of the system for economic growth. It is not obvious how a future, labor-oriented dictatorship would be able to solve this problem, which can only be expected to become increasingly important as capital becomes more mobile. On the other hand, a dictatorship which serves the interests of capital owners faces no such diffi-

---

[3] Boycko, Shleifer, and Vishny (1996) describe the privatization program. McFaul (1995) contains a good account of the consolidation of power of the old elite. Cottrell (1997) is a good account of the current state of the Russian economy.

culty. Moreover, the reduction in the price of labor and the imposition of labor discipline devices which are the hallmarks of these regimes serve to attract capital, raising the productivity of labor and, therefore, real wages in the long run. Real wages tripled in South Korea in the 1970–86 period (Dornbusch and Park 1987). So the system may be bad for the workers politically, but it has been good for them economically.[4]

A third interest group which may and often has controlled dictatorship is the *military*. The strange thing about military governments is that they tend to be short-lived and that they often end when the military voluntarily hands over power to a civilian regime. This seems odd for two reasons:

1. If the military is good at anything, it should be good at repression
2. If this is the primary instrument used by dictatorships to stay in power, one would expect military regimes to be relatively successful – that is, stable and long-lasting.

I explained this puzzle with the idea that the military is self-interested: Its main objective in seizing power is to raise the pay and budget of the military. There is nothing unusual about this – labor-dominated governments raise the price of labor, capitalist dictatorships raise the return to capital (privatization is a nice way to do this), and so forth. One additional point is that the members of the military tend to be a closed elite and to dislike the anarchy of political parties and other political organizations. As a result, they are not particularly good at buying the loyalty of other groups, which is a subtle process. Their comparative advantage is in repression, and they tend to use this instrument to stay in power. The dilemma facing military governments, then, is easily demonstrated: In the process of rewarding their supporters, they tend to raise the costs of repression, the primary instrument used to stay in power. If, for example, they doubled the pay scales of the military personnel, it will cost twice as much to stay in power as before. So the peculiar thing about military dictatorships is that in the process of rewarding their supporters, they tend to weaken rather than strengthen their own capacity to govern. It is therefore no surprise that military governments often hand the reins of government over to a civilian authority after some period of time. Having raised their pay scales (the chief objective of their rule), they

---

[4] The *apartheid* regime was not unfavorable to capital, and the pass system undoubtedly served to lower black wages, benefiting white capitalists (as argued in Chapter 8, especially Section 4). The regime collapsed not mainly because of this factor, but because of the enforcement costs of artificially separating the labor force into (high-paid) white workers and (low-paid) black workers.

realize that the rational strategy is to exit with suitable guarantees of immunity from prosecution for the crimes committed by the regime and with constitutional protection for their increased pay scales and budgets.

Finally, of all of the systems examined, dictatorship approaches its purest form in the role of a single individual, someone who is beholden to no interest group and who is not motivated by economic concerns. And as dictatorship approaches this form, it becomes progressively more dangerous and more interested in controlling a wider fraction of the economy and society. One reason for this is that the smaller the number of people in the governing coalition, the less need there is to compromise on the objectives of the government. Another reason is that the fewer people in the governing coalition, the greater the capacity of that coalition to divert the costs of government onto others. It follows that the most dangerous dictatorships are those in which power is personal – that is, either when the leader is charismatic or when he or she is clever enough to shift the coalitions required to deliver the necessary support.

This brings us to the general question of the limits to the power of a dictator over his or her people, a question which has been pursued throughout the book. The self-proclaimed aim of many regimes has been "perfect" domination, and some (the Nazis, for example) claimed to have achieved this goal. Other regimes have been much more modest in their ambitions. What limits a dictator's power? One limit comes from the use of repression. While a "little bit" of repression can actually increase loyalty, once the average level of repression is high, further repression can be counterproductive in terms of power-building. One reason is that, at very high levels of repression, fear and obedience tend to replace loyalty, because even loyal supporters of the regime become increasingly afraid to act independently (lest their actions are misinterpreted and mistaken for disloyalty). Ultimately, a point is reached at which more repression would reduce support by so much that it reduces power.

However, although this constrains the dictator's use of repression, it still does not limit his or her power, not as long as more power can be obtained by simply buying more loyalty. The true limit on power arises from the interaction between power and money. To glimpse this fact, let us note that dictators can always obtain more power if they can obtain more resources (which can be used to buy more loyalty). On the other hand, power can be converted into resources by the imposition of new tax bases, by war, or by selling rents or regulations like monopoly privileges, licenses, tariffs or quotas, and so on. Each of these processes is probably subject to diminishing (but not negative) returns. But the fact that the returns from both converting power into money and money into power are both ultimately diminishing means that an equilibrium exists which provides the limit to both the dictator's resources and his or her power simultaneously.

Another interesting implication can be drawn, one concerning the relationship between power and the economy. In the regimes studied here, there was typically a central institution which applied the power of dictatorship to the economy – the Apartheid Laws, the Seven Modernizations of Pinochet, the five-year plans of communism, and so on. In each case the book argues that if one wants to understand how the economy worked, how much government intervention there was, and so forth, the question is not "Is the application of power to the economic system good for the economy?" (i.e., for economic growth, efficiency, or the size of the government's budget) but "What is the *marginal* effect of the application of power on the economy?" For example, it seems clear (particularly with hindsight) that central planning – the application of power to the economy under communism – was economically inefficient. But at least in its heyday, at the margin, an increase in the power of the Communist party increased (rather than decreased) growth and efficiency. The absolute level of economic efficiency is relevant only insofar as the international competition among regimes is concerned. Indeed, one reason why dictators often promote nationalism and autarchic economic policies is precisely to avoid this competition.

The equilibrium level of power itself is determined by three factors:

1. the dictator's preferences (his or her "tastes" for power or consumption)
2. his or her capacity to turn money into power as determined by the regime's political organization
3. the effects of his or her power on the economy as determined by the workings of the central economic institutions just mentioned.

These three factors also decide whether a dictator behaves like a totalitarian, tyrant, or tinpot, a classification system which is useful for policy purposes – that is, for answering the question posed by the title of the next section.

4   What policies should be followed toward dictatorship by democratic regimes interested in promoting freedom?

This sort of question was brought into sharp relief by the analysis of Jeane Kirkpatrick, a political scientist who became ambassador to the United Nations under Ronald Reagan. She classified dictators into two types: totalitarians and traditional autocrats. In her way of thinking, dictators rule by repression alone, and so the main difference between the two types is in the level of repression. The first type – totalitarianism – is characterized by massive government intervention in the economic and social lives of citizens. The second type is what Kirkpatrick, following the political scientists Carl Friedrich and Zbigniew Brzezinski, calls traditional autocracies and what I called tinpot dictatorships (denoting their small-scale ambitions). In these regimes the level of repression is low.

In Kirkpatrick's model, dictators rule by repression alone, so what differentiates the two types is just the level of repression. She recommended that the United States and other countries interested in promoting democracy follow a "double standard" toward the different types, taking a relatively relaxed attitude toward tinpots and imposing sanctions on totalitarians. However, in my analysis there are two instruments for building power: repression and loyalty. Her framework can be translated into mine by simply assuming that tinpots are characterized by low levels of these variables, totalitarians by high levels. But then it becomes immediately obvious that there is a category which is ignored (what I called tyrants), regimes with high repression but little support or loyalty. Many of the regimes that were labeled traditional autocracies turned out – on measures of repression like numbers jailed or tortured – to be no less repressive than totalitarian regimes. So the world didn't divide up as neatly as Friedrich and Brzezinski and Kirkpatrick might have liked.

What policies should be followed toward dictatorship? Suppose, idealistically, that the only goal of Western policy is to reduce repression. The "weapons" in our arsenal are sanctions, trade agreements, imposing human rights constraints, and aid packages. Should we aid or trade with a tinpot like Ferdinand Marcos? Suppose Marcos' only goal is to consume as much as possible – in Marcos' case, this meant buying shoes for his wife, Imelda. What limits his consumption? Why doesn't he spend all of the GNP of the Philippines on shoes for her? The constraint is that he has to stay in office, so he cannot allow his power to fall so low that he is in danger of being deposed. So the levels of both repression and loyalty under his regime are just high enough to stay in office. Suppose that he is safely in office, which at one point, according to accounts of the regime (Wurfel 1988) as well as his own diaries (Renpel 1993), he felt he was. Then there is no point in giving him aid, because all he will do with the money is to buy more shoes. On the other hand, suppose he is in danger of being deposed. Then the aid simply props up the regime. So in neither case does the aid reduce repression. On the other hand, suppose the aid is tied to human rights observances. In order to keep receiving the aid, he must steadily relax repression over time. Then he has an incentive to use the aid to improve the welfare of his people, because if their welfare improves, loyalty or support for him will tend to increase. As a result, he can afford to relax repression and still buy the same number of shoes for Imelda as before. A trade agreement works in the same way.

With trade, it is sometimes argued that loyalty to the regime might fall, either because of the development of power centers in the private sector (which are independent of the government) or because trade tends to increase national income in the target country, thus leading people to demand more liberty as incomes rise. In that case, so the argument goes, the human rights constraint might be superfluous. But note that the increase in national income also tends to raise the revenues of the autocratic government, revenues which can be used to further extend its power. So even if loyalty to the regime does fall, the regime could make up for this loss of support with the extra resources at its disposal. Second, although the desire for freedom does tend to increase with income, the estimated size of the increase is very small (Londregan and Poole 1996). Finally, if on balance the regime's power and budgetary revenue were to fall as the result of trade or aid, this development implies that the dictator, in pursuing the aid or trade agreement, is either unaware of or deliberately acting contrary to his or her own self-interest, something which appears unlikely.

Now look at totalitarian regimes or tyrannies, defined as regimes whose rulers are interested not in consumption, but in power. Should we aid or trade with them? Again, suppose that as the result of the aid or trade agreement, economic growth improves. This growth gives the rulers an opportunity to accumulate more power, and since power is the only thing they care about, they take this opportunity, in the same way that a businessman who is already rich will grab an opportunity to make more money. So for these regimes, aid or trade without human rights constraint is not merely wasted; it is counterproductive, because repression *increases* when the economy improves. This is what happened under Hitler and Stalin: The more popular they were, the more they took these opportunities to put the screws to all those elements of the population whose absolute loyalty was uncertain. In the same way, the enormous economic growth in China has resulted in not the slightest degree of relaxation in the level of repression.

It might seem obvious that we would not aid these regimes, because the aid money would be spent on accumulating more power over the population – including repressing them. But again, if the aid is tied to a human rights constraint, which becomes progressively more stringent over time, the policy will work in the right direction. If the economy improves as a result of aid or trade, support increases, and the rulers can afford to relax repression and still have the same level of power as before. The human rights observances constraint is absolutely necessary if this is to lead to a fall in repression and not an increase. Of course, many of these regimes are too powerful to be dealt with in this way. In those cases a policy of sanctions might be recommended. But sanctions are not just the opposite of aid. They give the regime no chance to liberalize and will be resisted by the dictator. Under some circumstances they will cause a tightening of repression. They may perversely stimulate nationalistic support for the dictator and prop up his or her regime. They isolate the regime from Western influence. And their use requires a coordination of policy among the Western nations because businessmen and -women from other countries will want to move in to pick up the opportunities opened up by the sanctions. Trade or aid agreements are not accompanied by these problems.

So we have a very simple guide – *a single standard* – to the policies which should be pursued by foreign governments interested in reducing repression: to make human rights observance the cornerstone of Western policy. Trade or aid to any type of regime can be expected to produce beneficial effects provided it is accompanied by a long-term human rights constraint, one which becomes progressively more stringent over time. And it doesn't matter whether regimes can be accurately classified or not for policy purposes, because the policy is always the same. Without the human rights standard, the effects of aid or trade may be ineffective – and often perverse.

Some other simple implications which bear on how the democracies should deal with dictatorships suggested by the analysis may be worth mentioning. For example, this analysis suggests that democracies should never trust a reforming totalitarian – if the economy does improve, his or her incentive is to increase, not decrease, the level of repression. And they should never put faith in a seemingly benevolent dictator. The only way to tell if he or she is really benevolent is to check the level of repression under the regime. If it is high, he or she is a tyrant masquerading as a timocrat, a not uncommon disguise. Most dictators give gifts to their populations, and many pretend to be the "father" of their people. And if they really are benevolent, I have shown, they probably won't last long!

5   Who is responsible?

It is possible that more has been written on this subject than on any other aspect of dictatorship. The general idea is that dictatorships work by command or indoctrination. So no matter how heinous the crimes committed by the regime, it is difficult to hold anyone morally or criminally responsible for them. The people who committed them were just "following orders."

The classic and perhaps the most provocative analysis of this issue is the one presented by Hannah Arendt in her famous book on Adolf Eichmann's trial and on the Nazi bureaucracy, *Eichmann in Jerusalem* (1976). Her concepts, which have entered common parlance, of "bureaucracy as the rule of nobody" and "the banality of evil" were all more or less explicitly based on a common theory of bureaucracy. That theory states that in large organizations, orders typically emanate from the top and are implemented through a chain of command by subordinates at lower echelons of the organization. In such a context, even though the crimes perpetrated by the organization itself may be enormous, it is deemed difficult to assign individual responsibility for the crimes to anyone. Those at the top deny that orders were ever given (and they would seldom be written down, even if they were given). Those at the bottom say they were only following orders.

The same question has arisen repeatedly since then. Who is responsible for the deeds committed by the Stasi in East Germany and by secret police everywhere in Eastern Europe and the former Soviet Republics? Who should be prosecuted for the "disappearances" in Argentina or for the killings in Chile? Should the government of the newly enfranchised majority in South Africa prosecute the perpetrators of government violence under *apartheid*? If so, is the "I only acted under orders" defense credible? In all these cases the issue is identical to that which arose in the Eichmann case: "Who in the regime is and should be held responsible for the crimes against humanity committed under the dictatorship?"

The odd thing about this conception of dictatorial rule – and of the defense that rests on them – is that there is so little evidence for it. No one, to my knowledge, has produced any scientific evidence of any change in human consciousness as a result of exposure for over half a century to Communist propaganda. As far as criminal behavior is concerned, the crucial evidence required to support the command model is simple: We should see evidence that those who refused to take part in crimes against humanity (such as mass executions) were themselves subjected to severe punishment. No evidence like this has ever been produced.

There is a simple alternative explanation for the willingness to take part in such activities, one which has nothing to do with the command or the indoctrination models. This explanation rests on two principles:

1. Bureaucrats, like other people, are rational.
2. Bureaucracies don't run on the basis of orders, but on the basis of loyalty and competition.

In order to obtain higher salaries, promotions, perquisites, and other rewards, bureaucrats compete with each other by being entrepreneurial and finding ways to do things that advance the goals of their superiors. In dictatorships the elimination of political party competition does not eliminate bureaucratic competition; on the contrary, it may enhance it by blocking other (political) avenues of competition. In this book I summarized quite a bit of evidence that the Nazi and Soviet regimes were characterized by intense competition within the system for the rents controlled by the regimes. Bureaucratic competition is an important component in the machinery of dictatorship.

Because of the notoriety of his trial, we know a lot about Eichmann, and so it was easy to produce evidence from standard historical sources about the paradigm case of authoritarianism to buttress this theory. Like others, Eichmann was simply an energetic bureaucratic entrepreneur operating in a very competitive environment. He did not follow orders anymore than a businessman follows the "dictates" of the marketplace in order to make money. As a consequence, he and others like him (like any other rational actors) should be held responsible for their actions. What produced that behavior was the force of human rationality operating in a competitive environment in which most of the rewards of success were controlled by a political dictatorship. Perhaps this conception of the banality of evil is even more mundane (and therefore possibly even more frightening) than Arendt's. But, unlike hers, it accords with the evidence.

To conclude, let me emphasize that regimes like the Nazi one tend to bring out the worst in people. And to say that Eichmann could have been normal and rational doesn't mean that he is the same as everyone else, or that he was particularly nice. There is a self-selection process operating in dictatorships, in which the worst tend to rise to the top. But the principle that people are rational also means that they are responsible for their actions.

6   A brief speculation about the future

As this is written (at the beginning of 1997), we are living through what Samuel Huntington (1991) has referred to as a "wave" of democratization. The fall of communism in the former Soviet Union, the end of *apartheid* in South Africa, and the fall of dictatorships almost everywhere in Latin America have led many to hope – and some to believe – that dictatorship is a thing of the past, that democracy has won out and will eventually triumph everywhere.

In certain respects the analysis and arguments in this book support this prediction. The fears of the 1930s and 1940s – which saw the future in terms of either the triumph of Big Brother and his apparatus of surveillance or the chemical and drug-addicted passivity of an indoctrinated population – have largely proved groundless as the explosion of progress in the technology of communication has turned out to favor individual freedom rather than political mastery. Continued worldwide economic growth has also favored democracy, because the one solid piece of empirical evidence we have is the strong positive correlation between per capita income and political freedom.

At the same time there are reasons to be less sanguine. Although we cannot know the future, we can at least take a good look at the present. What kind of dictatorships are still prominent in the world as the next millennium approaches? Adrian Karatnycky, the president of Freedom House and the coordinator of its annual *Survey of Freedom*, summarizes the main results of the 1995 *Survey* on this question. He writes,

> In recent years, a clear pattern has emerged among the countries that are Not Free. Of the 54 countries that are Not Free, 49 – over 90% – share one or more of the following characteristics:
> (a) they have a majority Muslim population and frequently confront the pressures of Fundamental Islam;
> (b) they are multi-ethnic societies in which power is not held by a dominant ethnic group, i.e., a nation that represents more than two-thirds of the population;
> (c) they are neo-Communist or post-Communist transitional societies.
> Frequently, the Not Free countries have two or three of these characteristics. (1995, p. 7)

Combining this pattern with the analysis and the "images" of dictatorship presented in this book suggests the following speculations.

1. The continuance of ethnic conflict in many countries throughout much of the world means that democracy will function poorly in those countries, and it leaves ever-present the possibility of tyranny, perhaps the oldest and most common form of dictatorship in human history. Tyranny can also be sustained in the contemporary world on economic grounds, as the spectacular economic growth in China under "free-market communism" attests. And

of all of the forms of dictatorship, tyranny carries the most promise of being "good" for the economy because of its economic machinery.

2. Tinpots will always be around. Except in the most politically advanced countries, where democracy is entrenched, the possibility of a short-lived military (or other form of) takeover for the purpose of looting the country is simply a natural hazard.

3. Timocracy will be as elusive as ever.

4. The totalitarianism of the 1930s variety is gone. But totalitarianism, 1990s style, is very much alive. The two are formally identical, as readers can verify for themselves, for example, by reading Samir al-Khalil's[5] excellent (1989) analysis of Ba'thist Party propaganda and Party structure in Saddam Hussein's Iraq. The principles on which the party survives are identical to those analyzed in this book for the Nazi and Soviet regimes. But perhaps the greatest totalitarian threat in the near future is theocracy, as exemplified by the predominance of Islamic dictatorship in the autocratic world of the 1990s, which has been noted by Karatnycky.

Finally, at the most general level, the reason that dictatorship in all its forms can be expected to survive – and possibly prosper in the next millennium – is simply its appeal.

[5] The pseudonym for Kanin Makiya.

References

Abedian, I., and B. Standish, "Poor Whites and the Role of the State: The Evidence," *South African Journal of Economics* 35:2 (1985), 141–65.

Adam, Heribert, and Kogila Moodley, *South Africa Without Apartheid: Dismantling Racial Domination*. Berkeley: University of California Press, 1986.

Adorno, Theodor W., Else Fenkel-Brunswik, Daniel Levinson, and R. Nevitt Sanford, *The Authoritarian Personality*. New York: Harper, 1950.

Akerlof, George, "Labor Contracts as Partial Gift Exchange," *Quarterly Journal of Economics* 47 (1984), 543–69.

"Procrastination and Obedience," *American Economic Review* 81 (1991), 1–19.

Alchian, Armen A., and Harold Demsetz, "Production, Information Costs, and Economic Organization," *American Economic Review* 62 (December 1972), 777–95.

Aldrich, J. H., "A Downsian Spatial Model with Party Activism," *American Political Science Review* 77 (1983), 974–90.

Alesina, Alberto, "Credibility and Policy Convergence in a Two-Party System with Rational Voters," *American Economic Review* 78 (1988a), 796–807.

"Macroeconomics and Politics." *NBER Macroeconomics Annual 1988*. Cambridge: MIT Press, 1988b.

"Political Cycles in OECD Countries," *Review of Economic Studies* 59 (1992), 663–688.

"Elections, Party Structure, and the Economy," in J. Banks and E. Hanushek (eds.), *Modern Political Economy: Old Topics, New Directions*. New York: Cambridge University Press, 1995.

Alesina, Alberto, and A. Cukierman, "The Politics of Ambiguity," *Quarterly Journal of Economics* 105 (1990), 829–51.

Alesina, Alberto, and D. Rodrik, "Redistributive Politics and Economic Growth," Department of Economics, Harvard University (1990).

Alesina, Alberto, and H. Rosenthal, "Partisan Cycles in Congressional Elections and the Macroeconomy," *American Political Science Review* 83 (1989), 373–98.

Altemeyer, Robert, *Right Wing Authoritarianism*. Winnipeg, Man.: University of Manitoba Press, 1981.

Enemies of Freedom. San Francisco: Jossey-Bass Publishers, 1988.

The Authoritarian Specter. Cambridge: Harvard University Press, 1996.

Amsden, Alice, *Asia's Next Giant: South Korea and Late Industrialization*. New York: Oxford University Press, 1989.

Anderson, Gary M., and Peter J. Boettke, "Perestroika and Public Choice: The

Economics of Autocratic Succession in a Rent-Seeking Society," *Public Choice* 75 (1993), 101–18.

Arendt, Hannah, *The Origins of Totalitarianism.* 1951. New York: Harcourt, Brace, Jovanovich, 1951. New edition, 1973.

Eichmann in Jerusalem: A Report on the Banality of Evil (Rev. ed). New York: Penguin, 1976.

Arjomand, Said Amir, "Iran's Islamic Revolution in Comparative Perspective," *World Politics* 38 (1986), 383–414.

Arrow, K. J., "The Theory of Risk Aversion," in K. J. Arrow, *Essays in the Theory of Risk Bearing,* Chicago: Markham, 1971.

Arrow, K. J., "Models of Job Discrimination," in A. H. Pascal (ed.), *Racial Discrimination in Economic Life.* Lexington, MA: Heath, 1972.

Ash, Timothy Garton, *The Polish Revolution: Solidarity.* London: Penguin, 1991 (first published by Jonathan Cape, 1983).

Aslund, Anders, *Gorbachev's Struggle for Economic Reform: The Soviet Reform Process, 1985–88.* Ithaca, NY: Cornell University Press, 1989.

Aurelius, Marcus, *Meditations.* Translated by Maxwell Staniforth. London: Penguin Classics, 1964.

Axelrod, Robert, *The Evolution of Cooperation.* New York: Basic Books, 1984.

Azariadis, C., and A. Drazen, "Threshold Effects and Economic Development," *Quarterly Journal of Economics* 105 (1990), 501–26.

Bahry, D., and D. Silver, "Intermediation and the Symbolic Uses of Terror in the USSR," *American Political Science Review* 81 (1987), 1065–97.

Bandura, A., *Social Learning Theory.* Englewood Cliffs, NJ: Prentice Hall, 1977.

Banks, Jeffrey S., and Eric A. Hanushek (eds.), *Modern Political Economy: Old Topics, New Directions.* New York: Cambridge University Press, 1995.

Bardhan, Pranab, "Symposium on the State and Economic Development," *Journal of Economic Perspectives* 4 (1990), 3–7.

Barrow, R. H., *The Romans.* London: Penguin, 1949, 1987.

Bates, Robert H., *Markets and States in Tropical Africa: The Political Basis of Agricultural Policies.* Berkeley: University of California Press, 1981.

Becker, Gary, *The Economics of Discrimination* (2nd ed.). Chicago: University of Chicago Press, 1971.

"A Theory of Social Interactions," *Journal of Political Economy,* 82 (1974), 1063–93.

"Altruism, Egoism, and Genetic Fitness: Economics and Sociobiology," *Journal of Economic Literature* XIV (1976), 817–26.

"A Theory of Competition Among Pressure Groups for Political Influence," *Quarterly Journal of Economics* 98 (1983), 371–400.

Becker, Gary, and Kevin Murphy, "The Family and the State," *Journal of Law and Economics* 31 (1988), 1–19.

Bergson, Abram, *Productivity and the Social System – the USSR and the West.* Cambridge: Harvard University Press, 1978.

"Comparative Productivity," *American Economic Review* 77 (1987), 342–57.

"Communist Economic Efficiency Revisited," *American Economic Review* 82 (1992), 27–30.

Berliner, Joseph S., "Perestroika and the Chinese Model," in R. W. Campbell (ed.), *The Postcommunist Economic Transformation.* Boulder, CO: Westview Press, 1994.

Bernheim, B., A. Shleifer, and L. Summers, "The Strategic Bequest Motive," *Journal of Political Economy* 93 (1985), 1045–76.

Bialer, Seweryn, *Stalin's Successors*. Cambridge: Cambridge University Press, 1980.

The Soviet Paradox. New York: Alfred, A. Knopf, 1986.

Bilson, John, "Civil Liberties – An Econometric Investigation," *Kyklos* 35 (1982), 94–114.

Boettke, Peter J., *Why Perestroika Failed: The Politics and Economics of Socialist Transformation*. London: Routledge, 1993.

Borjas, George J., "Ethnic Capital and Intergenerational Mobility," *Quarterly Journal of Economics* 107 (1992), 123–50.

Borner, Silvio, Aymo Brunetti, and Beatrice Weder, *Political Credibility and Economic Development*. London: Macmillan, 1995.

Bowles, Samuel, "The Production Process in a Competitive Economy: Walrasian, Neo-Hobbesian, and Marxian Models," *American Economic Review* 75 (March 1985), 16–36.

Boycko, Maxim, "When Higher Incomes Reduce Welfare: Queues, Labor Supply and Macro Equilibrium in Socialist Societies," *Quarterly Journal of Economics* 107 (1992), 907–20.

Boycko, Maxim, Andrei Shleifer, and Robert Vishny, *Privatizing Russia*. Cambridge, MA: The MIT Press, 1996.

Bracher, Karl D., *The German Dictatorship: The Origins, Structure, and Effects of National Socialism*. New York: Praeger, 1970.

Turning Points in Modern Times: Essays on German and European History. Cambridge: Harvard University Press, 1995.

Brennan, G., and James Buchanan, *The Power to Tax: Analytical Foundations of a Fiscal Constitution*. Cambridge: Cambridge University Press, 1980.

Breton, A., G. Galeotti, P. Salmon, and R. Wintrobe (eds.), *The Competitive State: Villa Colombella Papers*. Boston: Kluwer Academic Press, 1991.

Nationalism and Rationality. New York: Cambridge University Press, 1996.

Breton, Albert, and Ronald Wintrobe, "The Equilibrium Size of a Budget-Maximizing Bureau," *Journal of Political Economy* 83 (1975), 195–208.

The Logic of Bureaucratic Conduct. New York: Cambridge University Press, 1982.

"The Bureaucracy of Murder Revisited," *Journal of Political Economy* 94 (1986), 905–26.

Broszat, Martin, *The Hitler State: The Foundation and Development of the Internal Structure of the Third Reich*. London: Longmans, 1981.

Bruce, Neil, and Michael Waldman, "The Rotten Kid Theorem Meets the Samaritan's Dilemma," *Quarterly Journal of Economics* 105 (1990), 155–65.

Buchanan, James, *The Limits of Liberty*. Chicago: University of Chicago Press, 1975.

Bullock, Alan, *Hitler and Stalin: Parallel Lives*. London: HarperCollins, 1991.

Bulow, Jeremy, and Lawrence Summers, "A Theory of Dual Labor Markets with Applications to Industrial Policy, Discrimination, and Keynesian Unemployment," *Journal of Labor Economics* 4 (1986), 376–14.

Burrowes, R., "Totalitarianism: The Revised Standard Version," *World Politics* 21 (1968), 272–94.

Callaghy, Thomas M., *The State Society Struggle: Zaire in Comparative Perspective*. New York: Columbia University Press, 1984.

Calvert, Randall, "Robustness of the Multi-Dimensional Model: Candidate Motivation, Uncertainty and Convergence," *American Journal of Political Science* 29 (1985), 69–95.

Camerer, Colin, "Gifts as Economic Signals and Social Symbols," *American Journal of Sociology* 94, supplement (1988), S189–S214.

Cassels, Alan, *Fascism*. Arlington Heights, IL: Harlan Davidson, 1975.

Chang, Chun, and Yijang Wang, "The Nature of the Township-Village Enterprise," *Journal of Comparative Economics* 19 (1994), 434–52.

Cheng, Hang Sheng, "Monetary Policy and Inflation in China," draft. Paper given at the conference, "Challenges to Monetary Policy in Pacific Basin Countries," at the Federal Reserve Bank of San Francisco (September 23–25, 1987).

Coase, R. H., "The Nature of the Firm," *Economica* 4 (1937), 386–405.

"The Problem of Social Cost," *Journal of Law and Economics* 3 (1960), 1–44.

Cobban, A., *Dictatorship: Its History and Theory*. New York: Haskell House Publishers, Ltd., 1971.

Cohen, Kathy J., and Michael C. Dawson, "Neighborhood Poverty and African American Politics," *American Political Science Review* 87 (1993), 286–302.

Coleman, James S., *Foundations of Social Theory*. Harvard University Press, 1990.

Collier, David (ed.), *The New Authoritarianism in Latin America*. Princeton, NJ: Princeton University Press, 1979.

Conot, Robert E., *Justice at Nuremberg*. New York: Harper and Row, 1983.

Constable, Pamela, and Arturo Valenzuela, *A Nation of Enemies: Chile Under Pinochet*. New York: W.W. Norton and Co., 1991.

Cottrell, Robert, review of "Kremlin Capitalism: The Privatization of the Russian Economy," *New York Review of Books*, March 27, 1997.

Coughlin, Peter, "Elections and Income Redistribution," *Public Choice* 50 (1986), 27–99.

Coughlin, Peter, Dennis Mueller, and P. Murrell, "Electoral Politics, Interest Groups and the Size of Government," *Economic Inquiry* 28 (1990), 682–705.

Dawidowicz, Lucy S., *The War Against the Jews, 1933–1945*. New York: Bantam, 1975.

The Holocaust and the Historians. Cambridge: Harvard University Press, 1981.

Degras, Jane, and Alec Nove (eds.), *Soviet Planning: Essays in Honor of Naum Jasny*. Oxford: Basil Blackwell, 1964.

Dornbusch, R., and S. Edwards, "The Macroeconomics of Populism in Latin America," *Journal of Development Economics* 32 (1990), 247–77.

The Macroeconomics of Populism in Latin America. Chicago: University of Chicago Press, 1991.

Dornbusch, R., and Y. C. Park, "Korean Growth Policy," *Brookings Papers on Economic Activity* 2 (1987), 389–454.

Downs, Anthony, *An Economic Theory of Democracy*. New York: Harper and Row, 1957.

Dudley, Donald, *Roman Society*. London: Penguin, 1975.

Easterly, W., and Stanley Fischer, "The Soviet Economic Decline: Historical and Republican Data," National Bureau of Economic Research Working Paper, Series No. 9735, 1994.

The Economist, "Sale of the Century" (May 14, 1994), 68–9.

Edwards, S., and Alejandra Cox Edwards, *Monetarism and Liberalization: The Chilean Experiment*. Cambridge: Ballinger Publishing Co., 1987.

Ellman, Michael, *Socialist Planning*. New York: Cambridge University Press, 1979.

Elster, Jon, *The Cement of Society: A Study of Social Order*. New York: Cambridge University Press, 1989.

Political Psychology. New York: Cambridge University Press, 1993.

Enelow, J. M., and M. J. Hinich, "Ideology, Issues, and the Spatial Theory of Elections," *American Political Science Review* 76 (1982), 493–501.

Ericson, Richard E., "The Classical Soviet-Type Economy: Nature of the System and Implications for Reform," *Journal of Economic Perspectives* 5 (1991), 11–78.

Fainsod, Merle, *How Russia Is Ruled*. Cambridge: Harvard University Press, 1967.

Fairbank, J., *China: A New History*. Cambridge: Harvard University Press, 1992.

Fallows, James M., *Looking at the Sun: The Rise of the New East Asian Economic and Political System*. New York: Pantheon, 1994.

Ferejohn, John A., *Pork Barrel Politics*. Stanford, CA: Stanford University Press, 1974.

Fernandez, R., and D. Rodrik, "Resistance to Reform: Status Quo Bias in the Presence of Individual-Specific Uncertainty," *American Economic Review* 81 (1991), 1146–55.

Ferrero, Mario, "Bureaucrats vs. Red Guards: A Politico-Economic Model of the Stability of Communist Regimes," in R. W. Campbell (ed.), *The Postcommunist Economic Transformation*. Boulder, CO: Westview Press, 1994.

Ferrero, M., and G. Brosio, "Nomenklatura Rule Under Democracy: When Government and Opposition Merge." *Journal of Theoretical Politics* (forthcoming). Paper originally presented at the 1992 Meeting of the European Public Choice Society, Turin, 1992.

Findlay, Ronald, and Mats Lundahl, "Racial Discrimination, Dualistic Labor Markets, and Foreign Investment," *Journal of Development Economics* 27 (1987), 139–48.

Finley, M. I., *The Ancient Economy*. Berkeley: University of California Press, 1973.

Finley, M. I., *Politics in the Ancient World*. New York: Cambridge University Press, 1983.

Fiorina, M., "The Reagan Years: Turning to the Right or Groping Through the Middle?" in Barry Cooper et al. (eds.), *The Resurgence of Conservatism in Anglo-American Democracies*. Durham, NC: Duke University Press, 1988.

Fischer, John, *Why They Behave Like Russians*. New York: Harper and Brothers, 1947.

Frank, Robert H., *Choosing the Right Pond*. Oxford: Oxford University Press, 1985.

Passions Within Reason. New York: W. W. Norton and Co., 1988.

Freedom House, "Freedom in the World: The Annual Survey of Political Rights and Civil Liberties," *Freedom Review*. New York: Freedom House, 1978 through 1997.

Friedrich, Carl, and Zbigniew Brzezinski, *Totalitarian Dictatorship and Autocracy*. Cambridge: Harvard University Press, 1965.

Freud, Sigmund, *Civilization and Its Discontents*. Original edition 1929. Reprinted in the Penguin Freud Library, vol. 12, *Civilization, Society and Religion*, 1991.

Galeotti, Gianluigi, "Political Exchanges and Decentralization." Villa Colombella Papers on Federalism. *European Journal of Political Economy* 3 (1987), special issue, 111–30.

"The Number of Parties and Political Competition," in A. Breton, G. Galeotti, P. Salmon, and R. Wintrobe (eds.), *The Competitive State: Villa Colombella Papers*. Boston: Kluwer Academic Press, 1991.

Galeotti, Gianluigi, and Albert Breton, "An Economic Theory of Political Parties," *Kyklos* 39 (1986) FASC.1, 47–65.

Galeotti, Gianluigi, and Antonio Forcina, "Political Loyalties and the Economy: the U.S. Case," *Review of Economics and Statistics* 71 (1989), 511–17.

Gay, Peter, *Weimar Culture*. London: Maitin Secker & Warburg 1968; Penguin 1974.

Gellner, Ernest, *Nations and Nationalism*. Ithaca, NY: Cornell University Press, 1983.

Gibbon, Edward, *The Decline and Fall of the Roman Empire* (Abridged Edition), D.A. Saunders (ed.). London: Penguin Classics, 1981.

Glazer, A. "The Strategy of Candidate Ambiguity," *American Political Science Review* 84 (1990), 237–42.

Glazer, I., and P. Moynihan, *Ethnicity*. Cambridge: Harvard University Press, 1975.

Goldhagen, Daniel J., *Hitler's Willing Executioners: Ordinary Germans and the Holocaust*. New York: Alfred A. Knopf, 1996.

Gordon, David, "Who Bosses Who? The Intensity of Supervision and the Discipline of Labor," *American Economic Review Papers and Proceedings* 80 (1990), 28–32.

Gordon, Sarah A., *Hitler, Germans, and the "Jewish Question."* Princeton, NJ: Princeton University Press, 1984.

Granick, David, "Institutional Innovation and Economic Management: The Soviet Incentive System, 1921 to the Present," in Gregory Guroff and Fred V. Carsteenen (eds.), *Entrepreneurship in Imperial Russia and the Soviet Union*. Princeton, NJ: Princeton University Press, 1983.

Grant, Michael, *History of Rome*. London: Weidenfeld and Nicholson, 1978.

The Antonines: The Roman Empire in Transition. London: Routledge, 1994.

Gregor, A. James, *The Ideology of Fascism*. New York: Free Press, 1969.

Grilli, V., D. Masciandaro, and G. Tabbelini, "Political and Monetary Institutions and Public Finance Policies in the Industrial Countries," *Economic Policy* 13 (1991), 342–76.

Grossman, Gregory, "Gold and the Sword: Money in the Soviet Command Economy" in Henry Rosovsky (ed.), *Industrialization in Two Systems*. New York: John Wiley, 1966, 204–36.

"The 'Second Economy' of the USSR," *Problems of Communism* 26 (1977), 25–40.

Grossman, Herschel I., "A General Equilibrium Model of Insurrections," *American Economic Review* 81 (1991), 912–21.

"Kleptocracy and Revolutions," unpublished manuscript, Brown University, September 1996.

Grossman, Herschel I., and Suk Jae Noh, "A Theory of Kleptocracy with

Probabilistic Survival and Reputation," *Economics and Politics* 2 (1990), 157–71.

Gumplowicz, Ludwig, *The Outlines of Sociology*. Translated by F. W. Moore. Philadelphia: American Academy of Political and Social Science, 1899.

Gwartney, James, Robert Lawson, and Walter Block, *Economic Freedom of the World: 1975–1995*. Vancouver, Canada: The Fraser Institute, 1995.

Haggard, Stephen, *Pathways from the Periphery: The Politics of Growth in the Newly Industrializing Countries*. Ithaca, NY: Cornell University Press, 1990.

Hagtvet, Bernt. "The Theory of the Mass Society and the Collapse of the Weimar Republic: A Re-examination," in Larsen, S., B. Hagtvet, and J. P. Mykelbust (eds.), *Who Were the Fascists? Social Roots of European Fascism*. Norway: Universitetsforlaget, 1980.

Hansson, I., and C. Stuart, "Voting Competitions with Interested Politicians: Platforms Do Not Converge to the Preferences of the Median Voter," *Public Choice* 44 (1984), 431–41.

Hawthorn, Geoffrey, "Liberalization and 'Modern Liberty': Four Southern States," *World Development* 21 (1993), 1299–312.

Hayek, Friedrich, *Collectivist Economic Planning*. London: Routledge and Kegan Paul, 1935.

The Road to Serfdom. Chicago: University of Chicago Press, 1944.

Hechter, Michael, *Principles of Group Solidarity*. Berkeley: University of California Press, 1987.

Hechter, Michael, Debra Friedman, and Satoshi Kanazawa, "The Attainment of Global Order in Heterogeneous Societies." Paper delivered at the 1992 meetings of the Public Choice Society, Tucson, Arizona.

Hewett, Edward A., *Reforming the Soviet Economy: Equality vs. Efficiency*. Washington, DC: The Brookings Institution, 1988.

Hibbs, Douglas A., "Political Parties and Macroeconomic Policy," *American Political Science Review* 71 (1977), 1467–87.

The American Political Economy. Cambridge: Harvard University Press, 1987.

Hicks, John, "The Theory of Monopoly," *Econometrica* 3 (1935), 1–20. Reprinted in G. J. Stigler and K. Boulding (eds.), *Readings in Price Theory*. Homewood, IL: Irwin, 1952, 361–83.

Hillman, A. L., and A. Schnytzer, "Illegal Economic Activities and Purges in a Soviet-Type Economy," *International Review of Law and Economics* 6 (1986), 87–100.

Hillman, A. L., and Avi Weiss, "A Theory of Illegal Immigration," paper presented at the European Public Choice Society Meetings, Tiberias, Israel, 1996.

Hirschman, Albert O., *Exit, Voice and Loyalty*. Cambridge: Harvard University Press, 1970.

Hirshleifer, J., "Shakespeare vs. Becker on Altruism: The Importance of Having the Last Word," *Journal of Economic Literature* XV (1977), 500–2.

Hobsbawm, E., *Nations and Nationalism Since 1780*. Cambridge: Canto, 1990.

Holborn, Hajo, *A History of Modern Germany*, 1840–1945, Vol. 3. New York: Alfred A. Knopf, 1969.

Holtfrerich, Carl-Ludwig, "Economic Policy Options and the End of the Weimar Republic," in Ian Kershaw (ed.), *Weimar: Why Did German Democracy Fail?* London: Weidenfeld and Nicholson, 1990.

Hough, Jerry, *The Soviet Union and Social Science Theory*, Cambridge: Harvard University Press, 1977.

Hough, Jerry, and Merle Fainsod, *How the Soviet Union Is Governed*. Cambridge: Harvard University Press, 1979.

Howitt, P., and Ronald Wintrobe, "Equilibrium Political Inaction in a Democracy," in A. Breton, G. Galeotti, P. Salmon, and R. Wintrobe (eds.), *Preferences and Democracy*. Dordrecht, The Netherlands: Kluwer Academic Press, 1993.

"The Political Economy of Inaction," *Journal of Public Economics* 56 (1995), 329–53.

Huntington, Samuel, *Political Order in Changing Societies*. New Haven, CT: Yale University Press, 1968.

No Easy Choice. Cambridge: Harvard University Press, 1976.

The Third Wave: Democratization in the Late Twentieth Century. Norman: University of Oklahoma Press, 1991.

The Clash of Civilizations and the Remaking of World Order. New York: Simon & Schuster, 1996.

Huntington, Samuel, and Clement H. Moore (eds.), *Authoritarian Politics in Modern Society: The Dynamics of Established One Party Systems*. New York: Basic Books, 1970.

Hutchcroft, Paul D., "Oligarchs and Cronies in the Philippine State: The Politics of Patrimonial Plunder," *World Politics* 43:3 (April 1991), 414–50.

Huxley, Aldous, *Brave New World*. New York: Harper and Row (first published 1946).

Brave New World Revisited. London: Flamingo, 1994.

Iannacconne, Laurence R., "Sacrifice and Stigma: Reducing Free Riding in Cults, Communes, and Other Collectives, *Journal of Political Economy* 100:2 (April 1992), 271–91.

James, Harold, "Economic Reasons for the Collapse of the Weimar Republic," in Ian Kershaw (ed.), *Weimar: Why Did German Democracy Fail?* London: Weidenfeld and Nicholson, 1990.

Jefferson, Gary H., and Thomas G. Rawski, "Enterprise Reform in Chinese Industry," *Journal of Economic Perspectives* 8 (1994), 47–70.

Jensen, Michael, and William H. Meckling, "The Theory of the Firm: Managerial Behaviour, Agency Costs and Ownership Structure," *Journal of Financial Economics* 3 (1976), 305–60.

Johnstone, F. A., *Class, Race, and Gold*. London: Routledge and Kegan Paul, 1976.

Joskow, Paul L., Richard Schmalansee, and Natalia Tsukanova, "Competition Policy in Russia During and After Privatization," *Brookings Papers on Economic Activity: Microeconomics*, 1994.

Kaempfer, William, and Anton Lowenberg, "The Theory of International Economic Sanctions: A Public Choice Approach," *American Economic Review* 78 (September 1988), 786–93.

Kahn, Herman, *The Emerging Japanese Superstate: Challenge and Response*. Englewood Cliffs, NJ: Prentice Hall, 1970.

Kandel, Eugene, and Edward Lazear, "Peer Pressure and Partnerships," *Journal of Political Economy* 100 (1992), 801–17.

Karatnycky, Adrian, "Democracies on the Rise, Democracies at Risk," *Freedom Review* 26 (January–February 1995), 7.

"Freedom on the March," *Freedom Review* 28(1), 6.

Kater, Michael, *The Nazi Party: A Social Profile of Members and Leaders, 1919–1945*. Cambridge: Harvard University Press, 1983.

Kennedy, Gavin, *The Military in the Third World*. New York: Scribners, 1974.

Kershaw, Ian (ed.), *Weimar: Why Did German Democracy Fail? Debates in Modern History*. London: Weidenfeld and Nicolson, 1990.

al Khalil, Samir, *Republic of Fear: The Inside Story of Saddam Hussein's Iraq*. Berkeley: University of California Press, 1989.

The Monument: Art, Vulgarity and Responsibility in Iraq. London: Andre Deutsch, 1991.

Kirk-Greene, A. M. H., "His Eternity, His Eccentricity, or His Exemplarity? A Further Contribution to the Study of H. E. the African Head of State," *African Affairs* 90 (1991), 163–87.

Kirkpatrick, Jeane, *Dictatorship and Double Standards: Rationalism and Realism in Politics*. New York: Simon & Schuster, 1982.

Klein, Benjamin, R. G. Crawford, and A. Alchian, "Vertical Integration, Appropriable Rents, and the Competitive Contracting Process," *Journal of Law and Economics* 21 (1978), 297–326.

Klein, Benjamin, and Keith Leffler, "The Role of Market Forces in Contractual Performance," *Journal of Political Economy* 89 (1981), 615–41.

Knack, Stephen, and Philip Keefer, "Institutions and Economic Performance: Cross-Country Tests Using Alternative Institutional Measures," *Economics and Politics* 7 (1995), 207–28.

Knight, J., and G. Lenta, "Has Capitalism Underdeveloped the Labour Reserves of South Africa?" *Oxford Bulletin of Economics and Statistics*, 42:3 (1980), 157–201.

Knight, J., and M. D. McGrath, "An Analysis of Racial Wage Discrimination in South Africa," *Oxford Bulletin of Economics and Statistics* 39:4 (1977), 245–71.

Koestler, Arthur, *Darkness at Noon*. Translated by Daphne Hardy. New York: Macmillan, 1941.

Kogon, Eugen, *The Theory and Practice of Hell: The German Concentration Camps and the System behind Them*. Translated by Heinz Norden. New York: Octagon Books, 1973.

Kornai, Janos, *Economics of Shortage*. Amsterdam: North Holland, 1980.

"Comments on Lipton and Sachs," *Brookings Papers on Economic Activity* 1 (1990), 138–142.

The Socialist System: The Political Economy of Communism. Princeton: Princeton University Press, 1992.

Kroll, Heidi, "Breach of Contract in the Soviet Economy," *Journal of Legal Studies* 16 (1987), 119–48.

Krueger, A. O., "The Political Economy of the Rent-Seeking Society," *American Economic Review* 64 (1974), 291–303.

Krugman, Paul, "The Myth of Asia's Miracle," *Foreign Affairs* 73 (1994), 62–78.

Kundera, Milan, *Life Is Elsewhere*. Translated by Peter Kussi. New York: Viking Penguin, 1986.

Testaments Betrayed. Translated from the French by Linda Asher. New York: HarperCollins Perennial, 1996.

Kuran, Timur, "Now Out of Never: The Element of Surprise in the East European Revolution of 1989," *World Politics* 44 (1991), 7–48.

Private Truths, Public Lies: The Social Consequences of Preference Falsification. Cambridge: Harvard University Press, 1995.

Lake, David A., "Powerful Pacifists: Democratic States and War," *American Political Science Review* 86 (1992), 24–37.

Landa, J., "A Theory of the Ethnically Homogeneous Middleman Group: An Institutional Alternative to Contract Law," *Journal of Legal Studies* 10 (1981), 49–62.

Landes, William, and Richard Posner, "The Independent Judiciary in an Interest Group Perspective," *Journal of Law and Economics* 18 (1975), 875–902.

von Lang, Jochen (ed.), *Eichmann Interrogated: Transcripts from the Archives of the Israeli Police.* Toronto: Lester and Orpen Denny, 1983.

Lange, Oskar, *On the Economic Theory of Socialism* (Minneapolis: University of Minnesota Press 1938; New York: McGraw-Hill, 1964).

LaPalombara, J., *Democracy, Italian Style.* New Haven, CT: Yale University Press, 1987.

Larsen, S., B. Hagtvet, and J. P. Mykelbust, *Who Were the Fascists? Social Roots of European Fascism.* Bergen, Norway: Universitetsforlaget, 1980.

Lazear, Edward, and Sherwin, Rosen, "Rank-Order Tournaments as Optimum Labor Contracts," *Journal of Political Economy* 89 (1981), 841–64.

Lewis, Stephen R., Jr., *The Economics of Apartheid.* New York: Council on Foreign Relations Press, 1990.

Linz, Juan, "Political Space and Fascism as a Latecomer," in S. Larsen, B. Hagtvet, and J. P. Mykelbust, *Who were the Fascists? Social Roots of European Fascism.* Bergen, Norway: Universitetsforlaget, 1980.

Linz, Juan J., and Alfred Stepan, *The Breakdown of Democratic Regimes.* Baltimore: Johns Hopkins University Press, 1978.

Lipton, D., and J. Sachs, "Creating a Market Economy in Eastern Europe: The Case of Poland," *Brookings Papers on Economic Activity* 1 (1990), 75–148.
   "Prospects for Russian's Economic Reforms," *Brookings Papers on Economic Activity* 2 (1992), 213–65.

Lipton, Merle, *Capitalism and Apartheid: South Africa 1910–1986.* Aldershott: Wildwood House Ltd., 1985.

Lipset, Seymour Martin, *Political Man.* New York: Doubleday, 1960.

Londregan, John, and Keith Poole, "Poverty, the Coup Trap, and the Seizure of Executive Power," *World Politics* 42 (1990), 151–83.

Londregan, John, and Keith Poole, "Does High Income Promote Democracy," *World Politics* 49 (1996), 1–30.

Lott, J. R., Jr., "Political Cheating," *Public Choice* 52 (1987), 169–86.
   "An Explanation for Public Provision of Schooling: The Importance of Indoctrination," *Journal of Law and Economics* 36 (1990), 199–231.

Lott, J. R., Jr., and Bruce Bender,"Legislator Voting and Shirking: A Critical Review of the Literature," *Public Choice* 87 (1996), 67–100.

Lowenberg, Anton, "An Economic Theory of Apartheid," *Economic Inquiry* 27 (January 1989), 57–74.

Lucas, R. E. B., "Mines and Migrants in South Africa," *American Economic Review* 75 (December 1985), 1094–108.

Lundahl, Mats, "The Rationale of Apartheid," *American Economic Review* 72 (December 1982), 1169–79.

Lundahl, Mats, and Daniel B. Ndela, *Apartheid in Theory and Practice: An Economic Analysis.* Boulder, CO: Westview Press, 1980.

MacFarquhar, Roderick, "Deng and China's Future," *New York Review of Books* (March 27, 1997), 14–17.

McFaul, Michael, "State Power, Institutional Change, and the Politics of Privatization in Russia," *World Politics* 47 (1995), 210–43.

McKee, Michael, and R. Wintrobe, "Parkinson's Law in Theory and Practise," *Journal of Public Economics* 51 (1993), 309–27.

McMillan, John N., and Barry Naughton, "How to Reform a Planned Economy: Lessons from China," *Oxford Review of Economic Policy* 8 (1992), 130–43.

MacMullen, Ramsay, *Corruption and the Decline of Rome*. New Haven, CT: Yale University Press, 1988.

Marshall, Alfred, *Principles of Economics* (9th ed.). London: Macmillan, 1961.

Matthews, Mervyn, *Privilege in the Soviet Union*. London: George Allen and Unwin, 1978.

Medvedev, Roy A., *Let History Judge*. New York: Random House, 1973.

Meltzer, Allan H., and Scott F. Richard, "A Rational Theory of the Size of Government," *Journal of Political Economy* 89 (1981), 914–27.

Merkl, Peter H., "Comparing Fascist Movements," in S. Larsen, B. Hagtvet, and J. P. Mykelbust, *Who Were the Fascists? Social Roots of European Fascism*. Norway: Universitetsforlaget, 1980.

Mesquita, Bruce Bueno de, Randolph M. Siverson, and Gary Woller, "War and the Fate of Regimes: A Comparative Analysis," *American Political Science Review* 86 (September 1992), 638–46.

Michels, Robert, *Political Parties*. New York: Dover, 1959.

Milgram, Stanley, *Obedience to Authority: An Experimental View*. New York: Harper and Row, 1974.

Mitchell, Neil J., and James M. McCormick, "Economic and Political Explanations of Human Rights Violations," *World Politics* 40 (1988), 476–98.

Montinola, Gabriella, Yingyi Qian, and Barry R. Weingast, "Federalism, Chinese Style: The Political Basis for Economic Success in China," *World Politics* 48 (1995), 50–81.

Moore, Barrington, Jr., *Soviet Politics – The Dilemma of Power*. New York: M.D. Sharp Inc., 1950.

Mosca, Gaetano, *The Ruling Class*. New York: McGraw-Hill, 1939.

Mueller, Dennis, *Public Choice II*. New York: Cambridge University Press, 1989.

Perspectives in Public Choice: A Handbook. New York: Cambridge University Press, 1997.

Murrell, Peter, and Mancur Olson, "The Devolution of Centrally Planned Economies," *Journal of Comparative Economics* 15 (1991), 239–65.

Murphy, Kevin M., Andrei Shleifer, and Robert W. Vishny, "The Transition to a Market Economy: Pitfalls of Partial Reform," *Quarterly Journal of Economics* 107 (1992), 889–906.

Nattrass, J., *The South African Economy: Its Growth and Change*. Cape Town: Oxford University Press, 1981.

Naumann, Bernd, *Auschwitz: A Report on the Proceedings against Robert Karl Ludwig Mulka and Others before the Court at Frankfurt*. New York: Praeger, 1966.

Nelson, Philip, "Information and Consumer Behavior," *Journal of Political Economy* 78 (1970), 311–29.

Niskanen, William A., Jr., *Bureaucracy and Representative Government*. Chicago: Aldine-Atherton, 1971.

Nordhaus, William, "Soviet Economic Reform: The Longest Road," *Brookings Papers on Economic Activity* 1 (1990), 287–309.

Nordlinger, Eric, *Soldiers in Politics: Military Coups and Government.* Englewood Cliffs, NJ: Prentice-Hall, 1977.

North, Douglass C., and Robert Paul Thomas, *The Rise of the Western World: A New Economic History.* New York: Cambridge University Press, 1973.

Structure and Change in Economic History. New York: W. W. Norton, 1981.

North, Douglass, and Barry Weingast, "Constitutions and Commitment: The Evolution of Institutions Governing Public Choice in Seventeenth Century England," *Journal of Economic History* XLIX (1989), 808–32.

Nove, Alec, *Was Stalin Really Necessary?* London: George Allen and Unwin, 1964.

The Soviet Economic System (2nd ed.). London: George Allen and Unwin, 1980.

O'Donnell, Guillermo, *Modernization and Bureaucratic–Authoritarianism: Studies in South American Politics.* Berkeley: Institute of International Studies, University of California, 1973.

"On the State, Democratization and Some Conceptual Problems: A Latin American View with Glances at Some Post-Communist Countries," *World Development* 21 (1993), 1355–69.

Ofer, Gur, "Soviet Economic Growth, 1928–85," *Journal of Economic Literature* 25 (1987), 1767–833.

Olson, Mancur, *The Rise and Decline of Nations.* New Haven, CT: Yale University Press, 1982.

"Dictatorship, Democracy and Development," *American Political Science Review* 87 (1993), 567–75.

Oppenheim, Lois Hecht, *Politics in Chile: Democracy, Authoritarianism and the Search for Development.* Boulder, CO: Westview Press, 1993.

Orwell, George, *1984.* London: Secker and Warburg, 1949 (the Alchian Press).

Paldam, Martin, "Inflation and Political Instability in Eight Latin American Countries, 1946–83," *Public Choice* 52 (1987): 143–68.

Pareto, V., *I Sistemi Socialisti,* Turin: Unione Tipografico–Editrice Torinese, 1954.

Perkins, Dwight, "Completing China's Move to the Market," *Journal of Economic Perspectives* 8 (1994), 23–46.

Perlmutter, Amos, and Valerie Plave Bennett, *The Political Influence of the Military: A Comparative Study.* New Haven and London: Yale University Press, 1980.

Persson, T., and Guido Tabellini, "Is Inequality Harmful for Growth" Theory and Evidence," University of California, Berkeley Center for Economic Policy Research Discussion Working Paper 581 (1991).

Plato, *The Republic* (2nd edition [revised]). Translated with an Introduction by Desmond Lee. London: Penguin Books, 1974.

Poggi, Gianfranco, *The State: Its Nature, Development and Prospects.* Stanford, CA: Stanford University Press, 1990.

Porter, Richard C., "A Model of the South African-Type Economy," *American Economic Review* 63:2 (1978), 287–95.

"South Africa Without Apartheid: Estimates from General Equilibrium Simulations," *Journal of International Development* 2:1 (1990), 1–59.

Posner, R. A., "The Social Costs of Monopoly and Regulation," *Journal of Political Economy* 83 (1975), 807–27.

Powell, G. B., Jr., "Extremist Parties and Political Turmoil: Two Puzzles," *American Journal of Political Science* 30 (1986), 357–78.

Powell, Raymond, "Economic Growth in the USSR," *Scientific American* 219 (1968), 17–23.

Przeworski, Adam, *Democracy and the Market: Political and Economic Reforms in Eastern Europe and Latin America*. New York: Cambridge University Press, 1991.

    "The Neo-Liberal Fallacy," *Journal of Democracy* 3 (1992), 45–59.

Przeworski, Adam, and Fernando Limongi, "Political Regimes and Economic Growth," *Journal of Economic Perspectives* 7 (1993), 51–70.

Putnam, Robert D., "Toward Explaining Military Intervention in Latin American Politics," *World Politics* 20 (1967), 83–11.

Putnam, Robert, *Making Democracy Work*. Princeton, NJ: Princeton University Press, 1993.

Ramet, Sabrina P., *Nationalism and Federalism in Yugoslavia 1962–91* (2nd ed.). Bloomington: Indiana University Press, 1992.

Remmer, Karen, *Military Rule in Latin America*. Boston: Unwin-Hyman, 1989.

    "The Political Economy of Elections in Latin America, 1980–1991," *American Political Science Review* 87 (1993), 393–407.

Rempel, William C., *Delusions of a Dictator: The Mind of Marcos as Revealed in His Secret Diaries*. Boston: Little, Brown, 1993.

Robinson, Jacob, *And the Crooked Shall Be Made Straight: The Eichmann Trial, the Jewish Catastrophe, and Hannah Arendt's Narrative*. London: Macmillan, 1965.

Rodrik, Dani, "Trade and Industrial Policy Reform in Developing Countries: A Review of Recent Theory and Evidence," NBER Working Paper #4417 (1993).

Rogowski, Ronald, "Causes and Varieties of Nationalism: A Rationalist Account," in Edward A. Tiryakin and Ronald Rogowski (eds.), *New Nationalisms of the Developed West: Toward Explanation*. Boston: Allen and Unwin, 1985, 87–108.

Root, Hilton, *The Foundation of Privilege: Political Foundations of Markets in Old Regime France and England*. Berkeley, CA: University of California Press, 1994.

Rosenberg, Harold, "The Trial and Eichmann," *Commentary* 32 (November 1961), 369–81.

Rueschemeyer, Dietrich, E. H. Stephens, and J. D. Stephens, *Capitalist Development and Democracy*. Chicago: University of Chicago Press, 1992.

Rutland, Peter, *The Myth of the Plan: Lessons of Soviet Planning Experience*. London: Hutchison and Co., 1985.

Sachs, Jeffrey, "Social Conflict and Populist Policies in Latin America," NBER Working Paper #2897 (1989).

Sachs, Jeffrey, and W. T. Woo, "Structural Factors in the Economic Reforms of China, Eastern Europe and the Former Soviet Union, *Economic Policy* 18 (1994), 101–46.

Salisbury, Harrison, "Gorbachev's Dilemma," *New York Times Magazine* (July 27, 1986).

Salmon, Pierre, "Trust and Trans-Bureau Networks in Organizations," *European Journal of Political Economy* 4 (1988), Extra Issue, 229–52.

Sanford, Nevitt, "The Authoritarian Personality in Contemporary Perspective" in Jeanne N. Kmutsoh (ed.), *Handbook of Political Psychology*. San Francisco: Jossey-Bass Publishers, 1973.

Sartori, Giovanni, *Parties and Party Systems*. New York: Cambridge University Press, 1976.

Sartre, Jean-Paul, *Anti-Semite and Jew*. New York: Grove Press, 1960; New York: Schocken Books, 1965.

Schaar, John H., "Loyalty," in David L. Sills (ed.), *International Encyclopedia of the Social Sciences* 9 (1968), 484–487. New York: The Free Press, 1968, 1991.

Schap, David, "Property Rights and Decision Making in the Soviet Union: Interpreting Soviet Environmental History," *Economic Inquiry* 26 (1988), 389–401.

Schapiro, Leonard, *The Communist Party of the Soviet Union* (2nd ed.). New York: Random House, 1971.

The Government and Politics of the Soviet Union. New York: Vintage Books, 1978.

Schatzberg, Michael G., *The Dialectics of Oppression in Zaire*. Bloomington, IN: Indiana University Press, 1988.

Schmitter, Phillipe C., "Military Intervention, Political Competitiveness and Public Policy in Latin America 1950–67," in Morris Janowitz and Jacques Van Doorn (eds.), *On Military Intervention*. Rotterdam: Rotterdam University Press, 1971.

Schnytzer, Adi, and Janez Susteric, "Why Do People Support Dictators? (Popularity vs. Political Exchange)," ms, Department of Economics, Bar Ilan University, 1996. *Public Choice*, forthcoming.

Schweller, Randall, "Domestic Structure and Preventive War: Are Democracies More Pacific?" *World Politics* 44 (1992), 235–69.

Shapiro, Carl, "Premiums for High-Quality Products as Returns to Reputations," *Quarterly Journal of Economics* 98 (1983), 659–79.

Shapiro, Carl, and Joseph E. Stiglitz, "Equilibrium Unemployment as a Worker Discipline Device," *American Economic Review* 74 (1984), 433–44.

Sheahan, John, *Patterns of Development in Latin America: Poverty, Repression, and Economic Strategy*. Princeton, NJ: Princeton University Press, 1987.

Shepsle, K., "The Strategy of Ambiguity," *American Journal of Political Science* 66 (1972), 555–68.

Shepsle, K., and Barry Weingast, "Structure-Induced Equilibrium and Legislative Choice," *Public Choice* 37 (1981), 503–19.

Shirer, William L., *The Rise and Fall of the Third Reich: A History of Nazi Germany*. New York: Simon & Schuster, 1960.

Shleifer, Andrei, and Robert W. Vishny "Reversing the Soviet Economic Collapse," *Brookings Papers on Economic Activity* 2 (1991), 341–65.

"Pervasive Shortages Under Socialism," *Rand Journal of Economics* 23 (1992), 237–46.

"The Politics of Market Socialism," *Journal of Economic Perspectives* 8 (1994), 165–76.

Sicular, Terry, "Plan and Market in China's Agricultural Commerce," *Journal of Political Economy* 96 (1988), 283–307.

"Public Finance and China's Economic Reforms," Harvard Institute of Economic Research Discussion Paper 1618 (1992).

"The Derailment of China's Two-Track System, or Pitfalls of Mixing Plan and Market During the Reform of Socialist Economies," ms (November 1993).

"Redefining State, Plan and Market: China's Reforms in Agricultural Commerce," *China Quarterly* 144 (1995), 1020–46.

"Why Quibble About Quotes? The Effects of Planning in Rural China," ms (1995).

Stepan, A., *The Military in Politics: Changing Patterns in Brazil*. Princeton, NJ: Princeton University Press, 1971.

Stigler, George, "Directors' Law of Public Income Redistribution," *Journal of Law and Economics* 13 (1970), 1–10.

"The Theory of Economic Regulation," *Bell Journal of Economics* 2 (1971), 3–21.

Stiglitz, Joseph E., *Whither Socialism?* Cambridge: MIT Press, 1994.

Strauss, Leo, *On Tyranny*. London: The Free Press, 1963, 1991.

Suetonius, Gaius Tranquillus, *The Twelve Caesars*. Translated by Robert Graves. London: Penguin, 1957.

Thompson, Leonard, *A History of South Africa*. New Haven, CT: Yale University Press, 1990.

Thompson, Leonard, and Andrew Prior, *South African Politics*. New Haven and London: Yale University Press, 1982.

Tilly, Charles (ed.), *Formation of the National States of Western Europe*. Princeton, NJ: Princeton University Press, 1975.

Toland, John, *Adolf Hitler*. New York: Ballantine, 1976.

Trevor-Roper, Hugh, *The Rise of Christian Europe*. London: Thames and Hudson, 1965.

Tullock, Gordon, "The Welfare Cost of Tariffs, Monopolies, and Theft," *Western Economic Journal* 5 (1967), 224–32.

Autocracy. Dordrecht: Martinus Nijhoff, 1987.

Ulam, Adam, "The Price of Sanity," in G. R. Urban (ed.), *Stalinism: Its Impact on Russia and the World*. Cambridge: Harvard University Press, 1986, 100–45.

Urban, G.R. (ed.), *Stalinism: Its Impact on Russia and the World*. Cambridge: Harvard University Press, 1982.

Veyne, Paul, *Bread and Circuses: Historical Sociology and Political Pluralism*. London: Penguin, 1990.

Vogel, Ezra F., *Japan As Number One: Lessons for America*. Cambridge, MA: Harvard University Press, 1979.

Wade, Robert, *Governing the Market: Economic Theory and the Role of Government in East Asian Industrialization*. Princeton, NJ: Princeton University Press, 1990.

Walder, Andrew G., *Communist Neo-Traditionalism: Work and Authority in Chinese Industry*. Berkeley: University of California Press, 1986.

Weber, Max, *Economy and Society: An Outline of Interpretive Sociology*. Edited by Guenther Roth and Claus Wittich. Berkeley: University of California Press, 1978.

Weingast, Barry R., "The Economic Role of Political Institutions: Market Preserving Federalism and Economic Growth," *Journal of Law, Economics, and Organization* 11 (1995), 1–31.

Weingast, Barry, and William J. Marshall, "The Industrial Organization of Congress, or Why Legislatures Like Firms, Are Not Organized as Markets," *Journal of Political Economy* 96 (1988), 132–63.

Weingast, Barry, Kenneth Shepsle, and Christopher Johnsen, "The Political Economy of Benefits and Costs: A Neoclassical Approach to Distributive Politics," *Journal of Political Economy* 89 (1981), 642–69.

Weitzman, Martin, "Industrial Production" in A. Bergson and H.S. Levine (eds.), *The Soviet Economy: Towards the Year 2000*. London: George Allen and Unwin, 1983.

Weitzman, Martin, and Chenggang Xu, "Chinese Township-Village Enterprises as Vaguely Defined Cooperatives," *Journal of Comparative Economics* 18 (1994), 121–45.

White, Stephen, "Economic Performance and Communist Legitimacy," *World Politics* (1986), 462–82.

Wiles, Peter, *The Political Economy of Communism*. Cambridge: Harvard University Press, 1962.

Williamson, John, "Democracy and the 'Washington Consensus,'" *World Development* 21 (1993), 1329–36.

Willerton, John P., Jr., "Patronage Networks and Coalition Building in the Brezhnev Era," *Soviet Studies* 39 (1987), 175–204.

Winiecki, Jan., *The Distorted World of Soviet-Type Economies*. London: Routledge, 1988.

Wintrobe, Ronald, "It Pays to Do Good But Not to Do More Good Than It Pays," *Journal of Economic Behaviour and Economic Organization* 2 (1981), 201–13.

"The Optimal Level of Bureaucratization Within a Firm," *Canadian Journal of Economics* 15 (1982), 649–68.

"Taxing Altruism," *Economic Inquiry* XXI (1983), 255–69.

"The Market for Corporate Control and the Market for Political Control," *Journal of Law, Economics and Organization* 3 (1987), 435–46.

"The Tinpot and the Totalitarian: An Economic Theory of Dictatorship," *American Political Science Review* 84 (1990), 849–72.

"Political Competition and the Rise of Dictatorship," in A. Breton, G. Galeotti, P. Salmon, and R. Wintrobe (eds.), *The Competitive State: Villa Colombella Papers on Competitive Politics*. Dordrecht, The Netherlands: Kluwer Academic Publishers, 1991.

"Some Economics of Ethnic Capital and Conflict," in A. Breton, G. Galeotti, P. Salmon, and R. Wintrobe (eds.), *Nationalism and Rationality*. New York: Cambridge University Press, 1995.

"Modern Bureaucratic Theory," in D. Mueller (ed.), *Perspectives in Public Choice: A Handbook*. New York: Cambridge University Press, 1997.

Wintrobe, Ronald, and Albert Breton, "Organizational Structure and Productivity," *American Economic Review* 76 (1986), 530–38.

Wittman, Donald, "Parties as Utility Maximizers," *American Political Science Review* 67 (1973), 490–98.

"Candidate Motivation: A Synthesis of Alternative Theories," *American Political Science Review* 77 (1983), 142–57.

Wolfe, Bertram D., *An Ideology in Power*. New York: Stein and Day. 1969.

Wurfel, David, *Filipino Politics: Development and Decay*. Ithaca, NY: Cornell University Press, 1988.

Xenophon, "Hiero, or Tyrannicus," reprinted in L. Strauss, *On Tyranny*. New York: Political Science Classics, 1948.

Young, Alwyn, "A Tale of Two Cities: Factor Accumulation and Technical Change in Hong Kong and Singapore,"in O. Blanchard and S. Fischer (eds), *NBER Macroeconomic Annual* 7 (1992), Cambridge. MA: MIT Press, 13–54.

"The Tyranny of Numbers: Confronting the Statistical Realities of the East Asian Growth Experience," *Quarterly Journal of Economics* 110 (August 1995), Issue 3, 641–80.

"The Razor's Edge: Distortions, Incremental Reform and the Theory of the Second Best in the People's Republic of China," ms, Department of Economics, Boston University (1996).

Name index

Abedian, I., 179
Adam, Heribert, 167–8
Adorno, Theodor, 9, 281, 296, 297, 298, 308
Aganbegyan, Abel, 232
Akerlof, George, 86, 310, 312, 313, 314, 315
Alchian, Armen, 297, 312
Aldrich, J.H., 267
Alesina, Alberto, 52n3, 83, 249, 250, 253, 267, 268, 270, 274
Altemeyer, Bob, 9, 281, 298, 300
Amsden, Alice, 148
Anderson, Gary M., 133
Arendt, Hannah, 8, 19, 47, 58, 59, 299n15, 302–3, 307n2, 308, 309, 310, 316, 319, 321, 323, 324, 326, 328, 329, 347, 348
Arjomand, Said Amir, 55
Arrow, K.J., 48, 287
Ash, Timothy Garton, 230
Aslund, Anders, 229, 232, 241
Aurelius, Marcus, 16
Axelrod, Robert, 130, 159n10
Azariadis, C., 83

Bahry, D., 62
Bandura, A., 301
Banks, Jeffrey, 52n3
Bardhan, Pranab, 146
Barrow, R.H., 36, 78, 84, 85, 90
Bates, Robert H., 83
Becker, Gary, 59, 86, 91, 101, 148, 150, 155–6, 167, 170, 288, 291
Bender, Bruce, 32
Bennett, Valerie, 56
Bergson, Abram, 10, 199, 200
Berliner, Joseph S., 233, 234, 240–1
Bernheim, B., 93–4, 291
Bialer, Seweryn, 34–5, 222, 225, 227
Bilson, John, 36, 55, 72, 179n3
Block, Walter, 146n3

Boettke, Peter J., 131, 133, 137
Borjas, George, 18n2, 287n4
Borner, Silvio, 36
Boulding, K., 96
Bowles, Samuel, 28, 139n10
Boycko, Maxim, 238, 340n3
Bracher, Karl D., 260, 305, 307n2, 317, 319, 320
Brennan, G., 52, 53, 132
Breton, Albert, 25, 30, 57, 138, 209, 210, 211, 212, 219, 222, 224, 269n9, 280n1, 285, 311n5, 315, 316, 326
Brewster-Smith, M., 298n14
Brosio, G., 271
Broszat, Martin, 59, 304, 317, 318, 324, 325
Bruce, Neil, 94n3
Brunetti, Aymo, 36
Brzezinski, Zbigniew, 8, 11, 25, 43, 44, 45, 47, 58, 219, 221, 344
Buchanan, James, 52, 53, 94, 132, 150
Bullock, Alan, 23, 34
Bulow, Jeremy, 28, 165, 182, 183
Burrowes, R., 47n2, 59n4

Callaghy, Thomas M., 24, 113
Calvert, Randall, 249
Camerer, Colin, 86
Cassels, Alan, 260
Chang, Chun, 130n6, 233
Cheng, Hang Sheng, 197
Chrysostom, John, 88
Coase, R.H., 311
Cobban, A., 37
Cohen, Kathy, 83n1
Coleman, James S., 25, 130, 301, 305, 310, 311, 312, 315, 316
Collier, David, 44
Conot, Robert E., 309, 318
Constable, Pamela, 153, 161
Coughlin, Peter, 148, 150, 158, 159
Crawford, R.B., 297
Cukierman, A., 268

Subject index